POINTS OF VIEW

POINTS OF VIEW

READINGS IN AMERICAN GOVERNMENT AND POLITICS

**Edited by ROBERT E. DiCLERICO
and ALLAN S. HAMMOCK**

West Virginia University

ADDISON-WESLEY PUBLISHING COMPANY

Reading, Massachusetts • Menlo Park, California

London • Amsterdam • Don Mills, Ontario • Sydney

Library of Congress Cataloging in Publication Data

Main entry under title:

Points of view.

1. United States--Politics and government--Addresses,
essays, lectures. I. DiClerico, Robert E. II. Hammock, Allan S., 1938-
JK21.P59   320.9'73'092   79-18040
ISBN 0-201-02990-1

ISBN 0-201-02990-1
BCDEFGHIJK-DO-89876543210

A NOTE TO
THE INSTRUCTOR

For some years now, both of us have jointly taught the introductory course to American government. Each year we perused the crop of existing readers, and while we adopted several different readers over this period, we were not wholly satisfied with any of them. It is our feeling that the fifty or so readers currently on the market suffer from one or more of the following deficiencies: (1) Some contain selections which are difficult for students to comprehend because of the sophistication of the argument, the manner of expression, or both, (2) In many instances, readers do not cover all of the topics typically treated in an introductory American Government course. (3) In choosing selections for a given topic, editors do not always show sufficient concern for how—or whether—one article under a topic relates to other articles under the same topic. (4) Most readers contain too many selections for each topic—indeed, in several cases the number of selections for some topics exceeds ten. Readers are nearly always used in conjunction with a textbook. Thus, to ask a student to read a lengthy chapter—jammed with facts—from a textbook and then to read anywhere from five to ten selections on the same topic from a reader is to demand that students read more than they can reasonably absorb in a meaningful way. Of course, an instructor need not assign all of the selections under a given topic. At the same time, however, this approach justifiably disgruntles students who, after purchasing a reader, discover that they may only be asked to read one-half or two-thirds of it.

Instead of continuing to complain about what we considered to be the limitations of existing American Government readers, we decided to try our own hand at putting one together. In doing so, we were guided by the following considerations:

Readability Quite obviously, students will not read dull, obtuse articles. As well as having something important to say, we feel that each of the articles in *Points of View* is clearly written, well organized, and free of needless jargon.

Comprehensiveness The fifteen topics included in *Points of View* constitute all the major areas of concern that are typically treated in the standard introductory course to American Government.

Economy of Selections We decided, in most instances, to limit the number of selections to two per topic, although we did include four selections for some topics that we deemed especially important. The limitation on selections will, we feel, maximize the possibility that students will read them. It has been our experience that when students are assigned four, five, or more selections under a given topic, they simply do not read them all. In addition, by limiting the selections for each topic, there is a greater likelihood that students will be able to associate an argument with the author who made it.

Juxtaposition The two selections for each topic will take *opposing* or *different* points of view on some aspect of a given topic. This approach was chosen for three reasons. First, we believe that student interest will be enhanced by playing one article off against the other. Thus, the "interest" quality of a given article will derive not only from its own content but also from its juxtaposition with the other article. Second, we think it is important to sensitize students to the fact that one's perspective on an issue will depend upon the values that he or she brings to it. Third, by having both selections focus on a particular issue related to a given topic, the student will have a greater depth of understanding about that issue. We think this is preferable to having five or six selections under a topic, with each selection focusing on a different aspect, and with the result that the student ultimately is exposed to "a little of this and a little of that"—that is, if the student even bothers to read all five or six selections.

While the readers currently available take into account one or, in some instances, several of the considerations identified above, we believe that the uniqueness of *Points of View* lies in the fact that it has sought to incorporate *all* of them.

Morgantown, West Virginia   R.E.D.
November 1979   A.S.H.

CONTENTS

CHAPTER 1 **DEMOCRACY**   1

How Democratic Is America?   2
Howard Zinn

How Democratic Is America? A Response to   15
Howard Zinn
Sidney Hook

CHAPTER 2 **THE CONSTITUTION AND THE FOUNDING FATHERS**   24

An Economic Interpretation of the Constitution   25
of the United States
Charles A. Beard

Charles Beard and the Constitution: A Critical   31
Analysis
Robert E. Brown

CHAPTER 3 **FEDERALISM**   37

Revenue Sharing Five Years Later   38
Amitai Etzioni

The New Federalism: Can the States Be Trusted?   43
Daniel J. Elazar

CHAPTER 4 **PUBLIC OPINION**   53

Public Opinion in a Free Society   54
Charles W. Roll and Albert H. Cantril

Do the Polls Serve Democracy?   61
John C. Ranney

CHAPTER 5   VOTING   67

Politics as Fraud: Voting in America   68
David Schuman

Why Vote?   74
William C. Mitchell

CHAPTER 6   CAMPAIGNS AND THE MEDIA   82

Politics as a Con Game   83
Joe McGinniss

The Impact of Televised Political Commercials   90
Thomas E. Patterson and Robert D. McClure

CHAPTER 7   ELECTIONS   99

The Case Against the Electoral College   100
Lawrence D. Longley

Four Reasons to Keep the Electoral College   106
Curtis B. Gans

CHAPTER 8   POLITICAL PARTIES   110

Let 100 Single-Issue Groups Bloom   111
David S. Broder

The Party's Only Begun   119
Richard E. Cohen

CHAPTER 9   INTEREST GROUPS   124

Who Governs? Leaders and Lobbyists   125
Michael Parenti

The Rise of Public Interest Groups: 1965-75   132
Andrew S. McFarland

CHAPTER 10   CONGRESS   146

Representation   146

Why We Should Limit Congressional Tenure   147
Dennis DeConcini

A Government as Good as Its People: Or, Do We   153
Really Want Farmer Jones to Be the Next Speaker?
Eric M. Uslaner

Congressional Ethics   161

Lawmakers as Lawbreakers   162
Mark J. Green, James M. Fallows, and David R. Zwick

Conflict of Interest: The View from the House   170
Edmund Beard and Stephen Horn

CHAPTER 11   THE PRESIDENCY   183

Presidential Power   183

The Myth of Presidential Power   184
H. Mark Roelofs

The Presidential Advantage   192
George E. Reedy

The President and the Press   198

The Presidency and the Press   199
Daniel P. Moynihan

Response to Daniel Moynihan   212
Max Frankel

CHAPTER 12   BUREAUCRACY   219

A Kind Word for the Spoils System   220
Charles Peters

A Kind Word for the Merit System   225
O. B. Conaway, Jr.

CHAPTER 13   THE JUDICIARY   232

The Supreme Court   232

In Support of Judicial Restraint   233
Sam J. Ervin, Jr.

In Support of Judicial Activism   241
Ramsey Clark

Courts and Criminal Justice   246

The Ineffectiveness of the Criminal Justice   247
System
Ernest van den Haag

Perry Mason in Wonderland: What Happens in   257
Criminal Court
Charles E. Silberman

CHAPTER 14   CIVIL LIBERTIES   271

Free Speech   271

Why Free Speech for Racists and Totalitarians   272
American Civil Liberties Union

Nazis: Outside the Constitution   277
George F. Will

Pornography   279

The Problem of Pornography: No Censorship   280
Murray Hausknecht

For Selective Censorship   285
Cynthia Fuchs Epstein

CHAPTER 15   CIVIL RIGHTS   289

The Case for Racial Quotas   290
Thurgood Marshall

Are Quotas Good for Blacks?   297
Thomas Sowell

CHAPTER 16   CHARACTERIZATIONS OF THE AMERICAN   305
              POLITICAL SYSTEM

The Power Elite   306
C. Wright Mills

Power Is Pluralistic   326
Arnold M. Rose

CHAPTER ONE

DEMOCRACY

Any assessment of a society's democratic character will be fundamentally determined by what the observer chooses to use as a definition of democracy. While the concept of democracy has commanded the attention of political thinkers for centuries, the following selections by Howard Zinn and Sidney Hook serve to demonstrate that there continues to be considerable disagreement over its meaning. Each of them has scanned the American scene and reached different conclusions regarding the democratic character of our society. This difference of opinion is explained primarily by the fact that each approaches his evaluation with a different conception of what democracy is.

For Zinn, the definition of democracy includes not only criteria which bear upon how *decisions get made, but also upon what* results *from such decisions. Specifically, he argues that such results must lead to a certain level of human welfare within a society. In applying these criteria of human welfare to the United States, he concludes that we fall short of the mark in several areas.*

Although Sidney Hook is willing to acknowledge that democracy may indeed function more smoothly in societies where the conditions of human welfare are high, he insists that these conditions do not themselves constitute the definition of democracy. Rather, he maintains that democracy is a process—a way of making decisions. Whether such decisions lead to the conditions of human welfare that Zinn prescribes is irrelevant. The crucial test, according to Hook, is whether or not the people have the right, by majority rule, to make choices about the quality of their lives—whatever those choices may be.

How Democratic Is America?

Howard Zinn

To give a sensible answer to the question "How democratic is America?" I find it necessary to make three clarifying preliminary statements. First, I want to define "democracy," not conclusively, but operationally, so we can know what we are arguing about, or at least what I am talking about. Second, I want to state what my criteria are for measuring the "how" in the question. And third, I think it necessary to issue a warning about how a certain source of bias (although not the only source) is likely to distort our judgments.

Our definition is crucial. This becomes clear if we note how relatively easy is the answer to our question when we define democracy as a set of formal institutions and let it go at that. If we describe as "democratic" a country that has a representative system of government, with universal suffrage, a bill of rights, and party competition for office, it becomes easy to answer the question "how" with the enthusiastic reply, "Very!" . . .

I propose a set of criteria for the description "democratic" which goes beyond formal political institutions, to the quality of life in the society (economic, social, psychological), beyond majority rule to a concern for minorities, and beyond national boundaries to a global view of what is meant by "the people," in that rough, but essentially correct view of democracy as "government of, by, and for the people."

Let me list these criteria quickly, because I will go on to discuss them in some detail later:

1. To what extent can various people in the society participate in those decisions which affect their lives: decisions in the political process and decisions in the economic structure?

From Howard Zinn, "How Democratic Is America?" in Robert A. Goldwin, ed., *How Democratic Is America?* (Chicago: Rand McNally & Co., 1971). Used with permission of Howard Zinn.

2. As a corollary of the above: do people have equal access to the information which they need to make important decisions?

3. Are the members of the society equally protected on matters of life and death—in the most literal sense of that phrase?

4. Is there equality before the law: police, courts, the judicial process—as well as equality *with* the law-enforcing institutions, so as to safeguard equally everyone's person, and his freedom from interference by others, and by the government?

5. Is there equality in the distribution of available resources: those economic goods necessary for health, life, recreation, leisure, growth?

6. Is there equal access to education, to knowledge and training, so as to enable persons in the society to live their lives as fully as possible, to enlarge their range of possibilities?

7. Is there freedom of expression on all matters, and equally for all, to communicate with other members of the society?

8. Is there freedom for individuality in private life, in sexual relations, family relations, the right of privacy?

9. To minimize regulation: do education and the culture in general foster a spirit of cooperation and amity to sustain the above conditions?

10. As a final safety feature: is there opportunity to protest, to disobey the laws, when the foregoing objectives are being lost—as a way of restoring them? . . .

Two historical facts support my enlarged definition of democracy. One is that the industrialized Western societies have outgrown the original notions which accompanied their early development: that constitutional and procedural tests sufficed for the "democracy" that overthrew the old order; that democracy was quite adequately fulfilled by the Bill of Rights in England at the time of the glorious Revolution, the Constitution of the United States, and the declaration of the Rights of Man in France. It came to be acknowledged that the rhetoric of these revolutions was not matched by their real achievements. In other words, the limitations of that "democracy" led to the reformist and radical movements that grew up in the West in the middle and late nineteenth centuries. The other historical note is that the new revolutions in our century, in Africa, Asia, Latin America, while rejecting either in whole or in part the earlier revolutions, profess a similar democratic aim, but with an even broader rhetoric. . . .

My second preliminary point is on standards. By this I mean that we can judge in several ways the fulfillment of these ten criteria I have listed. We can measure the present against the past, so that if we find that in 1960 we are doing better in these matters than we were doing in 1860 or 1910, the society will get a good grade for its "democracy." I would abjure such an approach because it supports complacency. With such a standard, Russians in 1910 could point with pride to how much progress they had made towards parliamentary democracy; as Russians in 1969 can point to their progress towards freedom of expression; as Americans could point in 1939 to how far they had come towards solving the problem of economic equality; as Americans in the South could point in 1950 to the progress of the southern Negro.

Or, we could measure our democracy against other places in the world. Given the high incidence of tyranny in the world, polarization of wealth, and lack of freedom of expression, the United States, even with very serious defects, could declare itself successful. Again, the result is to let us all off easily; some of our most enthusiastic self-congratulation is based on such a standard.

On the other hand, we could measure our democracy against an ideal (even if admittedly unachievable) standard. I would argue for such an approach, because, in what may seem to some a paradox, the ideal standard is the pragmatic one; it affects what we *do*. To grade a student on the basis of an improvement over past performance is justifiable if the intention is to encourage someone discouraged about his ability. But if he is rather pompous about his superiority in relation to other students (and I suggest this is frequently true of Americans evaluating American "democracy"), and if in addition he is a medical student about to graduate into a world ridden with disease, it would be best to judge him by an ideal standard. That might spur him to an improvement fast enough to save lives. . . .

My third preliminary point is a caution based on the obvious fact that we make our appraisals through the prism of our own status in society. This is particularly important in assessing democracy, because, if "democracy" refers to the condition of masses of people, and if we as the assessors belong to a number of elites, we will tend (and I am not declaring an inevitability, just warning of a tendency) to see the present situation in America more benignly than it deserves. To be more specific, if democracy requires a keen awareness of the condition of black people, of poor people, of young people, of that majority of the world who are not American—and we are white, prosperous, beyond draft age, and American—then we have a number of pressures tending to dull our sense of inequity. We are, if not doomed to err, likely to err on the side of complacency—and we should try to take this into account in making our judgments.

I. PARTICIPATION IN DECISIONS

We need to recognize first, that whatever decisions are made politically are made by representatives of one sort or another: state legislators, congressmen, senators, and other elected officials; governors and presidents;

also by those appointed by elected officials, like Supreme Court justices. These are important decisions, affecting our lives, liberties, and ability to pursue happiness. Congress and the president decide on the tax structure, which affects the distribution of resources. They decide how to spend the monies received, whether or not we go to war; who serves in the armed forces; what behavior is considered a crime; which crimes are prosecuted and which are not. They decide what limitations there should be on our travel, or on our right to speak freely. They decide on the availability of education and health services.

If representation by its very nature is undemocratic, as I would argue, this is an important fact for our evaluation. Representative government is *closer* to democracy than monarchy, and for this reason it has been hailed as one of the great political advances of modern times; yet, it is only a step in the direction of democracy, at its best. It has certain inherent flaws— pointed out by Rousseau in the eighteenth century, Victor Considerant in the nineteenth century, Robert Michels in the beginning of the twentieth century, Hannah Arendt in our own time. No representative can adequately represent another's needs; the representative tends to become a member of a special elite; he has privileges which weaken his sense of concern at others' grievances; the passions of the troubled lose force (as Madison noted in *The Federalist 10*) as they are filtered through the representative system; the elected official develops an expertise which tends towards its own perpetuation. Leaders develop what Michels called "a mutual insurance contract" against the rest of society. . . .

If only radicals pointed to the inadequacy of the political processes in the United States, we might be suspicious. But established political scientists of a moderate bent talk quite bluntly of the limitations of the voting system in the United States. Robert Dahl, in *A Preface to Democratic Theory*, drawing on the voting studies of American political scientists, concludes that "political activity, at least in the United States, is positively associated to a significant extent with such variables as income, socio-economic status, and education." He says:

> By their propensity for political passivity the poor and uneducated disfranchise themselves. . . . Since they also have less access than the wealthy to the organizational, financial, and propaganda resources that weigh so heavily in campaigns, elections, legislative, and executive decisions, anything like equal control over government policy is triply barred to the members of Madison's unpropertied masses. They are barred by their relative greater inactivity, by their relatively limited access to resources, and by Madison's nicely contrived system of constitutional checks. [1]

Dahl thinks that our society is essentially democratic, but this is because he expects very little. (His book was written in the 1950s, when lack of commotion in the society might well have persuaded him that no one else expected much more than he did.) Even if democracy were to be superficially defined as "majority rule," the United States would not fulfill that, according to Dahl, who says that "on matters of specific policy, the majority rarely rules."[2] After noting that "the election is the critical technique for insuring that governmental leaders will be relatively responsive to non-leaders," he goes on to say that "it is important to notice how little a national election tells us about the preferences of majorities. Strictly speaking, all an election reveals is the first preferences of some citizens among the candidates standing for office."[3] About 40 per cent of the potential voters in national elections, and about 60 per cent of the voters in local elections do not vote, and this cannot be attributed, Dahl says, simply to indifference. And if, as Dahl points out, "in no large nation state can elections tell us much about the preferences of majorities and minorities," this is "even more true of the interelection period." . . .

Dahl goes on to assert that the election process and interelection activity "are crucial processes for insuring that political leaders will be *somewhat* responsive to the preferences of *some* ordinary citizens."[4] I submit (the emphasized words are mine) that if an admirer of democracy in America can say no more than this, democracy is not doing very well.

Dahl tells us the election process is one of "two fundamental methods of social control which, operating together, make governmental leaders so responsive to nonleaders that the distinction between democracy and dictatorship still makes sense." Since his description of the election process leaves that dubious, let's look at his second requirement for distinguishing democracy: "The other method of social control is continuous political competition among individuals, parties, or both." What it comes down to is "not minority rule but minorities rule."[5]

If it turns out that this—like the election process—also has little democratic content, we will not be left with very much difference—by Dahl's own admission—between "dictatorship" and the "democracy" practiced in the United States. Indeed, there is much evidence on this: the lack of democracy within the major political parties, the vastly disproportionate influence of wealthy groups over poorer ones (the oil depletion allowance lobby wins out over the consumer for about five billion dollars a year in exorbitant fuel costs, *The New York Times* estimated in March);[6] the unrepresentative nature of the major lobbies (the wealthy doctors speaking for all through the A.M.A., the wealthy farmers speaking for the poorer ones through the American Farm Bureau Federation, the most affluent trade unions speaking for all workers through George Meany). All of this, and more, supports the idea of a "decline of American pluralism" that Henry Kariel has written about. What Dahl's democracy comes down to is "the steady appeasement of relatively small groups."[7] If these relatively small groups turn out to be the aircraft industry far more than the aged, the space industry far more than the poor, the Pentagon far more than the college youth—what is left of democracy?

Sometimes the elitism of decision-making is defended (by Dahl and by others) on the ground that the elite is enacting decisions passively supported by the mass, whose tolerance is proof of an underlying consensus in society. But Murray Levin's studies in *The Alienated Voter* indicate how much nonparticipation in elections is a result of hopelessness rather than approval. And Robert Wiebe, a historian at Northwestern University, talks of "consensus" becoming a "new stereotype." He approaches the question historically:

> *Industrialization arrived so peacefully not because all Americans secretly shared the same values or implicitly willed its success but because its millions of bitter enemies lacked the mentality and the means to organize an effective counterattack.* [8]

Weibe's point is that the passivity of most Americans in the face of elitist decision-making has not been due to acquiescence but to the lack of resources for effective combat, as well as a gulf so wide between the haves and have-nots that there was no ground on which to dispute. Americans neither revolted violently nor reacted at the polls; instead they were subservient, or else worked out their hostilities in personal ways. . . .

The national party conventions of 1968 were basically no different than the ones that have always taken place, but because of the intensity of national conflict over Vietnam and the race question, their distance from democracy stood out more starkly. Despite obvious public disaffection for the war (shown in public opinion polls, in Johnson's retirement, in many other pieces of evidence), both major parties nominated candidates who represented a continuation of the Johnson policies on the war. (Johnson's own election in 1964 on a peace platform and his subsequent escalation of the war was earlier evidence of how inadequately presidential elections permit popular control over foreign policy.) . . .

Furthermore, the candidate of the Democratic Party, Hubert Humphrey, was nominated against the evidence in polls and primaries that he was not wanted. The antiquated machinery that elects delegates to this national convention, the comic-tragic nature of the convention itself, is too well known to document. What we need to remind ourselves is that this absurd institution chooses the president of the United States, a man with power over the greatest accumulation of wealth in human history, a man with power of life and death not only over Americans, but over all the world.

With all the inadequacies of the representative system, it does not even operate in the field of foreign policy. In exactly those decisions which are the most vital—matters of war and peace, life and death—power rests in the hands of the president and a small group of advisers. We don't notice this when wars seem to have a large degree of justification (as World

War II); we begin to notice it when we find ourselves in the midst of a particularly pointless war.

I have been talking so far about democracy in the political process. But there is another serious weakness that I will only mention here, although it is of enormous importance: the powerlessness of the American to participate in economic decision-making, which affects his life at every moment. As a consumer, that is, as the person whom the economy is presumably intended to serve, he has virtually nothing to say about what is produced for him. The corporations make what is profitable; the advertising industry persuades him to buy what the corporations produce. He becomes the passive victim of the misallocation of resources, the production of dangerous commodities, the spoiling of his air, water, forests, beaches, cities.

2. ACCESS TO INFORMATION

Adequate information for the electorate is a precondition for any kind of action (whether electoral or demonstrative) to affect national policy. As for the voting process, Berelson, Lazarsfeld, and McPhee tell us (in their book, *Voting*) after extensive empirical research: "One persistent conclusion is that the public is not particularly well informed about the specific issues of the day.". . .

Furthermore, . . . there are certain issues which never even reach the public because they are decided behind the scenes. . . .

Consider the information available to voters on two major kinds of issues. One of them is the tax structure, so bewilderingly complex that the corporation, with its corps of accountants and financial experts, can prime itself for lobbying activities, while the average voter, hardly able to comprehend his own income tax, stands by helplessly as the president, the Bureau of the Budget, and the Congress decide the tax laws. The dominant influences are those of big business, which has the resources both to understand and to act.

Then there is foreign policy. The government leads the citizenry to believe it has special expertise which, if it could only be revealed, would support its position against critics. At the same time, it hides the very information which would reveal its position to be indefensible. The mendacity of the government on the Bay of Pigs operation, the secret operations of the CIA in Iran, Indonesia, Guatemala and other places, the withholding of vital information about the Tonkin Gulf events are only a few examples of the way the average person becomes a victim of government deception.

Furthermore, the distribution of information to the public is a function of power and wealth. The government itself can color the citizens' understanding of events by its control of news at the source: the presidential press conference, the "leak to the press," the White Papers, the teams of "truth experts" going around the country at the taxpayers' expense. As for private media, the large networks and mass-circulation magazines have the greatest access to the public mind. There is no "equal time" for critics of public policy. . . .

3. EQUAL PROTECTION

Let us go now from the procedural to the substantive, indeed to the *most* substantive of questions: the right of all the people to life itself. Here we find democracy in America tragically inadequate. The draft, which has been a part of American law since 1940 (when it passed by one vote) decides, in wartime, who lives and who dies. Not only Locke, one of the leading theorists of the democratic tradition, declared the ultimate right of any person to safeguard his own life when threatened by the government; Hobbes, often looked on as the foe of democratic thought, agreed. The draft violates this principle, because it compels young people to sacrifice their lives for any cause which the leaders of government deem just; further it discriminates against the poor, the uneducated, the young.

It is in connection with this most basic of rights—life itself, the first and most important of those substantive ends which democratic participation is designed to safeguard—that I would assert the need for a global view of democracy. One can at least conceive of a democratic decision for martial sacrifice by those ready to make the sacrifice; a "democratic" war is thus a theoretical possibility. But that presumption of democracy becomes obviously false at the first shot because then *others* are affected who did not decide. . . . Nations making decisions to slaughter their own sons are at least theoretically subject to internal check. The victims on the other side fall without any such chance. For the United States today, this failure of democracy is total; we have the capacity to destroy the world without giving it a chance to murmur a dissent; we are in fact right now destroying a part of southeast Asia on the basis of a unilateral decision made in Washington. There is no more pernicious manifestation of the lack of democracy in America than this single fact.

4. EQUALITY BEFORE THE LAW

Is there equality before the law? At every stage of the judicial process—facing the policeman, appearing in court, being freed on bond, being sentenced by the judge—the poor person is treated worse than the rich, the black treated worse than the white, the politically or personally odd character is treated worse than the orthodox. The details are given in the 1963 report of the Attorney General's Committee on Poverty and the Administration of Federal Criminal Justice. There a defendant's poverty is shown to affect his preliminary hearing, his right to bail, the quality of his counsel. The evidence is plentiful in the daily newspapers, which inform us that a Negro boy fleeing the scene of a two-dollar theft may be shot and killed by a pursuing policeman, while a wealthy man who goes to South America after a million dollar swindle, even if apprehended, need never fear a scratch. The wealthy price-fixer for General Motors, who cost consumers millions, will get ninety days in jail, the burglar of a liquor store will get five years. A Negro youth, or a bearded white youth poorly dressed, has much more chance of being clubbed by a policeman on the street than a well-dressed white man, given the fact that both respond with equal tartness to a question. . . .

Aside from inequality among citizens, there is inequality between the citizen and his government, when they face one another in a court of law. Take the matter of counsel: the well-trained government prosecutor faces the indigent's court-appointed counsel. Four of my students did a study of the City Court of Boston this past spring. They sat in the court for weeks, taking notes, and found that the average time spent by court-appointed counsel with his client, before arguing the case at the bench, was seven minutes.

5. DISTRIBUTION OF RESOURCES

Democracy is devoid of meaning if it does not include equal access to the available resources of the society. In India, democracy might still mean poverty; in the United States, with a Gross National Product over eight hundred billion dollars a year, democracy should mean that every American, working a short work-week, has adequate food, clothing, shelter, health care, education for himself and his family—in short, the material resources necessary to enjoy life and freedom. Even if only 20 per cent of the American population is desperately poor . . . in a country so rich, that is an inexcusable breach of the democratic principle. Even if there is a large, prosperous middle class, there is something grossly unfair in the wealthiest fifth of the population getting 40 per cent of the nation's income, and the poorest fifth getting 5 per cent (a ratio virtually unchanged from 1947 to 1966). . . .

Whether you are poor or rich determines the most fundamental facts about your life: whether you are cold in the winter while trying to sleep, whether you suffocate in the summer; whether you live among vermin or rats; whether the smells around you all day are sweet or foul; whether you have adequate medical care; whether you have good teeth; whether you can send your children to college; whether you can go on vacation or have to take an extra job at night; whether you can afford a divorce, or an abortion, or a wife, or another child. . . .

6. ACCESS TO EDUCATION

In a highly industrialized society, education is a crucial determinant of wealth, political power, social status, leisure, and the ability to work in one's chosen field. Educational resources in our society are not equitably distributed. Among high-school graduates of the same IQ levels, a far higher percentage of the well-to-do go on to college than the poor. A mediocre student with money can always go to college. A mediocre student without money may not be able to go, even to a state college, because he may have to work to support his family. Furthermore, the educational resources in the schools—equipment, teachers, etc.—are far superior in the wealthy suburbs than in the poor sections of the city, whether white or black.

7. FREEDOM OF EXPRESSION

Like money, freedom of expression is available to all in America, but in widely varying quantities. The First Amendment formally guarantees freedom of speech, press, assembly, and petition to all—but certain realities of wealth, power, and status stand in the way of the equal distribution of these rights. Anyone can stand on a street corner and talk to ten or a hundred people. But someone with the resources to buy loudspeaker equipment, go through the necessary red tape, and post a bond with the city may hold a meeting downtown and reach a thousand or five thousand people. A person or a corporation with a hundred thousand dollars can buy time on television and reach ten million people. A rich person simply has much more freedom of speech than a poor person. The government has much more freedom of expression than a private individual, because the president can command the airwaves when he wishes, and reach thirty million people in one night.

Freedom of the press also is guaranteed to all. But the student selling an underground newspaper on the street with a nude woman on the cover may be arrested by a policeman, while the airport newsstand selling *Playboy* and ten magazines like it will remain safe. Anyone with ten thousand dollars can put out a newspaper to reach a few thousand people. Anyone with ten million dollars can buy a few newspapers that will reach a few million people. Anyone who is penniless had better have a loud voice; and then he might be arrested for disturbing the peace.

8. FREEDOM FOR INDIVIDUALITY

The right to live one's life, in privacy and freedom, in whatever way one wants, so long as others are not harmed, should be a sacred principle in a democracy. But there are hundreds of laws, varying from state to state, and sometimes joined by federal laws, which regulate the personal lives of people in this country: their marriages, their divorces, their sexual relations, their right to bring up their children as they see fit, their right to smoke marijuana or grow their hair long. Furthermore, both laws and court decisions protect policemen and the FBI in their use of secret devices which listen in on private conversations, or peer in on private conduct.

9. THE SPIRIT OF COOPERATION

The maintenance of those substantive elements of democracy which I have just sketched, if dependent on a pervasive network of coercion, would cancel out much of the benefit of that democracy. Democracy needs rather to be sustained by a spirit in society, the tone and the values of the culture. I am speaking of something as elusive as a mood, alongside something as hard as law, both of which would have to substitute cooperation tinged with friendly competition for the fierce combat of our business culture. I am speaking of the underlying drive that keeps people going in the society. So long as that drive is for money and power, with no ceiling on either, so long as ruthlessness is built into the rules of the game, democracy does not have a chance. If there is one crucial cause in the failure of American democracy—not the only one, of course, but a fundamental one—it is the drive for corporate profit, and the overwhelming influence of money in every aspect of our daily lives. That is the uncontrolled libido of our society from which the rape of democratic values necessarily follows.

The manifestations are diverse and endless: the Kefauver hearings on the drug industry in 1961 disclosed that the drive for profit in that industry had led to incredible overpricing of drugs for consumers (700 per cent markup, for instance, for tablets to arthritic patients) as well as bodily harm resulting from "the fact that they market so many of their failures." . . . To take another random instance: in July, 1963, *The New York Times* reported: "Three men and two corporations were found guilty yesterday in Federal court of conspiring to sell blood plasma that had been manufactured in unlicensed laboratories."

If these were isolated cases, reported and then eliminated, they could be dismissed as unfortunate blemishes on an otherwise healthy social body. But the major allocations of resources in our society are made on the basis of money profit rather than social use. . . .

Recent news items buttress what I have said. The oil that polluted California's beautiful beaches earlier . . . was produced ·by a system in which the oil companies' hunger for profit has far more weight than the ordinary person's need to swim in clean water. This is not to be attributed to Republicanism overriding the concern for the little fellow of the Democratic Party. Profit is master whichever party is in power; it was the liberal Secretary of the Interior Stewart Udall who allowed the dangerous drilling to go on. . . .

In February, an Associated Press dispatch from Tooele, Utah, was headlined, "Utah Town Happily Coexists with Poison Gas." The army was storing nerve gas just outside the city, but "the people of Tooele generally shrug and accept it. Their discomfort is outweighed by the money the Tooele Army Depot means to the area. About 5,000 of the 15,000 residents work at the depot." According to the mayor, the town was so completely tied to the military, "it would blow away without it." When the essentials of life can only be guaranteed at such risk (this was where 6,000 sheep had died from the nerve gas because of the winds that day), something is wrong; and it is not assuaged by the fact that the residents of Tooele "voluntarily" choose it. That is as voluntary as miners choosing silicosis. Unnecessary death, unnecessary sickness, are inevitable in a society where business profit has priority over human life.

10. OPPORTUNITY TO PROTEST

The first two elements in my list for democracy—decision-making and information to help make them—are procedural. The next six are substantive, dealing with the consequences of such procedures on life, liberty, and the pursuit of happiness. My ninth point, the one I have just discussed, shows how the money motive of our society corrupts both procedures and their consequences by its existence and suggests we need a different motive as a fundamental requisite of a democratic society. The point I am about to discuss is an ultimate requisite for democracy, a safety feature if nothing else—neither procedures nor consequences nor motivation— works. It is the right of citizens to break through the impasse of a legal and cultural structure, which sustains inequality, greed, and murder, to initiate processes for change. I am speaking of civil disobedience, which is an essential safeguard even in a successful society, and which is an absolute necessity in a society which is not going well.

If the institutional structure itself bars any change but the most picayune and grievances are serious, it is silly to insist that change must be mediated through the processes of that legal structure. In such a situation, dramatic expressions of protest and challenge are necessary to help change ways of thinking, to build up political power for drastic change. A society that calls itself democratic (whether accurately or not) must, as its ultimate safeguard, allow such acts of disobedience. If the government prohibits them (as we must expect from a government committed to the existent) then the members of a society concerned with democracy must not only defend such acts, but encourage them. Somewhere near the root of democratic thought is the theory of popular sovereignty, declaring that government and laws are instruments for certain ends, and are not to be deified with absolute obedience; they must constantly be checked by the citizenry, and challenged, opposed, even overthrown, if they become threats to fundamental rights.

Any abstract assessment of *when* disobedience is justified is pointless. Proper conclusions depend on empirical evidence about how bad things are at the moment, and how adequate are the institutional mechanisms for correcting them. . . .

One of these is the matter of race. The intolerable position of the black person, in both North and South, has traditionally been handled with a few muttered apologies and tokens of reform. Then the civil disobedience of militants in the South forced our attention on the most dramatic (Southern) manifestations of racism in America. Now, it seems to require nothing *less* than civil disobedience (for riots and uprisings go beyond that) to make the nation see that the race problem is an American—not a Southern—problem and that it needs bold, revolutionary action.

As for poverty: it seems clear that the normal mechanisms of congressional pretense and presidential rhetoric are not going to change things very much. Acts of civil disobedience by the poor will be required, at the least, to make middle-class America take notice, to bring national decisions that begin to reallocate wealth.

The war in Vietnam is a particularly vivid example of how we cannot depend on the normal processes of "law and order," of the election process, of letters to *The Times*, to stop a series of especially brutal acts against the Vietnamese and against our own sons. Even the protests and demonstrations of the past few years have only brought small steps towards stopping the war. When people like Dr. Spock and Rev. Coffin engaged in rather mild acts of dissent, on the border of civil disobedience, they were prosecuted and convicted by a judge who spoke of "anarchy.". . .

The great danger for American democracy is not from the protesters. That democracy is too poorly realized for us to consider critics—even rebels—as the chief problem. Its fulfillment requires us all, living in an ossified system which sustains too much killing and too much selfishness, to join the protest.

NOTES

1. Robert A. Dahl, *A Preface to Democratic Theory* (Chicago: University of Chicago Press, 1963), p. 81.
2. *Ibid.*, p. 124.
3. *Ibid.*, p. 125.
4. *Ibid.*, p. 131.
5. *Ibid.*, pp. 131-32
6. *New York Times* (March 8, 1969).
7. Dahl, *A Preface to Democratic Theory*, p. 146.
8. Robert Wiebe, "The Confinements of Consensus," *TriQuarterly*, 1966. Copyright © by TriQuarterly 1966. All rights reserved.

How Democratic Is America?
A Response to Howard Zinn

Sidney Hook

I

There are a great many methodological errors and inconsistencies in Mr. Zinn's treatment of the theme. I shall focus on three.

First of all he confuses democracy as a political *process* with democracy as a political *product* or state of welfare, democracy as a "free society" with democracy as a "good society," where good is defined in terms of equality or justice (or both) or some other constellation of values. One of the reasons for choosing to live under a democratic political system rather than a nondemocratic system is our belief that it makes possible a better society. There is something that must be empirically established, something denied by critics of democracy from Plato to Santayana. The equality which is relevant to democracy as a political process is, in the first instance, political equality with respect to the rights of citizenship. Theoretically, a politically democratic community could vote, wisely or unwisely, to abolish, retain, or establish certain economic inequalities. Theoretically, a benevolent despotism could institute certain kinds of social and even juridical equalities. Historically, the Bismarckian political dictatorship introduced social welfare legislation for the masses at a time when such legislation would have been repudiated by the existing British and American political democracies. . . .

The second error in Mr. Zinn's approach to democracy is "to measure our democracy against an ideal (even if inadvertently unachievable) standard . . . even if utopian . . ." without *defining* the standard. His criteria admittedly are neither necessary nor sufficient for determining the presence of democracy since he himself admits that they are applicable to

From Sidney Hook,"How Democratic is America? A Response to Howard Zinn," in *How Democratic is America?*, ed. Robert A. Goldwin, Rand McNally & Company, 1971. Used by permission of the Public Affairs Conference Center, Kenyon College, Gambier, Ohio.

societies that are not democratic. Further, even if we were to take his criteria as severally defining the presence of democracy—as we might take certain physical and mental traits as constituting a definition of health—he gives no operational test for determining whether or not they have been fulfilled. For example, among the criteria he lists for determining whether a society is democratic is this: "Are the members of the society equally protected on matters of life and death—in the most literal sense of that phrase?" A moment's reflection will show that here—as well as in other cases where Zinn speaks of equality—it is impossible for all members to be equally protected on matters of life and death—certainly not in a world in which men do the fighting and women give birth to children, where children need *more* protection than adults, and where some risk-seeking adults require and deserve less protection (since resources are not infinite) than others. As Karl Marx realized, "in the most literal sense of that phrase," there cannot be absolute equality even in a classless society. . . .

The only sensible procedure in determining the absence or presence of equality from a democratic perspective is comparative. We must ask whether a culture is more or less democratic in comparison to the past with respect to some *desirable* feature of equality (Zinn ignores the fact that not all equalities are desirable). It is better for some people to be more intelligent and more knowledgeable than others than for all to be unintelligent and ignorant. There never is literally equal access to education, to knowledge and training in any society. The question is: Is there more access today for more people than yesterday, and how can we increase the access tomorrow?

Even Mr. Zinn should admit that with respect to some of his other criteria this is the only sensible approach. Otherwise they give arbitrary, unhistorical answers, the hallmark of the doctrinaire. He asks—criterion 1—"To what extent can various people in the society participate in those decisions which affect their lives?" and—criterion 7—"Is there freedom of expression on all matters, and equally for all, to communicate with other members of the society?" Why doesn't Mr. Zinn adopt this approach? Because it would lead him to inquire into the extent to which people are free to participate in decisions that affect their lives today, free to express themselves, free to organize, free to protest and dissent today, *in comparison with the past*. It would lead him to the judgment which he wishes to avoid at all costs, to wit, that despite the grave problems, gaps, and tasks before us, the United States is more democratic today than it was a hundred years ago, fifty years ago, twenty years ago, five years ago with respect to every one of the criteria he has listed. To recognize this is *not* an invitation to complacency. On the contrary, it indicates the possibility of broadening, deepening, and using the democratic political process to improve the quality of human life, to modify and redirect social institutions in order to realize on a wider scale the moral commitment of democracy to an equality of concern for all its citizens to achieve their fullest growth as persons. This commitment is to a process, not to a transcendent goal or a fixed, ideal standard.

In a halting, imperfect manner, set back by periods of violence, vigilantism, and xenophobia, the political democratic process in the United States has been used to modify the operation of the economic system. The improvements and reforms won from time to time make the still-existing problems and evils more acute in that people become more aware of them. The more the democratic process extends human freedoms, and the more it introduces justice in social relations and the distribution of wealth, the greater grows the desire for more freedom and justice. Historically and psychologically it is false to assume that reforms breed a spirit of complacency. . . .

The third and perhaps most serious weakness in Mr. Zinn's view is his conception of the nature of the formal political democratic process. It suffers from several related defects. First, it overlooks the central importance of majority rule in the democratic process. Second, it denies in effect that majority rule is possible by defining democracy in such a way that it becomes impossible. . . .

"Representation by its very nature," claims Mr. Zinn, "is undemocratic." This is Rousseauistic nonsense. For it would mean that no democracy—including all societies that Mr. Zinn ever claimed at any time to be democratic—could possibly exist, not even the direct democracies or assemblies of Athens or the New England town meetings. For all such assemblies must elect officials to carry out their will. If no representative (and an official is a representative, too) can adequately represent another's needs, there is no assurance that in the actual details of governance, the selectmen, road commissioners, or other town or assembly officials will, in fact, carry out their directives. No assembly or meeting can sit in continuous session or collectively carry out the common decision. In the nature of the case, officials, like representatives, constitute an elite and their actions *may* reflect their interests more than the interests of the governed. This makes crucial the questions whether and how an elite can be removed, whether the consent on which the rule of the officials or representatives rests is free or coerced, whether a minority can peacefully use these mechanisms, by which freely given consent is registered, to win over or become a majority. The existence of representative assemblies makes democracy difficult, not impossible.

Since Mr. Zinn believes that a majority never has any authority to bind a minority as well as itself by decisions taken after free discussion and debate, he is logically committed to anarchy. Failing to see this, he confuses two fundamentally different things—the meaning or definition of democracy, and its justification.

1. A democratic government is one in which the general direction of policy rests directly or indirectly upon the freely given consent of a majority of the adults governed. Ambiguities and niceties aside, that is what democracy means. It is not anarchy. The absence of a unanimous consensus does not entail the absence of democracy.

2. One may reject on moral or religious or personal grounds a democratic society. Plato, as well as modern totalitarians, contends that a majority of mankind is either too stupid or vicious to be entrusted with self-government, or to be given the power to accept or reject their ruling elites, and that the only viable alternative to democracy is the self-selecting and self-perpetuating elite of "the wise," or "the efficient," or "the holy," or "the strong," depending upon the particular ideology of the totalitarian apologist. The only thing they have in common with democrats is the rejection of anarchy.

3. No intelligent and moral person can make an *absolute* of democracy in the sense that he believes it is always, everywhere, under any conditions, and no matter what its consequences, ethically legitimate. Democracy is obviously not desirable in a head-hunting or cannibalistic society. But wherever and whenever a principled democrat accepts the political system of democracy, he must accept the binding authority of legislative decisions, reached after the free give-and-take of debate and discussion, as binding upon him whether he is a member of the majority or minority. Otherwise the consequence is incipient or overt anarchy or civil war, the usual preface to despotism or tyranny. Accepting the decision of the majority as binding does not mean that it is final or irreversible. The processes of freely given consent must make it possible for a minority to urge amendment or repeal of any decision of the majority. Under carefully guarded provisions, a democrat may resort to civil disobedience of a properly enacted law in order to bear witness to the depths of his commitment in an effort *to reeducate* his fellow citizens. But in that case he must voluntarily accept punishment for his civil disobedience, and so long as he remains a democrat, voluntarily abandon his violation or noncompliance with law at the point where its consequences threaten to destroy the democratic process and open the floodgates either to the violent disorders of anarchy or to the dictatorship of a despot or a minority political party.

4. That Mr. Zinn is not a democrat but an anarchist in his views is apparent in his contention that not only must a democracy allow or tolerate civil disobedience within limits but that "members of a society concerned with democracy must not only defend such acts, but encourage them." On this view, if Southern segregationists resort to civil disobedience to negate the long-delayed but eminently just measures adopted by the government to implement the amendments that outlaw slavery, they should be encouraged to do so. On this view, any group that defies any law that violates its conscience—with respect to marriage, taxation, vaccination,

education—should be encouraged to do so. Mr. Zinn, like most anarchists, refuses to generalize the principles behind his action. He fails to see that if all fanatics of causes deemed by them to be morally just were encouraged to resort to civil disobedience, even our imperfect existing political democracy would dissolve in chaos, and that civil disobedience would soon become quite uncivil. He fails to see that in a democracy the processes of intelligence, not individual conscience, must be supreme.

II

I turn now to some of the issues that Mr. Zinn declares are substantive. Before doing so I wish to make clear my belief that the most substantive issue of all is the procedural one by which the inescapable differences of interests among men, once a certain moral level of civilization has been reached, are to be negotiated. The belief in the validity of democratic procedures rests upon the conviction that where adult human beings have freedom of access to relevant information, they are, by and large, better judges of their own interests than are those who set themselves up as their betters and rulers, that, to use the homely maxim, those who wear the shoes know best where they pinch and therefore have the right to change their political shoes in the light of their experience. . . .

Looking at the question "How democratic is America?" with respect to the problems of poverty, race, education, etc., we must say "Not democratic enough!" but not for the reasons Mr. Zinn gives. For he seems to believe that the failure to adopt *his* solutions and proposals with respect to foreign policy, slum clearance, pollution, etc., is evidence of the failure of the democratic process itself. He overlooks the crucial difference between the procedural process and the substantive issues. When he writes that democracy is devoid of meaning if it does not include "equal access to the available resources of the society," he is simply abusing language. Assuming such equal access is desirable (which some might question who believe that access to *some* of society's resources—for example, to specialized training or to scarce supplies—should go not equally to all but to the most needful or sometimes to the most qualified), a democracy may or may not legislate such equal access. The crucial question is whether the electorate has the power to make the choice, or to elect those who would carry out the mandate chosen. . . .

When Mr. Zinn goes on to say that "in the United States . . . democracy should mean that every American, working a short work-week, has adequate food, clothing, shelter, health care, . . .," he is not only abusing language, he is revealing the fact that the procedural processes that are essential to the meaning of democracy, in ordinary usage, are not essential to his conception. He is violating the basic ethics of discourse. If democracy "should mean" what Zinn says it should, then were Huey Long or any other dictator to seize power and introduce a "short work-week" and distribute "adequate food, clothing, shelter, health care" to the masses, Mr. Zinn would have to regard his regime as democratic.

After all, when Hitler came to power and abolished free elections in Germany, he at the same time reduced unemployment, increased the real wages of the German worker, and provided more adequate food, clothing, shelter, and health care than was available under the Weimar Republic. On Zinn's view of what democracy "should mean," this made Hitler's rule more democratic than that of Weimar. . . .

Not surprisingly, Mr. Zinn is a very unreliable guide even in his account of the procedural features of the American political system. In one breath he maintains that not enough information is available to voters to make intelligent choices on major political issues like tax laws. (The voter, of course, does not vote on such laws but for representatives who have taken stands on a number of complex issues.) "The dominant influences are those of big business, which has the resources both to understand and to act." In another breath, he complains that the electorate is at the mercy of the propagandist. "The propagandist does not need to lie; he overwhelms the public with so much information as to lead it to believe that it is all too complicated for anyone but the experts."

Mr. Zinn is certainly hard to please! The American political process is not democratic because the electorate hasn't got enough information. It is also undemocratic because it receives too much information. What would Zinn have us do so that the public gets just the right amount of information and propaganda? Have the government control the press? Restrict freedom of propaganda? But these are precisely the devices of totalitarian societies. The evils of the press, even when it is free of government control, are many indeed. The great problem is to keep the press free and responsible. And as defective as the press and other public media are today, surely it is an exaggeration to say that with respect to tax laws "the dominant influences are those of big business." If they were, how can we account for the existence of the income tax laws? If the influence of big business on the press is so dominant and the press is so biased, how can we account for the fact that although 92 per cent of the press opposed Truman's candidacy in 1948, he was reelected? How can we account for the profound dissatisfaction of Vice-President Agnew with the press and other mass media? And since Mr. Zinn believes that big business dominates our educational system, especially our universities, how can we account for the fact that the universities are the centers of the strongest dissent in the nation to public and national policy, that the National Association of Manufacturers bitterly complained a few years ago that the economics of the free enterprise system was derided, and often not even taught, in most Departments of Economics in the colleges and universities of the nation?

Mr. Zinn's exaggerations are really caricatures of complex realities. Far from being controlled by the monolithic American corporate economy,

American public opinion is today marked by a greater scope and depth of dissent than at any time in its history. . . .

III

In justice to Mr. Zinn one should restate his position so that it becomes possibly more persuasive. It is demonstrable that democracy is healthier and more effective where human beings do not suffer from poverty, unemployment, and disease. It is also demonstrable that to the extent that property gives power, property in the means of social production gives power over the lives of those who must live by its use, and, therefore, that such property, whether public or private, should be responsible to those who are affected by its operation. Consequently one can argue that political democracy depends not only on the extension of the franchise to all adults, not only on its active exercise, but on programs of social welfare that provide for collective bargaining by free trade unions of workers and employees, unemployment insurance, minimum wages, guaranteed health care, and other social services that are integral to the welfare state. It is demonstrable that although the existing American welfare state provides far more welfare than was ever provided in the past—my own lifetime furnishes graphic evidence of the vast changes—it is still very far from being a genuine welfare state.

The basic issue that divides Mr. Zinn from others no less concerned about human welfare, but less fanatical than he, is how a genuine welfare state is to be brought about. My contention is that this can be achieved by the vigorous exercise of the existing democratic process, and that by the same coalition politics through which great gains have been achieved in the past, even greater gains can be won in the future.

For purposes of economy, I focus on the problem of poverty, or since this is a relative term, hunger. If the presence of hunger entails the absence of the democratic political process, then democracy has never existed in the past—which would be an arbitrary use of words. Nonetheless, the existence of hunger is always a *threat* to the continued existence of the democratic process because of the standing temptation of those who hunger to exchange freedom for the promise of bread. This, of course, is an additional ground to the even weightier moral reasons for gratifying basic human needs.

That fewer people go hungry today in the United States than ever before may show that our democracy is better than it used to be but not that it is as good as it can be. Even the existence of one hungry person is one too many. How then can hunger or the extremes of poverty be abolished? Certainly not by the method Mr. Zinn advises: "Acts of civil disobedience by the poor will be required, at the least, to make middle-class America take notice, to bring national decisions that begin to reallocate wealth."

This is not only a piece of foolish advice, it is dangerously foolish advice. Many national decisions to reallocate wealth have been made through the political process—what else is the system of taxation if not a method of reallocating wealth?—without resort to civil disobedience. Indeed, resort to civil disobedience on this issue is very likely to produce a backlash among those active and influential political groups in the community who are aware that normal political means are available for social and economic reform. The refusal to engage in such normal political processes could easily be exploited by demagogues to portray the movement towards the abolition of hunger and extreme poverty as a movement towards the confiscation and equalization of all wealth.

The simplest and most effective way of abolishing hunger is to provide a guaranteed annual wage for every family in the nation. This goal has already been adopted by several large trade unions. It has been widely discussed in public. The way has been prepared for it by the truly revolutionary principle, enunciated by the federal government, that it is responsible for maintaining a standard of relief as a minimum beneath which a family will not be permitted to sink. . . .

What is true for the guaranteed annual wage is true for a whole cluster of economic reforms that can increase the scope of the public sector of the economy, as well as extend social control of the private sector.

For reasons that need no elaboration here, the greatest of the problems faced by American democracy today is the race problem. Although tied to the problems of poverty and urban reconstruction, it has independent aspects exacerbated by the legacy of the Civil War and the Reconstruction period.

Next to the American Indians, the American Negroes have suffered most from the failure of the democratic political process to extend the rights and privileges of citizenship to those whose labor and suffering have contributed so much to the conquest of the continent. The remarkable gains that have been made by the Negroes in the last twenty years have been made primarily through the political process. If the same rate of improvement continues, the year 2000 may see a rough equality established. The growth of Negro suffrage, especially in the South, the increasing sense of responsibility by the white community, despite periodic setbacks resulting from outbursts of violence, opens up a perspective of continuous and cumulative reform. The man and the organization chiefly responsible for the great gains made by the Negroes, Roy Wilkins and the NAACP, are convinced that the democratic political process can be more effectively used to further the integration of Negroes into our national life than by reliance on any other method. . . .

The only statement in Mr. Zinn's essay that I can wholeheartedly endorse is his assertion that the great danger to American democracy does not come from the phenomena of protest as such. Dissent and protest are

integral to the democratic process. The danger comes from certain modes of dissent, from the substitution of violence and threats of violence for the mechanisms of the political process, from the escalation of that violence as the best hope of those who still have grievances against our imperfect American democracy, and from views such as those expressed by Mr. Zinn which downgrade the possibility of peaceful social reform and encourage rebellion. It is safe to predict that large-scale violence by impatient minorities will fail. It is almost as certain that attempts at violence will backfire, that they will create a climate of repression that may reverse the course of social progress and expanded civil liberties of the last generation.
. . .

CHAPTER TWO

THE CONSTITUTION AND THE FOUNDING FATHERS

Of the many books that have been written about the circumstances surrounding the creation of our Constitution, none generated more controversy than the publication of Charles Beard's An Economic Interpretation of the Constitution of the United States *(1913). A historian by profession, Beard challenged the belief that our Constitution was fashioned by men of democratic spirit. On the contrary, in what appeared to be a systematic marshalling of evidence, Beard sought to demonstrate: (1) that the impetus for a new constitution came from individuals who saw their own economic interests threatened by a growing trend in the population toward greater democracy; (2) that the Founding Fathers themselves were men of considerable "personality" (i.e., holdings other than real estate), who were concerned not so much with fashioning a democratic constitution as they were with protecting their own financial interests against the more democratically oriented farming and debtor interests within the society; and, finally, (3) that the individuals charged with ratifying the new constitution also represented primarily the larger economic interests with the society. While space limitations prevent a full development of Beard's argument, the portions of his book that follow should provide some feel for both the substance of his argument and his method of investigation.*

Beard's analysis has been subject to repeated scrutiny over the years. The most systematic effort in this regard came in 1956 with the publication of Robert Brown's Charles Beard and the Constitution: A Critical Analysis of an Economic Interpretation of the Constitution. *Arguing that the rigor of Beard's examination was more apparent than real, Brown accuses him of citing only the facts that supported his case while ignoring those that did not. Moreover, he contends that even the evidence that Beard provided did not warrant the interpretation he gave to it. Brown concludes that the best evidence now available does not support the view that "the Constitution was put over undemocratically in an undemocratic society by personal property."*

An Economic Interpretation of the Constitution of the United States

Charles A. Beard

Suppose it could be shown from the classification of the men who supported and opposed the Constitution that there was no line of property division at all; that is, that men owning substantially the same amounts of the same kinds of property were equally divided on the matter of adoption or rejection—it would then become apparent that the Constitution had no ascertainable relation to economic groups or classes, but was the product of some abstract causes remote from the chief business of life—gaining a livelihood.

Suppose, on the other hand, that substantially all of the merchants, money lenders, security holders, manufacturers, shippers, capitalists, and financiers and their professional associates are to be found on one side in support of the Constitution and that substantially all or the major portion of the opposition came from the non-slaveholding farmers and the debtors—would it not be pretty conclusively demonstrated that our fundamental law was not the product of an abstraction known as "the whole people," but of a group of economic interests which must have expected beneficial results from its adoption? Obviously all the facts here desired cannot be discovered, but the data presented in the following chapters bear out the latter hypothesis, and thus a reasonable presumption in favor of the theory is created.

Of course, it may be shown (and perhaps can be shown) that the farmers and debtors who opposed the Constitution were, in fact, benefited by the general improvement which resulted from its adoption. It may likewise be shown, to take an extreme case, that the English nation derived immense advantages from the Norman Conquest and the orderly administrative processes which were introduced, as it undoubtedly did; nevertheless, it does not follow that the vague thing known as "the advancement of general welfare" or some abstraction known as "justice" was the immediate, guiding purpose of the leaders in either of these great historic changes. The point is, that the direct, impelling motive in both cases was the economic advantages which the beneficiaries expected would accrue to themselves first, from their action. Further than this, economic interpretation cannot go. It may be that some larger world process is working through each series of historical events: but ultimate causes lie beyond our horizon. . . .

THE FOUNDING FATHERS: AN ECONOMIC PROFILE

A survey of the economic interests of the members of the Convention presents certain conclusions:

A majority of the members were lawyers by profession.

Most of the members came from towns, on or near the coast, that is, from the regions in which personalty was largely concentrated.

Not one member represented in his immediate personal economic interests the small farming or mechanic classes.

The overwhelming majority of members, at least five-sixths, were immediately, directly, and personally interested in the outcome of their labors at Philadelphia, and were to a greater or less extent economic beneficiaries from the adoption of the Constitution.

1. Public security interests were extensively represented in the Convention. Of the fifty-five members who attended no less than forty appear on the Records of the Treasury Department for sums varying from a few dollars up to more than one hundred thousand dollars. . . .

It is interesting to note that, with the exception of New York, and possibly Delaware, each state had one or more prominent representatives in the Convention who held more than a negligible amount of securities, and who could therefore speak with feeling and authority on the question of providing in the new Constitution for the full discharge of the public debt. . . .

2. Personalty invested in lands for speculation was represented by at least fourteen members. . . .

3. Personalty in the form of money loaned at interest was represented by at least twenty-four members. . . .

4. Personalty in mercantile, manufacturing, and shipping lines was represented by at least eleven members. . . .

5. Personalty in slaves was represented by at least fifteen members. . . .

It cannot be said, therefore, that the members of the Convention were "disinterested." On the contrary, we are forced to accept the profoundly significant conclusion that they knew through their personal experiences in economic affairs the precise results which the new government that they were setting up was designed to attain. As a group of doctrinaires, like the Frankfort assembly of 1848, they would have failed miserably; but as practical men they were able to build the new government upon the only foundations which could be stable: fundamental economic interests.[1] . . .

RATIFICATION

New York There can be no question about the predominance of personalty in the contest over the ratification in New York. That state, says Libby, "presents the problem in its simplest form. The entire mass of interior counties . . . were solidly Anti-federal, comprising the agricultural portion of the state, the last settled and the most thinly populated. There were however in this region two Federal cities (not represented in the convention [as such]), Albany in Albany county and Hudson in Columbia county. . . . The Federal area centred about New York city and county: to the southwest lay Richmond county (Staten Island); to the southeast Kings county, and to the northeast Westchester county; while still further extending this area, at the northeast lay the divided county of Dutchess, with a vote in the convention of 4 to 2 in favor of the Constitution, and at the southeast were the divided counties of Queens and Suffolk. . . . These radiating strips of territory with New York city as a centre form a unit, in general favorable to the new Constitution; and it is significant of this unity that Dutchess, Queens, and Suffolk counties broke away from the anti-Federal phalanx and joined the Federalists, securing thereby the adoption of the Constitution."[2]

Unfortunately the exact distribution of personalty in New York and particularly in the wavering districts which went over to the Federalist party cannot be ascertained, for the system of taxation in vogue in New York at the period of the adoption of the Constitution did not require a state record of property.[3] The data which proved so fruitful in Massachusetts are not forthcoming, therefore, in the case of New York; but it seems hardly necessary to demonstrate the fact that New York City was the centre of personalty for the state and stood next to Philadelphia as the great centre of operations in public stock.

This somewhat obvious conclusion is reinforced by the evidence relative to the vote on the legal tender bill which the paper money party pushed through in 1786. Libby's analysis of this vote shows that "No vote was cast against the bill by members of counties north of the county of New York. In the city and county of New York and in Long Island and Staten Island, the combined vote was 9 to 5 against the measure. Comparing this vote with the vote on the ratification in 1788, it will be seen that of the Federal counties 3 voted against paper money and 1 for it; of the divided counties 1 (Suffolk) voted against paper money and 2 (Queens and

Dutchess) voted for it. Of the anti-Federal counties none had members voting against paper money. The merchants as a body were opposed to the issue of paper money and the Chamber of Commerce adopted a memorial against the issue."[4]

Public security interests were identified with the sound money party. There were thirty members of the New York constitutional convention who voted in favor of the ratification of the Constitution and of these no less than sixteen were holders of public securities. . . .

South Carolina South Carolina presents the economic elements in the ratification with the utmost simplicity. There we find two rather sharply marked districts in antagonism over the Constitution. "The rival sections," says Libby, "were the coast or lower district and the upper, or more properly, the middle and upper country. The coast region was the first settled and contained a larger portion of the wealth of the state; its mercantile and commercial interests were important; its church was the Episcopal, supported by the state." This region, it is scarcely necessary to remark, was overwhelmingly in favor of the Constitution. The upper area, against the Constitution, "was a frontier section, the last to receive settlement; its lands were fertile and its mixed population were largely small farmers. . . . There was no established church, each community supported its own church and there was a great variety in the district."[5]

A contemporary writer, R. G. Harper, calls attention to the fact that the lower country, Charleston, Beaufort, and Georgetown, which had 28,694 white inhabitants, and about seven-twelfths of the representation in the state convention, paid £28,081:5:10 taxes in 1794, while the upper country, with 120,902 inhabitants, and five-twelfths of the representation in the convention, paid only £8390:13:3 taxes.[6] The lower districts in favor of the Constitution therefore possessed the wealth of the state and a disproportionate share in the convention—on the basis of the popular distribution of representation.

These divisions of economic interest are indicated by the abstracts of the tax returns for the state in 1794 which show that of £127,337 worth of stock in trade, faculties, etc. listed for taxation in the state, £109,800 worth was in Charleston, city and county—the stronghold of Federalism. Of the valuation of lots in towns and villages to the amount of £656,272 in the state, £549,909 was located in that city and county.[7]

The records of the South Carolina loan office preserved in the Treasury Department at Washington show that the public securities of that state were more largely in the hands of inhabitants than was the case in North Carolina. They also show a heavy concentration in the Charleston district.

At least fourteen of the thirty-one members of the state-ratifying convention from the parishes of St. Philip and Saint Michael, Charleston (all of whom favored ratification) held over $75,000 worth of public securities. . . .

CONCLUSIONS

At the close of this long and arid survey—partaking of the nature of catalogue—it seems worth while to bring together the important conclusions for political science which the data presented appear to warrant.

The movement for the Constitution of the United States was originated and carried through principally by four groups of personalty interests which had been adversely affected under the Articles of Confederation: money, public securities, manufactures, and trade and shipping.

The first firm steps toward the formation of the Constitution were taken by a small and active group of men immediately interested through their personal possessions in the outcome of their labors.

No popular vote was taken directly or indirectly on the proposition to call the Convention which drafted the Constitution.

A large propertyless mass was, under the prevailing suffrage qualifications, excluded at the outset from participation (through representatives) in the work of framing the Constitution.

The members of the Philadelphia Convention which drafted the Constitution were, with a few exceptions, immediately, directly, and personally interested in, and derived economic advantages from, the establishment of the new system.

The Constitution was essentially an economic document based upon the concept that the fundamental private rights of property are anterior to government and morally beyond the reach of popular majorities.

The major portion of the members of the Convention are on record as recognizing the claim of property to a special and defensive position in the Constitution.

In the ratification of the Constitution, about three-fourths of the adult males failed to vote on the question, having abstained from the elections at which delegates to the state conventions were chosen, either on account of their indifference or their disfranchisement by property qualifications.

The Constitution was ratified by a vote of probably not more than one-sixth of the adult males.

It is questionable whether a majority of the voters participating in the elections for the state conventions in New York, Massachusetts, New Hampshire, Virginia, and South Carolina, actually approved the ratification of the Constitution.

The leaders who supported the Constitution in the ratifying conventions represented the same economic groups as the members of the Philadelphia Convention; and in a large number of instances they were also directly and personally interested in the outcome of their efforts.

In the ratification, it became manifest that the line of cleavage for and against the Constitution was between substantial personalty interests on the one hand and the small farming and debtor interests on the other.

The Constitution was not created by "the whole people" as the jurists have said; neither was it created by "the states" as Southern nullifiers long contended; but it was the work of a consolidated group whose interests knew no state boundaries and were truly national in their scope.

NOTES

1. The fact that a few members of the Convention, who had considerable economic interests at stake, refused to support the Constitution does not invalidate the general conclusions here presented. In the cases of Yates, Lansing, Luther Martin, and Mason, definite economic reasons for their action are forthcoming; but this is a minor detail.
2. O. G. Libby, *Geographical Distribution of the Vote of the Thirteen States on the Federal Constitution*, p. 18. Libby here takes the vote in the New York convention, but that did not precisely represent the popular vote.
3. *State Papers: Finance*, Vol. I, p. 425.
4. Libby, *op. cit.*, p. 59.
5. *Ibid.*, p. 42-43.
6. "Appius," *To the Citizens of South Carolina* (1794), Library of Congress, Duane Pamphlets, Vol. 83.
7. *State Papers: Finance*, Vol. I, p. 462. In 1783 an attempt to establish a bank with $100,000 capital was made in Charleston, S.C., but it failed. "Soon after the adoption of the funding system, three banks were established in Charleston whose capitals in the whole amounted to twenty times the sum proposed in 1783." D. Ramsay, *History of South Carolina* (1858 ed.), Vol. II, p. 106.

Charles Beard and the Constitution: A Critical Analysis

Robert E. Brown

At the end of Chapter XI [of *An Economic Interpretation of the Constitution of the United States*], Beard summarized his findings in fourteen paragraphs under the heading of "Conclusions." Actually, these fourteen conclusions merely add up to the two halves of the Beard thesis. One half, that the Constitution originated with and was carried through by personalty interests—money, public securities, manufactures, and commerce—is to be found in paragraphs two, three, six, seven, eight, twelve, thirteen, and fourteen. The other half—that the Constitution was put over undemocratically in an undemocratic society—is expressed in paragraphs four, five, nine, ten, eleven, and fourteen. The lumping of these conclusions under two general headings makes it easier for the reader to see the broad outlines of the Beard thesis.

Before we examine these two major divisions of the thesis, however, some comment is relevant on the implications contained in the first paragraph. In it Beard characterized his book as a long and arid survey, something in the nature of a catalogue. Whether this characterization was designed to give his book the appearance of a coldly objective study based on the facts we do not know. If so, nothing could be further from reality. As reviewers pointed out in 1913, and as subsequent developments have demonstrated, the book is anything but an arid catalogue of facts. Its pages are replete with interpretation, sometimes stated, sometimes implied. Our task has been to examine Beard's evidence to see whether it justifies the interpretation which Beard gave it. We have tried to discover whether he used the historical method properly in arriving at his thesis.

If historical method means the gathering of data from primary sources, the critical evaluation of the evidence thus gathered, and the drawing of conclusions consistent with this evidence, then we must conclude that Beard has done great violation to such method in this book. He admitted that the evidence had not been collected which, given the proper use of historical method, should have precluded the writing of the book. Yet he nevertheless proceeded on the assumption that a valid interpretation could be built on secondary writings whose authors had likewise failed to collect the evidence. If we accept Beard's own maxim, "no evidence, no history," and his own admission that the data had never been collected, the answer to whether he used historical method properly is self-evident.

Neither was Beard critical of the evidence which he did use. He was accused in 1913, and one might still suspect him, of using only that evidence which appeared to support his thesis. The amount of realty in the country compared with the personalty, the vote in New York, and the omission of the part of The Federalist No. 10 which did not fit his thesis are only a few examples of the uncritical use of evidence to be found in the book. Sometimes he accepted secondary accounts at face value without checking them with the sources; at other times he allowed unfounded rumors and traditions to color his work.

Finally, the conclusions which he drew were not justified even by the kind of evidence which he used. If we accepted his evidence strictly at face value, it would still not add up to the fact that the Constitution was put over undemocratically in an undemocratic society by personalty. The citing of property qualifications does not prove that a mass of men were disfranchised. And if we accept his figures on property holdings, either we do not know what most of the delegates had in realty and personalty, or we know that realty outnumbered personalty three to one (eighteen to six). Simply showing that a man held public securities is not sufficient to prove that he acted only in terms of his public securities. If we ignore Beard's own generalizations and accept only his evidence, we would have to conclude that most of the country, and that even the men who were directly concerned with the Constitution, and especially Washington, were large holders of realty.

Perhaps we can never be completely objective in history, but certainly we can be more objective than Beard was in this book. Naturally the historian must always be aware of the biases, the subjectivity, the pitfalls that confront him, but this does not mean that he should not make an effort to overcome these obstacles. Whether Beard had his thesis before he had his evidence, as some have said, is a question that each reader must answer for himself. Certain it is that the evidence does not justify the thesis.

So instead of the Beard interpretation that the Constitution was put over undemocratically in an undemocratic society by personal property, the following fourteen paragraphs are offered as a possible interpretation of the Constitution and as suggestions for future research on that document.

1. The movement for the Constitution was originated and carried through by men who had long been important in both economic and political affairs in their respective states. Some of them owned personalty, more of them owned realty, and if their property was adversely affected by conditions under the Articles of Confederation, so also was the property of the bulk of the people in the country, middle-class farmers as well as town artisans.

2. The movement for the Constitution, like most important movements, was undoubtedly started by a small group of men. They were probably interested personally in the outcome of their labors, but the benefits which they expected were not confined to personal property or, for that matter, strictly to things economic. And if their own interests would be enhanced by a new government, similar interests of other men, whether agricultural or commercial, would also be enhanced.

3. Naturally there was no popular vote on the calling of the convention which drafted the Constitution. Election of delegates by state legislatures was the constitutional method under the Articles of Confederation, and had been the method long established in this country. Delegates to the Albany Congress, the Stamp Act Congress, the First Continental Congress, the Second Continental Congress, and subsequent congresses under the Articles were all elected by state legislatures, not by the people. Even the Articles of Confederation had been sanctioned by state legislatures, not by popular vote. This is not to say that the Constitutional Convention should not have been elected directly by the people, but only that such a procedure would have been unusual at the time. Some of the opponents of the Constitution later stressed, without avail, the fact that the Convention had not been directly elected. But at the time the Convention met, the people in general seemed to be about as much concerned over the fact that they had not elected the delegates as the people of this country are now concerned over the fact that they do not elect our delegates to the United Nations.

4. Present evidence seems to indicate that there were no "propertyless masses" who were excluded from the suffrage at the time. Most men were middle-class farmers who owned realty and were qualified voters, and, as the men in the Convention said, mechanics had always voted in the cities. Until credible evidence proves otherwise, we can assume that state legislatures were fairly representative at the time. We cannot condone the fact that a few men were probably disfranchised by prevailing property qualifications, but it makes a great deal of difference to an interpretation of the Constitution whether the disfranchised comprised ninety-five per cent of the adult men or only five per cent. Figures which give percentages of voters in terms of the entire population are misleading, since less than twenty per cent of the people were adult men. And finally, the voting qualifications favored realty, not personalty.

5. If the members of the Convention were directly interested in the outcome of their work and expected to derive benefits from the establishment of the new system, so also did most of the people of the country. We have many statements to the effect that the people in general expected substantial benefits from the labors of the Convention.

6. The Constitution was not just an economic document, although economic factors were undoubtedly important. Since most of the people were middle-class and had private property, practically everybody was interested in the protection of property. A constitution which did not protect property would have been rejected without any question, for the American people had fought the Revolution for the preservation of life, liberty, and property. Many people believed that the Constitution did not go far enough to protect property, and they wrote these views into the amendments to the Constitution. But property was not the only concern of those who wrote and ratified the Constitution, and we would be doing a grave injustice to the political sagacity of the Founding Fathers if we assumed that property or personal gain was their only motive.

7. Naturally the delegates recognized that the protection of property was important under government, but they also recognized that personal rights were equally important. In fact, persons and property were usually bracketed together as the chief objects of government protection.

8. If three-fourths of the adult males failed to vote on the election of delegates to ratifying conventions, this fact signified indifference, not disfranchisement. We must not confuse those who could *not* vote with those who *could* vote but failed to exercise their right. Many men at the time bewailed the fact that only a small portion of the voters ever exercised their prerogative. But this in itself should stand as evidence that the conflict over the Constitution was not very bitter, for if these people had felt strongly one way or the other, more of them would have voted.

Even if we deny the evidence which I have presented and insist that American society was undemocratic in 1787, we must still accept the fact that the men who wrote the Constitution believed that they were writing it for a democratic society. They did not hide behind an iron curtain of secrecy and devise the kind of conservative government that they wanted without regard to the views and interests of "the people." More than anything else, they were aware that "the people" would have to ratify what they proposed, and that therefore any government which would be acceptable to the people must of necessity incorporate much of what was customary at the time. The men at Philadelphia were practical politicians, not political theorists. They recognized the multitude of different ideas and interests that had to be reconciled and compromised before a constitution would be acceptable. They were far too practical, and represented far too many clashing interests themselves, to fashion a government weighted in favor of personalty or to believe that the people would adopt such a government.

9. If the Constitution was ratified by a vote of only one-sixth of the adult men, that again demonstrates indifference and not disfranchisement. Of the one-fourth of the adult males who voted, nearly two-thirds favored the Constitution. Present evidence does not permit us to say what the popular vote was except as it was measured by the votes of the ratifying conventions.

10. Until we know what the popular vote was, we cannot say that it is questionable whether a majority of the voters in several states favored the Constitution. Too many delegates were sent uninstructed. Neither can we count the towns which did not send delegates on the side of those opposed to the Constitution. Both items would signify indifference rather than sharp conflict over ratification.

11. The ratifying conventions were elected for the specific purpose of adopting or rejecting the Constitution. The people in general had anywhere from several weeks to several months to decide the question. If they did not like the new government, or if they did not know whether they liked it, they could have noted *no* and there would have been no Constitution. Naturally the leaders in the ratifying conventions represented the same interests as the members of the Constitutional Convention—mainly realty and some personalty. But they also represented their constituents in these same interests, especially realty.

12. If the conflict over ratification had been between substantial personalty interests on the one hand and small farmers and debtors on the other, there would not have been a constitution. The small farmers comprised such an overwhelming percentage of the voters that they could have rejected the new government without any trouble. Farmers and debtors are not synonymous terms and should not be confused as such. A town-by-town or county-by-county record of the vote would show clearly how the farmers voted.

13. The Constitution was created about as much by the whole people as any government could be which embraced a large area and depended on representation rather than on direct participation. It was also created in part by the states, for as the *Records* show, there was strong state sentiment at the time which had to be appeased by compromise. And it was created by compromising a whole host of interests throughout the country, without which compromises it could never have been adopted.

14. If the intellectual historians are correct, we cannot explain the Constitution without considering the psychological factors also. Men were motivated by what they believe as well as by what they have. Sometimes their actions can be explained on the basis of what they hope to have or hope that their children will have. Madison understood this fact when he said that the universal hope of acquiring property tended to dispose people to look favorably upon property. It is even possible that some men support a given economic system when they themselves have nothing to gain by it. So we would want to know what the people in 1787 thought of their class status. Did workers and small farmers believe that they were lower-class, or did they, as many workers do now, consider themselves middle-class? Were the common people trying to eliminate the Washingtons, Adamses, Hamiltons, and Pinckneys, or were they trying to join them?

As did Beard's fourteen conclusions, these fourteen suggestions really add up to two major propositions: the Constitution was adopted in a society which was fundamentally democratic, not undemocratic; and it was adopted by a people who were primarily middle-class property owners, especially farmers who owned realty, not just by the owners of personalty. At present these points seem to be justified by the evidence, but if better evidence in the future disproves or modifies them, we must accept that evidence and change our interpretation accordingly.

After this critical analysis, we should at least not begin future research on this period of American history with the illusion that the Beard thesis of the Constitution is valid. If historians insist on accepting the Beard thesis in spite of this analysis, however, they must do so with the full knowledge that their acceptance is founded on "an act of faith," not an analysis of historical method, and that they were indulging in a "noble dream," not history.

CHAPTER THREE

FEDERALISM

The making of decisions within the American governmental system has always been complicated by the fact that formal governmental powers are divided between the national government and the states. This arrangement, mandated by the Constitution, frequently has led to conflict between the states and the national government over which level of government should do what. Thus when government leaders in Washington have debated such things as health care for the elderly, the financing of public education, or civil rights protections for blacks and other minorities, they have had to ask not only "What should be done?" but also "At which level of government should we do it?" Indeed, it has often been the case that there has been more heated and time-consuming debate over who "should do it" than "what should be done."

The debate over which government is best able to do things in our political system continues to this day, as revealed by the next two selections. In one selection, Amitai Etzioni, a strong defender of national government action, took the occasion of the fifth anniversary of the Revenue Sharing Act to assess the record of the state governments. Looking at various statistical data on the performance of the states, Etzioni has serious misgivings about continuing federal revenue sharing, which provides federal money to the states and localities to spend with few restrictions.

Daniel Elazar, the second contributor, challenges Etzioni's conclusions, and the critics of the states generally, by arguing that the states have been the victims of a number of "myths" regarding state corruption and inefficiency. These "myths," he claims, have been perpetuated by those who have failed to examine all of the evidence. Thus, any assessment of the points of view expressed in these selections must take into account the nature of the "evidence" presented as well as the arguments themselves.

Revenue Sharing Five Years Later

Amitai Etzioni

LIBERAL ORIGINS

Revenue sharing's intellectual origins were chiefly liberal, and one of its main designers was Walter Heller, the chief Kennedy-Johnson economic adviser. Many liberals nowadays share with conservatives the dogma that small government is ipso facto better than big government.

As it was formed and implemented, however, revenue sharing has had a central thrust far different from the Kennedy-Johnson reformist goal of transferring income to the poor, to minorities, to the inner city and to other human services. Revenue sharing's thrust has been to free funds to local policy-makers to use as they wish.

Generally, those purposes are not reformist in nature. A study by Professors David Caputo of Purdue and Richard Cole of George Washington analyzed the use of $2.8 billion in revenue sharing funds mailed out to 32,685 governmental units. Of that sum, only $88 million was devoted to social services for the poor and aged.

The Treasury's Office of Revenue Sharing, which administers the program, has some revealing statistics of its own: 23 per cent of the funds go to public safety, 21 per cent to education, 15 per cent to public transportation, 10 per cent to construction, renovation and maintenance of public buildings, 7 per cent to health, 5 per cent to recreation, and 4 per cent to social services for the aged and poor. A former secretary of housing and urban development, Robert V. Wood, told a Senate committee that as $6 billion "new" dollars a year were offered to local governments under revenue sharing, 112 "old" federal social action programs costing $16.9 billion a year were either terminated or reduced.

This shift of emphasis from social reform toward conformity to the majoritarian local preferences is compounded by the manner in which revenue sharing funds are distributed.

It depends not on need but on the average per capita expenditure of the particular local government. The federal funds provide for no less than 20 per cent and no more than 145 per cent of that average. Thus, there is a windfall for affluent suburbs which spend a good deal of money per capita and relatively little in the way of money for areas in which the poor are concentrated.

Revenue sharing does have one major federal string. The monies are not to be used in a discriminatory fashion. The record here is far from magnificent.

The National Clearinghouse on Revenue Sharing, sponsored by four public interest groups, attempts to monitor the use of the shared funds. Fully half of the complaints it has filed dealt with channeling revenue sharing monies to parks and health centers that were "inaccessible to minority neighborhoods."

The group has also focused on the work of the Treasury's Office of Revenue Sharing. The office, according to the monitoring group, has been slow to investigate complaints, reluctant to act on violations when uncovered and almost never initiates studies of alleged violations on its own. The office's answer is that it is doing a "good job" when one considers the smallness of its staff. At one point the office director, Graham Watt, reported that he had two field workers to check civil rights compliance.

The Advisory Commission on Intergovernmental Relations, composed of private citizens and representatives of Congress and local and state governments, has complained that there are "insufficient" safeguards under revenue sharing against racial and sexual discrimination. The Civil Rights Commission has made the same point. And it was echoed recently in a study released by the National Revenue Sharing Monitoring Project.

POWER TO THE PEOPLE?

According to the anti-Washington refrain, the federal government is too remote and too rigidly bureaucratic to be responsible to varied local needs and values. The "new federalism" stresses decentralization. The relevant question, then, is whether revenue sharing does bring power closer to the people.

On the face of it, the answer would seem to be in the affirmative. Revenue sharing expenditures are controlled by state and local governments, bodies closer geographically to the people than Washington.

Actually, many Americans have less of a say in local affairs than in the nation's business. For the legislative oversight of most state and local administrators tends to be much weaker than that of Congress over federal agencies.

In 1970 a nonpartisan citizens' conference, using Ford Foundation funds, made a study of the 50 state legislatures. "Instead of operating as an independent or even important policy-making body," the report concluded, "the state legislature too often serves merely as a funnel or screen for outside initiative."

Legislatures and their members, the study noted, lack sufficient staff and access to information. Frequently, they must rely on lobbyists—or on the governor. According to the study in "most states" the governor is not simply chief executive but also "the chief legislator," the man best able to initiate and promote bills. . . .

Revenue sharing obviously cannot perform miracles in reforming state and local governments. The question is whether it creates greater opportunities for citizen participation in the decision-making process. The answer seems to be both yes and no.

Often, no hearings are held on the disposition of the funds. Sometimes, as a Minneapolis poverty worker put it, "public hearings just give citizens a chance to yell." However, a Brookings Institution study of the impact of a number of programs found that revenue sharing can lead to more budget hearings and to greater citizen participation in the political process. The hearings compel lobbyists to pay more attention to local budgets and politics; the issues become more "visible" to the public.

Yet a General Accounting Office study of the results of revenue-sharing in 240 cities and counties found increased citizen participation in the budgetary process in only about a third of the localities. Even there the increase was normal.

Returning power to the people raises the question: "Who are they?" In the nation's capitol many different pressure groups are at work, no single one controls. But in Detroit, certainly, the auto industry and the UAW between them are a dominant factor: in Delaware, Du Pont is influential and in Cincinnatti, Proctor and Gamble has a major voice. Blacks in Newark and whites in Buffalo may tend to have narrower vision than the federal bureaucrat. . . .

INEFFICIENCY AND WORSE

The stories of bureaucratic failings, follies and faults in Washington are often told. But advocates of a further dismantling of the federal machine must ask whether a shift to local government will relieve the problem—or exacerbate it. It costs more to collect local taxes than state taxes. It costs more to collect state taxes than federal taxes.

Congressional committees, in evaluating revenue sharing, have never conducted a systematic study comparing the incidence of fraud, nepotism and partisanship at the federal, state and local levels. One study of a pre-revenue sharing grant to local governments may be relevant. A House subcommittee, evaluating a $1.5 billion effort to upgrade law enforcement, concluded that the state programs were "riddled with inefficiency, waste, maladministration and in some cases, corruption." The probe took note of diversion of funds for political purposes, exorbitant consulting fees, the awarding of contracts without proper bidding and misappropriation of funds.

Most observers would agree that the FBI is more efficient and less corrupt than the average local police department. If it has been misused in the past, there are enough instances of abuse of local police authority. Thus, a Cook County grand jury found that police surveillance of six local community groups had "all the earmarks of a police state."

Medicare is a federally administered health care program. Medicaid is administered jointly by the federal, state and local governments. "The consensus," *Medical World News* reported in 1975, "is that Medicare has succeeded in insulating the aged from ruinous medical expenses but that Medicaid has largely failed to make good health care available to the poor and near-poor." A detailed examination of the two programs concluded: "What's to be done now, though, with the chaos that has ensued? The answer being heard more and more is that Medicaid should be federalized like Medicare."

The federal Social Security Administration recently ran into criticism for spending more than it takes in and for relatively poor administration of the new Social Security supplements, but it is still widely viewed as a highly efficient program compared to local human service administrations.

Forbes magazine, hardly a friend of big government, notes that the SSA "automated almost from the start and never did choke from feather-bedding and bureaucracy. It disburses its $75 billion a year with operating expenses of only about $1.4 billion . . . more efficiently than any private insurer." Locally administered welfare programs have frequently shown themselves to be burdened by people who receive and who ought not, and others who ought but don't, red tape, insensitivity and other bureaucratic failings.

Many lobbyists of regulated industries, failing to block a federal regulation, retreat to asking that it be locally enforced. They know that often local enforcement mechanisms are much weaker than federal ones. One reason the nursing homes scandal proved so immune to correction in New York State over the last decade is that influential state legislators acted as lawyers and lobbyists for the nursing homes.

Most experts on American local government agree that one of its great curses is this fragmentation into thousands of small jurisdictions. This often hobbles attempts to organize a battle against pollution, introduce a mass transit system or launch other endeavors requiring cooperation among several jurisdictions.

Revenue sharing helps this fragmentation by helping to finance the fragments. Most of the governmental units to benefit from revenue sharing are very small: half have less than 1,000 inhabitants, and four-fifths have less than 5,000. The amounts involved are small (about 2 per cent of the total revenue shared in 1973), but revenue sharing offers no inducement such as increased disbursement to governmental units which merge. About 13,000 of the units which receive revenue sharing funds, as "general governments," have little more responsibility than maintaining the local roads.

"MUDDLING THROUGH"

There are those who believe that revenue sharing in time will strengthen local governments. They argue that before revenue sharing local governments suffered from inexperience and relative lack of talented and professional manpower because 91 per cent of all tax revenues were spent by the federal government and the best and brightest were hired for federal positions. An expert on American government, Professor Daniel J. Elazar of Temple University, contends that the efficiency and integrity of local governments have never been so poor as critics maintain—and that, anyway, they are improving substantially. He points to several examples, but no statistical data has been brought forward to support this view.

Past experience, ranging from foreign aid programs to OEO local projects, suggests that injecting large amounts of funds into poor administrations with few strings attached as to how the funds shall be used, does not tend to lead to their reform, at least not to significant ones. A survey of 22 Iowa municipalities by the League of Women Voters found that revenue sharing had "no effect on the city's budget process," and the Institute of Public Administration of Pennsylvania State University concluded that revenue sharing encouraged "the continued use of 'muddling through' as the main method of local decision-making.". . .

. . . [Most] of our opinion makers seem to feel that as a matter of principle, revenue sharing is a fine thing. Most critics seek only to modify revenue sharing by changing its disbursement formula, its accounting methods, its rules governing citizen involvement. But such medicine is likely to prove a palliative, not a cure. Effective national control for reform of some 38,000 units of government is simply not practical. Local control of funds and concern for social reform do not go hand in hand in most communities. Local citizen involvement is likely to remain symbolic rather than real. We owe it to ourselves to consider alternatives to revenue sharing. . . .

It is an old failing of peoples and governments to become entrapped in a policy without ever attempting an unsentimental re-evaluation. The policy becomes sanctified. For years this country "renewed" cities with bulldozers and ignored the existence of China without asking whether the basic premise behind the original policy was still valid. It is time to ask that question about revenue sharing.

The New Federalism: Can the States Be Trusted?

Daniel J. Elazar

THE CRITICS' CASE

. . . In a single issue of *The New York Times* not long ago, Amitai Etzioni became the latest in a long succession of people who have attacked revenue sharing on the ground that state and local government is especially corrupt, and Arthur Schlesinger, Jr., questioned the entire idea of enhancing the power of local government by claiming, as many have before him, that, because the national government is no less the government of the people than local government, there is no reason to believe that anything is better done locally than nationally.

The Etzioni and Schlesinger myths are but two of many. In other quarters, there are those who still argue that strengthening the hand of the states and localities is a way of perpetuating racial discrimination. Others repeat the myth that the federal government grew in power originally because of state and local failures, and that there is therefore no reason to reward the states and localities today. Tied closely with that myth is another one that claims that, because the states and localities have not made sufficient effort to come to grips with their problems on their own, they do not deserve to be bailed out by Washington.

I submit that a careful reading of the record belies each and every one of these criticisms, revealing most of them to have been untruths from the first and the rest to be criticisms that, whatever their original value, have long since become obsolete. There is more than enough evidence to show that the states and localities, far from being weak sisters, have actually been carrying the brunt of domestic governmental progress in the United States ever since the end of World War II, and have done so at an

Reprinted with permission of the author from *The Public Interest* No. 35 (Spring 1974), pp. 89-102. © 1974 by National Affairs Inc. The author is Professor of Political Science, Bar-Ilan and Temple Universities; Senior Fellow, Center for the Study of Federalism, Temple University; President, Jerusalem Institute for Federal Studies.

accelerated pace since the advent of America's direct combat involvement in Vietnam. Moreover, they have been largely responsible for undertaking the truly revolutionary change in the role of government in the United States that has occurred over the past decade.

In making this claim, I do not intend to argue from single examples, as people usually do when they want to "prove" the failure of the states and localities. Generally, when the claim is made that the states or the cities are failing, the claimant then points to Mississippi or Newark or some other state or community that does provide a sufficiently horrible case in point. Such arguments are no more accurate than a claim that the states are the most progressive governments in the country—which could easily be substantiated if one looked exclusively at New York, California, Wisconsin, or Massachusetts, which have been over the last 80 years far more progressive in many ways than the federal government—or that the cities are far more compassionate than any other governments, a contention that would be sustained if one looked only at San Francisco, New Orleans, Berkeley, or New York, which have been far more tolerant of individual social differences and deviations than Washington or any state. In these pages, therefore, I propose to evaluate state and local government, not by citing a few extreme examples, but by looking at the general record which state and local governments as a whole have built in each of the areas their critics have pointed to.

THE MYTH OF URBAN-RURAL WARFARE

Criticism #1: The states are unmindful of local—particularly big-city—needs, while the cities distrust the states and refuse to cooperate with them. This argument had considerable merit during the two generations or so the country took to make the transition from rural to urban living. Not unreasonably, declining rural populations were reluctant to give up their dominance of state governments to the new urbanites, particularly since so many of the former genuinely believed in the moral superiority of rural life and so many of the latter belonged to ethnic or racial groups with decidedly different mores. Indeed, much of what posed as urban-rural conflict was really inter-ethnic conflict set in a discreet juridical framework. . . .

Since the rural-urban transition took place at different times in different parts of the country, different states have been undergoing its pains since the late 19th century. Consequently, in the memories of those now living there have always been horrible examples of rural-dominated state political systems interfering with the burgeoning cities within their borders, and these examples have obscured the ever-growing number of states that were politically responsive to their cities.

By 1970 few, if any, states had yet to enter the transition period. Put simply, the record reveals that the transition begins when at least 40 per cent of a state's population is urban and is completed when urban places account for over 60 per cent of the population total. No state is now below that 40 per cent figure, and only 11 (seven of them in the South) are less than 50 per cent urban, but these contain only a bit more than 10 per cent of the country's population. Another nine fall between 50 and 60 per cent. Before the 40 per cent mark is attained, big cities find it very difficult to gain consideration in their state capitols. This is hardly surprising in a democracy, where majorities rule and overwhelming majorities tend to rule easily. After the 40 per cent figure is reached, the cities can begin to bargain with increasing success. Georgia is a case in point, having passed the 40 per cent mark in 1960 and closed on the 50 per cent mark in 1970.

Past 60 per cent, there is no longer any real contest. Minnesota and Indiana are good examples. Since they passed 60 per cent of their legislatures, each in its own way, have opened up to every kind of pro-metropolitan legislation that has been proposed. Ten of the 50 states, containing some 79.4 million people (or nearly 40 per cent of the country's total population), are 75 per cent urban or more, which means that urban and state interests are essentially identical.

Cities—of varying sizes and with varying interests, to be sure—are in the saddle in virtually all of the states today, and rural-urban conflict has given way to new inter-urban conflicts in whose resolution the state government plays a legitimate and not unfair role, even if the losers, in the great tradition of American politics, holler "foul" at every opportunity. . . .

Even more significant than the fact of urban hegemony in contemporary state-city relations is the fact that state expenditures have grown extraordinarily since World War II, and that most of those expenditures, particularly in the last decade, have been funneled into urban areas, especially big cities. Unfortunately, the great fixed-cost programs such as public welfare, in which the fixed costs keep rising, have absorbed the greater part of these funds so that they are largely unavailable for more innovative uses. Worse for the public image of the states, the funds are so quickly absorbed in this manner that the public is not even aware that they have been increased—but this does not change the fact that they have been.

In fact, the states and the cities themselves have recognized that the day of conflicting state-city interests is past. For several years after it was seriously proposed, revenue sharing itself was held up by a dispute as to whether the cities would receive funds directly from Washington or through their states. In 1971, the Council of State Governments and the National League of Cities reached an agreement which ended the conflict. In a manner entirely consonant with the whole idea of American federalism, they agreed to request that Congress appropriate the monies to the states without even a fixed passthrough formula but with the provision that the states would have to negotiate with their local governments to arrive at a satisfactory distribution of the funds, thereby effectively affirming the cities' new feeling of confidence that the states will be alert to their needs through an ordinary negotiation process. While this was not the formula adopted by Congress, the agreement did pave the way for the passage of general revenue sharing legislation in 1972.

THE MYTH OF ADMINISTRATIVE INCOMPETENCE

Criticism #2: The states and localities are administratively incapable of properly utilizing any additional powers that might be transferred to them. This myth also has its roots in a partial truth of the past. When the role of government in American society underwent drastic expansion in the 1930's, Washington did indeed set the pace in the development of a proper bureaucracy to manage the new government programs. Many of the states and localities were either unprepared or too impoverished by the Depression to respond in kind, and some were still too small in size to require so extensive an administrative apparatus. Nevertheless, most states laid the foundations during the Depression years for an administrative system appropriate to the mid-twentieth century, and then built on those foundations after World War II, when the resources denied them by circumstances for 15 years or more became available again.

Today, in my own talks with officials of federal agencies that work with their state and local opposite numbers I have found, even among those not particularly disposed to turn their functions over to other planes of government, a growing consensus affirming the competence of state and local administration. These insiders' arguments in favor of retaining a strong federal presence are based on real or perceived policy differences between them and the states and localities, not on the question of competence. Nor should this cause any great surprise. The investigations of political scientists over the past decade—totally ignored by the mythologists, of course—have consistently found no substantial difference among the three groups of bureaucrats with respect to background, capability, and dedication to their respective programs. All the studies have shown that, in most program areas, the administrative officials of all three planes of government are drawn from the same professional backgrounds and are committed to the same professional goals.

Perhaps most important, within the past decade the executive agencies of general government in both the states and localities—that is, the offices of the governors and mayors—have generally been strengthened in a manner reminiscent of the strengthening of the President's office in the 1920's and 1930's. State planning agencies are being developed as arms of the office of governor; executive office staffing has improved in cities as well as in states; and mayors and governors are increasingly using their planning staffs as resources for controlling and coordinating the multifarious activities of their governments, much as our Presidents use the Office of Management and Budget.

A good deal of this improvement has been the consequence of simple growth. While the states range in population from California's 19.7 million to Alaska's 300,000, six states, containing 40 per cent of America's population, have over 10 million people each. Five more, containing some 15 per cent of the total, have over five million people each. States of this size are bigger than most sovereign countries in today's world (California is almost as populous as Canada or Argentina, Pennsylvania nearly equals Australia and surpasses Belgium or Chile, New Jersey is larger than Austria, and Michigan is larger than any of the Scandinavian countries or Switzerland). All told, fully half the states have more than three million inhabitants, which means that they are as large as or larger than Ireland, Israel, New Zealand, Norway, or Uruguay—all of them countries acknowledged to be able to sustain themselves as independent nations. This means that sheer growth in population has fostered a growth in social complexity and internal resources (human and material) that, in turn, has led to more sophisticated governmental responses.

It is true that smaller states may be unable to mobilize the resources necessary for across-the-board governmental sophistication (although all major programs, both in large states and small, are now managed by personnel of relatively equal competence). Yet in many such cases local norms and expectations do not encourage "sophisticated" government on the federal model. Supposed "deficiencies" in these states and localities are often mere reflections of the tastes and wishes of their citizens.

None of the foregoing is intended to suggest that there are no problems facing state and local administrations or that all business is efficiently conducted in the states and localities; but by the same token, no one is about to claim that the federal administration is without its serious problems either. Not many Americans would deny Washington the wherewithal to administer programs because of the TFX scandal or the Post Office mess or the lack of coordination within HEW. No government has a monopoly on efficiency—or inefficiency—in the United States today. Consequently, decisions as to where to locate responsibility must hinge on other criteria.

THE PROBLEM OF CORRUPTION

Criticism #3: Even if the states and localities now have enough in common and sufficient administrative skills to handle the additional powers, corruption and vested interests will prevent them from utilizing those powers well. The "local corruption" argument, another favorite myth in the American political repertoire, has at least two serious inadequacies. One is a question of fact. As a group, state and local governments today are far less corrupt in the usual sense of the term than at any time in the past 100 years. When it comes to "conventional" corruption, the same can be said of the federal

government. (The kind of corruption represented by Watergate is something new—and it is far more dangerous than old-fashioned graft and
influence-peddling.) A whole host of factors having to do with changes in
American society have operated to reduce at all planes of government the
relatively crude forms of political payoff common at the turn of the century
and earlier. . . .

The morality of public business—governmental or nongovern-
mental—is rightfully a matter of concern in the United States today, but
strengthening the position of the states and localities should not be
contingent on that question. It may indeed be argued with considerable
justice that supposed differences in the extent of corruption at the various
planes of government only reflect the fact that influence-peddling in
Washington is usually more genteel—since it involves the country's great
enterprises—than the simpler forms involving "common folk" in the states
and localities. By the same token, it may be that corruption closer to home
at least gets spread more widely among those who need money than
corruption in high places, which tends to reward the already privileged
only. And in any event, it is important to remember that corruption at the
federal plane affects the entire country, whereas at the state and local
planes the consequences stop at the state or city boundaries.

A second weakness of the "local corruption" argument is its tendency
to overestimate the extent to which corruption, where it exists, affects the
delivery of governmental services. There are many indications that corruption has far less influence on governmental performance today than it did
80 or 100 years ago. This is because the nature of corruption has changed;
the old days of straightforward bribery and "buying" of public officials
have generally disappeared. Today, practices are more subtle; characteris-
tically, they involve rewarding one's friends with favors rather than
blocking proposed government activities. The lucrative business today is in
the awarding of contracts for the delivery of services, a system which more
or less guarantees that services will be delivered one way or another.
Consequently, whether corruption exists or not, the services will.[1]

Corruption is a perennial governmental problem, and it is usually
related to norms rooted in the local culture. By all accounts, states like
Michigan, Minnesota, Virginia, and Utah are far less corrupt than the
federal government. New York, North Carolina, and Pennsylvania are
probably on a par with Washington in this respect, while Indiana,
Louisiana, New Jersey, and Texas are probably more corrupt. Even the
above list indicates that there is no simple correlation between corruption
and the quality of government.

Much the same argument can be made in the case of waste. There are
clearly no grounds for believing that one plane of government is more
wasteful than the others, though the way in which their wastefulness is
manifested may differ. Personal deficiencies of public officials cause waste

and inefficiency in some of the smaller states and localities, but no more than is generated by red tape in very large bureaucracies like the federal government today.

Nor do vested interests in the states and localities cause more "distortions" of public policy than those in Washington. This proposition has been well tested in recent years as the federal government has extended its regulatory powers over coal mining, boating, flammable clothes, and, most recently, industrial safety, supposedly in response to state "failures." It has become increasingly apparent that federal regulation has meant not higher standards in these areas but an adjustment of standards toward a national mean that suits the interests of the parties being regulated, often to the dismay of those who championed federal intervention in the first place on the ground that federal action would obviously mean higher standards.

WHY ARE FEDERAL FUNDS NEEDED?

Criticism #4: The states and localities have failed to assume their proper fiscal obligations, and there is no reason why the federal government should bail them out. If the truth be known, the states and localities have borne the brunt of the effort to cope with increased demand for domestic services since the end of World War II. No matter what base period is used, the fiscal data confirm this. Since 1946, state and local revenues from their own sources have risen from under $10 billion to over $100 billion, or by more than 10 times, while federal revenues have only quadrupled. Between 1960 and 1969—a decade of great expansion of federal activities—federal expenditures rose 69 per cent, including increases for the Vietnam war, but state and local expenditures rose 76 per cent. For only a few brief years during the mid-1960's at the height of the Great Society did federal expenditures increase at the same rate as those of the states and cities. . . .

The diversion of federal resources to the Vietnam war increased the burden on the states and localities to support domestic government activities. (Under the Constitution, this is how it should be; those who believe in strong state and local government cannot find fault in an arrangement whereby the states and localities provide something like two thirds of the funds for domestic purposes and the federal government approximately one third.) The states and localities did not shirk their responsibility to provide this larger share. In any given year, approximately four fifths of the states increase their taxes to pay for new services or added costs. Their problem is that they are caught either way. If they fail to provide adequate services, they are faulted for their failure. If they supply adequate services, the steady increase in fixed costs puts them near bankruptcy. . . .

At the same time, the federal government, with its foreign involvements taking precedence (and that is as it should be), has maintained its dominant role in the income tax field. There is where the crunch lies. Should Congress in its wisdom decide to drastically reduce the federal income tax, even without any formal provision for enhancing state revenues in the form of state tax credits or the like, there is little doubt that the states and localities would pick up the slack without any outside compulsion to do so. This thesis has even been tested in a limited way. When the federal government last cut taxes during the Kennedy Administration, state and local revenues increased automatically as the released funds poured into the economy to be taxed by those governments under existing levies; but, in addition, after a year's delay, no more, most states and localities raised their own taxes to absorb an even bigger share of the reduction, primarily because of the demands placed upon them by their own citizens.

Even the argument about the regressiveness of state taxes has lost potency in the last decade. Forty-five states now collect a state income tax, and several of the remaining states, which rely exclusively on the sales tax, have made that tax a far less regressive instrument than it once was by exempting such necessities as food, clothing, and medicine. . . . Only in the case of local reliance on property taxes is serious regressiveness still built into the system, but even here many states are now providing some relief for low-income taxpayers to the extent that they are fiscally able to do so. . . .

WILL FEDERAL MONEY BE WISELY USED?

Criticism #5: The states and localities will dissipate federal money given them without any strings attached instead of using the funds where they are most needed. The governmental functions which generate the heaviest drains on the country's fiscal resources—education, welfare, health, transportation—are precisely the ones whose necessity is generally accepted in all parts of the country or which have well-established clientele and interest-group support. The chances that any state or locality could easily ignore that public support is exceedingly slight. It has become entirely clear, in the study of federal aid programs, that once a program becomes routinized, there is rarely any difference of opinion among the planes of government as to the necessity for maintaining it. If anything, there is a tendency to freeze such programs in. There is absolutely no reason to doubt that the bulk of any shared revenues would be used to meet well-defined, well-established, and well-supported needs in these essential areas.

There is a historical precedent here which may be apt. In 1837, the federal government decided to distribute surplus revenue in the federal treasury to the states for use in meeting domestic needs that Congress felt the federal government was prohibited from undertaking directly. At that time, the great needs were for the creation of public elementary schools, the establishment of public welfare institutions, and the construction of internal improvements (particularly roads, canals, and railroads). There were those in Congress who wanted to specify, in the legislation granting the funds, that they would be used for these purposes, but the strict Constitutional constructionists of the time felt that this would be an improper exercise of federal power. The money was ultimately distributed with no formal strings but with the understanding that it would be used for such purposes—and indeed it was. While not every penny was well used (what government can ever make that claim?), a substantial share was; much of it was invested in permanent funds, with the interest to be used to support the functions in question for many years. Many of the state and local public school systems, public institutions, and even highways of today trace their origins to the surplus distribution of 1837, and more than a few are still benefiting from it. . . .

THE CASE FOR LOCALISM

There are those who assert that, since the national government is in many respects as close to the people as local government, there is no need to sacrifice the virtues of national uniformity for the will-o'-the-wisp of local control. Given the ease of nationwide communications today, it is reasonable to argue that national political figures can reach out to their constituents in ways that make them better known than their state and local counterparts. At the same time, however, one-way communication through the media is not the only—or even the best—measure of closeness. Granted that more people watch the President on television than the mayor, it is still questionable whether sheer visibility without the possibilities of interaction constitutes "closeness" in the sense that a democracy requires. Moreover, the sheer size of the national bureaucracy creates a degree of remoteness, inefficiency, and waste that rivals that of the least professionalized state government.

But efficiency is by no means the only value involved here. Part of the strength of the American political system derives from our understanding that where men are free it is not always necessary to use direct national action to achieve national goals. Often, they can be as effectively achieved through local or state action, and in such cases the results are almost certain to be more enduring because the decisions are more solidly rooted in public opinion. The history of the great innovations in the American federal system affirms the truth of this proposition. When we created a public education system in the United States over 100 years ago, we did so as a matter of national policy, but we accomplished the task through local action accompanied by state and national assistance of various kinds. Our highway and welfare systems were built in essentially the same way. This general technique is an aspect of the genius of American politics.

Today there is much discussion of, and growing support for, the idea of local control—of the restoration of local self-government insofar as that is possible in our complex world. I believe this is a responsible and hopeful movement of opinion. It is not a question of whether the federal government shall abdicate its role in domestic policy; that would be as impossible as it is undesirable. The growing demand of Americans today is rather that the federal role be adjusted to accommodate the goal of local self-determination. . . .

I do not doubt that, in some places, greater local responsibility for making and administering public policy will engender results that liberals and persons whose concern for a particular program is unmodified by other interests will find disagreeable. In other places, the result will be just as disturbing to conservatives and to those whose opposition to particular programs is untempered by any other interest. This is the price of democracy. No doubt it is a price worth arguing about. But those who choose to discuss the issue should do so on its merits, not on the basis of the myths which have hitherto obscured them. Today there is simply no justification for thinking that the states and localities, either in principle or in practice, are less able to do the job than the federal government. In fact, there is some reason to believe that, even with their weaknesses, they will prove better able to restore public confidence in America's political institutions.

NOTE

1. Massachusetts may well be a case in point. While its politics are often described as seamy, its governmental record actually makes it by any measure one of the most progressive governments in the Union, and in pioneering new programs or setting higher standards it often outdoes Washington. In the case of the Bay State, the combination of the moralistic commitment to "good government" stemming from its Puritan heritage and the desire to utilize politics to gain material advantage which is strong among many of its "ethnic" politicians has served to enhance the progressive character of that commonwealth when it comes to the delivery of services, even as it maintains its reputation for shady politics.

CHAPTER FOUR

PUBLIC OPINION

With the advent of modern high-speed computers, the discovery of the mathematical laws of probability, and the development of instant communication via television, public opinion polls have today become an integral part of the daily lives of citizens and public officials alike. Through the use of modern scientific polls, political decision makers can now be informed regularly on what the people feel about public issues. Polls, in short, have taken the guesswork out of lawmaking by making it possible for lawmakers to be well informed on what their constituents want.

In the following selections, two different points of view are expressed regarding public opinion polls and how they contribute to democracy. In the first selection, two experienced polling analysts, Charles W. Roll and Albert H. Cantril, reflecting on some thirty years of public opinion polling, conclude that polls have contributed greatly to the art of governing in a free society by making it possible for political leaders to be better informed on what the public is thinking. To these authors, a second and no less important benefit is that the public itself is better informed on the issues of the day through polls.

Our other author, John C. Ranney, writing at a time when polls were just beginning to come into widespread use (1946), examines how polls might actually be harmful to the operation of a democracy, especially if "democracy" is defined as an ongoing process of debate, discussion, and compromise. According to Ranney, polls may be harmful if they serve as a substitute for personal involvement in civic affairs. Ranney contends that the "heart of democracy" is to be found in active citizen participation in the "deliberative process," not in a public opinion poll.

Public Opinion Polling in a Free Society

Charles W. Roll and Albert H. Cantril

THE PLACE OF PUBLIC OPINION

The question is often asked about the circumstances under which political leaders should follow, lead, educate, cajole, or simply ignore public opinion. The issue is certainly not new, and while polling techniques have not raised any fundamentally new questions about the role of public opinion, they have indeed forced to the surface some of the traditional questions.

There were two points of view—each with its roots deep in European political tradition—which quickly emerged as the Founding Fathers framed our basic political institutions. One school of thought held that the determination of what was in the public interest could not be left to the people. They were held to be too ill-informed and too susceptible to momentary whims of passion to play a decisive role. This view was to be contrasted to the philosophy that the only legitimate source of judgment on major issues was to be found in the will of the people. The dilemma thus posed in these contending views was whether the nation's leaders were supposed to be responsible for the public's interest or to be responsive to the public's desires. . . .

THE COMPETENCE OF PUBLIC OPINION

The fundamental question raised by these conflicting strands of our political tradition basically is: What is the competence of public opinion? While this question calls for a philosophical answer, experience in the field of opinion research points up some of the considerations that should be borne in mind.

Excerpted from Chapter 7 of *Polls: Their Use and Misuse in Politics*, by Charles W. Roll, Jr., and Albert H. Cantril, © 1972 by Basic Books, Inc., Publishers, New York.

In our own view, the competence of public opinion is at the "feeling level." The public obviously cannot be expected to be informed and up-to-date in its understanding of complex issues, the implications of alternative courses of action, nor the advantages of specific instrumentalities by which a policy is effected. We agree with what Walter Lippmann wrote in 1925: ". . . when public opinion attempts to govern directly it is either a failure or a tyranny. It is not able to master the problem intellectually, nor to deal with it except by wholesale impact. . . . The intricate business of framing laws and administering them through several hundred thousand public officials is in no sense an act of the voters nor a translation of their will."[1]

However, when it comes to generalized impressions, in two areas the public's judgment usually proves sound and prophetic. The public is quick to spot a phony—the disingenuous politician who is facile and whose transparency soon betrays itself. The public is also very sensitive to the direction and adequacy of policies being pursued by its leaders. While public opinion takes longer to jell with regard to policies, once it becomes clear a policy is unworkable or simply getting too costly, the public will desert its leaders. . . .

Thus, in political research the crucial dimension from the public opinion standpoint is not whether people approve or disapprove of a given policy or the leader advocating a policy. Rather, it is the public's sense of trust and confidence in its leaders, when it comes to finding resourceful and effective ways of responding to problems. What it judges its leaders on, then, is less the substance of policies and programs than the overall impression of whether its leaders "are on top of things."

But Lippmann would argue in response: "The movement of opinion is slower than the movement of events. Because of that, the cycle of subjective sentiments on war and peace is usually out of gear with the cycle of objective developments. . . . The opinion deals with a situation which no longer exists."[2]

This forces a further differentiation regarding the public's competence to deal with matters of policy. We agree with Lippmann that the public cannot keep abreast of the twist and turn of events. But this does not mean that public opinion about these events is of political insignificance. When events or actions by leaders bring an issue home to the public, public opinion can quickly catch up to events, and when it does, it becomes all powerful. To quote Woodrow Wilson: "Opinion ultimately governs the world."[3] Opinion does not react to events unless they impinge in some meaningful way upon the level of basic individual concerns and individual self-interest.

Politicians often tend to exaggerate the degree to which the public pays attention to and cares about those procedural aspects of political life so important to them, e.g., the filibuster, seniority on Congressional committees, reapportionment, governmental organization, etc. However, on something less remote like school busing, which involves four sacred items to the American family—children, education, neighborhood, and the loss of hard-worked-for goals—the public's view sends politicians scurrying.

One major impact of television has been that it shortens the opinion lag to which Lippmann referred. TV undoubtedly helps hone the public's sensitivities to events and how its leaders are responding, and, also, it probably has helped the public become more alert to the difficulty of solving major problems. The medium has given the public a way to size up situations and individuals fairly quickly, and while the public's knowledge still lags behind the flow of events, TV will help keep current the public's impressions of the men at the helm and their policies, further cultivating its shrewdness of judgment.

Public opinion can be likened to a "system of dikes which channel public action or which fix a range of discretion within which government may act or within which debate at official levels may proceed."[4] This notion of the late V. O. Key "yields a different conception of the place of public opinion than does the notion of a government by public opinion in which, by some mysterious means, a referendum occurs on every major issue." . . .

The war in Indochina is the best single illustration of this concept. In a 1966 essay on public opinion about the war, Seymour Martin Lipset wrote: "To sum up the implications of the polls, it seems clear that the President holds the trump cards in dealing with the public on foreign policy matters. The public knows they do not know, and feel they must trust the President, for there is no one else on whom they can rely in the international field. . . . The President makes public opinion, he does not follow it. . . . The polls tell the President how good a politician he is."[5]

As events have since proven, Lipset greatly overstated the amount of latitude the President had. As Bill Moyers put it in an essay two years later:

> It should be obvious that a President faces no quest more difficult than the search for an accurate reading of how far and how fast he can lead the people. As difficult as the task is, he must try. He must try because there are questions on which governments dare not act without evidence of genuine support. When policies and laws outdistance public opinion, or take public opinion for granted, or fail to command respect in the conscience of the people, they lose their "natural" legitimacy. . . . Vietnam has proven that good intentions on the part of a nation's leaders will not substitute for the conscious involvement of the people in the decision to go to war.[6] . . .

LEADERSHIP OF OPINION

There is a tendency for people in positions of high leadership to develop an unbridled confidence in their own judgment. They have by and large survived political risks and made some basically sound calculations with regard to what is on the public's mind. Thus, they feel more competent than others to look over situations and make their own determinations as to what the state of public thinking is on an issue.

There is, therefore, an accompanying tendency for leaders to act quickly on the assumption that they have carefully weighed public opinion considerations. Decisions are announced or actions taken which often leave the public cold or in some instances spark outright opposition.

Three factors militate against sensitivity to the public opinion dimension of problems even on the part of seasoned political leaders. First, by definition political decisions are made amid great ambiguity. The choices are never easy. The alternatives are seldom clearly cut and they are often equally unattractive. In the words of the British Tory leader, Sir Gerald Nabarro, party politics is "the art of advocating something you know to be bad, as the only alternative to something you know to be a great deal worse."[7] The information available conflicts, special interests collide and staffers vie for the decision-maker's attention. The result is that subtle forces are at work to provide ways of reducing the ambiguity. In the extreme case, simplistic notions of what the relevant constituency consists of are propounded. Assumptions are made about "the silent majority," "the black vote," "youth," etc., as though these population groups can be thought of as segments of the population having an internal consistency of view.

This temptation is fed by a second factor we have touched upon earlier. This is the shared terms of reference with which national policies and priorities are debated. Politicians, journalists, bureaucrats, and the panoply of consultants-researchers-observers all tend to employ similar abstractions, words and information sources when commenting on the political scene. As the circle closes there are often mistaken assumptions made as to the state of public opinion.

Closely allied is a third factor, which is the frequently manifested cynicism of political leaders as to how suggestible the public is. It is often assumed that speeches, dramatic gestures, or good TV coverage will produce short-term gains with the public. Obviously, the public is often impressed. But consider that, after all the exposure given President Nixon on his visit to the People's Republic of China, there was no meaningful increase in those feeling he was doing a good job as President.[8]

The task of responsible leadership is to resist these influences, uncover the bases of consensus and cultivate a sense of community. . . .

In two principal respects, research into the state of public opinion can help. Research can help uncover the common ground amid the din of conflicting claims and help leaders find the bases for consensus. It can help elucidate the basic concerns of the people, place into context the topical issues of the moment and alert leaders to what it is in public opinion they had better pay attention to. As Lincoln put it: "What I want is to get done what the people desire to have done and the question for me is how to find that out exactly."[9]

At the other end of the process, research can provide a check on the claims of special interests which represent themselves as advocating the public interest. A superb example is found in the late 1940s. In 1947 the Republican Congress passed, over President Truman's veto, the Taft-Hartley Act with its strict regulation of organized labor. Truman, with the backing of labor leaders, attacked the law vigorously in the 1948 Presidential campaign and promised its repeal.

With Truman's surprise victory, Taft-Hartley appeared doomed. Robert Taft, up for reelection in 1950, looked to all equally doomed because of Ohio's large labor vote. However, a national poll was taken by the late Claude Robinson in early 1949 which showed that while two-thirds (69 percent) of labor union members did not "think the Congress should have passed this bill," overwhelming majorities approved of virtually every major provision of the bill when questioned about each separately. Armed with this knowledge, Taft carried his campaign right into union bailiwicks and confronted the issue head-on. Marked for sure defeat, Taft instead carried every industrial county in Ohio and defeated his popular challenger in a landslide with 57.5 percent of the vote.[10]

In our view this all suggests that opinion research—technically competent and sensitive to existing political realities—can enhance the strength of the democratic process by improving communication between the leader and the led. On the one hand, regular opinion soundings provide yet another way for the public's view to become known—particularly between elections. Were it not for the polls, President Johnson and others would not have known how profound the disaffection of the American people was with the war in Vietnam. In the absence of poll findings it would have been easier to dismiss the peace sentiment in the country as representing a few disenchanted and misdirected "peaceniks" and "doves."

On the other hand, insights obtained through opinion research can help alert leaders to stresses in their relationship with the public and uncover the sources of these stresses before it is too late. Research can thus contribute greatly to the stability of the political process.

With the speed and complexity of modern life these communication linkages are all the more important because it is all the more imperative that political leaders and the public understand one another. With the advent of opinion research it has been possible to reduce the time required for this transfer to take place. It is also now possible to remove much of the guesswork as regards how far ahead of or behind the public the nation's leaders are.

Opinion research can contribute in a number of specific areas:

1. Research can uncover areas of public ignorance, misunderstanding and indifference. At a time in which the Johnson Administration was

making some basic calculations with respect to U.S. policy in Southeast Asia, the finding of the Michigan Survey Research Center that one-fourth of the American public did not even know mainland China was ruled by communist regime could have been of the utmost importance.[11]

2. The public often does not understand how specific actions or policies relate to long-term objectives. Research can highlight these areas of confusion and help leaders then convey to the public what some of the considerations are that have been taken into account in the formulation of policies and why they show promise of being effective.

3. The public is usually ill-prepared for unexpected contingencies. Research that uncovers ignorance or indifference among the public can alert leaders to the need for preparing the public for eventualities that may lie ahead.

4. Conversely, the public may, in certain instances, have unrealistic expectations of what will follow from some action. We noted earlier how the popularity figures of Presidents tend to soar after periods of decisive Presidential initiatives. However, in all cases the luster soon vanishes as it becomes clear the action has not solved the problem of the moment. . . .

There is no doubt that the survey technique will be used in many new ways. The danger will always persist that the polls will be employed to ease the way for leaders who pander to the people's prejudices and exploit their many legitimate fears. Also, there will continue to persist the pollster who abuses the public trust with simplistic characterizations of the state of opinion.

The responsibility for the survey research community is immense. But so, too, is the obligation of those who use, report and follow the polls so closely. Now that the polls have come of age, the public has a need to know more about them. The more the potentialities—and limitations—of the polling technique are understood, the greater is the likelihood that opinion research will be employed in a responsible and meaningful fashion. . . .

We do not suggest that public opinion should be followed at every turn in decision making. We do suggest, however, that public opinion must be taken into account *before* decisions are made if there is to be any chance of their successful implementation. Far from constraining the options available to the decision-maker, reliable measurements of opinion can greatly enhance the range of choice and maneuver open to him. Without such insight, his initiatives can backfire or be misdirected as they collide with public misunderstanding, frustrations, resistances, and the many other barriers comprising the "system of dikes" to which V. O. Key referred.

It is not just a matter of finding in the polls a vivid and incisive device supportive of a kind of direct democracy. Rather, the polls can take the lead in helping the public and its leadership to understand one another better.

For the more faithfully the public's view is ascertained and taken into account, the greater is the chance that decisions of those at the helm will be both right and enduring.

NOTES

1. Walter Lippmann, *The Phantom Public* (New York: Harcourt, Brace and Co., 1925), quoted in Clinton Rossiter and James Lare, *The Essential Lippmann* (New York: Random House, 1963), p. 110.
2. Walter Lippmann, "Everybody's Business and Nobody's" from *Today and Tomorrow* (April 11, 1941), quoted in Rossiter and Lare, *Lippmann*, pp. 96-97.
3. Speech, April 20, 1915, quoted in *The Home Book of American Quotations*, ed. Bruce Bohle (New York: Dodd Mead and Co., 1967), p. 274.
4. V. O. Key, *Public Opinion and American Democracy* (New York: Knopf, 1964), p. 552.
5. Seymour Martin Lipset, "The President, The Polls and Vietnam," *Transaction* 3, no. 6 (September-October, 1966): 24.
6. Bill D. Moyers, "One Thing We Learned," *Foreign Affairs* (July 1968): pp. 661-662. (Italics provided.)
7. Quoted in *The New York Times*, October 12, 1969, in The Week in Review section.
8. The Gallup Poll found in interviewing just after the President's trip (March 3-5, 1972) that 56 percent approved of the job he was doing. In results from interviews February 4-7, the figure was 53 percent.
9. As quoted in Hadley Cantril, "Public Opinion in Flux," *Annals of the American Academy of Political and Social Science* (March 1942): 136.
10. Letter from L. Richard Guylay, January 20, 1972; and, Opinion Research Corporation, "The Taft-Hartley Law and Its Successor," from *The Public Opinion Index for Industry*, Vol. VII, No. 2 (February 1949).
11. Reported in A. T. Steele, *The American People and China* (New York: McGraw-Hill, 1966).

Do the Polls Serve Democracy?

John C. Ranney

Most of the current controversy over public opinion polls has centered about the question of their accuracy: the reliability of the sample taken, the impartiality of the sponsorship, the honesty of the interviewer and the person interviewed, the fairness of the questions, the measurement of intensities or gradations of feeling, and the validity of the analysis or interpretation. These are all, admittedly, important questions; but they tend to ignore or to beg one which is both more important and more theoretical: Assuming that the polls were to attain a miraculously perfect and unchallengeable accuracy, would they, even then, contribute significantly to the working of democracy?

One's first inclination is to take it for granted that the answer is "Yes." No principle, in democratic theory, has been more fundamental than the belief that political decisions ought to be made by the people as a whole or in accordance with their desires.[1] Yet no principle, in democratic practice, has proved more difficult of precise application. In theory, even when doubts are entertained as to the rationality, the objectivity, and the capacity of the ordinary citizen, modern democratic writers have continued to find the essence of democracy in popular participation in policy-making.[2] But in practice, it has long been apparent that our electoral system, as a reflection of popular wishes and as a channel for popular activity, leaves a good deal to be desired.

Various improvements have been suggested, ranging from the initiative and the referendum to proportional or functional representation. But none of these devices, except by placing an intolerable strain on the voter, has solved the problem of how to reflect simultaneously the great diversity of his interests and attitudes on different issues.[3] The result, under our present system, is that even if one assumes that the voter does anything

From John C. Ranney, "Do the Polls Serve Democracy?" *Public Opinion Quarterly* 10 (Fall 1946), pp. 349-351, 357-360. Reprinted by permission of the publisher.

more than choose between the personalities of rival candidates, an election approximates what has been called "plebiscitary democracy." It is a way of approving or disapproving in the most general terms the policies of the party or individual in office and of renewing or transferring this exceedingly vague mandate for the coming term of office.[4]

Such a check and consultation is much better than none at all. Notwithstanding its resemblance to some of the dictatorial plebiscites, it permits, in a free society, the expression of at least the major discontents. But consultations which are so sweeping and which occur at such rare intervals are only the thinnest caricature of the democratic belief that the health of the community depends upon the personal, active, and continuous political participation of the body of its citizens.

It is here that the polls are supposed to make their great contribution. By separating the issues from one another, by stating them simply and clearly, and by covering the electorate completely and continuously, they avoid the most obvious obscurities, strains, and distortions of the older procedures. If to these virtues one might add unchallengeable accuracy, the well-known dream of Bryce would be realized: the will of the majority of the citizens could be ascertained at all times; representative assemblies and elaborate voting machinery would be unnecessary and obsolete.[5]

ATTACKS ON THE POLLS

Not everyone has rejoiced over this possibility. Anyone who agrees with Hamilton, for example, that the people are turbulent and changing, seldom judging or determining right, is hardly likely to welcome a device to make the voice of the people (which decidedly is not the voice of God) more audible than ever. Nor is this attitude likely to surprise or disturb the genuine democrat.

What should disturb him, however, is the fact that there are many people who consider themselves good democrats and who nevertheless consider the polls a menace to democracy. . . .

THE POLLS AS A MISCONCEPTION OF DEMOCRACY

. . . [T]he most valid criticism which can be made of the polls is that they represent a fundamental misconception of the nature of democracy. Bryce's picture of a society in which the will of the majority of the citizens would be ascertainable at all times is neither a very profound nor a very realistic picture of democratic society. Democracy is not simply the ascertaining and the applying of a "will of the people"—a somewhat mystical entity existing in and of itself, independent, unified, and complete.[6] It is the whole long process by which the people and their agents inform themselves, discuss, make compromises, and finally arrive at a decision.[7]

The people are not the only element in this process, and they are not necessarily the agent which is best suited to each part of the task. In general, the executive and the administrative services are best fitted to see policy as a whole and to prepare a coherent program as well as to handle the technical details of legislation. The legislature provides a forum in which the different interests within the country can confront one another in a regularized way, as the people cannot, and acquire something of the mutual understanding and comprehensive outlook which is essential for the satisfactory adjustment of interests. The people themselves, finally, can express better than any other agency what it is they need and want.

None of these functions, it is true, belongs exclusively to any one agency, nor can any be separated rigidly from the others. The process of discussion and adjustment is a continuous one, carried on on all levels. There is a constant interweaving and interpenetration of talk and action subject to no precise demarcation but in which it is none the less essential that each agency refrain from functions which are beyond its competence.[8] In this process the operation of the polls may be positively harmful, not in interfering with "government by experts" as more frequently charged, but in emphasizing the content of the opinion rather than the way in which it is formed and in focussing attention on the divergency of opinion rather than upon the process of adjusting and integrating it.

To say this is not to urge a restriction on popular participation but to emphasize its real nature and function. Popular participation in government is thin and meaningless if it is nothing more than the registering of an opinion. It becomes meaningful to the extent that the opinion is itself the product of information, discussion, and practical political action. There is something not only pathetic but indicative of a basic weakness in the polls' conception of democracy in the stories of those who tell interviewers they could give a "better answer" to the questions if only they had time to read up a bit or think things over. It is precisely this reading up and thinking over which are the essence of political participation and which make politics an educational experience, developing the character and capacity of the citizens.[9]

The polls, however, except as their publication tends to stimulate political interest, play almost no part in this process. They make it possible for the people to express their attitude toward specific proposals and even to indicate the intensity of their feeling on the subject; and they can distinguish the attitudes of different social and economic groups from one another. But they provide no mechanism on the popular level for promoting discussion, for reconciling and adjusting conflicting sectional, class, or group interests, or for working out a coherent and comprehensive legislative program.

In fact, far less perfect instruments for discovering the "will" of the voters are often much more effective in arousing popular participation. The initiative and the referendum, for all their weaknesses, stir opponents and advocates of measures to unusual activity and stimulate a large proportion of the voters, rather than a small selected sample, to consider and discuss the issues.[10] Similarly, the privately-conducted British Peace Ballot proved to be an educational experience for the entire British people.[11] Even the much maligned *Literary Digest* Poll performed a greater service in arousing thought and discussion than did its more accurate competitors.

In short, the polls are not concerned with, and provide no remedy for, the gravest weaknesses in the democratic process. If one thinks of democracy in practical terms of discussion and political activity rather than of a disembodied "will," the great need is to get rid of the obstacles to popular education, information, debate, judgment, and enforcement of responsibility. To do this, there must be a multiple effort directed against a multiplicity of evils. To mention only a few of these, the political education in most of our schools, handicapped as they are by conventional school-boards and the fear of controversy, is wretchedly inadequate. In too many cities the sources of information are insufficient, the news itself distorted, and the free competition of ideas seriously restricted. In general, our facilities for discussion—clubs, unions, pressure organizations, forums, round-tables, and the radio—provide no adequate successor to the town meeting in the sense of active and responsible personal participation. More fundamentally, the undemocratic character of much of our economic and social life is a real hindrance to the growth of political democracy.

Moreover, even if our political education were magnificent, the channels of information completely clear, the facilities for discussion abundant, and the spirit of democracy universal, the obscurity and confusion in our political system, resulting from its checks and balances and its lack of party discipline, would make it almost impossible for the ordinary voter to understand what is going on, to pass judgment intelligently, and to place responsibility. Yet any government in which the people are to share must at a minimum be comprehensible. Obscurity and anonymity kill democracy. These defects, however, are present in our government, and about them the polls can do very little.

SUMMARY

The chief advantage of the polls is that, in an age of increasing strain upon traditional democratic procedures, they have made a constructive technical contribution by reflecting sensitively and flexibly the currents of public feeling, by making this information available to political leaders in a way which is neither rigid nor mandatory, and by testing the claims of special interests to represent the desires of the people as a whole. These are services performed by no other agency, and they should not be underestimated.

But if, in a democracy, the health of the community depends upon the personal, active, and continuous political participation of the body of its citizens, this contribution is a limited and even a minor one. Even when used with the greatest accuracy and intelligence, the polls cannot achieve any fundamental improvement until our political system itself is simplified, until the lines of responsibility are clarified, and until devices are discovered for increasing the direct participation of the people, not simply in the registration of their aims, but in the deliberative procedure which is the real heart of democracy.

NOTES

1. I do not intend to imply, of course, that this is the whole of democratic theory.
2. For some recent statements on this subject see Carl L. Becker, *Modern Democracy* (New Haven, 1941), p. 7; James Bryce, *Modern Democracies* (New York, 1924), Vol. I, p. 20; Francis Coker, *Recent Political Thought* (New York and London, 1934), p. 293; Carl J. Friedrich, *The New Belief in the Common Man* (Boston, 1942), pp. 31, 221; Harold J. Laski, "Democracy," *Encyclopaedia of the Social Sciences* (New York, 1932), Vol. 3, pp. 80, 84; John D. Lewis, "The Elements of Democracy," *American Political Science Review,* Vol. 34, p. 469 (June, 1940); A. D. Lindsay, *The Modern Democratic State* (London, New York, Toronto, 1943), Vol. 1, pp. 267-268; Charles E. Merriam, *The New Democracy and the New Despotism* (New York, 1939), pp. 11-12; Francis Graham Wilson, *The Elements of Modern Politics* (New York and London, 1936), pp. 189-190, 247.
3. John Dickinson, "Democratic Realities and the Democratic Dogma," *American Political Science Review,* Vol. 24, p. 300 (May, 1930); Pendleton Herring, *The Politics of Democracy* (New York, 1940), p. 329; E. E. Schattschneider, *Party Government* (New York, 1942), p. 33.
4. The electoral system is, of course, supplemented by the interpretive work of the pressure groups, and they provide an important instrument for popular political action. But it is obvious that many of them are at least as much concerned with misrepresenting or flouting public opinion on individual issues as with representing it.
5. *The American Commonwealth* (New York, 1920), Vol. 2, p. 262.
6. Dickinson, *op. cit.,* pp. 288-289; John D. Lewis, *op. cit.,* p. 471.
7. Ernest Barker, *Reflections on Government* (London, 1942), pp. 36, 67; C. Delisle Burns, *Democracy* (London, 1929), p. 90; Dickinson, *op. cit.,* pp. 291-292; Friedrich, *Constitutional Government and Democracy* (Boston, 1941), p. 255; Lindsay, *The Essentials of Democracy* (Philadelphia, 1929).
8. Barker, *op. cit.,* pp. 43-44; Dickinson, *op. cit.,* p. 301; Herman Finer, *The Theory and Practice of Modern Government* (New York, 1934), pp. 99-101, 369; Friedrich, *Constitutional Government,* pp. 255, 415; John D. Lewis, *op. cit.,* pp. 469-470; Merriam, *op. cit.,* pp. 120-121; John Stuart Mill, *Consideration on Representative Government* (New York, 1862), pp. 115-116.
9. To some, this is the greatest justification of democracy. Burns, *op. cit.,* pp. 7, 71-72, 88-89; Coker, *op. cit.,* p. 294; John Dewey, *The Public and Its Problems*

(New York, 1927), pp. 206-208; Mill, *op. cit.*, pp. 69-80, 170; Alexis de Tocqueville, *Democracy in America* (New York, 1838), p. 232.

10. Edwin A. Cottrell, "Twenty-Five Years of Direct Legislation in California," *Public Opinion Quarterly*, Vol. 3, pp. 30-45 (January, 1939). For a different opinion, see Waldo Schumacher, "Thirty Years of People's Rule in Oregon," *Political Science Quarterly*, Vol. 47, pp. 242-252 (June, 1932).

11. Dame Adelaide Livingstone, *The Peace Ballot* (London, 1935), pp. 19-29.

CHAPTER FIVE

VOTING

To some political observers, one of the more alarming developments within the American system in recent years has been the decrease in the percentage of persons going to the polls. At best, only slightly more than one-half of the eligible voters have voted in recent presidential elections—the election that tends to hold the most public interest. In other types of elections, such as congressional elections and those held at the state and local levels, the rates of participation are even lower. This development may be either good or bad, depending on how one views the value of the vote. The articles below highlight the problem of voter participation in America by examining the question of whether or not one should vote.

In the first selection, David Schuman views voting as currently practiced in America as anything but a positive virtue since it only serves to distract the masses from the real opportunities to participate and to affect policies in the American system. Schuman's argument turns principally upon his view that the two major parties, with their candidates and their campaigns, do not offer the American people a real choice. Schuman contends that the voter might as well stay home.

William C. Mitchell, on the other hand, offers a number of reasons why citizens ought to vote, not the least of which is the fact that staying home on election day is in itself a kind of vote.

But the principal difference between Mitchell's perception of voting and Schuman's is in what the two believe we can reasonably expect from the act of voting. Schuman seems to believe it ought to accomplish everything; Mitchell is much more modest in his expectations.

Politics as Fraud: Voting in America

David Schuman

It would be unreasonable to begin with the idea that voting in America is a positive virtue and then continue our study from there. Indeed, given the biases of society—Madisonian people, in an objective world, organized bureaucratically—we cannot understand voting out of its context. It would seem reasonable to argue that considering the way we have set up voting in America, voting is only a trivial distraction to keep the masses happy, to keep them occupied, to keep them powerless. . . .

THE VOTING FETISH

To begin to truly understand voting in America, we must put the whole discussion in context. We have got to know just how it fits into our view of the world. It may be best to discuss it by "pretending." Pretend that we are constructing a state. This state is to be inhabited by evil people; the population is to be motivated by self-interest. The world view is to be scientific. That is to say, realty and value are to be attributed only to those things that are physical and material, to those things that are countable and quantifiable. Finally, the population is to organize itself bureaucratically.

As good political scientists, as good creators, we would have to deal with a very fundamental problem: How do we keep citizens within the system? How can we give them an illusion of power so as to keep them content? How can we distract them from important questions—and possibly answers—while making trivial behavior seem important? The answer is deceivingly simple: Make voting a meaningless gesture (both to the individual and to the society), but also make voting a myth of important proportions.

Discussions of voting, and the questions asked about it, almost always

Reprinted by permission of the publisher, from David Schuman: *A Preface to Politics* (Lexington, Mass.: D.C. Heath and Company, 1977). For the full unabridged statement, see the original work.

miss the point. To look at how voting is discussed is an exercise in understanding how questions can predetermine answers. To understand the voting fetish, we must familiarize ourselves not only with the common questions and answers but also begin to ask questions not ordinarily asked.

The idea of voting is important in America, very important. The public schools pump our heads full of the importance of elections, the TV networks spend millions on their coverage, and we social scientists study and restudy elections and electors and the electorate. Even bars are closed on election day to insure that we become heady from voting and not drunk from liquor. Before one election has begun, people are making plans for the following one. There seems little doubt that elections—and voting—are the biggest games in town; but do they really mean anything? To put it differently, what does it mean to vote? How does it count?

Political scientists have worked hard studying elections. In part, elections are perfect to study if one believes in objective reality. Voting is an objective fact. A vote is something real, something that can be counted, computed, and "played with" in a variety of ways. Further, about the time one batch of votes is used up, there is another election and another batch. So we know a great deal about voting and we are told much about elections. For example, the distinguished political scientist Austin Ranney writes:

> . . . political scientists study the behavior of individual voters in order to understand the behavior of electorates, for their object is to comprehend the forces affecting the outcome of elections, which, as we shall see, are the principal democratic devices for holding government responsible to the people.[1]

It is all there—the myth of voting, that is. Let us examine the findings of those who study voting and elections, and see if we can understand the myth more clearly. More importantly, we could understand what they don't ask. . . .

The argument about voting often centers around the idea of democracy. In a simpleminded way, we are taught that to vote is democratic and that those who vote will have a say in determining policy. Political scientists are interested in who votes, in part to see which groups choose those who govern. Who votes? The more education a person has, the more likely the individual is to vote. The higher an individual's income, the greater the chances of his or her voting. More white people than black vote, and more white-collar than blue-collar workers vote. Finally, more men than women vote. ("One woman respondent told an interviewer, 'Woman is a flower for men to look after'; another said, 'I have never voted, I never will. . . . A woman's place is in the home'; and a third declared, 'Voting is for the men.' ")[2]

The suggestion has been made that the nonvoters—the black, the blue-collar, the "uneducated"—may not vote because they believe that elections make no difference.[3] Simply stated, these individuals hold that whoever—Democrat or Republican—holds power does not hold it for their benefit. On the other hand, the voter—the white, the "well-educated," the white-collar worker—may really believe that his or her vote makes a difference and that voting in national elections could change the world.

To understand the nature of elections and the nature of our party system is to begin to understand that the "uneducated" black who failed to vote may well be right. . . .

One basic criticism of elections is that they are not democratic. There is more than some truth in this contention. It is important to understand this point of view, and then to understand why it does not get us far enough.[4] To be democratic, elections should fulfill the following four requirements: First, either the parties or the candidates should offer clear-cut choices to the voters. Not a choice of hair color or of speaking style, but of politics and programs. Second, the voters must be concerned with and aware of the choices. Third, voting should somehow indicate how the majority feels about the issues. Finally, when a candidate is elected, he or she should somehow be bound by his or her promises. What we know about elections indicates that none of these conditions are met, or that they are even in very much danger of being met.

First things first: Are there policy alternatives? The answer is no. People do not run on issues; they run to be elected. Political parties are interested in winning the greatest number of votes, so they try to avoid taking stands which might offend or bringing up issues which seem to deviate too far from the center of things. When two parties equally intent on winning the election clash, the party that is the most vague may well triumph. Making clear the difficult issues is simply risky electoral politics. Our parties, our candidates, almost always play follow the leader; the funny part is that the leader never gets off dead center. . . .

Because the major parties deliberately try not to articulate the choices, the answer to our second condition is easy: The voters cannot be aware of policy alternatives when there are none. I blush at the redundance of the statement.

If people do not vote on issues, why do they vote? Generally speaking, people join the same party their parents joined. When elections come, most people, most of the time, vote for the candidate of their party. If people vote according to party, then what do the parties do, what functions do they serve?

Robert Dahl argues that political parties are of great help to the voter because they "present to voters a very small number of alternatives out of the total number theoretically available."[5] So that is what parties do! They help us to make rational choices by limiting those choices to two. They ease our anxiety over right and wrong—or, at least over who or what to vote for—by limiting our selection to an identical set of alternatives. Parties make it possible for us to choose between two representatives of the

system—and they make the choice relatively unencumbered by numbers.
. . .

Is it possible somehow for voting to indicate how the majority feels about the issues? The answer, of course, is no. With two—or three—candidates hedging on the issues, and each taking weak stands on many issues, it is simply naive to believe that a vote can be translated into support for a particular policy or set of policies. Our elections are not organized so that the voter can help decide what the major policies of the country will be. When an individual is elected, all that means is that he or she gets to hold office. Because the campaign promises were vague or silly or both, and because we do not really expect such promises to be kept, policies are not the result of elections.

So maybe that poor, black person is right not to vote. In 1968, 40 percent of the people who were eligible did not vote; in 1972, 44.6 percent didn't; by 1974 the percentage was up to 63.8. There just are not that many blacks in the country.

In the future the definition of an exciting election may change. Instead of being excited about who might win, we might be excited to see if anyone votes. . . .

Surely voting must do something, help someone. Oddly enough, it is not entirely clear just who does gain from elections. The voter may gain psychic satisfaction in knowing that he or she has "protected democracy" or whatever other symbol that citizen was serving. Someone gets elected, so certainly that someone is helped. In honesty, I believe the best we can do, the most we can say, is that voting contributes to the system. It symbolically hooks people to the process, at little or no risk to that process. Systems seek stability, and for us voting has uniquely served the status quo.

VOTING AND POLITICS

Up to here, two distinct arguments have been made. First, that our liberalism keeps us from an active involvement in politics. Second, that discussions on voting only show us that voting in America does not live up to the "requirements" of democracy. We have implied more than that. Certainly it seems possible to understand voting as fulfilling a stabilizing, symbolic function, as a method of keeping people from making important decisions and away from power. Few people ask what voting means if, in a bureaucratic society, most leaders are interchangeable anyway. But even that may not be the most important point.

If this is a book about politics, then it is necessary to ask at least one more question about voting in America. It is important to ask a very obvious question which is almost never asked: Is voting in America a political action? . . .

We have already discussed politics. To act politically, one must honestly work toward an eventual outcome. That means—more or less—that one must help frame the issues; one works for those issues; and, finally, one must help carry out the results of those issues. Ideally, this is done openly and with others. The argument, stated most simply, is that we make something legitimate, make something moral, by actively participating in it. By being political, we give meaning to what goes on. It is not a simple process of acquiescing; it is action.

In order to understand politics, we must understand what it means to take action. We can get at this by discussing the differences between behavior and action. Behavior is the normal, the routine, those things that are carefully closed by boundaries. To behave is to do the predictable, to do what has always been done. Pets behave; children "should" behave. In oddly similar ways, rats behave for scientists as voters behave for the system. . . .

To take action is to cut across traditional boundaries. It is to invent new methods, create new means, make new connections. It is to consciously help define who you are by what you do. It is an individual's way of relating to the whole, but in his or her own, unique, special way. You are what you do, if you act. You are what you are told to be, if you behave.

In order to act, one must have space. There must be political space provided by the state. Space metaphysically and actually. Space in which citizens may come together for creative political action, not simply for normal behavior. The greater the space available, the greater the opportunity for each citizen to act. But people must want and fight for and finally protect their political space. It is as much a human property as a property provided by the state. In other words, one of the reasons we have no political space is that it might endanger the system; another is that we are not actively working to get that space. . . .

Briefly, a person must have space in order to act creatively, in order to engage publicly in politics. But just what does that really mean?

For the purposes of our discussion, it simply means this: Voting as we practice it is not a political act. We know that we have no real say in who we vote for. All the candidates look the same. It is like being given a choice between identical twins in a beauty contest. We surely cannot feel creative, nor can we feel we are defining ourselves by what we do. There is no sense of participation.

The way voting has been set up, it is neither politics nor action. It is not even public. It is simply a fact that having three minutes alone in a three-foot by three-foot space once every few years neither furthers democracy nor enhances freedom. It is almost all those things we were taught that it was not. . . .

In many places, voting has come to mean behavior in the most confining sense. It is only a method of endorsing those who will keep doing the same old thing, in the same old way, according to the same old rules, under the same old system. It is the meaningless raised to important societal myth.

Voting keeps you where you are. It is not action, it is not politics; it is merely reaction, simply endorsement. The rules keep ruling, the people keep voting. The franchise has widened, eighteen-year-olds now vote. We have spread the novocaine; everyone gets deadened. The numbness of voting merely envelops more of us.

At the end of a creative political act, people should vote; but as it is now carried out, voting is a terrible fraud.

It is best we heed these words of Nietszche: "I say unto you: a man must have chaos yet within him to be able to give birth to a dancing star."

NOTES

1. Austin Ranney, *Governing* (New York: Holt, Rinehart & Winston, 1971), p. 141.
2. Ibid., p. 147. It is just such statements that point out how difficult the task of liberation will be.
3. Ibid., p. 148.
4. Thomas Dye and Harmon Zeigler, *The Irony of Democracy* (Belmont, Calif.: Wadsworth Publishing Co., 1970), p. 174.
5. Robert Dahl, *Pluralist Democracy in the United States* (Chicago: Rand McNally & Co., 1967), p. 250.

Why Vote?

William C. Mitchell

Although having vote power is now a fact, to exercise that power poses a dilemma in choice, at least for the voter who wishes to make the most of his vote. It would be foolish not to recognize the inherent dilemmas confronting a voter who, approaching the polls for the first time, wants to do good for himself, his generation, and the nation. . . .

Conventional voting studies by political scientists tell us that most voters are (1) not well informed, (2) apathetic if not cynical, (3) inclined to vote as their parents did, (4) inclined to vote as members of their social groupings previously have, and (5) inclined to be somewhat less than rational in their decision processes and their choices. Although evidence in favor of the first four generalizations is often highly impressive and persuasive, voters need not behave in these ways. Certainly this should not be true of students, who have acquired a vast social consciousness during the past decade and who are daily involved in intense emotional and intellectual experiences as students and young adults. If anyone has the opportunity and capacity to become intelligent voters it is today's 18 to 20 year old. The problems of choice and the decision processes should be well within his grasp. . . .

IS VOTING WORTHWHILE?

The answer to this question is *yes*, with the qualification that anyone's personal influence in any large arena is apt to be small. The new voter must not blithely assume that utopia has now arrived and that anything, and everything, he wants will be immediately forthcoming. With 140 million potential voters, a single voter's influence cannot, in itself, be impressive. In the 1968 Presidential election there were 73.2 million voters. Still, every

From William C. Mitchell, *Why Vote?* (Chicago: Markham Publishing Co., 1971), pp. 29-38, 43-46. Reprinted by permission of the author.

vote counts; the following pages will explain how much and under which conditions.

Voting is important in a number of ways. First, those who do not vote are, in effect, voting; they have decided *not* to support any of the competitors. Nonvoting can influence and has influenced many elections, especially close ones. Many elections are won by fewer than 1 percent of those casting ballots. We have had fourteen Presidents who won by less than popular majorities; in two cases the candidates (Tilden, 1876 and Cleveland, 1888) won the general election but lost the battle of the Electoral College. Twenty-one of our Presidential elections have been won by such small margins that a shift of not more than 1 percent could have changed the outcomes.[1]

A second factor in voting is the differential weights or importance of votes in different elections and districts. The influence of any voter is partially dependent on the size of the constituency in which he votes. For example, in senatorial contests all the voters choose the same number of senators (two) but the variance in the size of the voting populations is enormous. Each senator from New York obviously represents many more citizens than do the senators from Alaska or Nevada. Since all senators have the same voting power—one vote—each of their constituents might be said to have varying vote power or influence on public policy even though the magnitude of those differences may not appear very significant to a voter in New York or Nevada.

A third factor determining whether a vote is consequential depends to some extent upon the voter's *own* evaluation of his own action. A voter may consider his participation in the political life of the nation as rewarding in itself; voting makes him feel good. Or he may consider voting his sacred duty; violation of that duty makes him feel guilty. Many Americans do treat voting merely as a duty, while many more apparently feel good because they voted. The first group may become defensive and apologetic whenever they fail in these responsibilities. The others may derive satisfaction in the act of demonstrating their loyalties or allegiance to the nation and its heritage. Still others take some sporting pride in supporting their party and/or its candidates. Still others—perhaps less numerous—derive pleasure from the thought that they might influence the actual outcome of a close race.

Various bits of scholarly research on voting behavior and national loyalties—the "civil culture"—suggest that these rewards are not merely fanciful; in fact, at least one major cross-national study of five nations shows that fully 85 percent of Americans are extremely proud of their political institutions and do feel satisfaction when going to the polls.[2] Only 12 percent claimed "they never enjoy, never get angry, and never feel contempt during campaigns."[3] In fact, most citizens do have a sense of political involvement even when they do not vote.

Aside from these psychic rewards, the most important reason for voting is *the expectation of some tangible returns in the way of more favorable policies supporting or advancing one's way of life or ideals.* In short, the outcome of the election will make a difference for him—at least, he expects that it will do so. The significance a national election may have for each voter differs in terms of both the contents of policies and actions as well as the magnitude of policy differences. Although this difference will be minimal for some voters, for others the expected gains or losses may be material and considerable.

For still others the difference may, in fact, be zero; those voters are totally indifferent about who wins and about the subsequent policy outcomes. They may view all candidates and parties as equally bad or equally good. In this case, one obvious course of action is not to vote. Another is to support still another candidate, either by write-in or in preparation for a future election. But it is an obvious fact that the outcomes of national elections are a matter of indifference to countless citizens. Daily life is not always measurably affected by election results, and, in our system, those who vote for the loser are not excluded from the normal services of government. About all we can and ought to do with doubtful persons is attempt to persuade them that their low estimates of electoral outcomes are erroneous. . . .

CAN MY VOTE INFLUENCE THE ELECTORAL OUTCOME?

While it is necessary to demonstrate that expected electoral payoffs either maximize gains or minimize losses, these calculations are hardly sufficient inducements to vote. A voter should also be convinced that his vote will have some impact on deciding the outcome. . . . Surely not all who voted have been convinced that their votes were inconsequential or that the outcomes were unimportant, nor have those who stayed at home been motivated by their rational decisions that the elections were unimportant or that their chances of deciding the outcomes approached zero. Many did not vote because they were denied the opportunity to implement their voting decisions. . . .

These generalizations are portrayed in graphic form in Figure 1. The figure has both explanatory and normative implications, since it aids in accounting for voter turnouts and suggests the conditions under which a voter should or should not vote (aside from the costs incurred in voting, a problem we will consider shortly).

Using the graph, consider the most appropriate course of action for a potential voter. If he is convinced that the election is highly important (value of the outcome) and that he expects a close election in which his vote may be important (estimated probability of influencing the outcome) he should vote. This seems obvious. But what if a voter places a high value on

Estimated probability of
influencing the outcome

		Low	Medium	High
	High	VOTE	VOTE	VOTE
Value of the outcome	Medium	VOTE	VOTE	VOTE
	Low	?	VOTE	VOTE

Figure 1 Basic voter calculus.

the outcome but sees little chance of having his way? He should also vote, because even the slightest chance of achieving a high value should be pursued since there are no risks—nothing more is lost by participation than nonparticipation even if the outcome is unfavorable. By voting, each one increases the probability that his chosen candidate will be elected. Similarly, a voter who sees a high probability of influencing the outcome, but who does not highly value the outcome should also vote. He is almost certainly assured that he will win something, and something is better than nothing. In short, the voter should vote in almost all cases because he stands to gain. The only questionable cases are those in which the probabilities are exceedingly low and the return is very low. If, in addition, the voter's costs of voting outweigh the expected returns, he should not vote.

The estimates a voter places on both the probability that he can have a decisive effect on the election and the value of the outcome are *subjective estimates* that can only be provided by the voter himself. . . .

Although probability estimates are subjective, they can be well informed. A large part of the remaining pages . . . is devoted to presenting a variety of generalizations about various factors that affect electoral outcomes and, therefore, the chances that one's own vote will be decisive. Whether a single voter's action will determine the outcome is ultimately contingent upon the uncontrollable choices of both politicians and other voters. And we know a good deal about the factors that influence electoral outcomes.

Few voters will ever participate in elections that are decided by one vote. Many more will vote in relatively close contests. Even in a Presidential election, one vote *can* be critical. Rutherford B. Hayes moved into the White House in 1876 on the basis of a highly improbable sequence of one-vote decisions. He won in the Electoral College by one vote that was provided by an Indiana delegate—who had himself been elected to Congress by one vote. When the Electoral College vote was challenged a special commission was organized and Hayes was elected President— again by one vote. Hayes was merely one of several Presidents to assume office by exceedingly small margins during the latter quarter of the nineteenth century.

Although a voter casts only one of tens of millions of votes in a national election, the probability of affecting the outcome is somewhat higher than might be expected. The winner-take-all rule of the Electoral College enhances the value of votes, especially in large states with close elections. Richard Nixon won the 1968 Presidential election with 43.4 percent of the total popular vote, or a bare margin of 510,000. This means that a shift of 255,001 votes to Humphrey—in certain states—would have made him President. However, the Electoral College complicates things since Humphrey needed 79 more electoral votes to win the Presidency. If Humphrey had won Illinois (26), Ohio (26), New Jersey (17), and Missouri (12), he would have garnered 81 electoral votes and the Presidency; if he had won Illinois and Ohio the election would have been thrown into the House of Representatives. His losses in these states were small, but it is questionable whether he could have switched the necessary 32,000 votes in New Jersey or 68,000 in Illinois. In any case, small variations in turnouts and voter preferences can have large-scale effects.

The case was much more dramatic in 1960 when Nixon lost to Kennedy by 112,837 votes—*one* vote per precinct. Here a switch of only 56,413 votes in the proper states would have altered the order in which Nixon was to become President. Nixon needed just 51 more electoral votes to win the needed 270. Kennedy won 12 states by less than 1 percent and of those 12 the margin was less than .5 percent in 8 states. Very small shifts involving mere thousands of voters in such states as Arkansas, California, Illinois, Louisiana, Missouri, New Jersey, New Mexico, and Texas would have reversed the election outcome. Nixon would not have had to win all these states. He only needed a shift of 11,424 votes in five states—Illinois, Missouri, New Mexico, Hawaii, and Nevada—to win; a shift of just 8,971 votes in Illinois and Missouri could have sent the election into the House for a decision, just as a switch of 12,487 votes from Mr. Truman to Mr. Dewey in California and Ohio could have denied an electoral majority to either candidate and the election would have gone to the House. One student of Presidential elections claims that we have had 21 "hairbreadth" elections.[4] . . .

Close elections and outcomes are hardly confined to Presidential contests. . . . Many congressmen and senators gained their seats and have retained them or were defeated by mere handfuls of votes. Because city councils are usually very small, close votes are frequently a real possibility. The same is true of state legislatures. While voters do not directly participate in legislative roll calls, the importance of having a legislator who may cast the crucial vote is important to each voter.

CAN I INFLUENCE PUBLIC POLICY?

. . . The answer is complex but positive; voters can do something about policy. There is no guarantee, however, that each voter can either directly attain whatever he wants or prevent enactment of policies he disapproves of. Each voter will probably attain only a small portion of his preferred positions. . . .

Why is it that the individual voter cannot directly influence policy as much as he would like? The reasons are fairly apparent. In a free market situation, the consumer can spend his resources almost any way he likes. A music lover can visit his favorite store and purchase a Beatles record. Another may choose a recording by the Rolling Stones, and a third may buy an oldie—a Louis Armstrong recording from the 1930s. Each record buyer can purchase the record of his choice, if his income permits, without insisting that others buy the same record. This is not the case in political systems and for very sound reasons.

Public choice in democracies is not a free market situation. It must entail some degree of coercion because only one policy can be pursued in a given area at any given time. Obviously, every voter cannot direct public policy to suit himself, just as the United States . . . [could not] simultaneously withdraw completely and increase the scale of the Vietnam war. It is equally impractical for a citizen to visit City Hall once a week and purchase $10 of police protection, while another more fearful soul purchases $100 of the same service, and a paranoid demands $1,000 worth of services from the police. Individuals cannot purchase public services this way because government cannot provide discrete amounts to individual citizens. A public good, once created, is equally available to all citizens, whether they use it or not. While I am not forced to buy Beatles records, I am forced to help pay for public goods, programs, and activities I may have expressed myself as opposed to in elections and by other means. While it would be nice if individual citizens could have only those programs or policies they like, and only in the preferred amount, this is not possible in political systems, including democracies. . . .

A voter becomes more realistic as he recognizes serious limitations in his capacity to influence the workings of the system. But when he does he is in a better position to pursue whatever ends he chooses. This voter should also recognize that not everyone exercises the same amount of influence on policy in the United States. This revelation may be disheartening, but it can act as spur to more successful participation. Knowledge of where the power is and where it is not enables the interested citizen to concentrate his efforts in the most fruitful places.

In addition to the necessity for coercion in political systems and thus the denial of free choice in selecting public policies, individual citizens are confronted with the fact that our system is huge (140 million of voting age) and extraordinarily complex. No system this large and intricate could possibly be operated like a local free market in which individual choice is maximized. Just as a division of labor is necessary in the free market, representatives are a necessity in the public policy arena. U.S. voters have more than 521,760 elected representatives, or one for every 230 adult citizens. Each of these politicians must find some way of giving voice to the diversity of opinion among his constituents. Accordingly, the individual cannot directly choose public policies. He can at best attempt to influence the votes of his representatives. The exceptions are occasional referenda in which the voter can directly shape policy. Referenda are usually on local and state issues, and even here the voter has to face impressive constraints on his choices; the alternatives are restricted and his choice is limited to expressing a preference for or against the proposals offered on the ballot. Most of the time, on the national and state levels, public policy is bargained out among elected officials, who are representatives of interest groups and powerful individuals. The voter is in the position of a member of an audience. He is able to encourage and discourage producers by his purchase of tickets and actors with his applause. The extent of direct individual influence over national policy formation is miniscule.

If greater influence were possible would it be worth the sacrifice entailed by its adoption? Greater participation may be desirable from some viewpoints, but it is necessarily more costly both for the participant and the entire system. It extends the time necessary to make collective decisions and increases the resources an individual must devote to the participation. Town meetings cannot be operated on a scale much larger than a few hundred citizens. Furthermore, even town meetings result in majority-rule decisions, and coercion continues in any issue in which unanimity does not prevail. Those who vote against the proposals must concede to the victors; those who vote against a tax must pay the tax along with those who vote for it.

We began . . . optimistically contending that voting is normally worthwhile, but we have now conceded that the individual can do relatively little to directly attain the policies he prefers. So why vote? Just as the expenditure of a dollar in the market is a message to businessmen, the vote is a message to politicians, and although the message is ambiguous and brief, politicians know how to read it.

To expect that each individual can always have all that he wants, when he wants it, and in the form he wants, seems childish at best. Voters who suffer frustration because of lack of involvement should seek greater involvement by joining interest groups, becoming active in political parties, and perhaps running for public office, where their influence can be increased. . . .

NOTES

1. Neal R. Peirce, *The People's President* (New York: Simon and Schuster, 1968), pp. 317-21.
2. Gabriel A. Almond and Sidney Verba, *The Civic Culture* (Princeton: Princeton University Press, 1963), p. 146.
3. Almond and Verba, *The Civil Culture*, p. 146.
4. Peirce, *The People's President*, p. 317.

CHAPTER SIX

CAMPAIGNS AND THE MEDIA

Probably nothing has so transformed American politics as commercial television. What used to be the experience of only a few—hearing and seeing a candidate at some campaign rally, for example—is now an experience of many millions of Americans. Since television enables political candidates literally to be seen and heard in every living room in the country, it is no wonder that politicians devote so much time to its use in their campaigns.

What impact has television had on the voter? Can voters be manipulated into voting blindly for candidates because of clever image making on the television screen? Or are voters more discerning than the political advertising executives would have us believe?

While not all of the evidence is in on the impact of television on the American voter, two well-known books have dealt with this question and arrived at different conclusions. One book, The Selling of the President 1968 *by Joe McGinniss, from which excerpts are presented here, presents a first-hand account of the 1968 television campaign of former President Richard M. Nixon—a campaign that, according to McGinniss, featured a carefully packaged television image of Nixon. The success of the Nixon campaign in 1968, as compared to 1960, convinced McGinniss and many others that all political campaigning was now merely a matter of projecting the right image on the television screen and "selling" the politician to the public.*

Political scientists Thomas Patterson and Robert McClure, however, after studying the 1972 presidential election campaigns of George McGovern and Richard Nixon, conclude that the public, far from being manipulated, is actually better informed and is better able to make decisions as a result of exposure to televised political commercials.

What accounts for the seemingly contradictory results of these two studies? The answer is probably to be found in the different perspectives of the authors. McGinniss is writing from the point of view of an insider in the Nixon campaign. Patterson and McClure base their findings on the results of some two thousand interviews conducted during the 1972 campaign.

Politics as a Con Game

Joe McGinniss

Politics, in a sense, has always been a con game.

The American voter, insisting upon his belief in a higher order, clings to his religion, which promises another, better life; and defends passionately the illusion that the men he chooses to lead him are of finer nature than he.

It has been traditional that the successful politician honor this illusion. To succeed today, he must embellish it. Particularly if he wants to be President.

"Potential presidents are measured against an ideal that's a combination of leading man, God, father, hero, pope, king, with maybe just a touch of the avenging Furies thrown in," an adviser to Richard Nixon wrote in a memorandum late in 1967. Then, perhaps aware that Nixon qualified only as father, he discussed improvements that would have to be made—not upon Nixon himself, but upon the image of him which was received by the voter. . . .

Advertising, in many ways, is a con game, too. Human beings do not need new automobiles every third year; a color television set brings little enrichment of the human experience; a higher or lower hemline no expansion of consciousness, no increase in the capacity to love.

It is not surprising, then, that politicians and advertising men should have discovered one another. And, once they recognized that the citizen did not so much vote for a candidate as make a psychological purchase of him, not surprising that they began to work together. . . .

Advertising agencies have tried openly to sell Presidents since 1952. When Dwight Eisenhower ran for reelection in 1956, the agency of Batton, Barton, Durstine and Osborn, which had been on a retainer throughout his first four years, accepted his campaign as a regular account. Leonard Hall, national Republican chairman, said: "You sell your candidates and your programs the way a business sells its products.". . .

With the coming of television, and the knowledge of how it could be used to seduce voters, the old political values disappeared. Something new, murky, undefined started to rise from the mists. "In all countries," Marshall McLuhan writes, "the party system has folded like the organization chart. Policies and issues are useless for election purposes, since they are too specialized and hot. The shaping of a candidate's integral image has taken the place of discussing conflicting points of view.". . .

The television celebrity is a vessel. An inoffensive container in which someone else's knowledge, insight, compassion, or wit can be presented. And we respond like the child on Christmas morning who ignores the gift to play with the wrapping paper.

Television seems particularly useful to the politician who can be charming but lacks ideas. Print is for ideas. Newspapermen write not about people but policies; the paragraphs can be slid around like blocks. Everyone is colored gray. Columnists—and commentators in the more polysyllabic magazines—concentrate on ideology. They do not care what a man sounds like; only how he thinks. For the candidate who does not, such exposure can be embarrassing. He needs another way to reach the people.

On television it matters less that he does not have ideas. His personality is what the viewers want to share. He need be neither statesman nor crusader; he must only show up on time. Success and failure are easily measured: How often is he invited back? Often enough and he reaches his goal—to advance from "politician" to "celebrity," a status jump bestowed by grateful viewers who feel that finally they have been given the basis for making a choice.

The TV candidate, then, is measured not against his predecessors— not against a standard of performance established by two centuries of democracy—but against Mike Douglas. How well does he handle himself? Does he mumble, does he twitch, does he make me laugh? Do I feel warm inside?

Style becomes substance. The medium is the message and the masseur gets the votes. . . .

"The success of any TV performer depends on his achieving a low-pressure style of presentation," McLuhan has written. The harder a man tries, the better he must hide it. Television demands gentle wit, irony, understatement: the qualities of Eugene McCarthy. The TV politician cannot make a speech; he must engage in intimate conversation. He must never press. He should suggest, not state; request, not demand. Nonchalance is the key word. Carefully studied nonchalance.

Warmth and sincerity are desirable but must be handled with care. Unfiltered, they can be fatal. Television did great harm to Hubert Humphrey. His excesses—talking too long and too fervently, which were merely annoying in an auditorium—became lethal in a television studio. The performer must talk to one person at a time. He is brought into the living room. He is a guest. It is improper for him to shout. Humphrey vomited on the rug.

It would be extremely unwise for the TV politician to admit such knowledge of his medium. The necessary nonchalance should carry beyond his appearance while *on* the show; it should rule his attitude *toward* it. He should express distaste for television; suspicion that there is something "phony" about it. This guarantees him good press, because newspaper reporters, bitter over their loss of prestige to the television men, are certain to stress anti-television remarks. Thus, the sophisticated candidate, while analyzing his own on-the-air technique as carefully as a golf pro studies his swing, will state frequently that there is no place for "public relations gimmicks" or "those show business guys" in his campaign. Most of the television men working for him will be unbothered by such remarks. They are willing to accept anonymity, even scorn, as long as the pay is good.

Into this milieu came Richard Nixon: grumpy, cold, and aloof. He would claim privately that he lost elections because the American voter was an adolescent whom he tried to treat as an adult. Perhaps. But if he treated the voter as an adult, it was as an adult he did not want for a neighbor.

This might have been excused had he been a man of genuine vision. An explorer of the spirit. Martin Luther King, for instance, got by without being one of the boys. But Richard Nixon did not strike people that way. He had, in Richard Rovere's words, "an advertising man's approach to his work," acting as if he believed "policies [were] products to be sold the public—this one today, that one tomorrow, depending on the discounts and the state of the market."

So his enemies had him on two counts: his personality, and the convictions—or lack of such—which lay behind. They worked him over heavily on both. . . .

But Nixon survived, despite his flaws, because he was tough and smart, and—some said—dirty when he had to be. Also, because there was nothing else he knew. A man to whom politics is all there is in life will almost always beat one to whom it is only an occupation.

He nearly became President in 1960, and that year it would not have been by default. He failed because he was too few of the things a President had to be—and because he had no press to lie for him and did not know how to use television to lie about himself.

It was just Nixon and John Kennedy and they sat down together in a television studio and a little red light began to glow and Richard Nixon was finished. Television would be blamed but for all the wrong reasons.

They would say it was makeup and lighting, but Nixon's problem went deeper than that. His problem was himself. Not what he said but the man he was. The camera portrayed him clearly. America took its Richard Nixon straight and did not like the taste.

The content of the programs made little difference. Except for startling lapses, content seldom does. What mattered was the image the viewers received, though few observers at the time caught the point. . . .

What the camera showed was Richard Nixon's hunger. He lost, and bitter, confused, he blamed it on his beard. . . .

He was afraid of television. He knew his soul was hard to find. Beyond that, he considered it a gimmick; its use in politics offended him. It had not been part of the game when he had learned to play, he could see no reason to bring it in now. He half suspected it was an eastern liberal trick: one more way to make him look silly. It offended his sense of dignity, one of the truest senses he had.

So his decision to use it to become President in 1968 was not easy. So much of him argued against it. But in his Wall Street years, Richard Nixon had traveled to the darkest places inside himself and come back numbed. He was, as in the Graham Greene title, a burnt-out case. All feeling was behind him; the machine inside had proved his hardiest part. He would run for President again and if he would have to learn television to run well, then he would learn it.

America still saw him as the 1960 Nixon. If he were to come at the people again, as a candidate, it would have to be as something new; not this scarred, discarded figure from their past.

He spoke to men who thought him mellowed. They detected growth, a new stability, a sense of direction that had been lacking. He would return with fresh perspective, a more unselfish urgency.

His problem was how to let the nation know. He could not do it through the press. He knew what to expect from them, which was the same as he had always gotten. He would have to circumvent them. Distract them with coffee and doughnuts and smiles from his staff and tell his story another way.

Television was the only answer, despite its sins against him in the past. But not just any kind of television. An uncommitted camera could do irreparable harm. His television would have to be controlled. He would need experts. They would have to find the proper settings for him, or if they could not be found, manufacture them. These would have to be men of keen judgment and flawless taste. He was, after all, Richard Nixon, and there were certain things he could not do. Wearing love beads was one. He would need men of dignity. Who believed in him and shared his vision. But more importantly, men who knew television as a weapon: from broadest concept to most technical detail. This would be Richard Nixon, the leader, returning from exile. Perhaps not beloved, but respected. Firm but not harsh; just but compassionate. With flashes of warmth spaced evenly throughout.

Nixon gathered about himself a group of young men attuned to the political uses of television. . . .

Harry Treleaven, hired as creative director of advertising in the fall of 1967, immediately went to work on the more serious of Nixon's personality problems. One was his lack of humor.

"Can be corrected to a degree," Treleaven wrote, "but let's not be too obvious about it. Romney's cornball attempts have hurt him. If we're going to be witty, let a pro write the words."

Treleaven also worried about Nixon's lack of warmth, but decided that "he can be helped greatly in this respect by how he is handled. . . . Give him words to say that will show his *emotional* involvement in the issues. . . . Buchanan wrote about RFK talking about the starving children in Recife. *That's* what we have to inject. . . .

"He should be presented in some kind of 'situation' rather than cold in a studio. The situation should look unstaged even if it's not."

Some of the most effective ideas belonged to Raymond K. Price, a former editorial writer for the *New York Herald Tribune*, who became Nixon's best and most prominent speech writer in the campaign. Price later composed much of the inaugural address.

In 1967, he began with the assumption that, "The natural human use of reason is to support prejudice, not to arrive at opinions." Which led to the conclusion that rational arguments would "only be effective if we can get the people to make the *emotional* leap, or what theologians call [the] 'leap of faith.' "

Price suggested attacking the "personal factors" rather than the "historical factors" which were the basis of the low opinion so many people had of Richard Nixon.

"These tend to be more a gut reaction," Price wrote, "unarticulated, non-analytical, a product of the particular chemistry between the voter and the *image* of the candidate. *We have to be very clear on this point: that the response is to the image, not to the man.* . . . It's not what's *there* that counts, it's what's projected—and carrying it one step further, it's not what *he* projects but rather what the voter receives. It's not the man we have to change, but rather the *received impression.* And this impression often depends more on the medium and its use than it does on the candidate himself."

So there would not have to be a "new Nixon." Simply a new approach to television.

"What, then, does this mean in terms of our uses of time and of media?" Price wrote.

"For one thing, it means investing whatever time RN needs in order to work out firmly in his own mind that vision of the nation's future that he wants to be identified with. This is crucial. . . ."

So, at the age of fifty-four, after twenty years in public life, Richard

Nixon was still felt *by his own staff* to be in need of time to "work out firmly in his own mind that vision of the nation's future that he wants to be identified with."

"Secondly," Price wrote, "it suggests that we take the time and the money to experiment, in a controlled manner, with film and television techniques, with particular emphasis on pinpointing those *controlled* uses of the television medium that can *best* convey the *image* we want to get across . . .

"The TV medium itself introduces an element of distortion, in terms of its effect on the candidate and of the often subliminal ways in which the image is received. And it inevitably is going to convey a partial image— thus ours is the task of finding how to control its use so the part that gets across is the part we want to have gotten across. . . .

"Voters are basically lazy, basically uninterested in making an *effort* to understand what we're talking about . . . ," Price wrote. "Reason requires a high degree of discipline, of concentration; impression is easier. Reason pushes the viewer back, it assaults him, it demands that he agree or disagree; impression can envelop him, invite him in, without making an intellectual demand. . . . When we argue with him we demand that he make the effort of replying. We seek to engage his intellect, and for most people this is the most difficult work of all. The emotions are more easily roused, closer to the surface, more malleable. . . ."

So, for the New Hampshire primary, Price recommended "saturation with a film, in which the candidate can be shown better than he can be shown in person because it can be edited, so only the best moments are shown; then a quick parading of the candidate in the flesh so that the guy they've gotten intimately acquainted with on the screen takes on a living presence—not saying anything, just being seen. . . .

"[Nixon] has to come across as a person larger than life, the stuff of legend. People are stirred by the legend, including the living legend, not by the man himself. It's the aura that surrounds the charismatic figure more than it is the figure itself, that draws the followers. Our task is to build that aura. . . .

"So let's not be afraid of television gimmicks . . . get the voters to like the guy and the battle's two-thirds won."

So this was how they went into it. Trying, with one hand, to build the illusion that Richard Nixon, in addition to his attributes of mind and heart, considered, in the words of Patrick K. Buchanan, a speech writer, "communicating with the people . . . one of the great joys of seeking the Presidency"; while with the other they shielded him, controlled him, and controlled the atmosphere around him. It was as if they were building not a President but an Astrodome, where the wind would never blow, the temperature never rise or fall, and the ball never bounce erratically on the artificial grass.

They could do this, and succeed, because of the special nature of the man. There was, apparently, something in Richard Nixon's character which sought this shelter. Something which craved regulation, which flourished best in the darkness, behind clichés, behind phalanxes of antiseptic advisers. Some part of him that could breathe freely only inside a hotel suite that cost a hundred dollars a day.

And it worked. As he moved serenely through his primary campaign, there was new cadence to Richard Nixon's speech and motion; new confidence in his heart. And, a new image of him on the television screen.

TV both reflected and contributed to his strength. Because he was winning he looked like a winner on the screen. Because he was suddenly projecting well on the medium he had feared, he went about his other tasks with assurance. The one fed upon the other, building to an astonishing peak in August as the Republican convention began and he emerged from his regal isolation, traveling to Miami not so much to be nominated as coronated. On live, but controlled, TV.

The Impact of Televised Political Commercials

Thomas E. Patterson and Robert D. McClure

One minute after a product commercial fades from the television screen, most viewers have forgotten what was advertised. They cannot recall whether the ad trumpeted aspirin, shaving cream, or automobiles. A particularly clever or amusing commercial may draw some notice, and linger in their thoughts, but most product ads pass from the mind as quickly as from the screen.[1]

Presidential ads affect viewers differently. On television only a month or two every four years, their novelty attracts attention. Also their subject matter. They picture and discuss men seeking the nation's highest office, and most Americans feel that choosing a President deserves more consideration than selecting a brand of antacid. A clear indication of presidential advertising's attention-getting ability is that most viewers can rather fully recall the message of a presidential spot. When asked to describe a commercial they had seen during the 1972 election, 56 percent of the viewers gave a remarkably full and complete description of one, and only 21 percent were unable to recall anything at all from political ads.[2] In market research, any product whose commercials are recalled with half this accuracy is considered to have had a very successful advertising campaign.[3]

People also evaluate presidential advertising differently than product advertising. A study conducted for the American Association of Advertising Agencies in the 1960's discovered that television viewers judge product commercials more on *how* they communicate their message than on *what* they say about a product.[4] A commercial for a soft drink or a paper towel is regarded as good or bad by the television audience more on whether it is enjoyable to watch than on the truthfulness of its message or the value of the information it contains. People judge presidential ads, on the other hand, primarily on *what* they say, not *how* they say it. Whether the techniques used in presidential spots are visually appealing or unappealing seems to matter little. Viewers seem concerned mainly with whether the advertising message is truthful and worth knowing. Where the American Association of Advertising Agencies' study found that only 46 percent of viewer reactions to product ads related to the information communicated, 74 percent of viewer reactions to presidential commercials shown in 1972 centered on the information contained in the message.[5]

Thus, presidential spots get noticed, and the attention centers on the message. But to what end? Does the viewer learn anything about the candidates? Does he find out anything about the issues?

For years, most political observers have been certain they knew the answers: Advertising builds false political images and robs the American electorate of important issue information. On both counts, this orthodox view is wrong. In a presidential campaign, spot commercials do much more to educate the public about the issues than they do to manipulate the public about the candidates.

ADVERTISING'S IMAGE IMPACT

In presidential politics, advertising image-making is a wasted effort. All the careful image planning—the coaching, the camera work, the calculated plea—counts for nothing. Just as with network news appearances, people's feelings about the candidate's politics—his party, past actions, and future policies—far outweigh the influence of televised commercials.

Strong evidence for advertising's ineffectiveness comes from a look at *changes* in voters' images during the 1972 campaign. Just before presidential ads began appearing on television and again when the candidates' ad campaigns were concluding, the same people were asked to judge the images of Nixon and McGovern. They evaluated each candidate on seven traits associated with personality and leadership. Because the same people were questioned each time, an exact measure exists of how their images changed during the time when the candidates' ads were appearing on television.

These changes in voters' images indicate that advertising image-making had no effect. . . . Among people who preferred Nixon, his image showed a 35 percent improvement and McGovern's image a 28 percent decline. This happened among people exposed to many of the candidates' ads and to those seeing few commercials, if any. Among people backing McGovern, however, his image made a 20 percent improvement and Nixon's had an 18 percent decline. And again, no significant difference occurred in the image changes of people heavily and lightly exposed to presidential advertising.

Thus, whether people watched television regularly, and constantly saw the advertised images of Nixon and McGovern, had no influence on their impressions of the two candidates. Whatever people were getting from political spots, it was not their images of the candidates. . . .

By projecting their political biases, people see in candidates' commercials pretty much what they want to see. Ads sponsored by the candidate who shares their politics get a good response. They like what he has to say. And they like him. Ads sponsored by the opposing candidate are viewed negatively. They object to what he says. And they object to him.

A sampling of viewers' reactions to the series of image commericals used by George McGovern throughout the general election campaign illustrates how strongly political bias affects viewers. These spots pictured McGovern among small groups of people in natural settings, discussing their problems and promising to help them if elected. The commercials were intended to project an image of McGovern as a man who cared about people. Whether viewers received this image, however, had little to do with what happened on the television screen. It was all in their minds:[6]

He really cares what's happened to disabled vets. They told him how badly they've been treated and he listened. He will help them.

         —37-year-old, pro-McGovern viewer

McGovern was talking with these disabled vets. He doesn't really care about them. He's just using them to get sympathy.

         —33-year-old, pro-Nixon viewer.

It was honest, down-to-earth. People were talking and he was listening.

         —57-year-old, pro-McGovern viewer

Those commercials are so phoney. He doesn't care.

         —45-year-old, pro-Nixon viewer

McGovern had his coat off and his tie was hanging down. It was so relaxed, and he seemed to really be concerned with those workers.

         —31-year-old, pro-McGovern viewer

He is trying hard to look like one of the boys. You know, roll up the shirt sleeves and loosen the tie. It's just too much for me to take.

         —49-year-old, pro-Nixon viewer

I have seen many ads where McGovern is talking to common people. You know, like workers and the elderly. He means what he says. He'll help them.

         —22-year-old, pro-McGovern viewer

He's with all these groups of people. Always making promises. He's promising more than can be done. Can't do everything for everyone.

         —41-year-old, pro-Nixon viewer

These people were watching the same George McGovern, listening to the same words, and yet they were receiving vastly different impressions of the Democratic presidential nominee.

Even undecided voters are not influenced by advertising image-making. Just like partisans, the candidate images of undecided voters fluctuate with vote choice, not advertising exposure. In 1972, undecided voters' images changed very little and fit no definite pattern until *after* they had picked their candidate. Among those choosing Nixon, and only *after* they had done so, his image had a 35 percent improvement and McGovern's a 35 percent decline. This pattern of image change was the rule for those seeing many presidential ads and those seeing few or none. Likewise, for those picking McGovern, his image showed a 40 percent improvement and Nixon's a 55 percent decline. Again, there was no difference in this pattern based on the undecided voter's exposure to televised political commercials.

Spot ads do not mold presidential images because voters are not easily misled. They recognize that advertising imagery is heavily laden with something that is not intrinsically related to personal character at all—how the candidate looks on camera. This pseudocharacter, to some extent coached, posed, and created by the best media talent money can buy, is a "look" built into spots that is totally unreal. And viewers recognize its meaninglessness. Even the candid portrayals of presidential aspirants that sometimes appear in image appeals are ineffective. People's guards go up when a spot goes on. So no matter the style of presentation, when only 60 seconds are used to say that a candidate is big enough to handle the presidency, voters find the message skimpy, debatable, and unconvincing. They know that the candidate will display his strengths and mask his weaknesses and that a 60-second glimpse does not provide much of an insight into a man's fitness for the nation's highest office.

Symbolic manipulation through televised political advertising simply does not work. Perhaps the overuse of symbols and stereotypes in product advertising has built up an immunity in the television audience. Perhaps the symbols and postures used in political advertising are such patently obvious attempts at manipulation that they appear more ridiculous than reliable. Whatever the precise reason, television viewers effectively protect themselves from manipulation by staged imagery.

ADVERTISING'S ISSUE IMPACT

But where image appeals fail, issue appeals work. Through commercials, presidential candidates actually inform the electorate. In fact, the contribution of advertising campaigns to voter knowledge is truly impressive.

During the 1972 presidential election, people who were heavily exposed to political spots became more informed about the candidates' issue positions. . . . On every single issue emphasized in presidential commercials, persons with high exposure to television advertising showed a greater increase in knowledge than persons with low exposure. And on the typical issue, individuals who happened to see many commercials were nearly half again as likely to become more knowledgeable as people who saw few, if any, televised spots. Issue knowledge among people with considerable advertising exposure achieved a 36 percent increase compared with a 25 percent increase among those with minimal exposure. Persons heavily exposed to advertising were particularly aided in their knowledge about Nixon's position on China and military spending and about McGovern's position on military spending and taxes.

This information gain represents no small achievement. Televised political advertising has been widely maligned for saying nothing of consequence. Although the issue material contained in spots is incomplete and oversimplified, it also is abundant. So abundant in fact, that presidential advertising contributes to an informed electorate.

Advertising also educates voters because of the powerful way it transmits its issue content. Three basic advertising strategies—simplicity, repetition, and sight-sound coordination—combine to make presidential spots good communicators. Ads contain such simple messages that they leave almost no room for misunderstanding. . . .

THE EXTENT OF ADVERTISING MANIPULATION

Precise statistics on advertising's manipulative effects are hard to develop, because advertising, like other forms of media persuasion, works among and through a complex web of other influences. Seldom does a voter make his candidate choice for a single reason, whether the reason be political commercials, party loyalty, or a particular issue. Moreover, most people make up their minds about the candidates prior to the general election campaign, the time when presidential advertising saturates television programming. In 1972, as in previous elections where survey data have been gathered, about eighty percent of the electorate stayed with the choice it had decided upon before the general election began. Without doubt, some of these voters were reinforced in their initial vote choice by what they saw through television advertising. But how does one identify—among the people not changing their minds—those who would have changed their minds were it not for advertising? It is a treacherous task to assess whether people might have done something they did not do. So the effects of advertising on a voting decision are not that easily typed.

But some voters do decide their vote choice during a presidential general election and these people offer the best opportunity for understanding advertising's influence. In three interviews conducted with the same people during the 1972 general election, voters were asked which candidate they planned to support. If they changed their mind between one interview and the next, they were asked the reasons for the change and, if information about the candidates played some part in the change, where that information came from. By looking for advertising themes and sources in the reasons people gave for their vote changes, one way of estimating advertising's effects is provided. . . .

For three in every four people who arrived at their final vote choice during the 1972 general election, televised advertising had *no* discernible influence. . . . Some 42 percent cited important events, such as the Paris peace talks, as the reason why they selected their candidate; 11 percent said they decided to follow party allegiance, as did the factory worker who said, "I've always been a Democrat and McGovern is the Democrat;" 12 percent gave an old maxim, such as "not changing horses" or "it's time for a change," as their reason; 7 percent said they made their choice on the advice of their spouse or a friend or a co-worker; and 5 percent, although unable to provide a specific reason for choosing a candidate, did not watch much, if any, television during the 1972 campaign. In all of these decisions, televised advertising may have played some part, but at most, it was only a contributory influence. Additionally, 7 percent of vote changers present the situation of undetermined advertising effect. These people could give no clear reason for their candidate choice, but they were widely exposed to political ads during the campaign. Televised advertising, then, might have been the reason for their choice although other explanations, such as party loyalty or important political events, are also plausible.

So the first fact that must be recognized is that political advertising competes with other influences for the loyalties of indecisive voters. Before televised spots were used, less-informed voters were choosing candidates because they had a vague feeling that it was time for a change, because their father had pulled the same party lever years before, because an event triggered a reaction, because their spouse or union leader told them what to do. Today, most indecisive voters still select their candidate for such reasons.

Clear cases of advertising influence occurred among only 16 percent of those people making their candidate choice during the general election, or roughly 3 percent of the total electorate, since only one in five voters make up their minds during this time. But not even all these people can be labeled the victims of advertising manipulation. Indeed, the second fact about advertising influence is that simply because spot information helps people make up their minds does not mean manipulation occurs. True manipulation through advertising involves more than voters obtaining information that subsequently guides their vote choice. Spots are truly manipulative only when they convince the voter to act in the candidate's best interests and not the voter's. By this definition, of the 16 percent influenced by advertising, about half (9 percent) *were not* manipulated and about half (7 percent) *were* manipulated. To distinguish between these two types of advertising influence, here are the brief, but actual, voting histories of two people who during the 1972 general election made their vote choice from advertising information.

The first voter is a 74-year-old woman, who before she retired worked at an unskilled job. In 1972, she was deeply concerned about having enough income to live on; her social security and small savings forced her to make ends meet on only $3,000 a year. Asked at the beginning of the campaign what one political problem troubled her most, she replied: "The amount of social security. It is not enough for most people to live on." Asked the same question at the end of the campaign, she said that "taxes were too high for older people on fixed incomes."

This woman called herself an Independent, but her past voting behavior had been strongly Democratic. She claimed to have backed Kennedy, Johnson, and Humphrey in the three previous presidential elections. Her choice for the 1972 Democratic nomination was George Wallace, and when McGovern got the nod, she was undecided about whether to vote for him or Nixon. In late October, she made her choice. She selected McGovern and gave this reason:

> *I've seen many commercials where George McGovern wants to help older people, to get them more social security and otherwise help them all he could. Nixon has vetoed bills for helping older people and McGovern has shown a definite interest in doing something for us. If Nixon hasn't done anything in the last four years, he probably won't do it now. He looks after big business, not the worker. Nixon's funds are from big business and they'll try to put him in again. I've no use for him.*

The second voter is a 30-year-old hospital worker with two years of college. He is married and has one child. At the start of the general election, he was mainly concerned that the United States maintain a flexible foreign policy. At the campaign's end, he labeled unemployment the nation's major problem.

This man called himself a lukewarm Republican and in 1968 had not bothered to vote. But he registered to vote in 1972, and when the general election campaign began, he intended to support McGovern. By October, he had become undecided about McGovern, and just before the election day he switched to Nixon. He cited one particular commercial as the major reason:

> *I saw this ad where it says McGovern keeps changing his mind. It said he had first said this and then that. He did this last year and what about next year. It put a question in my mind about whether I wanted to vote for McGovern. He doesn't seem reliable as a person. He seems to be changeable with regard to the issues. So I eliminated him. Actually I guess Nixon has done okay the last four years. I'm not crazy about either one, but I'm voting for Nixon.*

Advertising did not manipulate the first voter. It did the second. The woman used the best information available to her to maximize her political values. Although McGovern was making the same arguments about the elderly in his campaign speeches and they were more fully reported and criticized in newspaper reports, the woman did not depend heavily on the news media. But she received from advertising the information she most needed. It informed her about the candidates' social security and other old-age benefits, and she chose the candidate who promised to do her the most good.

The man, on the other hand, was manipulated. He responded to the candidate's interest, not his own. Through commercials, this man's view of his stake in the political system was replaced by the candidate's view. He was concerned about America's role in world affairs and unemployment, and yet he cast his vote on the basis of an idea placed in his head by advertising and seemingly unrelated to his own political concerns. He was used. He had no strong feelings that the nation needed decisive leadership and no firm ground for assuming McGovern would not provide it. His view of politics simply came to mimic the view of a Nixon advertisement.

America can tolerate the effect that advertising has on people like this man. Counting for one or perhaps two voters in every hundred that got to the polls, this man and others like him will select a candidate for trivial reasons with or without advertising. (Before being persuaded by the Nixon commercial, the man indicated his vote for McGovern was premised on the fact that "McGovern had got a raw deal because of all the criticism about Eagleton.") And besides, since their reasons for choosing a candidate seem randomly selected, their votes distribute about equally between the candidates.

The benefits provided other voters by televised political advertising far exceed this kind of cost. Not only do more Americans, like the woman who learned which candidate was best for her, obtain information that helps them determine how their self-interest can be served, but many more people acquire information that helps them to validate a prior decision. And then there are people who simply learn a little more from ads than what they would have otherwise been able to learn. . . .

NOTES

1. Leo Bogart, *Strategy in Advertising* (New York: Harcourt & Brace & World, 1967), p.139.
2. Respondents were first asked whether they had seen a Nixon or McGovern commercial. If they indicated seeing an ad, they were then asked: "Would you tell me what you can about the Nixon (McGovern) commercial you remember best?" Those remembering nothing about the ad were classified as "unable to recall." Other replies were classified as partial or full recall depending on whether respondents stated the central message of the commercial they had seen.

3. Bogart, op. cit., p. 139.
4. Raymond A. Bauer and Stephen A. Greyser, *Advertising in America* (Boston: Harvard University Press, 1968), chapter 7.
5. Ibid. Percentages based on a reconstruction of data contained in source.
6. Responses come from interviews conducted with potential voters during the 1972 general election. Responses have been edited to improve readability. Ages and occupations have been changed to protect identities of respondents.

CHAPTER SEVEN

ELECTIONS

At least once every four years, at the time the president of the United States is being elected, political commentators raise the issue of the electoral college as a method of electing the president, claiming that something ought to be done to correct the defects of that system. Lawrence Longley, a professor of political science at Lawrence University, is one of many to have taken up the argument. In a paper presented to his fellow political scientists in 1977, a portion of which is reproduced here, Longley argues that the electoral college is not only undemocratic, but also politically dangerous. In his view it is dangerous because it permits candidates in a close electoral vote situation to upset the normal political stability of the electoral process by challenging electoral votes, calling for recounts in selected states, and otherwise calling into question the votes of selected electors.

Longley's views are shared by others, including Senator Birch Bayh, Democrat of Indiana, who has sponsored an amendment to abolish the electoral college and instead choose the president through direct election.

The author of the second selection, Curtis Gans, thinks we ought to take a long hard look before we pass such an amendment. Aside from the fact that he thinks the present system contributes to the operation of our pluralist system, he maintains that it might be better to keep an imperfect system that works than to trade it in on something the consequences of which are not known.

The Case Against the Electoral College

Lawrence D. Longley

The contemporary electoral college is a curious political institution.[1] Obscure and even unknown to the average citizen,[2] it serves as a crucial mechanism for transforming popular votes cast for President into electoral votes which actually elect the President. If the electoral college were only a neutral and sure means for counting and aggregating votes, it would likely be the subject of little controversy. The electoral college does not, however, just tabulate popular votes in the form of electoral votes. Instead, it is an institution that operates with noteworthy inequality—it favors some interests and hurts others. In addition, its operations are by no means certain or smooth. The electoral college can—and has—deadlocked, forcing a resort to extraordinarily awkward contingency procedures. Other flaws and difficulties with the system can also develop under various electoral situations. In short, the electoral college system has important political consequences, multiple flaws, possible grave consequences, and inherent gross inequalities. Yet, it continues to exist as a central part of our Presidential electoral machinery. . . .

THE FAITHLESS ELECTOR

The first characteristic arises out of the fact that the electoral college today is not the assembly of wise and learned elders as assumed by its creators, but is rather a state by state assembly of political hacks and fat cats.[3] Neither in the quality of the electors nor in law is there any assurance that the electors will vote as expected. Pledges, apparently unenforceable by law,[4] and party and personal loyalty seem to be the only guarantee of electoral voting consistent with the will of a state's electorate.

From Lawrence D. Longley, "The Case Against the Electoral College," paper delivered at the annual meeting of the American Political Science Association, Washington, D.C., 1977. Used with permission.

The problem of the "faithless elector" is neither theoretical nor unimportant. Republican elector Doctor Lloyd W. Bailey of North Carolina, who decided to vote for Wallace after the 1968 election rather than for his pledged candidate Nixon, and Republican elector Roger MacBride of Virginia who likewise deserted Nixon in 1972 to vote for Libertarian Party candidate John Hospers, are two examples of "faithless electors." In the recent 1976 election, we once again had a faithless elector—and curiously enough once again a deviant Republican elector. Washington Republican Mike Padden decided, six weeks after the November election, that he preferred not to support Republican nominee Ford, and cast his electoral vote for Ronald Reagan. Similar defections from the voter expectations also occurred in 1948, 1956 and 1960, or in other words, in six of the eight most recent Presidential elections. Even more important is that the likelihood of this occurring on a multiple basis would be greatly heightened in the case of an electoral vote majority resting on one or two votes—a very real possibility in 1976 as in other recent elections.

In fact, when one looks at the election returns for the recent 1976 election, one can observe that if about 5,560 votes had switched from Carter to Ford in Ohio, Carter would have lost that state and had only 272 electoral votes, two more than the absolute minimum needed of 270. In that case, two or three individual electors seeking personal recognition or attention to a pet cause could withhold their electoral votes, and thus make the election outcome very uncertain.

A startling reminder of the possibilities inherent in such a close electoral vote election as 1976 was provided recently by Republican Vice-President nominee Robert Dole. Testifying before the Senate Judiciary Committee on January 27, 1977 in *favor* of abolishing the electoral college, Senator Dole remarked that during the election count:

> We were looking around on the theory that maybe Ohio might turn around because they had an automatic recount.

> We were shopping—not shopping, excuse me. Looking around for electors. Some took a look at Missouri, some were looking at Louisiana, some in Mississippi, because their laws are a little bit different. And we might have picked up one or two in Louisiana. There were allegations of fraud maybe in Mississippi, and something else in Missouri.

> We need to pick up three or four after Ohio. So that may happen in any event.

> But it just seems to me that the temptation is there for that elector in a very tight race to really negotiate quite a bunch.[5]

THE WINNER-TAKE-ALL SYSTEM

The second problem of the contemporary electoral college system lies in the almost universal custom of granting all of a state's electoral votes to the winner of a state's popular vote plurality—not even a majority. This can lead to interesting results, such as in Arkansas in 1968 where Humphrey and Nixon together split slightly over 61% of the popular vote, while Wallace, with 38%, received 100% of the state's electoral votes. Even more significant, however, is the fact that the unit voting of state electors tends to magnify tremendously the relative voting power of residents of the larger states, since each of their voters may, by his vote, decide not just one vote, but how 41 or 45 electoral votes are cast—if electors are faithful.

As a result, the electoral college has major impact on candidate strategy—as shown by the obsession of Carter and Ford strategists, in the closing weeks of the 1976 campaign, with the nine big electoral vote states with 245 of the 270 electoral votes necessary to win. Seven of these nine states were, in fact, to be exceedingly close, with both candidates receiving at least 48% of the state vote.

The electoral college does not treat voters alike—a thousand voters in Scranton, Pennsylvania are far more strategically important than a similar number of voters in Wilmington, Delaware. This also places a premium on the support of key political leaders in large electoral vote states. This could be observed in the 1976 election in the desperate wooing of Mayors Rizzo of Philadelphia and Daley of Chicago by Carter because of the major roles these political leaders might have in determining the outcome in Pennsylvania and Illinois. The electoral college treats political leaders as well as voters unequally—those in large marginal states are vigorously courted.

The electoral college also encourages fraud—or at least fear and rumor of fraud. New York, with more than enough electoral votes to elect Ford, went to Carter by 290,000 popular votes. Claims of voting irregularities and calls for a recount were made on election night, but later withdrawn because of Carter's clear national popular vote win. If fraud was present in New York, only 290,000 votes determined the election; under direct election, at least 1,700,000 votes would have to have been irregular to determine the outcome.

The electoral college also provided opportunity for third-party candidates to exercise magnified political influence in the election of the President when they can gather votes in large, closely balanced states. In 1976, third-party candidate Eugene McCarthy, with less than 1% of the popular vote, came close to tilting the election through his strength in close pivotal states. In four states (Iowa, Maine, Oklahoma, and Oregon) totaling 26 electoral votes, McCarthy's vote exceeded the margin by which Ford defeated Carter. In those states, McCarthy's candidacy *may* have swung those states to Ford.[6] Even more significantly, had McCarthy been on the New York ballot, it is likely Ford would have carried that state with its 41 electoral votes, and with it the election—despite Carter's national vote majority.

THE CONSTANT TWO ELECTORAL VOTES

A third feature of the electoral college system lies in the apportionment of electoral votes among the states. The constitutional formula is simple: one vote per state per Senator and Representative. A significant distortion from equality appears here because of "the constant two" electoral votes, regardless of population, which correspond to the Senators. Because of this, inhabitants of the very small states are advantaged to the extent that they "control" three electoral votes (one for each Senator and one for the Representative), while their population might otherwise entitle them to but one or two votes. This is weighting by states, not by population—however, the importance of this feature, as shown below, is greatly outweighed by the previously mentioned winner-take-all system.

THE CONTINGENCY ELECTION PROCEDURE

The fourth feature of the contemporary electoral college system is probably the most complex—and probably also the most dangerous in terms of the stability of the political system. This is the requirement that if no candidate receives an absolute majority of the electoral vote—in recent years 270—the election is thrown into the House of Representatives for voting among the top three candidates. Two questions need to be asked: is such an electoral college deadlock likely to occur in terms of contemporary politics?, and would the consequences likely be disastrous? A simply answer to both questions is yes.

Taking some recent examples, it has been shown that, in 1960, a switch of less than 9,000 popular votes from Kennedy to Nixon in Illinois and Missouri would have prevented either man from receiving an electoral college majority.[7] Similarly, in 1968, a 53,000 vote shift in New Jersey, Missouri, and New Hampshire, would have resulted in an electoral college deadlock, with Nixon receiving 269 votes—one short of a majority. Finally, in the recent 1976 election, if slightly less than 11,950 popular votes in Delaware and Ohio had shifted from Carter to Ford, Ford would have carried these two states. The result of the 1976 election would then have been an exact tie in electoral votes—269-269. The Presidency would have been decided *not* on election night, but through deals or switches at the electoral college meetings on December 13, or the later uncertainties of the House of Representatives.

What specifically might happen in the case of an apparent electoral college non-majority or deadlock? A first possibility, of course, is that a faithless elector or two, pledged to one candidate or another, might switch at the time of the actual meetings of the electoral college so as to create a majority for one of the candidates. This might resolve the crisis, although it is sad to think of the Presidency as being mandated on such a thin reed of legitimacy.

If, however, no deals or actions at the time of the December 13 meetings of the electoral college were successful in forming a majority, then the action would shift to the House of Representatives, meeting at noon on January 6, 1977, only 14 days before the Constitutional scheduled Inauguration Day for the new President.

The House of Representatives contingency procedure which would now be followed is an unfortunate relic of the compromises of the writing of the Constitution as discussed earlier. Serious problems of equity exist, certainly, in following the constitutionally prescribed one-vote-per-state procedure. Beyond this problem of voter fairness lurks an even more serious problem—what if the House itself should deadlock and be unable to agree on a President?

In a two candidate race, this is unlikely to be a real problem; however, in a three candidate contest, such as 1968, there might well be enormous difficulties in getting a majority of states behind one candidate, as House members agonized over choosing between partisan labels and support for the candidate (especially Wallace) who carried their district. The result, in 1968, might well have been no immediate majority forthcoming of 26 states and political uncertainty and chaos as the nation approached Inauguration Day.

THE UNCERTAINTY OF THE WINNER WINNING

Besides the four aspects of the electoral college system so far discussed: "the faithless elector," "the winner-take-all system," "the constant two votes per state," and "the contingency election procedure," one last aspect should be described. This is that under the present system, there is no assurance that the winner of the popular vote will win the election. This problem is a fundamental one—can an American President operate effectively in our democracy if he has received *less* votes than the loser? I suggest that the effect upon the legitimacy of a contemporary Presidency would be disastrous if a president were elected by the electoral college after losing in the popular vote—yet this *can* and *has* happened two or three times, the most recent undisputable case being the election of 1888, when the 100,000 popular vote plurality of Grover Cleveland was turned into a losing 42% of the electoral vote.

Was there a real possibility of such a divided verdict in 1976? An analysis of the election shows that if 9,245 votes had shifted to Ford in Ohio and Hawaii, Ford would have become President with 270 electoral votes, the absolute minimum,[8] despite Carter's 51% of the popular vote and margin of 1.7 million votes.

One hesitates to contemplate the consequences of a non-elected

President being inaugurated for four more years despite having been rejected by a majority of the American voters in his only Presidential election. . . .

NOTES

1. Some of the material contained in this paper was originally prepared and presented as "Statement of Lawrence D. Longley Before the Committee on the Judiciary, United States Senate," *Hearings on the Electoral College and Direct Election,* 95th Congress, 1st Session, February 1, 1977, pp. 88-105. Earlier research drawn upon for this paper include: Lawrence D. Longley and Alan G. Braun, *The Politics of Electoral College Reform* (New Haven: Yale University Press, 1972, second edition, 1975); Lawrence D. Longley, "The Electoral College," *Current History,* LXVII (August, 1974), pp. 64-69 ff; and John H. Yunker and Lawrence D. Longley, *The Electoral College: It's Biases Newly Measured for the 1960s and 1970s* (Beverly Hills, Ca.: Sage Professional Papers in American Politics, 1976).

2. In another publication, the following "man-on-the-street" interviews are cited: "Every boy and girl should go to college, if they can't afford Yale or Harvard, why, Electoral is just as good, if you work"; "The group at the bar poor-mouth Electoral somethin' awful. Wasn't they mixed up in a basketball scandal or somethin'?" quoted in Longley and Braun, p. 1.

3. See: Lawrence C. Longley, "Why the Electoral College Should be Abolished," Speech to the 1976 Electoral College, Madison, Wisconsin, December 13, 1976. Despite being referred to as "political hacks and fat cats," the Wisconsin electors there assembled proceeded to go on record supporting the abolishment of their office.

4. Only sixteen states have laws requiring electors to vote according to their pledge, and these laws themselves are of doubtful constitutionality. See James C. Kirby, Jr., "Limitations on the Power of State Legislatures over Presidential Elections," *Law and Contemporary Problems* 27 (Spring, 1962), pp. 495-509.

5. "Testimony of Honorable Robert Dole, U.S. Senator from the State of Kansas," *Hearings on the Electoral College and Direct Election,* 95th Congress, 1st Session, January 27, 1977, pp. 36-37. (These hearings are hereafter cited as February 1977 Senate Hearings.)

6. Testimony of Neal Peirce, *National Journal,* Author, February, 1977 Senate Hearings, p. 248.

7. Neal R. Peirce, *The People's President: The Electoral College in American History and The Direct-Vote Alternative* (New York: Simon & Schuster, 1968), pp. 317-21. The concept of hairbreadth elections is also discussed in Longley and Braun, op. cit., pp.37-41.

8. This analysis assumes, of course, the non-defection of Republican elector Mike Padden of Washington. If he had nevertheless declined to vote for Ford, then the election would have been inconclusive and would have gone to the House in January, 1977.

Four Reasons to Keep the Electoral College

Curtis B. Gans

What do Richard Nixon, John F. Kennedy, Harry S. Truman, Woodrow Wilson, Abraham Lincoln, Andrew Jackson and eight other American presidents have in common?

Each received less than a majority of the votes cast in the election which elevated him into the White House.

What do all presidents have in common?

None has ever received the votes of a majority of the adult population living in the United States at the time of his election.

It is in the context of these two questions that the U.S. Senate should consider Sen. Birch Bayh's constitutional amendment to abolish the electoral college and substitute direct presidential elections.

The American republic has survived quite nicely, thank you, despite the electoral college, occasional minority presidencies and even at least one president (Rutherford B. Hayes) who was elected while receiving fewer popular votes than his opponent.

It is by no means clear that the American polity would be nearly so healthy if the electoral college were abolished, especially in this, the television age.

The arguments *for* direct elections and Sen. Bayh's amendment are simple, clear and persuasive:

- Why should every person's vote not be equal, and what better way to guarantee that equality than through direct elections?

- How more efficaciously can the country protect itself against the possibility of electing a president who receives fewer votes than his

From Curtis B. Gans, "Four Reasons to Keep the Electoral College," *The Washington Post*, July 2, 1978. Copyright Curtis B. Gans, Director, Committee for the Study of the American Electorate. Used with permission of the author.

opposition than to abolish the electoral college which makes such an outcome possible?

- Should not American democracy protect itself from the demagogue—the George Wallace who succeeds—who might invalidate the vote of the people and throw an election into the House of Representatives?

Very simple, clear, persuasive. Not, however, compelling.

For abolishing the electoral college might well bring about greater equality and more direct democracy, but it would likely do so at the expense of American political stability.

The case for keeping the electoral college is not nearly so clear and simple, but it is, in the end, more persuasive and compelling.

The case for retention of the electoral college rests upon four words—pluralism, federalism, participation and manipulation.

Pluralism The success of the American political experiment has always rested on a delicate balancing of the will of the majority with the rights and needs of minorities. The electoral college has served to protect the latter.

American blacks, for instance, are, in the aggregate, only a small part of the total national eligible vote, and this might be ignored in a politician's national political calculations. Blacks, however, account for nearly half the popular vote in almost every southern state, nearly 80 percent of the vote in the District of Columbia and a substantial portion of the vote in every northeastern urban state. In the state-by-state competition for electoral votes, no politician can afford to bypass the black vote.

Farmers comprise an even smaller percentage of the population than blacks, but they hold the key to a critical set of midwestern and western electoral votes. A politician ignores them at his peril.

Hispanic Americans, urban dwellers, rural dwellers, union members, small businessmen, industrialists, environmentalists and other groups of Americans might see their concerns go unaddressed were presidential elections one giant political free-for-all. What insures that the needs and desires of significant minorities will be taken into account is the one aspect of the American political system that forces national candidates to compete for votes on the state and local levels—the electoral college.

Federalism Until recently, federalism was a reason many liberals gave for opposing the electoral college. The way, they said, to rid the nation of states' rights obstructionism on such issues as civil rights was to reduce the power of the states by abolishing the electoral college.

More recently, even liberals have come to see that a burgeoning, bureaucratic, all-too-powerful and perhaps all-too-cumbersome federal government is not an unmixed blessing. Perhaps more pertinently, they have come to see that state and local governments are sources for innovation—that only state and local government can ban nuclear power, establish off-track betting, create universal voter registration, provide for neighborhood government or experiment with varying educational modes. They serve not only as a potential social and political laboratory, but also as a bulwark against unwarranted concentration of political power.

Those who drew up the Constitution did not, perhaps, envision warrantless wiretaps, "enemies lists" or other perversions of presidential power. They did, fortunately, buffer presidential power by making it necessary to conduct presidential politics state-by-state through the electoral college. States may not be the most rationally planned units of subfederal governance, but, given the alternative of overweening and unimaginative national power, they surely deserve the protection the electoral college affords them.

Participation For nearly two decades, while American politics has become increasingly nationalized, the level of political participation has been dwindling. Nearly 70 million Americans now do not vote in presidential elections; nearly 15 million eligible voters have dropped out of the political process during the last decade.

Survey results indicate that many of these non-participants feel alienated by the conduct of their leaders, confused by the growing complexity of the issues that face them and powerless in the face of large and growing institutions and forces. Many no longer believe that their vote can make a difference in any election or that any election can make a difference in their lives.

In the face of this, it seems absurd to revise America's system of choosing a president to make the individual voter feel even more impotent and meaningless.

For an individual voter may well be persuaded that his vote *can* make the difference between winning and losing the electoral votes of his state. No individual in his right mind will ever be bullied into believing that his individual vote is likely to make a difference among 70 million or more.

Manipulation Of all the changes in American political life, the advent of television has wrought the most profound and far-reaching alterations in the American political landscape.

During the period of television's growing impact, many traditional community institutions have atrophied, political parties have decayed and the grass roots structure of American politics—local clubs, reform and regular organizations and community and precinct leadership—have all diminished in importance. In their stead is a proliferation of single-issue organizations, polarizing attempts to attract the attention of television cameras and political candidates whose charisma quotient is seen as a more important personal attribute than competence and character.

Whether all of this is directly attributable to television is a subject of some debate. What is not debatable is that, in the actual conduct of American political campaigns, television has become an increasingly important factor. Money that went to precinct organizations, volunteer workers, travel for candidates to meet with local political, civic, religious and ethnic leaders is now being husbanded to pay for television commercials.

A whole new generation of media experts, with their attendant political pollsters, have become a dominant force in American politics by virtue of their ability to manipulate images in order to bring out the vote for their candidates. Managers of campaigns have made increasing use of paid television because, unlike volunteer organization and precinct politics, the video image reaches everyone and is easy to control. The larger the scale of the campaign—from local to state to national—the greater the growing dependence on television, and the less people and their desires, needs and involvement have anything to do with the American political enterprise.

The only thing keeping the dependence on television in national campaigns from being total is the need to compete for the electoral votes in various states and therefore the need to relate to local political organizations and leadership and to mount an organizational effort to get a maximum turnout.

Unless the American people wish to turn their politics completely over to the Rafshoons and Garths and the Caddells and Teeters—to the media experts and the pollsters—they had better give serious thought to retaining the electoral college and the human factor in American politics.

When the debate on the electoral college begins in the Senate, proponents of the Bayh amendment will likely make much of a Gallup Poll which shows that 84 percent of Americans want direct elections for the presidency.

But those Americans were not asked whether they wanted to vitiate the federal system, weaken the pluralistic underpinnings of American democracy, decrease the level of political participation or turn American politics over to media manipulation. Had they been so asked, the results might have been quite different.

The issue before both Senate and nation is sufficiently complex so that polls are of little relevance. The debate over the electoral college presents a conflict of fundamental and competing values, in which neither side has a corner on the market of wisdom.

But what seems clear is that the Senate and the several states should think long and hard before trading in an imperfect system that has worked for the illusion of greater perfection that may not.

CHAPTER EIGHT

POLITICAL PARTIES

Many years ago a distinguished political scientist by the name of V. O. Key, Jr., characterized politics in the one-party South as a "free-for-all" in which individual candidates, backed by their "friends and neighbors," engaged in a rabble-rousing campaign style that approached political demagoguery. The road to success for most Southern politicians, in the absence of orderly two-party politics, was to play on the emotions of the people on some single issue—usually the race issue.

Today, the single-issue candidate and the single-issue interest group have become a prominent part of national politics, not just the politics of the South. In the first selection, David Broder, syndicated columnist for the Washington Post, *takes note of this development and argues that it is likely to have a destructive effect on our political system. Contrary to what the title of Broder's article suggests, he is not in favor of a political system in which all politicians and groups are atomized, in which no compromise or muting of positions is possible. Instead, his advocacy of the single-issue group is merely a way of bringing to the attention of politicians the dangers inherent in single-issue politics with the hope that the politicians will reinstate a more traditional party system before it is too late.*

Richard Cohen, staff correspondent of the National Journal, *takes issue with Broder, arguing that single-issue groups have made it possible to have a new openness in our politics. Cohen believes that the American public does not need political party "kingmakers," but rather politicians, reporters, and citizens who can cooperate to advance a new politics that is less costly and more participatory.*

Let 100 Single-Issue Groups Bloom

David S. Broder

Some call them special-interest groups. Some call them single-interest groups. Whatever the name, it's agreed that they're a shame. "Strident and self-righteous," as one senator terms them, the single-issue groups are accused of fragmenting the political consensus, whipsawing conscientious public officials with non-negotiable demands, and generally playing havoc with responsible government and politics.

But if single-cause groups are an evil, they are a necessary evil. In fact, rather than hoping that they can be curbed, as some members of Congress have proposed, it may be better to let such groups flourish and exasperate politicians as much as possible.

I say this in the belief that American politics has reached the point where it has to get worse before it can get better. Specifically, it must become more painful and difficult for politicians and officeholders. And because single-interest groups are making it more painful and difficult, they are helping create the conditions in which responsible politics and government may be reborn.

TWIN PERILS

The complaints about single-interest groups are abundant, if sometimes overstated. When Democratic Sen. Edward M. Kennedy of Massachusetts declared last October that "the Senate and House are awash in a sea of special interest campaign contributions and special interest lobbying," he was probably mixing dreadnaughts and dories, if apples and oranges do not suit his nautical metaphor.

He cited as evidence the growth in political action committees and in their contributions to congressional campaigns.

From David S. Broder, "Let 100 Single-Issue Groups Bloom," *The Washington Post*, January 7, 1979. © The Washington Post. Reprinted with permission of David Broder.

It is true that the $76 million reported spent by 1,911 independent, non-party groups in the 1978 elections were records, both in dollars and in numbers of organizations. But many of the largest spenders—the AFL-CIO, the National Conservative Political Action Committee, the American Medical Association, for example—have broad political and policy agendas.

Nevertheless, there are certainly narrow, one-cause groups—the opponents of gun control, most notably, but also some conservation, arms-control and equal rights amendment advocates—that raised and spent substantial sums.

The concern about their influence is not misplaced. Groups like these—or the right-to-life organizations, which depend on volunteer workers rather than dollars for their influence—can effectively threaten officeholders with political retaliation because of stands on a single question.

They have demonstrated a capability—at least in some states and some races—to upset not only individual careers but also powerful party organizations. For example, the Minnesota Democratic Farmer-Labor Party, a rich source of national leadership for the past generation, has been riddled by infighting between pro- and anti-abortion groups.

When admitting the destructive power of single-interest groups, however, it is important to stress that their rise represents the *second* stage in the demolition of the party system in the United States, not the first.

The first stage came in the 1950s and 1960s, when ambitious office-seekers found that they could bypass the party and win office from the courthouse to the White House on their own. Now, in the 1970s, issue-concerned citizens are applying the same lesson—not to gain office but to force their policy views on the government. Like the candidates, they are bypassing the party structure and "taking their case directly to the people."

The result is that independent, autonomous officeholders are confronting independent, autonomous interest groups in a kind of unmediated power struggle that leaves the national interest in shreds and helps persuade voters to express their dissatisfaction in the most dramatic way possible—by not voting.

What is not generally perceived is that single-issue groups and single-shot candidates are twin perils to responsible politics and government. In reality, the Gun Owners of America Campaign Committee is no more narrow or selfish in its aims than was the Carter-for-President Committee. The League of Conservation Voters is fundamentally no different in this respect than the Committee for the Re-election of the President. One has the single interest of seeing a certain policy adopted, the other of having a certain candidate elected.

That is an alien notion, I know. But it may be more easily understood by following a short historical trail to see how we arrived at this point in our politics.

BREAKING THE PATTERN

In the innocent days of the 1940s or 1950s, what would a young man eager for public office do? In most places, he would decide first whether he felt more comfortable as a Democrat or Republican, and then present himself to a party screening or slating committee.

After examining his credentials, the party elders might offer him their support for supervisor or sheriff, for prothonotary or (at a different level) president. But they also might say, "Doubtless you are all the things you claim, but we already have a good candidate for senator, so why don't you run for clerk this year and we'll see how you do in that job." In that way, the party maintained its members' loyalties and fresh ambitions were channeled into useful roles.

The young man, of course, understood that he had acquired certain advantages and taken on certain obligations upon being embraced by the party.

His campaign costs would be met in whole or part by the party, which collected contributions from supportive citizens and interest groups. Party precinct workers would push his candidacy as they made the rounds. He would be cloaked with a label, Democrat or Republican, which had broad significance for voters, so that even if they did not know him, they would know he was (or was not) "their kind of candidate."

At the same time, the young man knew that he was no longer a free agent. He had acquired obligations to help promote his party and win votes for his ticket-mates, whatever he thought of their individual merits. A degree of loyalty was expected. His disagreements with party leaders would be expressed privately or, if publicly, in muted tones. When they needed help, he would be available.

He also knew that when the party was popular, he might benefit from the "coattails" of its leaders, and when the party lost the public's confidence, he might be booted out of office—no matter how conscientiously he had done his own job for his constituents.

That is roughly the way the game was played for most of American history in most places in this country.

But after World War II, the pattern changed. It changed because certain smart fellows discovered that they could achieve their ambitions without going through all this rigamarole. Sen. Kennedy's brother John probably wasn't the first, but he was an important trend-setter.

When he returned to Boston from Navy service, Gov. Maurice Tobin and other Democratic Party elders invited the 29-year-old novice to go on the ticket for lieutenant governor. It was a flattering offer, but one Kennedy could refuse. His goal was the House of Representatives, and he plunged into a 10-man primary without asking anyone's permission. While his father pulled strings to mollify some of the old-guard politicians, Kennedy and his young friends put together the organization of political amateurs and volunteers that won the campaign.

It worked for him not only in that first House race, but in later campaigns for the Senate and the presidency—and he was not alone.

Jerry Ford did the same thing in Grand Rapids, taking a House nomination away from a Republican incumbent. Richard Nixon launched his career in California with the same sort of volunteer effort. Jimmy Carter followed the pattern in Georgia.

They and their counterparts made a number of discoveries. They found that volunteers worked harder and were more persuasive in campaigns, than patronage-oriented "soldiers" of the old political machines.

They found that interest groups preferred to give money directly to candidates rather than through the party. They found that people of means who would never have "dirtied their hands" with party politics would contribute to a candidate who had a tasteful cocktail party or after-theater reception. Later, with the development of direct-mail techniques, people like Barry Goldwater, George Wallace and George McGovern found that the wallets of thousands of less affluent citizens could also be tapped to finance individual candidacies.

The new candidates then discovered more powerful ways of communicating with the voters. Radio and television ads, telephone banks and computerized, targeted mailings carried much more impact than the slate-cards precinct captains used to hand out at the polls.

They discovered—or intensified the use of—an old trick: door-to-door personal campaigning. If they were willing to spend enough time with the voters themselves before a primary, they found, they could beat the organization-backed candidate.

So individuals eager for public office no longer "submit" themselves to a party screening process. They organize to capture a nomination with a full-time, extended primary campaign, and then they announce, as the most recent product of that process announced to his party on the evening he captured its nomination: "My name is Jimmy Carter, and I am running for president of the United States."

A POLITICAL PARTY OF ONE

In office, these new-style politicians behave with an independence appropriate to their manner of acquiring office. They are under no obligation to anyone—and certainly not to others who claim to be "leaders" of their party. This independence of House members has made the job of lining up votes for Democratic legislation far more difficult than it used to be. Those legislators do not feel their fate rests with the voters' judgment on their party, but on them as individuals, and they vote as best suits their individual interests.

Elected executives are no different. Cleveland Mayor Dennis Kucinich ran against the party "establishment" and carried his policy differences with the Democratic city council to the point of forcing his city into bankruptcy. Newbreed governors from West Virginia's Jay Rockefeller to Illinois' Jim Thompson to California's Jerry Brown have been at odds with their legislatures as often as Carter has with Congress.

What really has developed is a system of independent, autonomous candidates and officeholders, each with a political and governmental agenda of his own—a political party of one.

And now those officeholders are raising a cry of alarm about the invasion of their turf by independent, autonomous issue groups.

"Single-issue politics," says Democratic Sen. John Culver of Iowa, "has, in my judgment, disturbing implications for the nature and quality of political representation in this country."

"Increasingly," he says, "splinter lobbies are forcing upon elected officials and candidates . . . loyalty tests on wide ranges of peripheral matters . . . We have vocal, vehement and well-orchestrated lobbies on abortion, consumer agencies, gun control, labor law reform and a host of other subjects," each judging the officeholder not on his overall record but "by a single litmus test of ideological purity."

More and more, officeholders are demanding protection from what one of them has called the "issues extortionists." They are asking why there is nothing to provide some defense against this crossfire of non-negotiable, special-interest demands.

The blunt answer is that they themselves helped destroy the one institution that historically filled that function—the political party. The officeholders are now being victimized by people who have borrowed their own campaign techniques to use against them.

THE RISE OF THE VIGUERIES

In the old system, the parties served to screen the demands of interest groups as well as to regulate the ambitions of candidates. All groups were invited to present their proposals at platform time, but all understood that platform-writing, like ticket-balancing, was a matter of compromise and tradeoff. Individual goals were likely to be subordinated to the overall aim of maintaining the party in power.

In the last 10 years, however, the issue constituencies, witnessing the success of candidates who bypassed the party, decided they could do the same thing. If your aim was to clean up the rivers, you did not have to establish that as a priority with the Democratic or Republican platform committees. You could form the League of Conservation Voters and run campaigns against "the dirty dozen." So it went if you wanted to ban guns or protect guns, stop abortions or make them more available.

Like the candidates, these groups discovered the effectiveness of organizations built on the disciplined enthusiasm of volunteers. They learned that door-to-door canvassing and church or shopping center leaflets can have tremendous impact when targeted for or against particular candidates.

And they learned even better than the candidate organizations of the 1950s and 1960s how to use computerized direct-mail techniques. It is the ability of these groups to generate mail and money, literally at the push of a button, to support or oppose a particular legislative issue or candidate that makes officeholders most upset.

Richard Viguerie, the owner of the most active direct-mail company, has become, in an astonishingly short time, a political power in his own right. He did his first right-to-work mailing in 1969 and his first antiabortion mailing two years later. But it is only since 1975, he says, that he had begun to "focus in on special-interest clients," and his success so far guarantees an expansion of the technique. . . .

A THERAPEUTIC VALUE

For lawmakers subjected to the computerized power of single-interest groups, it can be a frightening experience. Suddenly their offices are flooded with mail warning that unless they vote a particular way on an approaching issue, "we will defeat you next time you run." Suddenly their campaign organizations pick up reports of the district being flooded with disparaging letters—not by their opponent but by some organization they never knew was there.

The politicians' pleas for protection, however, must be scrutinized with care. There are important constitutional rights involved here; the right to petition the government applies equally to organizations with computer mailing techniques as without.

Moreover, there is a therapeutic value in letting the politicians experience the dangers of the kind of politics we have today—a primal struggle for control among single-shot candidates and single-interest groups.

To be sure, it is a brutal, ugly kind of politics, and it is helping turn off the American people in massive numbers. The people are not issue ideologues. They are not candidate fanatics. They are what they have always been—reasonably broad-minded, practical and progressive.

What they hear in the last 10 days of a campaign, whenever they turn on a radio or TV set, is a babble of voices saying "vote for me, vote for me, vote for me." What they read, whenever they open their mail, are injunctions to "vote for this, vote for that." Being sensible, most of them are covering their ears against the din, shutting their eyes to all the commands, and tuning out this self-serving racket by turning away from the polls.

What is missing from our politics is the mechanism which once helped organize those voter choices in a sensible fashion, which channeled the individual ambitions of eager aspirants and the conflicting claims of various interest groups into a coherent ticket and platform. That agency was the political party, and it is in a shambles today.

The destruction of the political parties began with the individual office-seekers, and it is they who keep the parties weak today.

They loved free-lance, individualistic politics—until the techniques of free-lance, individualistic politics were turned against them. Now they are saying that something dangerous has been unleashed. They are right—but about 20 years late in their discovery.

The first reaction among officeholders was to try in 1978 to curb the influence of single-interest groups by reducing the amount of money their political-action committees could contribute to congressional campaigns. Their second ploy—sure to be repeated this year—was an attempt to expand taxpayer financing of individual campaigns beyond the presidential level to House and Senate contests.

But before any curbs are put on the role of single-issue groups and before any more public funds are given to single-shot candidates, it seems reasonable to expect officeholders to demonstrate that they are prepared to sacrifice some of their own precious autonomy.

It really has to be one way or the other. If individual candidates are to be allowed to play their own games for their own ends, with blithe disregard of the effects on the governmental and political system, then single-interest groups are not to be denied the same destructive freedom. If single-issue groups are to be brought back within the constraints of party politics, then the candidates must, too.

FRANKLIN'S CHOICE

The tests of their seriousness about reconstructing the party system are very clear:

• Are they prepared to submit their own credentials to serious screening by party leaders, or will they continue to insist on their absolute right to pursue any office any time the desire strikes them? Will they continue to legislate increasing numbers of primaries, thereby adding to the incentive for full-time candidates to bypass the party endorsement process, or will they cut back on that destructive change in the nominating system?

• As nominees, are they prepared to campaign as members of a party ticket, rather than set up a private political organization of their own? Are they prepared to defend the record of their party, or just their own work on behalf of their own constituents?

• Are they prepared to raise money for their party and partake of the party treasury, or will they keep all the funds they can gather for themselves? Will they channel public campaign subsidies through the political parties, rather than giving them to individual campaign committees, as is the case now?

• Will they accept a responsibility to cooperate with the leaders of their own party—both legislative and executive—in carrying out the party program? Or will they insist that they are free agents on every vote, responsible only to their own conscience and constituents?

My guess is that few candidates or officeholders are ready to sacrifice their own freedom of action to rehabilitate their party. But it may be that when more of them have been bullied by single-issue lobbyists, threatened by single-interest mailings, and beaten by single-interest machines, they will perceive their need for the protections political parties once offered against these ideological buccaneers.

There is no way to put the genie of single-issues groups back in the bottle. But they are not new to our politics. From the anti-Masons of the 1830s to the anti-saloon leagues of the 1920s, such groups have flourished. In a pluralistic society, with a constitutional guarantee of freedom of speech and association, they have an inevitable and proper role to play.

What is different now is that the political parties are not strong enough to play their equally essential role. As Anthony King, the British journalist and political scientist, has observed, the threat to American government is not partisanship but hyperpluralism. Political parties function to build coalitions, but in today's politics, to use King's phrase, "they are only coalitions of sand."

The lesson the officeholders have to learn was stated at the beginning of the republic by Benjamin Franklin: Either they hang together or they hang separately.

Give them a few more years of the rigors of single-shot candidacies and single-issue movements, and even the dullest politicians will discover the need to reinvent political parties.

The Party's Only Begun

Richard E. Cohen

There has been a lot of moaning recently from some politicians and reporters that politics just isn't what it used to be. Their basic complaint: a proliferation of special interests, single-issue groups, political action committees, and grass-roots lobbyists has changed the nature of politics from building coalitions to protecting narrow self-interests.

As articulated by one of its most forceful advocates, *Washington Post* political writer David S. Broder, the case seems to rest on three main points:

1. A decline in the strength of political parties in the 1950s and 1960s, when candidates found they could win elections without party assistance, left room for special-interest groups to grow in number and sophistication.

2. The old-fashioned style of politics featuring strong party leadership served the public interest. Although the style is no longer in vogue, the nation should and will return to it.

3. The new politicians, principally Democrats, "behave with an independence appropriate to their manner of acquiring office," making the enactment of legislation far more difficult.

Broder perversely argues that the single-interest groups should be allowed to "flourish and exasperate politicians as much as possible" so that American politics sinks to a level from which politicians will flee to the security of the old party system. The theory has several problems: It ignores not only simple facts but also social, economic and political changes that have taken place in America since the supposedly halcyon days when the political parties reigned.

Used with permission of Richard E. Cohen. This article is based on an article that appeared in the *National Journal* on January 13, 1979.

Single-interest groups are hardly new to American history. Whether it was the abolitionists before the Civil War, prohibitionists following World War I, or civil rights groups during the 1960s, there have always been—as is appropriate and desirable in a democracy—individuals and groups that feel passionately about an issue and make their case to public officials. Their supporters have cast their election votes strictly on the basis of the candidates' views on their single interest.

It may be true that there are more of these groups on all sides of the political spectrum now than in the past and that they have become more sophisticated. But several factors other than the decline in political parties may be responsible.

First, recent decades have witnessed a diversification of issues in the public sector. Government disposed of the most pressing social issues, which enjoyed a broad consensus on the need for government action, in the New Deal. The issues that confront government today are much more divisive. For example, there was not much doubt in the 1930s that social security was a valuable program, but no such consensus exists now on the need for public jobs programs.

The broader discussion of issues may also result from a greater openness in society and willingness to bring issues before the public. It was not many years ago that discussion of abortion or gay rights, for example, was taboo.

The Supreme Court has made clear that the Constitution guarantees interest groups the right to make their views known in the manner they see fit. In numerous decisions during the past few years, the Court has taken a skeptical view toward limiting any form of speech in a political environment. This attitude has encouraged groups to express their viewpoints. One important ruling came April 26, 1978, in the case of *The First National Bank of Boston* v. *Bellotti*. The Court ruled unconstitutional a Massachusetts law that barred corporations from making cash contributions to influence the outcome of a public referendum. Writing for the majority, Justice Lewis F. Powell, Jr., said: "The inherent worth of the speech in terms of its capacity for informing the public does not depend upon the identity of its source, whether corporation, association, union or individual. . . . The fact that advocacy may persuade the electorate is hardly a reason to suppress it."

Undoubtedly, the new focus on single issues also reflects the power of the press, principally broadcasters, to present issues to the public quickly and understandably, if somewhat superficially.

Finally, the civil rights and Vietnam debates witnessed a development of many special techniques to gain public and political attention. As they gained legitimacy because of their effectiveness, these tactics have been copied by interest groups of all stripes.

Even if it can logically be argued that any of these conditions resulted from the weakening of political parties—a dubious proposition—it hardly seems likely that they will be reversed and that the single-interest groups will disappear. Nor should they. There is no question of the sweeping turnover in House and Senate membership during the last several years. Undoubtedly, many of the new groups have been more willing than their predecessors to go their own way and to challenge leadership.

When the 96th Congress convened January 15, 1979, it had lost 223 of the 435 House members serving in 1974 and 48 of the 100 Senators serving then. Those who left had many reasons including defeat, boredom, inability or lack of desire to keep up with the demanding physical pace, plans to make more money elsewhere, or a combination of these and other factors.

In both the House and Senate, the new members of both parties generally have been independent of almost everyone—the president, their own leaders, and committee chairmen. In the House, the seventy-five freshmen Democrats made their point quickly in 1975 when they joined with a few of their senior colleagues to oust three powerful and crusty committee chairmen. The three barons were stripped of their powers, not so much because of their political views, but because they operated their committees in an autocratic fashion, usually ignoring the concerns of younger colleagues.

The 1975 revolt has had a lasting effect in both the House and Senate. Committee chairmen now usually bend over backward to make sure that everyone, sometimes even a Republican, has a chance to pursue his or her special interest or register a viewpoint. Subcommittee chairmen also have gained far more power to shape legislation and nurture it to enactment, thus increasing the number of persons getting a share of the power.

Some problems are created, of course, not the least of which is the president or congressional leaders can no longer make a deal with just two or three persons to assure a pet proposal has easy passage.

Broder seems particularly distressed by the unwillingness of young Senate and House members to follow their leaders, although he does not explain why they should have to subordinate their views in the "go along to get along" spirit. One significant explanation is that about two-thirds of the freshmen Democrats elected in the House in 1974 took seats previously held by Republicans.

William Schneider and Gregory Schell discussed the effect of these changes in their article on "The New Democrats" in the November/December 1978 issue of Public Opinion, published by the American Enterprise Institute for Public Policy Research. In many suburban and rural areas, they wrote, the party "extended itself into areas remote from (its) base and, in so doing, changed the ideological complexion of the party's representation in the House." Because these new seats were less secure than those forming the party's base, it should not be surprising that Democrats from previously Republican districts tended to be "mavericks" compared to those from areas more traditionally Democratic.

Nor should it be ignored that Democrats elected 291, 292, and 277 of their party to the House in the 1974-78 elections. Only twice before since 1940 were there more than 263 Democrats. While the high numbers create organizational and leadership problems, there are worse difficulties that a party can face.

Despite the reduction in party power, congressional leaders have been able to adjust so that they still retain considerable influence over what takes place. But they would be the first to agree that the days are over when a few senior lawmakers can run Congress.

House Speaker Thomas P. O'Neill, Jr., of Massachusetts leads by building coalitions that shift from one issue to another. Rep. Philip R. Sharp, an Indiana Democrat who has been chosen by O'Neill for several assignments, says O'Neill's style is to "entrust" his colleagues to do something, not to "direct" them. He carefully picks his lieutenants to help him persuade other House members on a particular vote and to mediate disputes among warring factions of the House. He is an exceptional and sympathetic listener, a trait which helps him to gauge the sentiment of the House and then to shape its action.

In the Senate, Majority Leader Robert C. Byrd of West Virginia has a similar capacity to work with all sides and perform the necessary functions that will enhance the prospects for enacting Democratic Party legislation. Often he helps to identify a consensus position among differing factions and gets agreement on that position.

Many senators have become intimately involved with legislative dealings far sooner after they entered the Senate than was the case a decade or two earlier. These senators, many of whom were elected through their own political appeal and organization rather than as candidates of a strong state party machine, have demonstrated that diligence and intelligence can carry the day, on occasion. As a group, they have made the era of the crusty and powerful Senate barons a relic of the past and have brought more informed and meaningful debate of the nation's issues to the Senate.

There is no denying the importance of political parties in an earlier American era. For many Americans they provided crucial assistance in finding jobs or housing and protecting their rights. But Tammany Hall— the Democratic organization in New York City that flourished in the first half of this century—had its seamy side too, and in any case it seems farfetched to hope for its revival.

Yet Broder closes his article with several proposals that would have made Boss Tweed proud—steps he says must be taken before his goal of reconstructing the party system can be achieved. He says candidates should submit their credentials to screening by party leaders. But who elects these bosses? To whom are they accountable? Why do we need latter-day godfathers? The idea that the public would stand aside for political king making is wishful thinking and a bit presumptuous. While no one denies parties or other groups interested in politics the right to recommend standards for public service or policy, the public has a right and responsibility to choose its own leaders. Broder says candidates should campaign as members of a party ticket. Why should someone be forced to pledge support of obvious hacks? He says they should accept responsibility to carry out the party system. But does the voter elect a person or a party?

Politics is a process of negotiation and accommodation. It is unrealistic and unfair to expect that party members should commit themselves to their fellow candidates and a common platform. Instead, all elected officials should pledge themselves to foster the public—and not the party—interest.

As a Broder book title stated, *The Party's Over.* Rather than try to revive a corpse, politicians, reporters, and citizens should cooperate to assure that the new party system is less costly for participants and more egalitarian for all.

CHAPTER NINE

INTEREST GROUPS

According to most recent public opinion polls, the average American is skeptical of the politicians who run the government. Much of this skepticism is no doubt attributable to the fact that Americans are confronted almost daily with the news of yet another political scandal—some congressman or senator has received an under-the-table contribution from a special-interest group in exchange for political favors. Such political scandals invite the public to conclude that the government is controlled by the wealthy few.

Is this an accurate picture? Michael Parenti, a long-time critic of American politics, argues that it is. In his article below, Parenti describes what he believes to be the consequences of a pressure system that is skewed in favor of the rich and powerful—special tax benefits for oil interests, tariff protection for the automobile industry, the leasing of public land to lumber companies, the easing of pollution standards for the nation's chemical companies, and many more. Moreover, public interest groups, supposedly organized to look out after the public interest, have done little more than produce cosmetic changes in the present system, nothing fundamental.

Andrew McFarland, on the other hand, claims that new public interest groups such as Common Cause, Nader, and the environmental groups have been much more successful than Parenti is willing to concede. He attributes the success to the public's skepticism of government, the growth of computer technology, and the availability of money for public relations. Ironic though it may seem, it is probably for these same reasons that Parenti's special interests have been so successful in recent times.

Who Governs? Leaders and Lobbyists

Michael Parenti

LOBBYISTS AND THEIR WAYS

Lobbyists are persons hired by organized interest groups to influence legislative and administrative policies. Some political scientists see lobbying as essentially a "communication process." They argue that the officeholder's perception of a particular policy is influenced solely or primarily by the information reaching him. The lobbyist's role is one of providing that information. By this view, the techniques of the "modern" lobbyist consist mostly of disseminating data and "expert" information and making public appearances before legislative committees rather than the obsolete tactics of secret deals and bribes.[1] The students of lobbying who propagate this image of the influence system overestimate the changes that have occurred within it. *The development of new lobbying techniques does not mean that the older, cruder ones have been discarded.* Along with the slick brochures, expert testimonies and technical reports, corporate lobbyists still have the slush fund, the kickback, the stock award, the high-paying job offer in private industry, the lavish parties and prostitutes, the meals, transportation, housing and vacation accommodations and the many other hustling enticements of money. From the lowliest city councilman to the White House itself, officeholders accept money and favors from lobbyists in return for favored treatment. "Members of the House Banking and Currency Committee," complained its chairman, the late Wright Patman (D.-Tex.), "have been offered huge blocks of bank stocks free of charge and directorships on bank boards. Freshmen members have been approached within hours of their arrival in Washington and offered quick and immediate loans. In one instance that was reported to me, the bank told the member, 'Just write a check, we will honor it.' "[2] "Everyone has a price," Howard Hughes once told his associate Noah Dietrich, who later recalled

From Michael Parenti, *Democracy for the Few*, 2nd ed. (New York: St. Martin's Press, Inc., Macmillan & Co., Ltd., 1977). Used with permission.

that the billionaire handed out about $400,000 yearly to "councilmen and county supervisors, tax assessors, sheriffs, state senators and assembly-men, district attorneys, governors, congressmen and senators, judges—yes, and vice-presidents and presidents, too."[3]

Many large corporations have a special division dedicated to perform-ing favors for officeholders. The services include everything from free Caribbean trips on private jet planes to loans, private contracts and illegal gifts. An employee at ITT's congressional liaison section publicly com-plained about the way Congressmen continually called her office for favors "on a big scale." This situation "shocked" her, she said, even though "very little in Washington would shock me."[4]

The case of Claude Wild, Jr., is instructive. As a vice-president for Gulf Oil and a lobbyist, Wild had the full-time job of passing out, over a twelve-year period, about $4.1 million of Gulf's money to politicians like Lyndon Johnson, Hubert Humphrey, Richard Nixon and Gerald Ford. The money was delivered to Wild from Gulf offices around the country in cash packets of $25,000 each, to be divided about equally among federal, state and local politicians.[5] Other oil companies made illegal contributions to public officeholders in return for special tax favors and protection against the growing agitation to break up the monopolized oil industry. Airline companies, heavily dependent on federal regulations and subsidies, pas-sed along large sums, as did companies that were major suppliers to the federal government. In addition to the millions contributed at home, the multinationals paid hundreds of millions in bribes and contributions to right-wing governments and militarists in countries like Iran, South Korea, Bolivia and Taiwan.[6]

The big-time Washington lobbyists are usually attorneys or business people who have proven themselves articulate spokespersons for their firms, or ex-legislators or former bureaucrats with good connections. Whatever their varied backgrounds, the one common resource lobbyists should have at their command in order to be effective is—money. Money buys what one House aide called that "basic ingredient of all lobbying"—*accessibility* to the officeholder[7] and, with that, the opportunity to shape his judgments with arguments of the lobbyist's own choosing. Accessibility, however, involves not merely winning an audience with a Con-gressman—since even ordinary citizens sometimes can get to see their Representatives and Senators—but winning his active support. In one of his more revealing moments, Woodrow Wilson pointed out:

> *Suppose you go to Washington and try to get at your Government. You will always find that while you are politely listened to, the men really consulted are the men who have the big stake—the big bankers, the big manufacturers, and the big masters of commerce. . . . The masters of the Government of the United States are the combined capitalists and manufacturers of the United States.*[8] *. . .*

Surveying the organized pressure groups in America, E. E. Schattschneider notes: *"The system is very small.* The range of organized, identifiable, known groups is amazingly narrow; there is nothing remotely universal about it."[9] The pressure system, he concludes, is largely dominated by business groups, the majority of citizens belonging to no organization that is effectively engaged in pressure politics. Almost all organized groups, even nonbusiness ones such as community, religious, educational and professional associations, "reflect an upper-class tendency";[10] low-income people rarely have the time, money or expectation level that would enable them to participate.

The pressure system is "small" and "narrow" only in that it represents a highly select portion of the public. In relation to government itself, the system is a vast operation. "Most of the office space in Washington that is not occupied by government workers is occupied by special-interest lobbyists, who put in millions of hours each year trying to get special legislation enacted for the benefit of their clients," writes Richard Harris. "And they succeed on a scale that is undreamed of by most ordinary citizens."[11] A favorable adjustment in rates for interstate carriers, a new tax writeoff for industry, a special tax benefit for a family oil trust, a high-interest bond issue for big investors, a special charter for a bank, a tariff protection for auto producers, the leasing of some public lands to a lumber company, emergency funding for a faltering aeronautics plant, a lenient occupational health code for employers, a postal subsidy for advertising firms, a soil bank for agribusiness, the easing of safety standards for a food processor, the easing of pollution controls for a chemical company, an investment guarantee to a housing developer, a lease guarantee to a construction contractor—all these hundreds of bills and their thousands of special amendments and the tens of thousands of administrative rulings which mean so much to particular interests and arouse the sympathetic efforts of legislators and bureaucrats will go largely unnoticed by a public that pays the monetary and human costs, and has not the organization, information and means to make its case—or even discover that it has a case.

Public interest groups, professing to speak for the great unorganized populace, make many demands for reform but have few of the resources that could move officeholders in a reformist direction. In any case, most public interest groups accept the capitalist system as a given, hence the kinds of "within-the-system" changes they advocate are usually of a cosmetic nature or, at best, offer only marginal improvements: thus the advocacy of seat belts and pollution devices for automobiles rather than a nonprofit, publicly owned mass transportation system; better labeling of commercial products rather than an attack on the waste and abuses of commercialized consumerism; the elimination of no-deposit throwaway beverage bottles rather than the elimination of the profit system and its war against the environment; public exposure of lobbying spending rather than an end to the concentration and use of private wealth for public power.

In limiting their critiques, most public interest groups betray the limitations of their liberal politics and their commitment to the very system which creates the problems they deplore. A "people's lobby" like John Gardner's Common Cause, for instance, while supposedly designed as a counterbalance to corporate influence, accepts the corporate system as one to be "improved" and is closely associated with leading capitalists. For years Gardner has been one of the few nonfamily trustees of the Rockefeller Brothers Fund, a fact omitted from his lengthy official biographies. Furthermore, Common Cause received most of its original funding, some $70,000, from various members of the Rockefeller family and the Chase Manhattan Bank.[12]

Pressure group activities are directed not only at officeholders but encompass entire segments of the public itself. Grant McConnell offers one description of this "grass-roots lobbying":

> The electric companies, organized in the National Electric Light Association, had not only directly influenced Congressmen and Senators on a large scale, but had also conducted a massive campaign to control the substance of teaching in the nation's schools. Teachers in high schools and grammar schools were inundated with materials. . . . Each pamphlet included carefully planted disparagement of public ownership of utilities. The Association took very active, if inconspicuous, measures to insure that textbooks that were doctrinally impure on this issue were withdrawn from use and that more favorable substitutes were produced and used. College professors . . . were given supplemental incomes by the Association and, in return, not infrequently taught about the utility industry with greater sympathy than before. . . . Public libraries, ministers, and civic leaders of all kinds were subjected to the propagandistic efforts of the electric companies.[13]

The purpose of grass-roots lobbying is to build a climate of opinion favorable to the corporate giants rather than to push a particular piece of legislation. The steel, oil and electronics companies do not advertise for public support on behalf of the latest tax depreciation bill—if anything, they would prefer that citizens not trouble themselves with thoughts on the subject—but they do "educate" the public, telling of the many jobs the companies create, the progress and services they provide, the loving care they give to the environment, etc. This kind of "institutional advertising" attempts to place the desires of the giant firms above politics and above controversy—a goal that is itself highly political.

CORRUPTION AS AN AMERICAN WAY OF LIFE

In recent years there have been reports on corruption involving federal, state and local officials in every state of the Union. In Congress, "Corruption is so endemic that it's scandalous. Even the honest men are corrupted—usually by and for the major economic-interest groups and the wealthy individuals who together largely dominate campaign financing."[14] In some states—Louisiana, for instance—scandals are so prolific that exposure of them has absolutely no impact," reports one observer.[15] A Republican member of the Illinois state legislature estimated that one-third of his legislative colleagues accepted payoffs.[16] In 1970-1971, officials in seven of New Jersey's eleven urban counties were indicted or convicted for graft and corruption, along with the mayors of the two largest cities, the minority leader of the state assembly, the former speaker of the state assembly, a prominent state senator, a state prosecutor, a former secretary of state, and a Port Authority commissioner.[17] At about the same time, major scandals were occurring in Texas, Illinois, West Virginia, Maryland and New York. . . .

On a still grander scale in Washington, the Nixon administration was implicated in major scandals involving the sale of wheat, an out-of-court settlement with ITT, price supports for dairy producers, corruption in the Federal Housing Administration, stock market manipulations, and political espionage—the Watergate Affair. And Vice-President Spiro Agnew resigned from office because of charges of bribery, extortion and corruption.[18]

Campaigning for President in 1976, Jimmy Carter made a plea for honesty in government at a \$100-a-plate dinner in Miami while beside him on the dais sat a mayor recently imprisoned for tax evasion, a couple of Florida state senators who had just pleaded guilty to conflict of interest, a commissioner facing trial for bribery, and three other commissioners charged with fraud.[19]

Corruption in America is so widespread that, as Lincoln Steffens pointed out long ago, throwing the rascals out only means bringing more rascals in. . . .

NOTES

1. Lester Milbrath, *The Washington Lobbyists* (Chicago: Rand McNally, 1963), p. 185 and *passim*. See also Douglass Cater's comparison of the "new" with the "old" NAM in his *Power in Washington* (New York: Random House, 1964), p. 208. For a good critique of the Milbrath view of lobbying, see Ernest Yanarella, "The Military-Industrial Complex, Lobbying and the ABM Decision: Some Notes on the Politics of Explanation," unpublished monograph.
2. Quoted in Robert Cirino, *Don't Blame the People* (New York: Vintage, 1972), p. 144.
3. Howard Kohn, "The Hughes-Nixon-Lansky Connection: The Secret Alliances of the CIA from World War II to Watergate," *Rolling Stone*, May 20, 1976, p. 44. Hughes contributed heavily to Nixon's campaigns in 1968 and 1972 and, according to his close aides, Robert Maheu and John Meier, sought to have the Vietnam war prolonged until he had made sufficient profits on his helicopter

program; *New York Times,* April 9, 1975. Hughes has been romanticized as a "cowboy capitalist" by some; I have a better name for him.

4. Quoted in the *New York Times,* March 31, 1972. For a fascinating eyewitness account of corruption and special influence in Washington by a former lobbyist, see Robert Winter-Berger, *The Washington Pay-Off* (New York: Dell, 1972). See also Drew Pearson and Jack Anderson, *The Case Against Congress* (New York: Simon and Schuster, 1968); Lawrence Gilson, *Money and Secrecy* (New York: Praeger, 1972); and *New York Times,* April 28, 1975. For a description of how local politicians are bought off by large corporations, see Jack Sheperd, "The Nuclear Threat Inside America," *Look,* December 15, 1970, pp. 24-25.

5. Since the contributions were illegal, the money was first laundered by Gulf through a Caribbean subsidiary and then a Canadian bank. See the *Wall Street Journal,* November 17, 1975; and *Philadelphia Evening Bulletin,* November 12, 1975.

6. *Workers World,* March 5, 1976, has a summary of some of these expenditures. Lockheed admitted to having paid $22 million in overseas bribes, including $7 million to the leader of an ultra-right militarist political faction in Japan. *New York Times,* February 5, 1976. Boeing admitted to $70 million in bribes during a five-year period. Gulf paid $4 million to the South Korean dictatorship in 1966, and Exxon made secret payments of $51 million to conservative leaders in Italy over an eight-year period. See Anthony Sampson, "How the Oil Companies Help the Arabs to Keep Prices High," *New York,* September 22, 1975, p. 48.

7. Quoted in Richard Harris, "Annals of Politics: A Fundamental Hoax," *New Yorker,* August 7, 1971, p. 55. Winter-Berger emphasizes this in *The Washington Pay-Off.*

8. Quoted in D. Gilbarg, "United States Imperialism," in Bill Slate (ed.), *Power to the People* (New York: Tower, 1970), p. 67.

9. E. E. Schattschneider, *The Semi-Sovereign People* (New York: Holt, Rinehart and Winston, 1960), p. 31. Italics in the original.

10. *Ibid.,* pp. 33-34, and the studies cited therein.

11. Harris, "Annals of Politics," p. 56.

12. Richard Reeves, "The City Politic," *New York,* December 2, 1974, p. 12.

13. Grant McConnell, *Private Power and American Democracy* (New York: Knopf, 1966), p. 19.

14. George Agree, director of the National Committee for an Effective Congress, quoted in Harris, "Annals of Politics," p. 62.

15. Martin Waldron, "Shadow on the Alamo," *New York Times Book Review,* July 10, 1972, p. 2. See also Peter Cowen, "Graft Held Fact of Life in Boston,"*Boston Globe,* October 2, 1972.

16. Paul Simon, "The Illinois State Legislature," *Harper's,* September 1964, p. 74.

17. For revealing accounts of corruption in states like West Virginia, Maryland and New Jersey, see the articles by John Rothchild, Mary Walton, Thomas B. Edsall and Michael Rappeport published together under the title "Revenue Sharing with the Rich and the Crooked," *Washington Monthly,* February 1972, pp. 8-38.

18. Agnew pleaded guilty to income-tax evasion, . . . was fined $10,000 and given three years probation. In return for his guilty plea and resignation from the vice-presidency, the Justice Department dropped the other charges. Regarding the influence peddling and criminal behavior of the Nixon people, see Howard Kohn, "The Hughes-Nixon-Lansky Connection . . . ," pp. 40-90.

19. *Workers World*, May 7, 1976.

The Rise of Public Interest Groups: 1965-75

Andrew S. McFarland

PUBLIC INTEREST GROUPS: OLD OR NEW?

It is easy to waste time arguing whether the present generation of public interest groups is a new phenomenon or merely the latest manifestation of an old phenomenon. Enthusiastic proponents of public interest groups sometimes state or imply that these groups represent an entirely new political force on the American scene—thereby dramatizing the accomplishments of these groups. Critics of public interest groups ordinarily point to the tradition of public interest reform in American politics—the Progressives, generations of proponents of good government, and so forth—and view Common Cause, Nader, and the others as the latest manifestation of this tradition. These critics, whose observations are commonly infused with antagonism, argue that since such reform groups have failed to achieve their goals in the past, the current set of such groups is also bound to fail and therefore need not have much attention paid to them.

The recent upsurge of power on the part of public interest groups is in fact the present manifestation of a tendency in American politics that surely dates back at least to the 1890s. The aims of the public interest movement today are not new: Municipal reformers of the 1890s advocated reforms similar to some of those advocated by Common Cause (ceilings on expenditures in political campaigns, for example), and the Muckrakers of the era 1905-15 exposed corporate infringements of the general public welfare in a way that foreshadowed Nader's dramatic investigatory journalism and public interest research. What is new is the amount of influence that public interest groups have acquired in a relatively short time. Ten years ago environmentalists were still conservationists, Common Cause

From Andrew S. McFarland, *Public Interest Lobbies: Decision Making on Energy* (Washington, D.C.: American Enterprise Institute for Public Policy Research, 1976). © American Enterprise Institute, 1976. Reprinted with permission.

did not exist, and Ralph Nader was a newcomer on the national political scene.

As evidence of the influence of public interest groups, consider these events of the last decade: A coalition of environmentalist groups delayed the construction of the Alaskan oil pipeline for four years, even though the project was supported by the oil industry and the incumbent administration of the federal government.[1] A group of political unknowns in California succeeded in gaining a majority of 70 percent in support of a referendum which changed the rules for elections and lobbying, despite the opposition of business *and* labor *and* political party leaders.[2] In 1965, the American automobile industry was generally independent of federal regulation. During the last decade the industry has become subject to a great many regulations—with respect to safety equipment, gas mileage, and, increasingly, emissions—and this regulation was precipitated by Nader's exposures of safety defects, exposures which undercut the industry's public prestige.[3] Incessant lobbying efforts by Common Cause, in combination with activity by congressional reformers, have led to restrictions on the financing of political campaigns that could not have been predicted in 1970 or even in 1972 (though perhaps Richard Nixon and Watergate are partly responsible for these reforms).[4] Things have changed since the early 1960s, when cars came without seat belts, no one was concerned about the safety hazards created by nuclear power plants or the land laid waste by strip mining, the Kennedy administration tried to kill legislation introduced by Estes Kefauver to ensure that new drugs were adequately tested before they were prescribed to the public,[5] and neither political scientists nor members of Congress could remember the details of legislation regarding campaign finances, since such laws as were on the books were never enforced.

In the last few years, public interest groups, and the type of public opinion that they express, have been more influential in American politics than at any time since the entry of the United States into the First World War ended the so-called Progressive Era. Like the Progressives, the supporters of the recent public interest movement, whom we shall henceforth call the new civic reformers, come from the white middle classes. . . .

How can we understand this tradition of middle-class civic reform in America? What motivated the Progressives? What motivates the civic reformers of today? . . .

CAUSES OF THE NEW CIVIC REFORM MOVEMENT

Let us consider seven factors which may help in understanding the increase in the influence of public interest groups in recent years. These are: (1) the increase in middle-class participation in American politics in the 1960s and 1970s; (2) the corresponding increase in the politics of issues and systems of beliefs as opposed to the politics of party identification, personality, or patronage; (3) the growth of "civic skepticism"—the disbelief in the utility of existing politics and public administrative practices in solving important social problems; (4) skillful leadership of public interest groups; (5) technical advances in communications; (6) economic prosperity; and (7) initial success bringing more success.

The Increase of Middle-Class Participation

We might also call this factor the increase of college education in America. Political scientists have demonstrated that the level of a person's education is directly correlated with the extent of his participation in American politics. For example, Sidney Verba and Norman H. Nie found in their nationwide survey that those with "some college or more" were found twice as often in the group of "complete activists" as would be expected from their proportion in the total sample. Conversely, those with "grade school or less" were found in the activist sample only half as often as would be expected from their proportion of the population.[6] The term *complete activists* designated those who were active in all four types of participation: voting only, political campaigning, activity in community-oriented groups, and making contact with government officials.

Available evidence indicates that supporters of public interest groups generally fall into the 11 percent of the public designated as "complete activists." In a careful survey done for the management of Common Cause, a majority of the supporters of Common Cause in Massachusetts were found to be active in partisan politics. Contribution to one or more public interest groups—multiple contributions are a frequent phenomenon—indicate a particularly high psychological involvement in politics, unless the contribution is to one of those groups who repay their members with financial savings, such as Consumers Union. It seems safe to say that the majority of contributors to Common Cause, Nader, and the environmentalist movement also vote, occasionally try to persuade a friend to vote for a favorite candidate, and communicate with a government official about some matter. . . .

The Politics of Issues and Systems of Beliefs

Political scientists conventionally categorize motivations for voting and other political acts according to party identification, attraction to a personality, patronage incentives, and issue orientation.[7] For instance, one who voted for Eisenhower in 1952 might have done so chiefly because the voter was a loyal Republican, or because he was attracted to Eisenhower as a person even though he normally voted Democratic, or because he preferred the Republican candidate's stand on some issue—such as the possibility of ending the Korean War. Patronage has been found to be a factor in local elections; the citizen votes for a politician because of some favor the politician has done for the voter.

Survey research has found that only a small percentage of the American voting public has been motivated by the issues—about 10 percent in the 1950s.[8] From 1964, however, the frequency of motivation by the issues increased to the point that in 1972 researchers found that issues were more important than party loyalty and almost as important as reactions to the candidates' personalities in the Nixon-McGovern election.[9] The greater frequency of issue voting is probably the result of the fact that there is a greater atmosphere of criticism and debate than there was during the 1950s. But the increasing number of college-educated, middle-class citizens is likely to be another factor producing an increase in the proportion of issue-motivated political actions. The college educated are much more likely to be concerned about issues than those with less education.[10] Until contradictory evidence is found, we can presume that the great majority of contributors to public interest groups (whom we know to be college-educated) have an issue orientation to politics. . . .

. . . From our observations of public interest groups, I conclude that most leaders and most followers of such groups believe in something I will call civic balance, to give it a deliberately bloodless name. Later I observe that beliefs concerning civic balance help the leaders of public interest groups decide what positions to take on complex energy issues, such as the question of deregulation of natural gas.

The elements of the civic-balance system of beliefs are these: the political system is seen as complex, fragmented into numerous areas of policy; such policy areas are often controlled by unrepresentative elites, however, who act to further their own special interests to the detriment of the interests of the great majority of the public; such public interests frequently go unrepresented in policy making, either because public interests, such as those of consumers, are inherently hard to organize, or oligopolies or bureaucracies, acting singly or in combination, defeat those agents working "in the public interest"; hence there is a need for citizens to organize into groups and participate in the political process in order to balance the power of the special interests. . . .

Civic-balance theory permeates the political communications issued by many public interest groups. To illustrate what I mean by civic-balance beliefs, let us examine recent mass mailings sent from Common Cause and from Ralph Nader. Such mailings represent a major organizational invest-ment. They are written with great care. I am confident that they state actual beliefs of John Gardner and of Ralph Nader. While the statements below were written with the intent to persuade, they are similar to numerous other public statements of Mr. Gardner and Mr. Nader.

Let us turn to a recent Common Cause mailing: "Common Cause: Modern Americans Fighting for Principles as Old as the Republic." It is an elegant ten-page brochure, designed to fit inside a standard business envelope. Between 1 and 10 million copies will be mailed, depending on its success in obtaining new members. The text begins with a statement of the theme of special interests versus the "people's interests" and the need for citizens' organizations to attain a more representative form of government:

> *Our nation's founders did not leave us a completed task . . . they left us a beginning. It is our obligation to define and dislodge the modern obstacles to the fulfillment of our founding principles. Because, as visionary as they were, our founders could not have foreseen* how dominant special interests would become *through the accumulation of wealth and power, and through skillful secret dealings with government officials.*

> *In the face of this, people like you and me—people who reject apathy and cynicism—must join forces to fight for open and accountable government. How? By joining Common Cause and supporting our efforts to create direct and immediate changes in the political system.* [Emphasis added; ellipsis points in original; paragraphing adjusted.]

The next section of the text faces a full-page picture of a founding father, Benjamin Rush, "Treasurer of the U.S. Mint," who is quoted as having said: "The influence of wealth at elections is irresistible." The text is a particularly direct statement of the civic-balance belief system:

> *THANKS TO COMMON CAUSE, THE INFLUENCE OF WEALTH IN ELECTIONS IS SHRINKING. In Benjamin Rush's day, money could influence elections. A century and a half later, it could dominate them. By lavishing contributions on candidates, well heeled* special interests *came to exercise decisive leverage over the outcome of elections. Matched against this enormous power, the principle of fair elections often proved a feeble challenger.*

> *That is, until Common Cause changed the odds by strengthening the* people's *interest through election reforms. Our members threw themselves behind the cause of campaign finance reform. Our highly skilled lobbyists* pressured *Congress. Our volunteers monitored campaigns throughout the country. And our staff disclosed the cozy relationships between candidates and* special interest *contributors.* [Emphasis added; paragraphing adjusted.]. . .

Civic-balance theory is further expounded on the next page of text, where it is applied to Congress:

> *Congress was never intended to be a bulwark against* the people's interests. *But a self-perpetuating system of favors and rewards caused its committee structure to become just that. Committee chairmen who favored* special interests *were richly rewarded with campaign contributions. With better financing than their challengers, they repeatedly won re-election. In turn, they used the power of their seniority to side with* the special interests. *Common Cause was determined to dismantle this structure by toppling its two strongest pillars: seniority and secrecy.* [Emphasis added; paragraphing adjusted.]

The following mailing on behalf of Nader's Public Citizen organization was sent in 1974. Its opening litany of complaints uses the "special interests versus people's interests" type of language. The implication is that special interest rule is at least partly to blame for the social ills cited in the letter.

> *From: Ralph Nader*
>
> *Dear Friend:*
>
> *Recently, a young woman asked me whether there was anything bigger than the Watergate scandal in Washington. I replied: "Yes, the 'citizen gap.' "*
>
> *A "citizen gap" opens when business or governmental abuses prevail without citizens doing anything about them.*
>
> *Just about everybody has experienced "citizen gap."*
>
> *—Have you ever felt there was a wall around City Hall?*
>
> *—Have you wondered why Congress so often responds to the monied interests instead of the peoples' interest?*
>
> *—Have you grumbled about high taxes for the many and large loopholes for the favored corporations and millionaires?*
>
> *—Have you had the helpless feeling against inflation, especially fast rising food, energy, medical and housing prices?*
>
> *—Have you gotten sick over the poisonous pollution of our priceless air, water and soil which sustain human life and health?*
>
> *—Have you felt unable to do anything at all about shoddy consumer goods and companies who don't respond to your legitimate complaints?*
>
> *—Do you wonder how our country could have so many problems when it has such wealth, talent and know-how to overcome them?*
>
> *—Do you feel an uneasy frustration over the growing concentration and secretiveness of economic and political power?*
>
> *If you identify with any of these reactions, you're experiencing "citizen gap.". . .*

The Growth of Civic Skepticism

During the last decade, the decline in popular trust of our national political institutions, as indicated by survey research, is quite shocking. Increasing skepticism extends not only to national institutions in general but to such specific institutions as the Congress and the political parties.[11] After inspecting the data in Table 1, one may very well conclude, in the words of the old popular song, "something's gotta give." These and other data indicate an extraordinary decline in the level of trust in national political institutions as expressed to survey research interviewers. But of course what people *say* when interviewed and what they actually *do* is another matter. For example, skeptical responses do not necessarily imply that the respondent will drop out of politics. On the contrary, he might become active in support of a candidate who expresses a skeptical point of view and who appears to be different from the usual breed of "untrustworthy" politicians.

Table 1

Decline of popular trust in social institutions: Harris Survey responses, 1966-1974

Q. I want to read you some things some people have told us they have felt from time to time. Do you tend to feel or not to feel—	Percentage of voters agreeing			
	1966	1972	1973	1974
The rich get richer and the poor get poorer?	45	68	76	79
Special interests get more from the government than the people do?	n.a.	n.a.	74	78
The tax laws are written to help the rich, not the average man?	n.a.	74	74	75
The people running the country don't really care what happens to you?	26	50	55	63
Most elective officials are in politics for all they personally can get out of it for themselves?	n.a.	n.a.	60	62
What you think doesn't count much anymore?	37	53	61	60
You feel left out of things going on around you?	9	25	29	32

n.a. Not available.

Source: "Public Disaffection at Record High," *The Harris Survey,* released 27 June 1974. Cited by Jack Dennis, "Trends in Support for the American Party System," *British Journal of Political Science,* vol. 5 (April 1975), p. 227.

Another type of action suitable for citizens skeptical of existing political institutions is to support a public interest group. Many must have done so, although their number constitutes only a small fraction of the total number of skeptics. But this growth of skepticism can be seen as another factor inducing the recent growth and influence of public interest groups.

. . .

In a mass mailing for recruitment, dated October 1974, Ruth C. Clusen, president of the League of Women Voters, started her letter with explicit references to the extent of skepticism and allying the league with such skeptics:

Dear Fellow Citizen:

I think you'll agree that the last few years have left a lot of Americans feeling disillusioned about their government and public institutions. Pollsters report, in fact, that the current mood of disenchantment is so pervasive that a

majority of every major segment of the populace is turned off by politics, and
questions the fairness of our economic system and the role accorded the
individual in our society. According to a Harris poll taken earlier this year, a
significant 63 percent believe "The people running the country don't really
care what happens to you." And 60 percent said, "What you think doesn't
count much anymore."

We at the League of Women Voters and League of Women Voters
Education Fund hope that you're not only disillusioned, but disturbed and
concerned enough to want to do something. WE ARE!

Another expression of skepticism is found in the following excerpts
from a mass mailing sent by the Natural Resources Defense Council in June
1974:

At this very moment, gigantic monsters are tearing away at some of the most
picturesque and fertile land in our country . . . they are engaged in one of the
most ruinous assaults ever unleashed on the environment: strip mining. . . .
Because years of efforts to legislate the abolition of stripping have ended in
abject failure, the Natural Resources Defense Council took the Tennessee
Valley Authority to court last year over its failure to comply with the National
Environmental Policy Act. . . . Rarely has there been a better opportunity or a
more urgent need to safeguard our vanishing heritage.

It is important to note that this letter expresses disillusionment in the
possibility of congressional action to deal with the "monster" of strip
mining. Nor will government agencies, such as the Tennessee Valley
Authority (TVA), necessarily follow the law. The letter clearly implies that
laws often go unenforced. . . .

From the historical point of view, it is important not to confuse the
attitudes held by the Progressives and by the New Dealers toward
government and politics with the civic skepticism that prevails today. The
Progressives believed that they could establish government agencies and
regulatory commissions that would administer progressive reforms in a
neutral, scientific manner in the public interest. They believed that it is
possible to take politics out of administration.[12] Until the time of Lyndon
Johnson's presidency, New Dealers and liberals had a different idea. They
thought that great social reforms could be achieved through the establishment of a powerful, political executive branch, unified and directed by a
powerful President, and supported by a similarly minded Congress and
political party. The leaders of the public interest groups of today have still
another idea, however.

They are for reform, but reform through ad hoc coalitions. In the view
of the new civic reformers, pressure must be put on the President,
Congress, and the executive branch from outside if reform laws are to be
implemented. True, these reformers press for the creation of new
agencies—such as Nader's demand for a consumer protection agency or

Common Cause's insistence that a powerful federal elections commission be established. But neither Mr. Nader nor Mr. Gardner imagines that such new agencies, designed to implement public interest reforms, will be effective unless they are supported by political power from the outside, including backing from public interest groups.[13]

Reform laws, and agencies to implement them, are backed by ad hoc coalitions, limited as to subject matter and in time. Typically one of the larger public interest groups will take the lead in lobbying for a bill. Nader, for example, will take the lead in calling for creation of a consumer protection agency, Common Cause will take the lead in support of legislation to regulate campaign financing, and so forth. . . . The public interest group leader will work with congressmen who exercise leadership with respect to a particular issue (Nader with Senator Ribicoff on auto safety, Common Cause with Congressmen Morris Udall and John Anderson on campaign-finance legislation). The congressmen and the public interest group then form links with journalists, concerned pressure groups, officials in the executive branch, and individual citizens. In sum, an ad hoc coalition is formed around the public interest issue—the public interest group that is leading in support of the issue, other public interest groups, congressmen, members of the executive branch, other interest groups, journalists, and individual citizens. Such a coalition may be formed around the goal of getting a bill passed by Congress, or it may be formed to ensure enforcement of some reform legislation, a much more difficult task.

Another aspect of action through outside pressure and ad hoc coalitions is public interest litigation.[14] This tactic is now familiar to politically aware Americans, but its use became widespread only in 1966, with the emergence of Nader as a national figure. Government agencies are sued for failure to enforce existing legislation, injunctions are obtained against public works projects pending the satisfactory submission of environmental impact statements, and so forth. Public interest litigation is a tactic viewed as effective by most persons who follow politics, although the degree of effectiveness is a matter of dispute: Are such lawsuits only delaying tactics, or are they a new institution that has been added to our political system? This question cannot be answered here. But public interest litigation is much more effective when it is conducted by well-organized, influential public interest groups than it is when suits are initiated by individual citizens who happen to be aggrieved by some practice affecting consumers, the environment, or the electoral system. Lawsuits are expensive and require considerable legal and technical skills, which are best furnished by an established organization. The defense by Common Cause of the 1974 campaign reform act has cost about $150,000 so far; so much documentation was necessary that it had to be wheeled into court in a shopping cart. Public interest lawsuits frequently are a type of ad hoc coalition activity; they have specific goals and are often the result of the efforts of several supporting groups. . . .

Leadership

It is hard to imagine the public interest movement in its present form without the figures of Ralph Nader and John Gardner. Their activities have constituted an important stimulus for the appearance of influential public interest lobbies.

Nader has both charisma and technical skills. The ascetic, dedicated prophet of the public interest is the object of widespread admiration. Thousands of young persons desire to emulate him. . . . His long hours of study have made him well informed, although perhaps in the sense of an advocate arguing one side of a case. He has the journalist's instinct and skill for spotting news and conveying it dramatically to the public.

Such abilities enable Nader to raise $2 million a year for his cluster of about fifteen organizations in Washington. He has assembled a group of fifty to seventy-five talented persons who work full time in Washington for the various causes that he advocates. Within reasonable limits, Nader can publicize any issue and put it on the national political agenda. These are impressive accomplishments. But his most impressive accomplishment is his contribution to the practice of ad hoc coalition politics in the public interest, which puts the new civic reformers a step ahead of the Progressive and the New Deal liberals. Working with friendly congressmen, journalists, tipsters within the executive branch, dedicated staffers, and volunteers, Nader has been able to place issues before Congress and has thus been prominent in the effort to protect the consumer and to regulate big business. He has demonstrated thereby the possibilities for effective coalition politics in the interests of the public, using techniques of data gathering, publicity, lobbying, and lawsuits.

The founding of Common Cause in the summer of 1970 was an impressive feat of leadership on the part of John Gardner. . . . Gardner gained his following among the policy elite through his activity as an innovator in educational policy while he was president of the Carnegie Foundation. As secretary of health, education, and welfare (1965-68), he impressed most observers with his performance in that hot seat of American government, which generally lowers the reputation of those who sit in it.

Contrary to the opinion of most sophisticated observers, Gardner decided that it would be possible to establish a mass-membership, citizens' lobbying effort. He was right. Common Cause was an immediate success. One reason for its success was a heavy reliance, in the newspaper advertisements and mass mailings that were the basis of membership recruitment, on Gardner's reputation for moral leadership and political skill. (Nader was one of those who thought a mass-membership solicitation wouldn't work, and thus the Common Cause effort preceded the Public Citizen effort by about a year.)

Since 1970, Common Cause has flourished, with membership ranging from 200,000 to 320,000 and budgets ranging from $4 million to $6 million.

Such success has been due in large part to Gardner's sagacious leadership. Thus, internal conflict was minimized and political impact was maximized by the emphasis of Common Cause on government-reform issues. With the help of his right-hand men, Jack Conway and David Cohen, Gardner assembled a group of highly skilled persons for the national staff, which included lobbyists, public relations experts, direct-mail specialists, political organizers, writers, computer operators, and policy analysts. . . .

Technology

Certain advances in technology are one of the reasons that national public interest lobbies achieved influence only in 1970, rather than, say, 1950. Communications technology is particularly important to the existence of public interest groups, because the interests they represent are typically widespread but not immediately perceived by those whom they affect. Such issues as the environment, consumer protection, good government, and now energy frequently require explanation, and even dramatization, before people can be aroused to action in regard to them.

News programs on television are important in the development of support for public interest issues. Nader is highly telegenic, and the issues he supports thus get wide publicity. The environmentalist movement was strengthened by televised news. Few persons have seen a strip mine, an oil spill, Alaska, or a nuclear power plant, but these things can be made objects of immediate perception by means of television journalism. It is thus easier now for environmentalists to attract supporters beyond their basic constituency of conservationists, hikers, and sportsmen than it would have been in the 1940s.

As noted earlier, computer-based mass-mailing techniques are used to gain members and contributions for public interest organizations. Common Cause got about 80 percent of its 275,000 members by means of direct-mail promotion; Consumers Union nearly tripled its membership by using the same techniques; Nader's Public Citizen is purely a mail operation; the American Civil Liberties Union has greatly expanded its membership by the use of direct-mailing techniques. Common Cause has sent out about 40 million solicitations for membership; this organization could not have existed in its present form if it had had to depend on hand typing of address labels and hand filing of address lists.

The development of relatively cheap, reliable, and quick (direct distance dialing) telephone communications gives a new advantage to national political organizations. Common Cause in particular uses five Wide Area Telephone System (WATS) lines, thereby renting five long-distance lines at a flat monthly rate. A basic part of the lobbying organization of Common Cause is the link between about 250 volunteers in the national headquarters and a representative in each of the 350 congressional districts in which Common Cause maintains a local organization. Thus when the national office wants to pressure Congress on an issue, it can make immediate contact with its local members by telephone. The local members are organized into telephone networks (one person calls seven), so that when Washington calls the district, letters and telegrams are soon on their way. Computer technology helps with the telephoning. Every month the membership of Common Cause is analyzed by congressional districts, and fresh lists of members are sent to local organizations, so that the local leaders know who has joined, who has withdrawn, who has moved out or in, and what their addresses and phone numbers are.[15]

Prosperity

This factor requires little explanation. Fifteen-dollar membership contributions are frequently among the first items to be cut from the budgets of middle-class families striving to maintain their standards of living during inflation. The successful attraction of widespread contributions by Common Cause (1970) and Nader's Public Citizen (1971), as well as the expansion of Consumers Union, occurred during a time of relative economic prosperity. But 1974 and 1975 were years of budget cuts for most public interest groups. It would have been much more difficult to launch a mass-membership public interest group in 1975 than it was in 1970-71.

Initial Success Brings More Success

First let us examine success in the sense of gaining mass support. Well-publicized legal victories by environmentalists in 1969 meant that donors to such groups as the Sierra Club, the Natural Resources Defense Council, or to any of thousands of ad hoc local efforts could expect an effective use of their money. By the time of Nader's mass mailing in behalf of Public Citizen in 1971, he had gained a reputation for effectiveness in putting issues before Congress, and thus, again, a donor could expect that his money would be used effectively. About 125,000 persons joined Common Cause before that group had achieved its initial successes in opposing the SST and in helping to organize antiwar congressmen in the House to get a vote of overall approval or disapproval of the war effort. (Speakers McCormack and Albert had blocked such a vote for six years.) Many of these persons might have dropped their membership however—about 65 percent renewed—if they had not had some assurance from the leaders of Common Cause that their lobbying was effective. This assurance was given in mail solicitations and in newsletters by quoting public statements of Senators Kennedy, Scott, Mondale, and others complimenting the Common Cause lobby in opposition to the SST.

Another way in which success brings more success is illustrated by the fact that a reputation for power and effectiveness in the past helps one gain power in the present.[16] Politicians are more readily persuaded by lobbyists who have some reputation for "clout." It is my impression, on the basis of twenty interviews with members of the House on a tangential matter, that most congressmen do not want to be quoted publicly in criticism of Nader, Common Cause, or the League of Women Voters. These groups are evidently seen as capable of causing at least minor difficulties for a congressman. The great surge in support for environmentalism and ecology in early 1969 meant that for two or three years most politicians felt that they had to give the impression of support for environmental questions or else be criticized by future political opponents, letter writers, demonstrators, local newspaper and TV editors, ministers, high-school and college teachers, scientists, and others.

But, of course, countervailing factors will check the success of public interest groups. After a few years, the public became aware of the costs of environmentalism in increased prices and increasing uncertainty of employment. Nader overextended himself in 1971-72 in his massive study of Congress, out of which a monograph on each congressman was produced. These evaluations appeared to have little effect on the 1972 congressional elections however. One chairman of a House committee reported to me that this failing effort reduced Nader's reputation for clout, since it showed that he could not readily influence congressional elections on a mass basis.

Finally, success may undercut itself, particularly in times of economic trouble. Some donors might expect that others would begin to contribute to a successful public interest organization, thereby relieving the first group of responsibility for continuing their contributions. The view "they don't need my money" can hurt public interest groups. . . .

NOTES

1. See Mary Clay Berry, *The Alaska Pipeline* (Bloomington: Indiana University Press, 1975); Richard Corrigan, *The Trans-Alaska Pipeline: A Case Study in Energy Politics* (Washington, D.C.: American Enterprise Institute, forthcoming).
2. See a forthcoming Ph.D. dissertation on Proposition 9 by Ken Smith, Department of Public Administration, University of Southern California. Mr. Smith was one of the principal leaders of the Proposition 9 campaign.
3. See Paul J. Halpern, "Consumer Politics and Corporate Behavior: The Case of Automobile Safety" (Ph.D. diss., Harvard University, 1972).
4. See *Congressional Quarterly Almanac*, vol. 30 (1974), pp. 611-33.
5. J. B. Gorman, *Kefauver: A Political Biography* (New York: Oxford University Press, 1971).
6. Sidney Verba and Norman H. Nie, *Participation in America* (New York: Harper & Row, 1972), p. 100.
7. Angus Campbell, Philip E. Converse, Warren E. Miller, Donald E. Stokes, *The American Voter* (New York: John Wiley & Sons, 1960).
8. Ibid., p. 249.
9. Arthur H. Miller, Warren E. Miller, Alden S. Raine, Thad A. Brown, "A

Majority Party in Disarray: Policy Polarization in the 1972 Election," Paper delivered at the 1973 meeting of the American Political Science Association, New Orleans. This paper appeared in revised form in the *American Political Science Review*, vol. 70 (September 1976), pp. 753-78.

10. Campbell et al., *The American Voter*, p. 250.

11. See Jack Dennis, "Trends in Support for the American Party System," *British Journal of Political Science*, vol. 5 (April 1975), pp. 187-230; Arthur H. Miller, "Political Issues and Trust in Government: 1964-1970"; Jack Citrin, "Comment"; and Miller, "Rejoinder," *American Political Science Review*, vol. 63 (September 1974), pp. 951-1001.

12. For a criticism of such views, see Dwight Waldo, *The Administrative State* (New York: Ronald Press, 1948).

13. Interview with John W. Gardner, October 1975. Also see Charles McCarry, *Citizen Nader* (New York: Saturday Review Press, 1972), pp. 75-96.

14. See Joseph L. Sax, *Defending the Environment* (New York: Alfred A. Knopf, 1971).

15. Statements about Common Cause are based upon the author's ongoing study of that organization.

16. Richard E. Neustadt, *Presidential Power* (New York: John Wiley & Sons, 1960); Reputation for power, however, a power base, should not be confused with power itself: Andrew S. McFarland, *Power and Leadership in Pluralist Systems* (Stanford, Cal.: Stanford University Press, 1969), pp. 5-6.

CHAPTER TEN

CONGRESS

REPRESENTATION

In the aftermath of Watergate, political reformers both in and out of government are calling for ways to limit the power of those who hold public office. One suggestion has been to limit the term of office of public officials. While the 22nd Amendment to the Constitution limits the term (and hence the power) of presidents (though, according to some, not nearly enough), no such limitation applies to members of Congress.

In an effort to remedy this supposed shortcoming, Dennis DeConcini, U. S. Senator from the state of Arizona, has proposed a constitutional amendment that would allow senators to serve for no more than fourteen years and congressmen for no more than fifteen. According to Senator DeConcini, such an amendment is needed to remove the electoral advantage of incumbents as well as to reduce the importance of seniority in the operations of Congress.

In a response to Senator DeConcini, political scientist Eric Uslaner argues that not only would such an amendment deny the public the right to choose whomever it wants to be its representative, it would have the effect of seriously weakening the congressional leadership, which is already operating under a number of handicaps, not the least of which is an inexperienced membership in the present Congress. Senator DeConcini's advocacy of a nonprofessional Congress thus must be balanced off by Uslaner's concern over having a person experienced in the legislative process serve as Speaker.

Why We Should Limit Congressional Tenure

Dennis DeConcini

SENATE JOINT RESOLUTION 27—PROPOSED AMENDMENT TO CONSTITUTION

MR. DECONCINI. Mr. President, I rise today to introduce a joint resolution proposing an amendment to the Constitution of the United States. I am joined in this endeavor by my friends and colleagues from Missouri and New Mexico, Mr. Danforth and Mr. Schmitt.

The amendment I propose limits the terms of service for Members of the U.S. Senate and House of Representatives.

The Constitution of the United States, which has served to bind this Nation together for two centuries, should not be tampered with for inconsequential reasons. It should not be the vehicle for transitory policy decisions. Our Constitution was a document forged to provide a large, sprawling, heterogenous society with a flexible framework within which diverse elements could resolve matters of national concern.

The Constitution should remain neutral in terms of policy. Its function and purpose is to define the parameters and rules within which our society struggles with the issues of the day. The amendment I propose does not violate this conception of our Constitution.

Limiting the terms of service of legislators will strengthen the representative nature of our two legislative bodies. In taking this action, I want to make it quite clear that I am not casting, directly or indirectly, aspersions on any Member of the Senate or the House of Representatives. My action is founded in personal philosophy regarding the nature of government and the proper role of legislators.

The Constitution as it was originally written did not specify a maximum length of service for Members of the House and Senate or the President. In practice, this has allowed individuals to occupy Senate and House seats for unlimited periods of time. I cannot argue that this has

Taken from U.S. Congress, Senate, Committee on the Judiciary, Subcommittee on the Constitution, *Congressinal Tenure*, 95th Congress, 2nd Session, 1978, pp. 3-9. Used with permission of Dennis DeConcini.

brought us bad government. Nor would I try to make any case which disparaged the superb leadership which both Houses of the Legislature have provided the Nation.

The argument I will make in support of my amendment is essentially philosophical. I believe the amendment will further perfect a system of government so well rooted in the nature and character of the American people that it has survived and prospered under the most adverse of circumstances; and a system of government that has preserved personal freedom not just for one generation or two but for eight generations.

The amendment would limit each person to two terms of service as a U.S. Senator plus an additional 2 years of an unexpired term to which the individual may have been appointed. No person would be allowed, thus, to serve more than a total of 14 years.

The amendment would limit each person to seven terms of service as a Member of the House of Representatives plus an additional year of an unexpired terms to which the individual may have been appointed. No person would be allowed to serve more than a total of 15 years.

The numbers may be different, but the objectives of my amendment are the same as those that led to the adoption of the 22d amendment to the Constitution. As a people, we have decided that no person should serve as President for more than 10 years. In ratifying that amendment, we recognized that we were condemning no individual; rather, we were perfecting the fundamental law that governs us.

There are differences between the Office of President and the Office of Representative or Senator. It is understandable why we sought, first, to deal with the Office of President. For the person who holds that office commands an awesome power; power that any democracy must view skeptically and cautiously. Recent events, unfortunately, have demonstrated how that power can be abused. But now that we have disposed of that question, we need to turn our attention to the legislature.

It was the purpose of the framers of the Constitution to insure that all Americans were represented equally and fairly in the House of Representatives. In the Senate, representation was to be by State—but, again, equally and fairly. The 17th amendment to the Constitution has not changed this: and a multitude of Supreme Court decisions have reaffirmed the rights of Americans to be represented equally.

Scholars agree that one of the most significant trends in the 20th century has been the tendency for Senators and Representatives to serve longer and longer terms. Nineteenth century politics was marked by a lively rotation of legislative seats. This was true for both the popularly elected House of Representatives and the State-appointed Senate.

The 20th century, however, has seen the average length of congressional terms increase rather dramatically. Other indicators of increased longevity point in the same direction. For example, in 1877, 46 percent of the Members of the House were first-termers; by 1977, the proportion had decreased to 15 percent.

Analysts disagree over what caused this change and, hopefully, some of the reasons for these modifications in our electoral structure will emerge from these hearings. There is one thing, though, about which everyone agrees: The value of incumbency—the value of simply being in power, being visible, and having at one's command the resources of political office—has greatly contributed to what has come to be an increased rigidity in the political process. On the average, 90 percent of all congressional incumbents are returned to office. More importantly, research has shown that incumbency itself has become a much more important factor in the American voters' choice of Senators over the last three decades.

Some would argue that American voters still have a choice; they can, if they so desire, "throw the rascal out." My contention is that the powers of incumbency are so great that the voter is really offered only the illusion of choice. It has been estimated that the value of being the incumbent in a House race is worth roughly $500,000. While it is more difficult to calculate such a figure for the Senate because each Senator's allowance varies according to the size of his State, a figure on the average of $1 million would not seem to be far off. Furthermore, political interest groups funnel most of their campaign contributions to incumbents, thereby reinforcing their already substantial advantages.

The rise of the incumbency factor is but one reason for limiting Senate and House Terms.

[I]n ways unforeseen by the Founding Fathers, the absence of any limitation on service in the Legislature has worked against equal and fair representation. The imperative to organize each Chamber in a reasonable and responsible fashion has over the decades evolved into what is now known as the seniority system. Under this rule, responsibilities within the committee structure of the two Houses are allocated on the basis of length of tenure in office.

In recent years, there have been abundant attacks on the seniority system, some sincere, some self-serving, and some merely the result of personal antipathies. My own view is that it is pernicious, but not necessarily for many of the reasons often cited. I believe that the men and women who have served as chairmen of our legislative committees have served well: they have often provided us with an independent source of national leadership. In most cases, they have exercised their power with moderation, and in the pursuit of national, not personal interest.

My own brief experience in this body confirms that observation, and I feel compelled to underscore again that the position I am taking is totally independent of my strong positive personal feelings toward my colleagues and the leadership in this body.

However, the seniority system does tend to diminish the equal representation of individuals and States that is so close to the heart of the meaning of democracy, and which the men at the Philadelphia Convention were so anxious to preserve. Under it, we do not stand as equals. Therefore, the States and the people we represent do not stand as equals.

Every Member of this body clearly understands that to be chairman, for example, of a standing committee confers immense benefits. Not only does it bring personal power and prestige; it enables that person to insure that the people he represents will receive benefits out of proportion to a purely rational allocation of Federal resources. It puts at the disposal of the chairman vast staff resources that practically insure his success in passing legislation of interest to him and his constituents.

Each of us, at one time or another, has witnessed or been involved in an election in which that was a central issue. Incumbents have appealed for votes on the grounds that their seniority insured that more of the Federal dollar would be spent in their State or district than would otherwise be true. Or, that seniority would allow the incumbent to pass legislation that a new Member could not conceivably be expected to shepherd through the complex legislative process. And in most instances, these are not vacuous or idle boasts; the nature of the seniority system makes them true. The question at issue is whether it should be thus; whether longevity of tenure in office should be the criterion for legislative success and constituent service; and whether this is the best a democracy can offer.

Our constituents complain—and we complain—about the Federal bureaucracy. It is entrenched. It is unresponsive. It is practically immune to change. We often ask of these professional civil servants whether they exist to serve us, or we them? At the same time that we launch these verbal assaults, we are anxious to perpetuate an entrenched, institutionalized legislature. What is the difference between a professional bureaucracy and a professionalized legislature?

Neither the delegates to the 1789 Constitutional Convention nor the American public today believes that we are best served by a professional legislature. But that is precisely the system we have created. We should not be career legislators; nor should we make a career of the legislature. The theory of democracy demands that as many members of society as possible should be given the opportunity to serve. In some of the early Greek experiments with democracy, community service was demanded; in some cases, public offices were routinely rotated.

Because of the size and complexity of American society, we have moved away from direct democracy to representative democracy. Even though it is impossible for all citizens to participate in public service, we ought to insure that as many individuals as possible have the opportunity for such service. Limiting the number of years any single individual can serve would be an important step in that direction.

It is not sufficient to answer that if the electorate wanted change it would mandate a change by its vote. None of us is so politically naive that we do not understand the advantages of incumbency. The extent and nature of these advantages vary from region to region, but they exist everywhere. Political party officials are often well aware of the advantages of seniority; and they will work diligently to insure the continued success of the incumbent.

In those States or districts where competition is keenest, the reward for the earnest practice of democracy is self-defeating. We espouse the virtues of party and intraparty competition for public office; yet, the Senators and Representatives from regions where this occurs usually find themselves perpetually doomed to the bottom of seniority lists.

All power is subject to abuse, even the power of Senators and Congressmen. I am loathe to quote Lord Acton's dictum about the corrupting nature of power because I do not believe that any Member of this Chamber or of the House of Representatives has been corrupted by power. It is the possibility that exists; and it is that possibility that we must guard against.

Our constitutional structure with its delicate checks and balances rests on the prudent assumption that men are corruptible and that power may be misused. This is a healthy skepticism; one that keeps us constantly aware of how fragile freedom really is. We have placed the power of the Congress as a check against the power of the Executive, with the Federal courts occupying the third point on the triad. In diffusing power among different groups and persons, we have tried to insure that no individual will dominate the Government and destroy our liberty.

To be true to our commitment that shared power is responsible power, we need to address ourselves to the subtler dimensions of the problem. The 22d amendment to the Constitution removed an inherent contradiction in our system by limiting the terms a President can serve. That same contradiction persists in the unlimited terms for legislators. True, the potential for damage is less; the principle, however, is nonetheless valid.

Adoption of the amendment I propose should be viewed from two different perspectives. First, it would eliminate present disparities between Senators and Representatives based upon length of tenure. It would place each State, each district, each citizen on a more nearly equal footing. Simultaneously, it would add an additional safeguard against possible abuse of power.

The second perspective is the one I would emphasize. It is the positive side of the amendment. By limiting the length of service in the Legislature, we will be embracing the idea that new people should be brought constantly and consciously into the system. By opening the doors of the Legislature to people from every walk of life and every age group, we will be providing far more opportunities for everyone to participate. I am especially committed to the youth of today as the hope of tomorrow. That youth should be encouraged to serve the Nation; it is our responsibility to insure that as few barriers as possible stand in the way.

Two thousand years ago, Plato rejected democracy because he believed the decisions of government should not be made by amateurs. He said we needed philosopher kings to guide us—divinely annointed experts who clearly saw truth. I reject that view because in the realm of politics there is no truth as such. The best we can do is to seek modes of compromise and accommodation so we can live together fruitfully and in harmony. The Legislature is the bar of the people; the forum in which we continue the great experiment in self-government. This is not an exercise that requires any special expertise; it requires commitment to the values of democracy.

In the act of creating an institutional structure which insures maximum participation, we will have reaffirmed our faith in the representative nature of our political institutions. We will have reaffirmed our faith that the laws which govern this great land should be made by men and women who truly reflect and represent the attitudes, values, and more of each generation of Americans, and the many different perspectives they represent.

I ask unanimous consent, Mr. President, to have the text of my amendment printed in the RECORD.

The ACTING PRESIDENT pro tempore. Without objection, it is so ordered.

A Government as Good as Its People: Or, Do We Really Want Farmer Jones to Be the Next Speaker?

Eric M. Uslaner

A constitutional amendment to limit the number of terms which members of the House and Senate could serve can only be based upon a fundamental distrust of human nature. In proposing such an amendment, Senator Dennis DeConcini (D., Ariz.) does not specifically charge the members of our national legislature with malfeasance in office; instead, he warns us of the "possibility" that such misconduct may occur. Nor does the senator condemn the voters who continually reelect representatives and senators, although he professes little faith in their ability to replace ne'er-do-wells with less senior members. It seems, then, that the problem is with the system, which engulfs both legislators and the mass public, specifically the seniority system in Congress.

Can we blame all of the problems of the contemporary Congress on "the system"? A former presidential press secretary once remarked to a group of political scientists:

> *You people have this congressional reform business all wrong. What's wrong with Congress is not the rules, seniority, and all those things. What's wrong with Congress is the* people *in it. You're not going to change anything until you change that.*[1]

There simply is no system apart from the men and women who serve in the Congress and the electorate which sends them to Washington. To insist upon a limitation of terms by a constitutional amendment then must be to challenge frontally both the ability of members of Congress to perform their tasks and the capacity of the electorate to hold their representatives accountable. And if both the members of Congress and the electorate are held lacking, then where is the contingent of new legislators who must arise every decade and a half to save us from ourselves?

Prepared especially for this volume by Eric M. Uslaner. The assistance of Robert DiClerico is gratefully acknowledged, as is support from the General Research Board, University of Maryland—College Park.

The proposal for a constitutional limitation on the number of terms which representatives and senators may serve is first a direct assault on our representative institutions. Telling me how many terms my senator (representative) may serve, in essence, tells me for whom I cannot vote in at least some elections. I can understand why convicted felons, the criminally insane, those under a certain age, or noncitizens might be barred from holding high public office. But it is far more puzzling to me that I might not be able to vote for a person simply because he or she has held that office before. Why should I have to select an inexperienced person to make my laws when I can choose an experienced mechanic to work on my car? I am more wary of the mechanics I have dealt with than the members of Congress I have known. In either case, however, the integrity of the person is not necessarily related to the length of time served in the profession.

Furthermore, as we shall see below, the senator's arguments fundamentally misconstrue the nature of the current seniority system and the charges which were levied against it in the past. Thirdly, the proposal does not conform to what a majority of the public sees as the appropriate reform for much of the contemporary congressional malaise; indeed, the public seems to have a completely contrary perspective to that of Senator DeConcini as to what the role of a member of Congress should be. Finally, I shall argue that the DeConcini proposal would seriously weaken congressional leadership and thus make the legislative situation even worse than the senator currently believes it is. The unfortunate argument against the "system" must be rejected, as also must be the references to what the intentions of the Founding Fathers were in 1787. These prescriptions are hardly relevant to the contemporary Congress, since the framers of the Constitution had no idea that 200 years later the country would have a population of over 200 million people, have a Congress of 535 members, be engaged in many "entangling alliances" (which George Washington warned against in his farewell address), and have a senator (actually, two) from some place called Arizona. Just as we would not send the Congress back to New York, we would not want to employ outdated criteria for judging its performance and capabilities today.

First, let us consider the seniority system. What the system does, or more appropriately did, is assign committee rankings (including the position of chairman) according to the single criterion of the amount of consecutive time served on that body. This worked to the advantage of members from electorally safe seats, who could accumulate years of seniority on important committees while their colleagues often had to serve on less critical committees with greater pork-barreling opportunities in order to get reelected. Members from marginal districts were not likely to be around nearly as long anyway. However, by 1971, both the Democrats and Republicans in the House and the Senate had adopted policies which permitted selection of chairman and ranking minority member by criteria other than seniority. The full party caucus would vote on the filling of each position and Democrats provided a mechanism for secret ballot. In the House, even subcommittee chairmanships on the important Appropriations Committee have been subject to caucus ratification since 1975. In that year, three sitting chairmen were deposed by the caucus (F. Edward Hebert of Armed Services, W. R. Poage of Agriculture, and Wright Patman of Banking) of House Democrats and were replaced by men with less seniority; in the case of Patman, he was succeeded by a representative third in line behind the chairman with respect to committee seniority. Furthermore, subcommittees in both the House and the Senate have been permitted to select their own chairmen (as well as hire their own staffs); in 1979, there were two very important upsets for subcommittee leadership on the House Interstate and Foreign Commerce committee and another on Government Operations.

The Senate has not actually "violated" seniority since 1971, but it is far from clear that we can draw any conclusions about the representativeness of the two institutions from this fact alone. A major argument against seniority, echoed in the remarks of Senator DeConcini, is that the rewards that accrue to members from safe seats are not distributed equitably among the 435 members of the House and the 100 members of the Senate, indeed not even among the members of the majority party. Thus, the ranks of Democratic chairmen have traditionally overrepresented the south, long a one-party area, in comparison with the percentage of Democratic members of Congress who come from that region.[2] But, in the 96th Congress (1979-1980), southerners hold only a fifth of Senate chairmanships and little more than a third of House chairmanships. Thus, whatever are the ills of the contemporary Congress, they cannot be blamed on the seniority system.

We have been able to overcome many of the problems of seniority without amending the constitution. How has this occurred? The answer, quite simply, is membership change. Without any statutory limit on the number of terms members may serve, there has been a marked turnover in both the House and Senate. At the beginning of the 96th Congress (January, 1979), fewer than half of the members of the House had served more than three two-year terms, while over half of the Senate, including the twenty new members (the largest freshman class this century), were serving their first terms. A variety of factors have led to this turnover, including voluntary retirements and changing electoral trends. Many observers believe that "juniority," the lack of of experience, is a more critical problem facing the contemporary Congress than is seniority.[3] In any event, the most objectionable part of the seniority system was that it *automatically* elevated the member who had the longest consecutive service on a committee to a position of leadership. It failed to differentiate between the member who had spent years studying the intricacies of a particular policy area and "deserved" the reward of leadership and a colleague whose major achievement was sheer survival. The presidential press secretary was correct: the critical element in reform is the people who make it work (or who work against it). There is bound to be disagreement as to whether the Congress is performing better or worse now that seniority is no longer automatic and also now that there are so many new faces. But very few people think that a constitutional amendment is needed either to restore the old system or to rid the vestiges of it from the Congress.

If the Congress has been quite successful in changing the seniority system, it has been less so with respect to improving its own public image. Confidence in Congress continues to plummet, and the House and the Senate are both under greater pressure than before to police the ethical standards of members. Senator DeConcini recognizes that we cannot adopt a direct democracy in such a large and complex society, but he does worry about the creation of a "professional legislature," a set of chambers composed of "career legislators." The argument, with roots traced back to the Constitutional Convention, maintains that the longer a member serves, the greater are the inducements towards corruption. In other words, get rid of the rascals before they learn how to steal from the public till. Unlike the auto mechanic I discussed above, the national legislator holds a public trust. There is an underlying suspicion that public officials either are more likely to raid the national treasury than a private account, that the sort of people who are attracted to politics constitute, as Mark Twain called them, "America's only native criminal class," or that the amount stolen from the public treasury will be larger than a heist from, say, a bank. These arguments are all fascinating; yet, there is not a scintilla of evidence to support them. It is not that our legislators are angels, but only that we hear much more about the arrest and/or conviction of one of them than we do about some corporate executive who does not have to face the electorate.

A more plausible argument is that being too close to the center of power in our nation's capital may tend to corrupt people, including members of Congress. But is the nation better served by: (1) letting a member be reelected to the House (Senate) as often as he or she can do so, with the support of industry (group, union, etc.) X; or (2) putting a limit on the number of terms a member can serve and then setting him or her free to work much more directly for industry X, perhaps as a lobbyist or as corporate executive? If we do have a deep distrust of our elected representatives, we ought to do everything possible to keep them under our diligent surveillance. The easiest way to accomplish this is to require them to face the voters every two years for the House, six for the Senate. Occasionally, a member convicted of a crime (such as Rep. Charles Diggs [D., Mich.] in 1978) will be reelected anyway; but, more generally, even the suggestion of scandal is enough to end a member's career.

The appeal for a citizen legislature rather than a professional one stems from our own democratic heritage which tells us that any boy or girl can grow up to become a member of Congress, or even president. One does not have to be a professional legislator in order to represent a constituency. Congressional staffs draw up the complex pieces of legislation, the argument runs, so there is really little need for "lifetime" members of Congress. On the other hand, a new member of Congress does not rush out and pass bill after bill. Most subjects are sufficiently complex that even professionals have difficulty in putting together legislative proposals on most policy areas; furthermore, these proposals must be able to command a majority not only in committee, but also in the floor of both the Senate and the House. Creating these majorities requires a type of political skill which is unlikely to be learned outside of legislative politics.

The gentleman farmer who would spend a few months in the capital working on affairs of state, as many framers of the Constitution had imagined, is simply an anachronism. The Congress meets virtually year-round, so it is highly unlikely that an average citizen could give up his or her job to serve for a brief stretch in the Congress. The gentleman farmer of the late 18th century is involved in agribusiness in the late 20th century; even the family farmer now owns several thousand acres of land. Those who are not rich and seek political office often do so in the hope of making it into a full-time career.[4] Others who want to make forays into politics generally have to be rich enough that they can take a leave from the regular occupations (such as being a Rockefeller or a Kennedy—or even a Percy, chairman of the board of Bell and Howell). Would a limitation on the number of terms not discourage the former type of member and make entry barriers into politics even stronger for those who are not rich? We build up so many myths like that of the citizen legislator that we tend to forget that the era in which we did have a distinctly part-time Congress (from 1789 until the mid-1820's) there was constant bickering within the chambers, and many members found their limited duties and equally restricted compensation so insufficient that they resigned their seats.[5]

What does the public think about these arguments? As mentioned above, the public tends to have a strongly negative attitude about congressional performance, as measured by public opinion polls. Here we examine the results of a survey taken by the Louis Harris organization in January, 1977 for the House Commission on Administrative Review. The public had a 65-22 percent negative opinion (the remainder being undecided) on overall congressional performance, but individuals rated their own representative positively by a margin of 40 percent to 23 percent, with seven times as many people arguing that their member was better than the average instead of holding that he or she was worse. Voters thus do seem satisfied with the type of representation they get personally, but not with the performance of the institutions. When asked more detailed questions about why things needed improvement and what steps should be taken, ethical considerations were offered by many respondents. Yet, by 54 percent to 34 percent, respondents thought that being a member of Congress should be a full-time job.[6] Apparently, many people agreed with the argument that it is better to provide adequately for members of Congress so that they do not have to depend upon outside sources of income to meet their expenses. It is the part-time legislature which may lead one into temptation, rather than the full-time chamber.

When Senator DeConcini argues against the evils of the full-time legislature, he cites the many things that incumbents do to keep themselves in office, including pressing for legislation that would directly benefit the districts they represent, working to pass legislation so that they can claim credit for such activity in their next reelection bid, and solving a multitude of personal problems for constituents. Just how devious are these incumbents? Are they conniving their own reelection efforts, as at least one student of Congress has argued?[7] The evidence is again far from conclusive. The Harris survey for the House Commission on Administrative Review indicated that these activities are the ones given the highest priority for members by the voters themselves! What supporters of a term limit for members of the House and Senate fail to realize is that most members get reelected time and time again precisely because they do what their constituents want them to do.

Finally, amendment supporters have not considered what effects on leadership their plan might have. Had such an amendment been operative, every House majority and minority leader, as well as every Speaker, would have either been retired from the Congress or in his last term for all such leaders *in this century*.[8] The effects on the Senate would be less dramatic, although every leader except Lyndon B. Johnson would have been in his last term before assuming the key slot. Senator DeConcini argues persuasively that we need new blood in the Congress, but the men and women of the two chambers who have put members with substantial service in leadership positions are doing far more than rewarding people for time served. The country is unhappily short on leaders such as Henry Clay; Clay served seven terms in the House in the early 19th century, interrupted three times, but *only* served as Speaker. In contrast, two contemporary Speakers who developed reputations as outstanding leaders, Sam Rayburn (1940-1947, 1949-1953, 1955-1961) and Thomas P. O'Neill (1977—) served long apprenticeships and learned not only a great deal about specific policies but also how to get them enacted. With seniority comes a knowledge of the institution and of the mood of the country, so that a truly gifted leader can have greater power than the President of the United States. The twenty-second amendment to the constitution limited the number of terms a president could serve to two; since its adoption, only one president has served even that long (Dwight D. Eisenhower). We were so preoccupied with the possibility that a man such as Franklin D. Roosevelt might become a lifetime president (which he did) that we failed to realize that the more pressing problem has been our dearth of great leaders. The situation is more acute in the legislative branch than in the executive and the term limitation would only ensure that we have more leaders, not better ones.

Thus, the arguments offered by Senator DeConcini are deficient on a number of grounds. An appeal to history does not suffice to justify a constitutional amendment for the 1980's and beyond. And the history of the part-time legislator is hardly as glorious as the myth that sustains it. The seniority system is no longer sacred and there has been sufficient turnover in the House and the Senate in recent years to suggest that no amendment is needed. The available survey evidence also shows that people are getting pretty much the kind of government they want, even if they are dissatisfied with the results. This dissatisfaction remains a puzzle not only to politicians but also to students of the Congress and the electorate. Perhaps it might even be inevitable in a democracy. But, whatever its cause, we should be very careful in proposing a "remedy" through the mechanism of a constitutional amendment. We can throw the rascals out of an unpopular Congress rather easily, but an amendment, once adopted, takes many years to repeal. Stimson Bullitt, an erstwhile candidate for public office, commented, "A constituency would have low standards or bad luck to elect a politician whose wisdom and knowledge were not above the average of the whole."[9] If we restrict the available pool of candidates for office, we then might be lucky to settle for a government as good as its people.

NOTES

1. Quoted in David Price, *Who Makes the Laws?* (New York: Schenkman, 1972), p. 11.
2. Cf. Barbara Hinckley, *The Seniority System in Congress* (Bloomington: Indiana University Press, 1971), pp. 36-46.
3. See Alan L. Otten, "Errand Boys," *Wall Street Journal,* August 18, 1977.
4. A good example is Senator Edmund S. Muskie (D., Me.). See Bernard Asbell, *The Senate Nobody Knows* (Garden City, N.Y.: Doubleday, 1978), pp. 238-240.
5. See James Sterling Young, *The Washington Community* (New York: Columbia University Press, 1966), especially chapters 1-3.
6. The classic statement on the different ways constituents see the Congress and their Representative is that of Richard F. Fenno, Jr., "If, as Ralph Nader says, Congress Is 'The Broken Branch,' How Come We Love Our Congressmen So Much," in Norman Ornstein, ed., *Congress in Change* (New York: Praeger, 1973), pp. 277-287. Also see Glenn Parker and Robert H. Davidson, "Why Do Americans Love Their Congressmen So Much More Than Their Congress?" *Legislative Studies Quarterly* 4 (February 1979): 53-61. The data from the House Commission on Administrative Review reported here were taken from various reports of the Commission in the 95th Congress. For the question on the full-time legislators in particular, see the testimony of Louis Harris in House Commission on Administrative Review, *Financial Ethics* (Washington: Government Printing Office, 1977), p. 171.

7. See Morris P. Fiorina, *Congress: Keystone of the Washington Establishment* (New Haven: Yale University Press, 1977).

8. These figures taken from Robert L. Peabody, *Leadership in Congress* (Boston: Little, Brown, 1976), pp. 32, 36-37, 328.

9. Stimson Bullitt, *To Be a Politician* (New Haven: Yale University Press, 1977, revised ed.), p. 74.

CONGRESSIONAL ETHICS

With the notoriety given to some celebrated cases of wrongdoing by certain members of Congress, it is no wonder that the popular perception of the average congressman is that he is at least guilty of conflict of interest, and perhaps even a crook.

Researchers for the Ralph Nader Congress Project, Mark J. Green, James M. Fallows, and David R. Zwick, make a strong case for the proposition that a good many, if not most, congressmen engage in activities that violate the public trust and, indeed, frequently border on the illegal. For example, the Nader group points to the widespread practice of congressmen maintaining their law practice while serving in Congress—a situation that almost inevitably invites conflict of interest problems.

If Nader and his associates are upset over this aspect of congressional ethics, the perceptions of congressmen themselves on this matter appear to be a bit different. Edmund Beard and Stephen Horn of the Brookings Institution, after conducting interviews with a sample of congressmen, conclude that what is called conflict of interest by outside observers is not always defined that way by members of Congress. And if some members of Congress view a particular action as a conflict of interest, as for example, when a congressman accepts a ride on an airplane owned by a corporation, it is not considered a conflict by other congressmen.

Given the mixed views that congressmen have, it is hardly surprising that they have had difficulty policing conflict of interest, even though the public seems to demand a higher standard of ethics and accountability today than ever before.

Lawmakers as Lawbreakers

Mark J. Green, James M. Fallows,
and David R. Zwick

"What this country needs is a little law and order." The cry comes from many quarters, but there is little agreement about who the violators of law and order really are: wise-guy protesters, troublesome blacks, street criminals, executives whose firms exploit and pollute, governmental agents who trample over the law in an attempt to enforce it. Yet a good place to start would be the American Congress. The most obvious reason is symbolic: if chosen men have the power to make the law, then they should respect the law. If they do not, they can scarcely expect that others will.

Corruption involving criminal conduct has shaken Congress at least since 1873, when the House censured two members for their roles in the Crédit Mobilier stock scandal. While Congress and the country have passed through fundamental metamorphoses since then, one constant theme has been the public's suspicion of the people it sends to Washington. This was not the constitutional mistrust that had plagued the Founding Fathers—the gnawing fear that men in power would become tyrants. Instead, it was the suspicion of personal venality, that the men in government were somehow turning a profit. In 1965, Gallup pollsters found that four times as many people thought that "political favoritism and corruption in Washington" were rising as thought them falling. Two years later, as Congress washed its hands of Adam Clayton Powell, Gallup asked whether the revelations about Powell had surprised the public. Sixty percent thought that Powell's offenses—which the questionnaire called "misuse of government funds"—were fairly common. (Twenty-one percent disagreed.) Powell had protested, in victimized anguish, that he was only one public scapegoat among many quiet offenders. "There is no one here," he said to his accusers, "who does not have a skeleton in his closet."

The skeletons vary in size. The smallest are the personal

peccadilloes—which are the stuff of public amusement, scorn, and regular exposure by Washington columnists. Outweighing these in importance are the systematic violations of Congress's own rules and laws, offenses which are not quite crimes, but which are not quite cricket, either. Conflicts of interest are the next biggest skeletons in congressional closets. Finally, there is the *summum malum* of congressional crime, instances of bribery, perjury, and influence-peddling. Taken together, the pervasiveness of lawbreaking amounts to a grim commentary on those who govern us.

NOT QUITE A CRIME: PECCADILLOES, RULES, AND LAWS

Congressmen are people, and subject to the same temptations and flaws as other people. At times, their visibility makes them suffer more for their failings than they otherwise would. An omission or mistake which would pass unnoticed in a plumber may become big news when attached to a politically important name. This does not excuse congressional misconduct. Just as the public expects higher standards of personal morality from those who instruct its children than from those who fix its drains and pipes, so it expects high standards from those who make its laws.

In order to assure them freedom to exercise their duties free from harassment, congressmen are granted immunity from arrest for statements made, or actions taken, in Congress, or while coming from or going to Congress. This desirable privilege, however, has frequently been abused by congressmen caught in unsavory escapades. In his prepresidential days, for example, Senator Warren Harding was surprised by two New York policemen while visiting friend Nan Britton in a hotel room. As the police prepared to arrest him on charges of fornication, carnal knowledge, and drunken driving, Harding successfully argued that as a senator he could not be arrested. It was hardly what the Constitution intended for congressional immunity, but it worked well here.

Several years ago, Texas Congressman Joe Pool rammed his car into the back of another car stopped at a red light. Pool refused to accept a traffic ticket from a policeman and, later, from his sergeant. Instead, he repeated over and over, "I am a congressman and I cannot be arrested." Unimpressed, the police held him for six hours before releasing him. "He kept saying he was a congressman," said the policeman, "but he didn't look like one or sound like one." Later, Pool confided to a friend, "I thought they couldn't arrest a congressman unless he'd committed a felony. But it turns out they *can* unless he's en route to or returning from a session of Congress."

They *can*, but they *don't*. On the way to a party in the summer of 1972, Mississippi Congressman Jamie Whitten—who normally conducts himself with decorum—ran a stop sign in Georgetown and struck a car, an iron fence, two trees, a brick wall, and another car on the other side of the wall. Whitten said his accelerator stuck, but an investigating officer said at the scene, "The guy's been drinking; there's alcohol on his breath. I don't think he's drunk. But he's shook up." No arrest was made and no charges were filed. "The first thing [Whitten] did," said the owner of the wall, "was to get out of the car and begin shaking everyone's hand.". . .

Annoying as these cases might be, they are small potatoes. They involve single, unplanned romps, not deliberate self-enrichment or serious affairs of state. If this were the extent of congressional lawlessness, we could all sleep a little easier at night.

But it's not. Worse is the hypocrisy of congressmen violating their own rules. A classic illustration is junketing. Congressmen who legislate about foreign affairs or military bases may do a better job if they've seen some of the areas for themselves. That's the theory. In practice, however, many trips are personal vacations (with family) rather than public fact-findings. In 1971, 51 percent of Congress, or 53 senators and 221 representatives, took foreign trips at public expense; the total cost to taxpayers was $1,114,386. Hong Kong and the Caribbean turned out to be favorite destinations for those supposedly seeking self-education. "Scratch hard in December," one congressman joked, "and you'll come up with a quorum in Hong Kong." There may even be motives beyond the chance of a vacation. "Those who do get away," Jerry Landauer has written in the *Wall Street Journal,* "will enjoy little-known opportunities [double-billings, for example] for lining their own pockets—opportunities that some have exploited in the past.". . .

Large-scale juggling of committee rules and committee staff is also widespread. Committee chairmen . . . can be tyrants. When it serves their purposes, they can simply ignore the rules, or, when it serves their purposes, they can become maniacal defenders of every conceivable rule and technicality. "It's my game, baby," Chairman Adam Clayton Powell once explained to the grumbling members of his House Labor and Public Welfare Committee.

But one rule is almost universally violated: committee chairmen use staff members who are assigned to the committee as if they were their own personal employees. . . . This springs less from any special avarice in the chairmen's souls than from the committee and seniority systems themselves. The fond references that a chairman will make to "my" committee shows how deep the confusion runs. . . .

Congressmen suffer equally mild twinges of conscience about using their own staff members for political campaigns. The element of abuse is clear: staff men are paid by the government, not by the senator or representative; they are paid to serve *the office,* not to help the man who happens to be in office to stay there. In 1968, the two Senators Kennedy admitted that twenty of their staffers were working on Robert Kennedy's presidential campaign. If other senators do not reveal how many of their staffers serve reelection drives, it is probably because no one realizes it's wrong. When interviewers from the Nader Congress Project asked about this practice, few congressmen realized it was illegal. But it *is* illegal: Public Law 89-90 says an assistant can't be paid "if such does not perform the services for which he receives such compensation, in the offices of such Member . . ." Because the law is so widely violated, violation becomes custom, and custom replaces law. There are many instances of this phenomenon. Nearly all congressmen violated the archaic 1925 Federal Corrupt Practices Act (replaced in 1972), which aimed to limit campaign funding and to require some disclosure of campaign finances, yet no one has ever been prosecuted for it. An 1872 law directs House and Senate officials to deduct from a member's salary a day's pay for each day's absence, except for illness; in the last hundred years this has been done exactly twice, although there are absentees daily. . . .

CONFLICTS OF INTEREST

Congress correctly demands a high standard of impartiality from those it confirms for executive and judicial appointments. In 1969, when President Nixon tried and failed to get Judge Clement Haynsworth onto the Supreme Court, the most compelling reason against the nomination was that Haynsworth had tried cases involving business in which he held small bits of stock. When industrialist David Packard was nominated as assistant secretary of defense, Congress required that he put $300 million of his personal fortune in a "blind trust," one which manages the money entirely out of Packard's sight. The ex-president of GM, Charles Wilson, and the ex-president of Ford, Robert McNamara, had to unload $2.7 million and $7.1 million respectively of their companies' stock before being confirmed as secretary of defense. The rationale behind these requirements is biblical and clear: since no man can serve two masters, Congress insists that federal officials put their private interests aside before assuming public duties.

Unfortunately, this diligence stops when it comes to the congressmen themselves. No one scrutinizes their stock holdings to check for potential conflicts; no one insists that members sell sensitive shares. The only group with the power to screen the members—their voting constituency—is usually too ill-informed to make any serious judgment. And such conflicts are not considered a crime. In many states they violate the law, but not in Congress, simply because Congress, which writes the laws, chooses not to call what it does illegal.

With so few barriers against it, potential conflict of interest becomes commonplace in Congress. "If everyone abstained on grounds of personal interest," former Senator Robert Kerr claimed, "I doubt if you could get a quorum in the United States Senate on any subject." Kerr's own position neatly illustrated the problem. As a millionaire oilman from Oklahoma,

Kerr stood to lose or gain huge sums, depending on the government's tax rules for oil. As a powerful member of the Senate Finance Committee, Kerr was one of the men who decided what the tax laws would be. It does not take long to see the conflict. "Hell," Kerr bragged, "I'm in everything."

Conflicts of interest in Congress take two main forms: business dealings and legal practice. Banks are the most obvious illustration of the first. In 1971, according to the National Committee for an Effective Congress, one hundred representatives held stock in or were officials of some financial institution. A dozen also served on the House Banking Committee. Nine of them had at some time accepted loans at special reduced rates from the National Bank of Washington.

Indeed, favors from banks to congressmen are frequent. In 1962, the first new national bank to receive a District of Columbia charter since 1931 let Senator John Sparkman—then heir-apparent to the chairmanship of the Senate Banking Committee—buy $10,500 of its shares at preferred terms. Congressman Seymour Halpern got even more personal attention. While struggling to pay off loans outstanding, Halpern in 1969 managed to get another $100,000 from banks in unsecured loans. His committee was considering banking legislation at the time. The First National City Bank of New York, for one example, loaned $40,000 to Halpern while its lobbyists were pushing for a mild version of the bill Halpern was considering.

The same pattern extends to other business holdings. From evidence turned up in 1969 financial disclosure forms, *Congressional Quarterly* estimated that 183 congressmen had interests in companies which either did business with the federal government or were subject to federal legislation. Eleven had interests in airlines, for example, 59 in firms with substantial defense contracts, 54 in oil and gas, 25 in power and light, 20 in radio and television, 19 in farms and timberland, and 16 in real estate. Clarence Brown of Ohio, for specific example, holds the majority stock in a broadcasting station—and sits on the House subcommittee regulating broadcasting. Brown may be a wise enough man to keep his personal affairs out of public decisions. But whenever he takes a stand—such as his opposition to public television—his financial stake in the outcome gives at least the appearance of impropriety. He is not alone. The late Robert Watkins, a former Republican congressman from Pennsylvania, was the chairman of an interstate trucking firm whose profits depended on rules passed by Watkins's House Commerce Committee. James Eastland, the Alabama Democrat who is president pro tempore of the Senate, and his wife received $159,000 in 1971 in agricultural subsidies; at the same time, he sits on the Agriculture Committee and votes against ceilings on farm subsidies.

One of the few congressmen who have bothered to defend such self-serving behavior openly is Senator Russell Long of Louisiana. Like Kerr, Long is an oilman. In the five years before 1969, his income from oil was $1,196,915. Of that, $329,151 was tax-free, thanks to the curious oil depletion allowance. Long is also chairman of the Senate Finance Committee, which recommends tax plans, including oil depletion clauses, to the Senate. A conflict of interest? Not to Long. "If you have financial interests completely parallel to [those of] your state," he explained, "then you have no problem." Even if it were true that the interests of a state and all its people can be lumped with that of one giant industry—which it is not—the haughty premise that lies behind this reasoning is alarming. What Long is saying is that each senator is alone the sufficient judge of his own propriety. Once he convinces himself that his companies are really in the best interest of his folks back home, "then you have no problem." It must ease Long's conscience to know that he is helping others when he helps himself.

Occasionally there are men for whom even these lush fringe benefits of political office are not enough. They count the moments wasted which they must spend on the tedium of bills and votes. Such a man was George Smathers. Even while serving as Florida's senator, Smathers was melancholy. "A person with my background can make more money in thirty days [as a lobbyist]," he said, "than he can in fifteen years as a senator."

In preparation for the easy days ahead, Smathers spent the closing days of his Senate career collecting IOUs from private interests. According to *Newsday*, Smathers led a posse of Florida congressmen in a secret attempt to salvage a floundering Florida company, Aerodex. Because of what the Air Force called "poor quality work which was endangering the Air Force pilots and aircraft," the Defense Department wanted to cancel a multimillion-dollar contract with Aerodex. After Smathers's effort, the contract stood.

In 1969, when Smathers retired, he claimed his reward. He became a director of Aerodex and got an attractive deal on stock: $435,000 worth of it for $20,000. The company also put Smathers's Washington law firm on a $25,000-a-year retainer. Smathers is now comfortably installed as a lobbyist, fulfilling his earlier exuberant prediction that "I'm going to be a Clark Clifford. That's the life for me."

The second important type of conflict of interest comes from congressmen who maintain legal practices. The moral problem here is subtler than that of the oilmen or bankers. A lawyer's business, like a doctor's or writer's, is built on reputation and skill. But when a lawyer also holds government office, his clients might conclude that he can do more for them than another person of similar talent. A widely circulated, widely respected study by the New York City Bar Association strongly condemns the lawyering congressmen. They are the fiduciaries of the public—administrators of public functions, the Bar study says. Accordingly, they must administer this public trust for the public's benefit, not their own. Instead, "law practices have played a disproportionate role in the history of congressional scandals."

More than a century ago, New Hampshire's Daniel Webster kept in practice for his Senate orations by appearing as a private lawyer for the Bank of the United States. He argued the private bank's case some forty-one times before the Supreme Court. There was no Committee on Ethics then, and Webster did not have to conceal the relation. When, in his senatorial role, he was considering legislation to extend the bank's charter, he wrote his clients to remind them that "my retainer has not been received and refreshed as usual." While the standards change, certain practices do not. The irrepressible Thomas Dodd, writing to his Hartford law firm for more money, stated the problem candidly. "I'm sure you know that there's a considerable amount of business that goes into the office because of me. Many men in public life receive a steady income from their law practices because of the value of their association [and] my name and association is a realistic fact which definitely has value."

Dodd is gone, but (according to Common Cause) there were still fifty-seven congressmen affiliated to law firms in May, 1972. One was Sam Gibbons of Florida. He sits on the House Ways and Means Committee; there he judges tax bills whose clauses can mean profit or loss for corporations. Gibbons's local law firm in Florida has among its clients six of the country's largest insurance firms; the second biggest car rental firm; and the biggest grocery chain in the South. Congressman Joshua Eilberg also has a law firm. One of its clients is the National Liberty Corporation, a mail-order health insurance firm. Eilberg lauded National Liberty in the pages of the *Congressional Record*. Customers trying to choose an insurance plan could thereafter read advertisements claiming "National Liberty commended in the *Congressional Record* of the United States Congress." (Eilberg later repudiated this insertion, saying National Liberty had misused it.)

If a congressman can endure the Bar Association's frowns, there is little to stop him from keeping up his law practice. There is a point, however, when the law imposes a limit. An 1863 statute forbids congressmen-lawyers from representing clients who have claims before the federal government. To avoid embarrassing problems while keeping the business thriving, congressmen have therefore devised an ingenious "two-door" system. On the front door of the law firm is the congressman's name; through this door come the many clients who value his help. Another door is just the same, except the congressman's name is missing. Here enter those proscribed clients with claims before the government. The ruse is within the letter of the law, but it still irritates purists. Journalist Robert Sherrill, for example, has said that Congressman Emanuel Celler's double doors are "one of the longest-standing and most notorious embarrassments to Congress." To this, Celler has had a standard reply. "Your constituents are the final arbiter of any conflicts, and I'm always reelected."

In 1972, after fifty years in the House, Emanuel Celler lost in his Brooklyn Democratic primary. . . .

It would be polite to end a discussion of congressional lawlessness by stressing that, while there are a few rotten apples, the overwhelming majority of congressmen are honest. This may be true, but how would we know? Their public financial disclosures do not tell us enough, nor are the ethics committees vigilant enough, to make us sanguine. By failing to police itself, Congress has not elevated itself above suspicion. A critical observer can hardly take heart at the number of congressmen and staff who have been caught. There are no cops regularly patrolling Capitol Hill corridors, and no law enforcement agencies devote resources to congressional crime. The luckless few are exposed more by fluke than investigation. Until the two houses put themselves in order, friends and cynics will continue to wonder not what congressmen do but how they do it.

Conflict of Interest: The View from the House

Edmund Beard and Stephen Horn

Any congressional behavior that is not designed to advance the common interests of constituents and country might be termed conflict of interest. But this generalization is not useful, neglecting as it does the many complexities and ambiguities of congressional service. At one extreme, conflict of interest becomes corruption; at the other, it merges with the legitimate representation of constituents.

A congressman is approached by many people other than the residents of his district—his own or the opposing party's leadership, colleagues, the President or his agents, and a host of representatives of private interests seeking the congressman's voice and vote. These groups can create divided loyalties for the congressman, and they can also offer a variety of material and nonmaterial rewards for his cooperation.

Congressmen lament about the special burdens and contradictions that characterize their responsibilities—problems they feel the public and the media do not recognize. A legislator is simultaneously expected to represent the interests of his constituency and of the nation as a whole, but these interests may not always be identical, and, even when they are substantially complementary, other claims to limited federal resources may be more valid. This ambiguity of role creates some of the most intense ethical dilemmas faced by congressmen.

The problem of conflicting national and constituent interests is complicated because most legislators feel that if they consistently oppose the interests of the constituency, even when those interests are quite narrowly conceived, their prospects for continued tenure are bleak, and they are likely to be replaced by more compliant representatives. This situation forces a pattern of ad hoc compromise whereby competing images of constituency interests and national interests are held in tandem while the representative sometimes attempts to "educate" his district and at other times works wholeheartedly for narrow constituent benefits. Some legislators see their role merely as that of a promoter of constituency interests and never confront such conflicts. For a great many legislators, however, such dilemmas are a real part of congressional life.

Related problems arise over the meaning of "constituency." Is a constituency simply a majority of the population or of the voting-age population? Is it the members of one's own party since the other party would have elected someone else and in many cases worked actively in opposition? Is the constituency composed primarily of those who contributed the major part of one's campaign expenses and without whom one might not have been elected? Is the district characterized by its largest employers? These are questions that confront all legislators and that touch in one way or another on many of the unresolved issues discussed in this study. . . .

FIVE POSSIBLE CONFLICTS

One analyst of the executive branch conflict of interest law passed in 1961 has defined five areas of possible conflict: self-dealing by a public official, discretionary transfer of economic value to a public official from a private source, assistance by public officials to private parties dealing with the government, post-employment assistance by former public officials to private parties dealing with the government, and private gain derived from information acquired in an official capacity.[1] Using this list as a guide, we will illustrate the distinction claimed . . . between the executive and congressional situations and the difficulty in defining congressional conflict of interest.

Self-Dealing by a Public Official

The implication of "self-dealing by a public official" is that public officials ought to disqualify themselves when a particular course of government action might significantly affect their personal economic interest. The difficulty with this notion when applied to the House of Representatives is that, unless congressmen are to have no source of income other than their salaries, it may be difficult for them to avoid situations that affect their own interests. A member of the executive branch charged with overseeing only one policy area may without undue hardship avoid personal holdings in that field. Congressmen cannot handle the problem that easily. As the late Senator Robert Kerr said, "If everyone abstained from voting on grounds of personal interest, I doubt if you could get a quorum in the United States Senate on any subject."[2]

In a recent study two researchers attempted to examine "associations between the personal financial holdings of members of the Ninetieth Congress and their roll-call responses on votes relevant to those holdings."[3] They analyzed eleven fields of interest: finance, defense, the antiballistic missile system, farming, transportation, broadcasting, electrical power, law, airlines, petroleum, and capital gains. Although the authors found apparent correlations between personal holdings in an industry and pro-industry voting patterns in the case of electrical power and airlines, they found the opposite pattern in the case of farming, transportation, capital gains, and petroleum. In general they discovered "few if any examples of self-serving in the U.S. House of Representatives."

The authors of the study did find differences between interested and disinterested members (those with or without relevant financial holdings) with respect to the size of winning coalitions. Members with relevant financial holdings showed a tendency to favor those holdings in close votes and were more likely than others to change their votes when a compromise alternative was offered. The authors pointed out in addition that "record votes on the floor are but a small part of the total legislative process" and that there may be errors in their findings because overly stringent standards may have caused them to overlook potentially interesting results. Furthermore, there may have been shortcomings in the financial data available or in the nature of the inquiry itself.

On the other hand, the findings may be accurate. As another observer has commented: "In the ordinary ranges of stock ownership the rewards from favoritism or worse are simply inadequate. The official runs all the risks of detection and obloquy but receives only one-thousandth or one-millionth of the proceeds. Even a narrow, grasping man will find this disproportion between risks and profits uninviting."[4] The benefits a congressman might get from favoring his stock holdings are not worth the risks he runs. A congressman risks less if he favors an interest for other deferred compensation such as future employment, which we will discuss later. In addition, a legislator's vote in favor of a certain stock holding may also benefit his constituents (depending on how they are defined). . . .

Congressmen believe that it is a common practice for their colleagues to promote personal interests that coincide with constituent interests [See Table 1]. Item 3, for example, in which a legislator owning $100,000 worth of savings and loan stock votes for a tax amendment favoring the savings and loan industry, was the most disapproved item in this group, presumably because of the size of the stock holding, yet the respondents did not believe that disapproval would prevent such behavior on the part of their colleagues. In general these questionnaire responses support the interview conclusions that congressmen are not particularly worried about promoting personal interests that coincide with constituent interest. . . .

Outside business interests do present unnecessary and avoidable conflicts, but congressmen disagree widely about their legitimacy. There

Table 1
Mean scores on questionnaire items, group 6:
promoting personal interests that coincide with constituent interests

Questionnaire item	Mean Score	
	Judgement of practice*	Extent of practice**
(3) A legislator owns $100,000 worth of stock in a hometown saving and loan association and votes in favor of an amendment to a tax bill that benefits the savings and loan industry as a whole.	2.28	2.24
(37) A legislator owns 2,000 acres of cotton-producing land. He represents a constituency in which cotton is the major agricultural crop. He receives as assignment to the Committee on Agriculture where he actively works for higher price supports for cotton.	2.48	2.23
(38) A legislator is president of a local labor union. He wins election to Congress and is granted a two-year leave by his union executive board, which continues his pension and retirement rights. He is appointed to the committee with jurisdiction over labor matters. He works actively for repeal of the right-to-work laws and less restrictive federal controls over labor organizations.	2.56	2.20
(2) A legislator owns $5,000 worth of stock in a hometown savings and loan association and votes in favor of an amendment to a tax bill that benefits the savings and loan industry as a whole.	2.65	1.74

* Scoring for judgement of practice:
   1 = clearly unethical   3 = probably ethical
   2 = probably unethical 4 = clearly ethical

** Scoring for extent of practice:
   1 = most congressmen   3 = few
   2 = many   4 = none

are three distinct opinions in Congress about such interests: that any time spent away from congressional business is improper; that although outside income is desirable, law practice is very conflict prone; and that outside business is acceptable, including law practice, which is no different from any other business and should not be discriminated against.

One northeastern Republican put the first case forcefully.

People invariably think of a conflict of financial interest, but the conflict in time is more important. Unless you give to the job all your time and energy, I think you have a conflict of interest. When I see it, it bothers me as I know I need between seventy and seventy-five hours a week to do this job. I just don't think a member should have outside professional and business interests.

A western Democrat exemplified the second position.

I have to maintain outside interests. What if I'm defeated tomorrow? What do I do? My business might be a fiction, but I keep it like a security blanket. It's something that I might have to use. I think the big problem is the lawyer/legislator. If I did what they do, I could be put in prison.

This critique was echoed by a southern Democrat.

The biggest criticism I can see is those attorneys who maintain an active law practice. A large percentage of that practice is generated because of their position in Congress. They are also the active members of the Tuesday-to-Thursday Club. If we could get them to come down here and work a five-day week, why we would be done with our work three months earlier.

Despite what several lawyer members saw as an apparent injustice in condemning law practice while allowing other business interests, many other members felt quite strongly that law ties presented special difficulties. As one western Democrat said bluntly: "The similarity of legal practice and congressional behavior is so close that it is an obvious channel for sanitized bribery and influence peddling. Every major bribery effort of a public official goes through a law firm." "Double door" law firms with one "door" listing a congressman's name as a partner (for the nonfederal business) and another eliminating the name (for federal business) were often unfavorably mentioned.

Both of the positions above—that of abstaining totally from outside occupations and that of prohibiting only law practice—were disputed by several lawyer members. As a southern Democrat put it:

I think a member should have an outside interest. The worst single mistake I made, besides probably running for Congress, was to give up my law practice. I think you need—at least I need—an adequate income to support a family when you have several children in college at one time as I do.

Other members cited another important reason for maintaining an outside occupation and income. "I could survive without having a law firm partnership," one said, "but I think having the partnership gives me a feeling of independence as to what I do here. Otherwise my future will be up to the whims of local party officials." This argument also applies to independence from special interests. As a northern Republican noted:

> I think that if you have a business or income connection, you can be very much more independent as a member of Congress. If you're defeated, you can go back to your profession. If you're a professor, you can get a job in a university. If you have nothing to go back to, why you may become more dependent and less independent.

Several members said that a legislator from a rural area may have more time to pursue an outside interest than one from an active urban district may have. The time conflict was not seen as much of a problem if, in fact, a members district not put time demands on him. This position overlooks the possibility that a member less pressed by constituent demands could spend more time on substantive legislative business. Nevertheless, several members did make the distinction. . . .

In their responses to questions about ties with law firms, congressmen recognized the ethical problems an active law practice can entail, or even encourage. They also recognized, however, that a junior congressman who may not be reelected should not have to cut himself off from his legal career. The respondents saw a difference between a congressman who simply maintains ties with his law firm and one who allows his law firm to profit from his congressional service. . . .

Judging from the responses to the questions in this study, congressmen are unlikely to voluntarily limit the range of outside activities open to them. There is a widespread feeling in Congress that outside business interests (with the possible exception of a law practice) are legitimate and necessary, either for personal financial security or for legislative independence. Coupled with the unwillingness of congressmen to interfere with their colleagues' personal habits or relations with their constituents, these attitudes protect even law affiliation. The difficulty of regulating one particular activity, which will certainly be considered unfair discrimination by those most affected, makes it unlikely that outside law practice will be formally prohibited. . . .

Discretionary Transfer of Economic Value

The most extreme form of discretionary transfer of economic value from a private source to a public official—the second area of possible conflict—is bribery, which is illegal. There are many less extreme forms, however, that also raise questions.

Even in cases of demonstrated bribery, the congressional situation is unique. Congressmen are protected under the Constitution from arrests in civil suits and for words written or spoken in the execution of their office. Former Congressman John Dowdy of Texas was convicted of bribery, conspiracy, and perjury in a case involving the protection of a home improvement firm accused of fraud. In April 1973 an appeals court overturned the bribery and conspiracy convictions. The court did not find that Dowdy was innocent of the acts charged; rather it ruled that his acts could be interpreted as being in the line of his duty on a subcommittee and as such would be protected legislative acts, even if he was being bribed to so act.[5] The perjury conviction was left standing.

In 1963 the conviction of Congressman Thomas L. Johnson of Maryland on charges of receiving a bribe in exchange for giving a speech on the House floor was also overturned on these constitutional grounds. Johnson's speech, extolling savings and loan institutions, was reprinted and distributed by officers of a Maryland savings and loan company then under indictment. . . . Congressman Johnson was later convicted for a second time on federal conflict of interest charges and was sentenced to six months in prison.

The difficulties of trying to regulate behavior such as Johnson's floor speech are enormous. To be able to convict Johnson on the basis of his speech would jeopardize, for example, a member from an urban district who received large campaign contributions from labor interests and subsequently gave a speech in the House favorable to those interests. The latter is an example of legitimate political behavior and the promotion of constituency interests, as well as a common method of rewarding contributors. . . .

Many other unique circumstances surrounding congressional rewards from private sources blur the charge of conflict of interest. Just as no laws forbid congressmen to engage in outside business activity, none forbid them to accept honorariums, although legislation in 1974 limited payments for each speech or article to $1,000 and the total annual income from such activities to $15,000. Legislators commonly receive stipends for speaking before private groups, including those concerned with legislation before their committees. Two questionnaire items addressed this issue. One asked about a member who accepted a $1,000 honorarium from a group with which he had long been identified. The other asked about a member who accepted the same sum from a group, new to him, that was interested in upcoming legislation, while he was undecided how to vote on the issue. The respondents deemed the first situation probably ethical and widely practiced. They considered the second more unethical . . . but also fairly likely to be practiced. . . .

Honorariums can be treated as direct income. They are an obvious, and for many a very lucrative, discretionary transfer of economic value to a public official. Campaign contributions are a different matter. Nevertheless, they fall in the same category and may present many of the same conflicts.

Members of the House of Representatives must run for reelection every two years. In a closely contested district the costs of a primary and general campaign may run over $100,000. A congressman earning less than half that sum a year could not hope to manage such expenses on his own, and he is not expected to. He can use his salary and associated allowances to partially support his campaign, but he must raise a campaign fund to meet the bulk of his expenses. Although the amounts of money needed in an election campaign and the methods employed for raising funds vary greatly among members, the funds all come from the private sector.

Campaign funds and personal finances may complement each other, with an unclear line between expenses that should be charged to one or the other. Unexpended campaign funds can be used for political as opposed to personal expenses between campaigns. However, if a congressman does not have unused campaign funds, he pays for political expenses vital to his performance (or continuance) in office out of his own pocket. Many respondents reported that they used considerable amounts of their own funds to run their offices and to serve their constituents.

In addition to the trips that congressmen are authorized to take to their districts at government expense each year, they can use unexpended campaign funds to pay for additional trips home by including one political function. By visiting the district office, meeting with supporters, or addressing a local organization, a congressman can claim that the trip was political and charge it to excess funds, whether he spends most of the time at leisure with his family or not.

The respondents agreed that the use of campaign funds for activities that bear little relation to any campaign is improper. . . . The responses clearly reveal congressional disapproval of improper diversion of campaign money. When the activity in question has more to do with constituency service, congressmen approve it more. This pattern appeared often in this study and indicates distinctions that should be considered in reform proposals. . . .

In the interviews, we asked questions about the extent to which congressmen would accept special favors from lobbyists. Specific questions referred to lobbyists paying the entertainment costs of legislators or lending them planes for personal travel or campaign purposes. Other questions dealt with the leasing or selling of automobiles to legislators at substantial discounts and the provision of free hotel rooms in the legislators' districts.

Overall, the congressmen saw very little wrong in most of these practices. Many reported that lobbyists had never paid for entertainment for groups of constituents or for political gatherings; others mentioned that it happened once in a while or that they had been to parties that were probably paid for by private interests. Those who recognize the practice were not particularly upset by it, believing it to be a legitimate campaign-associated activity.

The practice of using private planes for personal travel or campaigning also raised few eyebrows. Slightly less than half of the sample admitted to using planes that had been put at their disposal, although the majority stated that they did so occasionally rather than frequently. More than 10 percent of the sample, however, said that they used such planes often. Only a small number of congressmen said such activity was wrong. A western Republican said he was "wary of the practice," and a midwestern Republican said he considered it "questionable," but many others who did not report using private planes said this practice was inconvenient or unnecessary. (One southern legislator reported simply, "I don't go home.")

A midwestern Republican gave a typical response to a question about using airplanes belonging to others: "I think these planes come in handy. Nobody ever tried to collect from me because they hauled me around to a speech. Firms in my area do it for the Democratic senator and the national committeeman as well as myself." Another Republican from a border state agreed. "I don't think there is any real problem on this. I don't think anybody really expects anything. You are just one person on a committee, and unless you are the chairman I don't see how you can be too much help to them."

Most congressmen in the sample looked upon the provision of planes as a convenience that they would be foolish to ignore and as the sort of activity that does not create difficult bonds or debts. One eastern Republican who did not engage in the practice said, "I really can't think why I haven't done it, since I would do anything for the company anyhow because they're in my constituency." He added, however, "I guess it would look bad if I did take a ride on the plane." A large proportion of his colleagues did not agree. Much more common were comments such as this one from a western Democrat: "I was offered a trip on a DC-6, but it would take a week across the country in a DC-6. Both [major air frame companies] that have plants in my district made the offer. I turned it down for inconvenience. I don't think it's any problem."

Scarcely any congressmen thought it was wrong to accept free hotel rooms in their districts. Many reported that they enjoyed such benefits and considered it perfectly legitimate behavior. Many others said they did not receive such treatment and wished they did. A number of congressmen mentioned that it was possible to offend a constituent by refusing the offer of a hotel room or a complimentary dinner in a restaurant.

Many members thought that it was improper to accept discounts on car leases. One reported that he used to get the free use of a car from one of the major auto companies but that he "Certainly cut it out once the Dodd case happened." Even though they disapproved, members knew of such arrangements, indicating that the practice was not completely rejected. In several cases the main complaint was that the discounts were a privilege reserved only for committee chairmen. "I told a friend of mine in Congress who has such an arrangement to send the person around, but he never came by. I'd certainly like to take advantage of it," one legislator said.

We asked the congressmen if they participated in inaugural airline trips. (An inaugural trip takes place when an airline opens service to a new location. The airline invites dignitaries on the initial flight. This can constitute a free vacation.) Very few saw anything wrong with accepting the trip. On the contrary, most members believed that travel helped them in their work by contributing to their understanding of world conditions. No one was offended by the junketing aspect of the trips, although several admitted to that dimension. A typical comment was:

> I don't think it's a problem. I found it very helpful. I went to India on a TWA flight. I had never been there. We spent ten days there and I learned much more about India than I had ever known before. TWA has never asked me for a thing, and I have a better understanding of the country.

Others stated that they had not taken trips, but in the words of one: "It's been a matter of time, not ethics. I think it would be a good thing." Another noted: "I've never been invited on any and I regret it. It's all very disillusioning never to have been asked."

In a general discussion of government-paid travel by congressmen that grew out of the inaugural flight questions, most respondents said that much work did get done on the trips and that the diligent members on study/work trips well outnumbered those along for pleasure. Work and relaxation may enjoy a peaceful coexistence, however, as one comment demonstrates:

> I can remember when I was on the Agriculture Committee, and the committee was going to Europe to investigate Public Law 480, and I found out they were taking two of the best-looking secretaries along who weren't necessarily the most competent. I protested to the chairman and told him that either they stayed home or I did. The result was that I stayed home.

Despite such reports, most of the congressmen resented the "junketing" label given to congressional travel and the skeptical attitude taken by many journalists. They felt that press stories often create unfair public bias against travel that damages hard-working members who seriously need to learn the effects of American policies abroad or to witness firsthand the practices and conditions in other nations. Former Speaker Sam Rayburn's boast that he had never been outside the United States was often cited by the congressmen as indicative of an unfortunate parochialism, not far removed from xenophobia. . . .

A common although initially surprising finding was that lobbyists paid little or no attention to many members. "As I said, I have never had a lobbyist take me to lunch and I'm frankly amazed, because it is different in my state legislature," was a common refrain. Those members who had served in state legislatures before being elected to Congress believed that standards of conduct were much lower in the state capitals than in Washington.

The apparently higher standard at the national level is not simply due to the fact that the greater responsibility or the year-round term of a national legislature brings out the best in its members or to the fact that there is much more probing and sophisticated journalistic coverage of Washington politics. One reason for the higher level of conduct may be that the average member of Congress is ordinarily not worth as much to a lobbyist as the average member of a state legislature is. The House is a large and in many ways unwieldy body. The division of labor into committees and subcommittees that takes place in all legislatures is much greater in the 435-member House of Representatives than in, say, the 100-member Senate. House members usually serve on only one major committee, but in the U.S. Senate and in many state legislatures it is normal to serve on two, three, or even more committees. As a consequence, House members feel more remote from much of the legislation and from even the daily operations of Congress. . . .

The Other Potential Conflicts

With respect to the third possible conflict under consideration—public officials giving assistance to private parties dealing with the government— the dilemma caused by the demands of the legislator's role is immediately apparent. Constituents expect most congressmen to offer assistance in dealing with a huge and seemingly unresponsive government, and legis- lators view such service as vital to reelection.

The fourth possible conflict can occur when former public officials give assistance to private parties dealing with the government. Again the situations of congressmen and executive branch personnel are different. The latter presumably could offer special access to government delibera- tions only in the field (and indeed perhaps only in the bureau) in which they had been previously employed. Thus to legislate a required period during which they could not deal with the bureau that had formerly employed them would be neither difficult nor excessively discriminatory. Congress, however, is not a bureau. A comparable prohibition would debar former members from lobbying Congress itself. Yet to prohibit retired or defeated members from such practice might be discriminatory. Moreover, the potential for the misuse of an executive official's knowledge of contemplated administrative actions has few parallels on the legislative side.

In any case, members are unlikely to vote such a restriction. Some of them look upon the possibility of service as a Washington representative as a form of insurance. The legislative process is what they know best. To preclude congressmen from this field would be unfair in their view.

In a related area, members of Congress were asked about the extent and effectiveness of former legislators serving as lobbyists, particularly because of their access to the House floor. The general response was that, with certain exceptions, ex-legislator lobbyists did not abuse their privileges. Several members noted that the floor is not a good place to lobby because members often leave the floor quickly when they are not needed so that they can attend to other responsibilities. . . .

Only in the last of the five suggested conflicts of interest—deriving private gain from the use of information acquired in an official capacity—is the situation of a congressman similar to that of a nonelected official. Clearly congressmen should refrain from using inside information. It is as improper for them to use information gained from executive sessions of a committee as it is for a member of a regulatory commission to do so. Because congressmen deal with many issues, however, they might consider themselves a special case and believe that they should not be prohibited from using inside information. But the organization of Congress, with its division of labor through the committee system, generally limits a congressman's access to useful inside information to those activities that come under the jurisdiction of his committee. Requesting a congressman to refrain from dealing in those specific matters would not constitute the same penalty as a more generalized prohibition. This might also prove a satisfactory way of limiting lobbying by ex-congressmen.

When we questioned congressmen about using information obtained in executive sessions of a committee for private gain, few of them cited evidence of members benefiting from such information. The responses were quite uniform: "There isn't much opportunity really—if you read the *Washington Post* you know as much as we do," or "You'd have to really hustle out of the committee room to have it work," or "There are a lot easier ways of getting rich around here if you really want to cheat." Congressmen generally suggest that rewards from committee assignments, if there are any, come in other forms. As one said, "I think you get a lot more of this in terms of campaign contributions.". . .

The range of possible congressional conflicts of interest is considerable. At one extreme are the unavoidable conflicts. As one member observed:

> *Obviously, I have conflicts of interest in terms of Medicare, since I have a mother who is very old. I have a conflict of interest on education legislation since I have a little boy six months old. I have a conflict of interest on social security, since my mother is on it, and I'll eventually be on it.*

Most Americans recognize the inevitability of such conflicts and do not expect congressmen to disqualify themselves from votes on these issues. In a representative system conflicts of this kind are bound to appear since the legislators are selected from the population they represent. But the other extreme, of course, is outright bribery.

Once outside the boundaries of bribery and overt self-dealing, there is very little consensus, at least among our respondents, about what constitutes a legitimate or an illegitimate business or political transaction. . . .

NOTES

1. Roswell Perkins, "The New Federal Conflict of Interest Law," *Harvard Law Review*, vol. 26 (April 1963), pp. 1118-19.
2. Cited in Laurence Stern and Edwin Knoll, "Congress: When the Private Life of a Lawmaker Becomes a Public Affair," *Esquire*, April 1964, pp. 82-84.
3. James W. Lindeen and Shirley A. Lindeen, "Conflict of Interest in the U.S. House of Representatives: Some Preliminary Findings" (paper delivered at the Annual Meeting of the Midwest Political Science Association in Chicago, May 1973).
4. George Stigler, "The Economics of Conflict of Interest," *The Journal of Political Economy*, vol. 75 (February 1967), pp. 100-101.
5. Article 1, Section 6 of the Constitution protects legislators against being "questioned in any other place" for legislative acts. This is commonly referred to as the "speech or debate" clause.

CHAPTER ELEVEN

THE PRESIDENCY

PRESIDENTIAL POWER

In the first of the two selections that follow, Mark Roelofs notes that several scholars of the presidency have attributed rather extraordinary powers to this office. Some of these scholars take great comfort in this fact, while others view such power with alarm. Roelofs, however, contends that both points of view are in error as he proceeds to argue that presidential power is more a myth than a reality.

The second selection is written by journalist George Reedy, who served for a time as Lyndon Johnson's press secretary. He maintains that the function of the presidency has evolved into something considerably more than the rather narrowly confined managerial role that the Founding Fathers intended. The net result of this evolution, according to Reedy, is that the president now dominates the federal establishment.

The Myth of Presidential Power

H. Mark Roelofs

. . . [I]t is fashionable in some circles to say that in the post-Watergate era we must demythologize the presidency. The American people must learn to reduce their reliance on the White House. But it is not fashionable in any circles to take that charge with full, analytic seriousness, to go beyond "cutting the office down to life-size," to insist in fact that the American presidency's actual powers are and have been from the beginning radically incongruous with the hopes even moderates place in the office or that critics fear in it. Moreover, it can be argued that the talk of Washington, Lincoln, Wilson, and Roosevelt and the monuments and sculptures in mountains are not so much measures of heroic achievement as enduring expressions of the nation's underlying anxiety, of a will to believe myth in the face of the facts.

As mythic heroes, the "great" presidents have welded the nation into the unity of its dreams. That is a political function of considerable significance, sometimes admirable, sometimes dangerous. But operationally, in terms of practical achievement, even the greatest of the great presidents were continually hamstrung by the structural logic of the political system they sought to dominate. In their times of desperation and crisis, and through their soaring words and acts, myth mightily challenged ideology, but myth inevitably lost. This is not the fault of the great presidents or of their advisors. Even under the most inspired leadership, myth in America cannot command and organize resources for the victory it craves. Consequently the great presidents were, without exception, tragic figures. They were dragged back from the fulfillment of their inspirations not by personal failure but by the tides of history, by patterns of events they had no hand in creating.

To make these points in analytic detail, we should begin by confronting and defining the myth of presidential power, the notion that the presidential office is a grand place filled best by great men, saviors of the people. This myth in the American political mind gives rise to all the symbolism, rhetoric, and legend crowded around the nation's memory of the great presidents. In the works of certain scholars, this broad, vague evidence takes on surprising precision.

These scholars divide into critics of presidential power and admirers of it. Both groups are prominently represented in the corpus of scholarship on the presidential office that has developed since Edward S. Corwin published *The President: Office and Powers* in 1940. This book has been enormously influential. Through innumerable reprintings and a number of revisions, it virtually defined the field of contemporary presidential studies. Corwin was a critic, and his book carried on its title page a statement by Secretary of State Seward.

We elect a king for four years, and give him absolute power within certain limits, which after all he can interpret for himself. [1]

Corwin argued that over the years the presidency had accumulated enormous powers, and as the long administration of Franklin Roosevelt came to an end, he became greatly concerned about the degree to which Roosevelt had enveloped the office with his personality and a perpetual sense of crisis. Corwin feared that the enhanced powers of the national government generally and of the presidency in particular gravely exposed personal and private rights and violated the constitutional separation of powers.

Corwin's charge that Roosevelt had "dangerously personalized"[2] presidential power is mild compared to the swelling fury of some contemporary scholars toward particular uses of it of which they disapprove. For example, when American war planes were bombing Hanoi in December of 1972 at President Richard Nixon's command, Arthur Schlesinger, Jr., published an article which began by quoting an old letter on presidential powers by Abraham Lincoln: " . . . see if you can fix *any limit* to his power. . . ." and then went on to declare, in his own words, that Mr. Nixon, by greatly extending a long-term trend among activist presidents, had

. . . by 1973 made the American President on issues of war and peace the most absolute monarch (with the possible exception of Mao Tse-tung of China) among the great powers of the world. [3]

Lest it be thought that this is a scholar losing his objectivity to partisan heat, it may be noted that the same crisis prompted David Apter and Robert Dahl, two of the most respected names in American political science at the time, to comment in a jointly signed public letter that President Nixon's ordering out the bombers,

> . . . *reveals more starkly than ever before the complete breakdown of the American constitutional system in the domain of foreign policies involving the employment of military forces.*
>
> *In this domain the arbitrary power of the President has over three decades swelled to a magnitude flatly inconsistent with both the intentions of the Founders and the requirements of a democratic political order.* [4]

These frightened comments should be compared to positive appreciations of supposed presidential powers of vast magnitude. The major expression of this view remains the work of Clinton Rossiter. Rossiter wrote his doctoral dissertation on presidential government under Corwin's direction and gave it the title *Constitutional Dictatorship*. Later, in his most important book, *The American Presidency*, he more glorified than questioned the office and set out to present

> . . . *the American Presidency as what I honestly believe it to be: one of the few truly successful institutions created by men in their endless quest for the blessings of free government.* [5]

More analytically, the first chapter of this book is a serial explanation of presidential powers listed under these headings:

Chief of State	Voice of the People
Chief Executive	Protector of the Peace
Commander in Chief	Manager of Prosperity
Chief Diplomat	World Leader (or, less
Chief Legislator	grandly, President of
Chief of the Party	the West)

Although the heading of the chapter refers to these titles as "powers," the text often refers to them as "roles" or "functions" of the presidential office, implying that actual presidents have been able to summon up the powers and other wherewithall to carry them out more or less sufficiently. This implication is strengthened by Rossiter's repeated insistence that the president is not each of these roles separately but all of them in sum, bringing to the execution of each the aura of his possession of all the rest.

No other writer, past or present, has matched the expansive terms Rossiter used to describe the capacities of the presidential office for greatness. But it is not belaboring of the point to stress his rhetoric. His approach to the office through an analysis of its supposed roles has become common in the academic literature and is clearly the dominant approach in the textbook field. Moreover Rossiter's language in *The American Presidency* and his feelings about the presidency accurately project nationally held beliefs and sentiments about the office. [6]

Significant variations from Rossiter's central theme appear among those scholars who have found, regretfully, that in actual practice the presidency does not quite come up to his expectations. Under the Madisonian Constitution, actual presidents simply cannot carry out with any semblance of success all those roles Rossiter assigned them. A vivid anecdote in Richard Neustadt's study, *Presidential Power*, illustrates the disillusionment that attends realization of this fact.

> *In the early summer of 1952, before the heat of the campaign, President Truman used to contemplate the problems of the General-become-President should Eisenhower win the forthcoming election. "He'll sit here," Truman would remark (tapping his desk for emphasis), "and he'll say, 'Do this! Do that!'* And nothing will happen. *Poor Ike—it won't be a bit like the Army. He'll find it very frustrating."*[7] . . .

It remains to show that the myth of presidential greatness is both false and inoperative. The myth is false primarily because it presupposes the presidency capable of generating a kind of political power it does not and could not possess and, beyond that, a kind of political power alien to the operative American political system generally. Talk of a national government led by the president to the achievement of national priorities, talk of the president as tribune of the people, talk of the president taking the nation, by a new deal or across a new frontier to a rendezvous with destiny and the great society, is talk envisioning a political figure of the dimensions of Napoleon, Lenin, or Castro. It is not unreasonable to suppose such figures seeking to mass, organize, release, and totally control the energies of an entire society in the systematic pursuit of major community objectives. Such figures might bind up a nation's divisions, reconcile its failures, and lead it forward into patterns of broad social renewal. Or they might fail at such tasks. But it would not be absurd to think of them trying to do such things. It is absurd to talk except rhetorically of actual American presidents attempting this kind of work.

Operationally, the American president is a baron; he is bigger, more visible, and certainly louder than most, but in terms of broad social power, he is no stronger than any because he is as individualized as any. The constitutional basis for presidential power is narrow indeed; it does little more than make him a participant *ex officio* in the political process along with other designated elements of the government. Most of the president's actual and supposed powers are political in origin, that is, they devolve upon him from precedent, statute, and above all, daily practice. Hence presidential powers, contrary to the myth and even when swollen by mythic misrepresentation, are no more than what that daily practice can generate. That means that the president's powers, like those of barons generally, are mostly personal, episodic, and negative.

The president has very considerable personal power. It comes to him immediately because of the highly personalized character of presidential elections, and the White House is a fine vantage point from which to exercise it. With a far broader reach than any other baron, the president can get himself involved in an extraordinary number and variety of political activities. There are few areas of public life immune to presidential intervention. But these interventions are invariably of a personal sort. Given the dispersed character of the political system generally, no president can build up and extend his authority into objective patterns of sustained control. In consequence, it is seriously misleading to suggest that he is "chief" of anything, except for the purely ceremonial role of "Chief of State." He is a principal figure in the legislative process, but he is certainly not in charge of it and rarely sets its general pace. He is the most prominent member of his party, but often enough, especially when running for re-election, he has to be reminded of its existence. As for the federal bureaucracy, the first thing to be remembered is that it does not constitute some massive monolith which could support a chief at its pinnacle. It is a vast, dispersed melange, and the president is best pictured as scrambling somewhere in the middle to control this or that aspect of it.

This is obvious commentary but it may seem to fail to support the general argument in two prime areas. First, it may seem that the president is truly by constitutional warrant, "Commander in Chief" of the nation's military might. This point, however, is easily refuted. The president can order out the bombers. Nixon did so against the judgment of most of his advisors, although there were other occasions when the bombers went without being ordered. But giving commands of this sort is a long way from "running the Pentagon." Pentagon politics is a book in itself, not always a pretty one, and many of its pages are notable for the total absence of the president or his influence.

Second, it is often asserted that the firmest base of the president's general prestige is his virtually exclusive authority in foreign affairs. But this observation more underlines the personal character of presidential power than the opposite. On the world stage the president can walk with an extraordinary individual eminence, to his great personal political benefit. But that is a very different thing from managing, in an ongoing comprehensive pattern, the nation's foreign relations. To the contrary, the persistent presence in presidential entourages of special advisors and envoys of the order of Colonel House, Harry Hopkins, and Henry Kissinger, are testimony to the difficulties presidents have had in this area.

Largely because of the personal nature of presidential power, his use of it is bound to be episodic. He can veto a bill here, browbeat a congressman there, fight a senatorial committee chairman, in a dramatic confrontation, to a standstill, or bully some segment of the bureaucracy into doing his will on a particular issue. Above all, or at least most noticeably, he can from time to time, in a clarion call to his public at large, chart a new course for the nation. The initiation of debates on national issues is perhaps the president's outstanding power. But to plan, program, and systematically allocate resources in a sustained pattern of national

4. Letter to the Editor, *The New York Times,* January 4, 1973, p. 36.
5. Second rev. ed., Mentor, New York, 1962, p. 13.
6. "The President, in short, is the one-man distillation of the American people. . . ." (p. 16) "The final greatness of the Presidency lies in the truth that it is not just an office of incredible power but a breeding ground of indestructible myth." (p. 103) "It is a priceless symbol of our continuity and destiny as a people. Few nations have solved so simply and yet so grandly the problem of finding and maintaining an office of state that embodies their majesty and reflects their character." (p. 250).
7. *Op. cit.,* p. 9.
8. Quoted by Rossiter, *op. cit.,* p. 81.
9. "There is a Presidency in our future . . ." Rossiter, p. 229.

The Presidential Advantage

George E. Reedy

. . . The theory of democracy is that power shall reside in the people and that they shall have an opportunity to register their desires at periodic intervals. But since the mood of the people is subject to repeated and unforeseen changes, the great problem has always been to combine the necessary continuing authority to rule with the necessary checks to prevent that rule from becoming despotic. The contribution of the men who wrote the American Constitution was the thesis that power could be divided and lodged in different institutions—the executive, the legislative, the judiciary—in such a way that no one of these institutions could ever gain a monopoly. The success of this thesis has been little short of amazing in that the United States has remained a reasonably democratic nation since 1789. But it is equally interesting that, in the process of history, the American government has undergone changes which have taken it far from the concepts set forth by the men of Philadelphia. The most interesting change has been in the power and the authority of the president.

The men who wrote the Constitution very obviously ascribed to the president a lesser role than the legislative in the field of policy. It was clear that he would manage the affairs of the government, both military and civil, and that he would represent the United States in its dealings with other nations. But his management was assumed to be within limits laid down by legislation; and in dealing with other nations what he represented was supposed to be determined by Congress. There was little realization that his role as an activist would place the president in an advantageous position from which his domination of the Federal establishment became an inevitability.

In our managerial-oriented society, where administrative techniques have been raised to the status of an intellectual discipline in leading universities, we are all conscious of the direct relationship between the capacity to launch action and the control over the instruments and resources which make the action possible. To us it is self-evident that the chief executive officer, who administers payrolls, the collection and disbursement of funds, and the activities of production and sales, will determine the policies of a corporation until he is replaced by a successor. He can be harassed by stockholders, his life can be made difficult by an unfriendly board of directors. But even though the stockholders, and their representatives on the board of directors, can cause a shift in policy by firing their chief executive officer and bringing in a replacement, it is still *the new man* who will make corporate policy. Presumably, he will take into account the forces that placed him in office. But the extent to which he *must* do so is determined only by his political skill. And he is in a position almost daily to make commitments for the corporation of such a nature that the stockholders and directors have little alternative other than to acquiesce. They can, of course, get rid of him but this is a step that is usually taken only when provocation is extreme. Once he has his basic budget approved, he has the power of initiative—the power to initiate lawsuits, specific expenditures, sales campaigns, and new production models, and all these steps have self-perpetuating forces built into them. It is entirely possible for any corporate manager to lead his firm in a direction diametrically opposite from that intended by his stockholders without abusing any of his authority or usurping any undue prerogatives. He can do it merely by day-to-day decisions which *must* be made by someone and which *cannot* be made by a committee.

This concept was not very clear to the founding fathers. They thought of usurpation of power only in terms of bad law, ignored law, or violated law. They felt that the capacity of human reasoning to determine or alter human destiny was limited only by the quality of the intellects that could be brought to bear, by the physical environment, and by the relative balance of coercive powers in a society. As sophisticated men, they had little faith in human wisdom but thought it was perfectible through discussion. They accepted the physical environment philosophically as having both advantages and disadvantages (difficult trade routes from Europe to the New World were also difficult invasion routes). And they sought to create a balance of coercive powers which would cancel each other out. Their reaction was both rational and adequate to the times. No one then could have foreseen the rise of our interdependent society with its almost minute division of labor creating social forces that have a life of their own.

They made the president commander-in-chief of the armed forces. But they counterbalanced his power by lodging in the Congress the authority to raise and support those forces and by guaranteeing the people the inviolable right to bear arms.

They made the president the sole spokesman in the field of foreign affairs. But they counterbalanced this power by lodging in the Senate the sole right to pass upon the validity of treaties.

They made the president responsible for staffing the executive agencies which would administer the nation's business. But they counterbalanced this power by lodging in the Senate the right to approve or disapprove his key appointees and in the House of Representatives the right to initiate appropriation of the funds needed to run the government.

They made the president (of course, acting through an agent) the prosecutor of offenses against the government. But they specified that adjudication of the charges would be handled through an independent judiciary.

When to all this was added the power of impeachment (carefully structured so it could not be managed in a frivolous fashion), it would appear that the founding fathers had performed a superb job of employing reason to devise safeguards for freedom. What they had not reckoned with was the ability of the "manager" to make commitments which could not easily be revoked.

The clearest example in our history was presented by Theodore Roosevelt, who in 1907 wanted to send America's navy around the world on a "goodwill" tour. The proposal engendered a considerable amount of heat. Roosevelt's propensity for extravagant and somewhat overly masculine language had aroused fears as to his intentions. It was felt that he was uncomfortably enamored of foreign adventures and might be preparing to annex foreign territory in accordance with the traditions already established by the great imperialistic powers of Western Europe. The debate raged in Congress. Roosevelt could not send the navy (then known as the "Great White Fleet") completely around the world because he did not have the necessary money. Unfortunately for the opposition, the president did have enough funds to send the navy halfway around the world. He did so. Congress suddenly, and without warning, found itself confronted not with the choice of sending or not sending the navy but with the choice of leaving it somewhere in Asia or bringing it home. There were loud cries of "arrogance" and "bully-boy tactics." But they were futile cries and the opposition knew it. Congress dutifully voted the necessary funds and the Great White Fleet completed its round-the-world tour. The influence of this trip on America's position in world affairs may have been questionable, but its influence on Roosevelt's position domestically was clear. He was a hero simply because he had been able to act decisively, and it is a good general rule that people prefer decisive leaders. The most that Congress could do was to grumble—and grumbling has yet to win a single election.

Theodore Roosevelt, of course, was not the first president to use the power of the initiative to extend the scope of the office far beyond anything that was conceivable by the founding fathers. From the very beginning of the republic, presidents have found that it is a relatively simple matter to place Congress in a position where it has no alternative other than to back the president. This was the case in the punitive expeditions against the Barbary pirates; in the Louisiana Purchase; in the Indian wars in southern Georgia and Florida; and, more recently, in the landing of troops in the Dominican Republic and the escalation of the undeclared war in Vietnam. The president has the capacity to order troops into any area of the world, and as long as the troops are loyal, the orders will be obeyed. And once Americans are placed in a position of difficulty or peril by such orders, Congress has no alternative other than to bail them out. . . .

The president's power of initiative, of course, is subject to certain checks. But in the field of foreign affairs and defense, these checks are almost entirely in the nature of a review. Theoretically, Congress can always hamper his activities by refusing to grant the necessary appropriations to pay for the acts taken by the executive. It is inconceivable though that Congress would refuse appropriations to support men who are fighting in the name of their country's freedom. It is also inconceivable that Congress would withhold appropriations that are essential to sustain the nation's prestige. And it is even more inconceivable that Congress would fail to approve a president's action against an avowed enemy.

The war in Vietnam . . . rested for years on the Gulf of Tonkin resolution, which gave carte blanche to President Johnson to take virtually unprecedented steps in Southeast Asia. Some senators have since stated that had they known what was to follow, they would not have voted for it. This, of course, is not only hindsight but nonsense. The resolution was passed following an effort to torpedo an American naval vessel in the Gulf of Tonkin and after strong U.S. air retaliation against North Vietnamese torpedo boats in Haiphong. It is unthinkable that very many members of Congress would have been willing under such circumstances to tell the world that the United States would not support its leader in a moment of national peril (actually, only two senators took that course).

In domestic affairs, however, the president's power of initiative is far less effective. This is simply because there are very few domestic crises which require an immediate affirmation of national unity. In the domestic field, Congress is willing to repudiate a president because this is something that rests within the family. It does not assume that catastrophe will follow clear evidence of division. Even here, presidents have developed techniques which give them an iniative over the legislative branch of the government. These include preparation of the budget, at which Congress can only nitpick; the establishment of revolving funds, which go a long way toward negating the appropriation authority; and the use of executive orders which have limited force of law but which can completely bypass Congress.

A most dramatic example of the latter was the executive order by which President Kennedy set up an Equal Employment Opportunity Commission that had far more drastic authority to enforce nondiscrimination than could possibly have been accorded to a legally established Fair Employment Practices Commission. This was done by the simple device of permitting the commission to cancel any government contracts if the contractor was held guilty of bigotry in his hiring practices. Congress has no adequate countermeasures to such an act. It can only react, and while the reaction can be violent, that is not equivalent to having the edge that comes with the initiative.

Almost, but not quite, as important as the power of the initiative is the ability of the chief executive to place his views before the public. This is one arena in which he has no equal from the standpoint of opportunity. When he has a point of view, that point of view can be communicated instantly to the American people, and it has behind it all the power of the nation speaking through the voice of one individual. Furthermore, the president has the capability of shaping his words as he wants them without the necessity of sifting them through a "committee" process, which hampers any similar expression of views on the part of the Congress or the courts.

The president's ability to place his views before the public is important primarily because he can usually set the terms of the national debate—and anyone who can set the terms of a debate can win it. An outstanding example was the manner in which Harry S. Truman converted certain defeat into unexpected victory in 1948.

At the beginning of the year, no one conceded Mr. Truman any chance for re-election. He had been plagued by deep divisions within the Democratic party and by the strains placed upon the economy by the postwar readjustment. In 1946 the voters had signaled their disapproval by the election of the first Republican Congress in fourteen years, and there was no reason to believe that they were dissatisfied with their decision. The situation was so serious that leading Democrats debated the almost unheard-of possibility of denying renomination to Mr. Truman. Important leaders of the party had even proposed that General Eisenhower be asked to be the Democratic standard bearer (at that time no one had any idea of General Eisenhower's politics). The Democratic convention in Philadelphia was dispirited and lackluster, with the only heartening note a remarkable speech by Senator Alben W. Barkley, of Kentucky—a speech which secured for him the vice-presidential nomination. There was, of course, no real alternative to Mr. Truman's renomination and the delegates went along reluctantly.

But Mr. Truman was a fighter. He startled the convention and the country by declaring immediate war on the "do-nothing, good-for-nothing, Republican-controlled, Eightieth Congress." He whistle-stopped the nation, lambasting the Republican Congress at every crossroads and every train station. The issue became the Congress itself, and the Republican candidate, who considered his victory a foregone conclusion, made the mistake of not rallying to its defense. The outcome was Mr. Truman's election, a result so unexpected that one American newspaper found itself on the stands with a banner headline ("Dewey Wins Election") which had been set in advance and released before the results were in. Mr. Truman had taken advantage of an important power of the presidency and had proved its effectiveness. . . .

The third source of presidential power is basically the ability to place others in a position of authority or prestige. This is something more than the power of appointment. A lawyer who is known to dine privately with the president (for example, Clark Clifford before he became secretary of defense) is raised to a position of eminence in the legal profession. An author who is known to be favored by the president or his family (for example, Truman Capote) finds that his readership increases overnight. A businessman who is seen at the president's elbow on more than one occasion (for example, banker Arthur Krim) finds his place in the business community enhanced. And all three are quite likely to use their newfound prestige to promote the cause of the president. By careful manipulation of such favors, a president can establish a network of Americans from coast to coast ready and anxious at any hour of the day or night to explain his cause, form supporting committees, or raise the money without which politics would be impossible. It may well be that an early sign in the decline of presidential power is the decline in the caliber of the people immediately around him.

All these powers added together are truly formidable. It is unlikely that any president could be defeated for re-election if he exercised them wisely. Franklin D. Roosevelt secured four terms in office, and it is not adequate to explain his dominance solely on the fact that he was a war-time president. Basically, he was a man who maintained his grip on reality and knew how to recover quickly from such mistakes as the Supreme Court packing bill. A president who suffers a defeat or a loss does so because he has made the wrong decisions and has not acted to recover from his errors.

The trend is clear. Over the passage of the years, what was little more than managerial authority has become power over the life of the nation itself. The right to check this power still rests in Congress and the courts. But the ability to check assumes the capacity to offer alternatives, to explain them to the public, and to manage a structure that carries them out. In the modern age, when action with little time for reflection becomes increasingly urgent, these capabilities are lessened with each passing day for every arm of the government except the presidency.

THE PRESIDENT AND THE PRESS

Throughout our history, there has always existed an element of tension in the relationship between the president and the press. Indeed, it could hardly be otherwise, for presidents understandably seek to present their administrations in the most favorable light possible. Such efforts, however, are viewed by the press as attempts to manage the news. On the other hand, the press feels it has the responsibility to report the negative as well as the positive aspects of an administration and, not surprisingly, presidents perceive the press as doing a good deal more of the former than the latter.

Although the relationship between the president and the press has traditionally been an adversary one, Daniel Patrick Moynihan suggests that the tension between the two has become unusually severe in recent years. He attributes this development to certain trends in the composition and reporting habits of the national press. Should these trends persist, Moynihan fears that presidents will be significantly handicapped in their ability to lead the nation.

Moynihan's observations appeared as an article in Commentary *magazine. Among the many journalists who read them was Max Frankel, then Chief Correspondent for the* New York Times. *Sufficiently disturbed by what he had read, Frankel decided to respond to Moynihan in the form of a letter to the editor of* Commentary. *In this letter, a portion of which appears as the second selection in this section, Frankel attempts a point-by-point refutation of Moynihan's arguments.*

The Presidency and the Press

Daniel P. Moynihan

As his years in Washington came to an end, Harry S. Truman wrote a friend:

> *I really look with commiseration over the great body of my fellow citizens, who, reading newspapers, live and die in the belief that they have known something of what has been passing in the world in their time.*

A familiar Presidential plaint, sounded often in the early years of the Republic and rarely unheard thereafter. Of late, however, a change has developed in the perception of what is at issue. In the past what was thought to be involved was the reputation of a particular President. In the present what is seen to be at stake, and by the Presidents themselves, is the reputation of government—especially, of course, Presidential government. These are different matters, and summon a different order of concern.

There are two points anyone would wish to make at the outset of an effort to explore this problem. First, it is to be acknowledged that in most essential encounters between the Presidency and the press, the advantage is with the former. The President has a near limitless capacity to "make" news which must be reported, if only by reason of competition between one journal, or one medium, and another. (If anything, radio and television news is more readily subject to such dominance. Their format permits of many fewer "stories." The President-in-action almost always takes precedence.) The President also has considerable capacity to reward friends and punish enemies in the press corps, whether they be individual journalists or the papers, television networks, news weeklies, or whatever these individuals work for. And for quite a long while, finally, a President who wishes can carry off formidable deceptions. (One need only recall the barefaced lying that went with the formal opinion of Roosevelt's Attorney General that the destroyer-naval-base deal of 1940 was legal.)

With more than sufficient reason, then, publishers and reporters alike have sustained over the generations a lively sense of their vulnerability to governmental coercion or control. For the most part, their worries have been exaggerated. But, like certain virtues, there are some worries that are best carried to excess.

The second point is that American journalism is almost certainly the best in the world. . . . What in most other countries is known as the "provincial" press—that is to say journals published elsewhere than in the capital—in America is made up of a wealth of comprehensive and dependable daily newspapers of unusually high quality.

The journalists are in some ways more important than their journals—at least to anyone who has lived much in government. A relationship grows up with the reporters covering one's particular sector that has no counterpart in other professions or activities. The relationship is one of simultaneous trust and distrust, friendship and enmity, dependence and independence. But it is the men of government, especially in Washington, who are the more dependent. The journalists are their benefactors, their conscience, at times almost their reason for being. For the journalists are above all others their audience, again especially in Washington, which has neither an intellectual community nor an electorate, and where there is no force outside government able to judge events, much less to help shape them, save the press.

That there is something wondrous and terrible in the intensities of this relationship between the press and the government is perhaps best seen at the annual theatricals put on by such groups of journalists as the Legislative Correspondents Association in Albany or the Gridiron in Washington. To my knowledge nothing comparable takes place anywhere else in the world. These gatherings are a kind of ritual truth telling, of which the closest psychological approximation would be the Calabrian insult ritual described by Roger Vailland in his novel *The Law*, or possibly the group-therapy practices of more recent origin. The politicians come as guests of the journalists. The occasion is first of all a feast: the best of everything. Then as dinner progresses the songs begin. The quality varies, of course, but at moments startling levels of deadly accurate commentary of great cruelty are achieved. The politicians sit and smile and applaud. Then some of them speak. Each one wins or loses to the degree that he can respond in kind; stay funny and be brutal. (At the Gridiron John F. Kennedy was a master of the style, but the piano duet performed by Nixon and Agnew in 1970 was thought by many to have surpassed anything yet done.) A few lyrics appear in the next day's papers, but what the newspapermen really said to the politicians remains privileged—as does so much of what the politicians say to them. The relationship is special.

How is it then that this relationship has lately grown so troubled? The immediate answer is, of course, the war in Vietnam. An undeclared war, unwanted, misunderstood, or not understood at all, it entailed a massive deception of the American people by their government. . . .

But there are problems between the Presidency and the press which have little to do with the cold war or with Vietnam and which—if this analysis is correct—will persist or even intensify should those conditions recede, or even dissolve, as a prime source of public concern. The problems flow from five basic circumstances which together have been working to reverse the old balance of power between the Presidency and the press. It is the thesis here that if this balance should tip too far in the direction of the press, our capacity for effective democratic government will be seriously and dangerously weakened.

I

The first of these circumstances has to do with the tradition of "muckraking"—the exposure of corruption in government or the collusion of government with private interests—which the American press has seen as a primary mission since the period 1880-1914. It is, in Irving Kristol's words, "a journalistic phenomenon that is indigenous to democracy, with its instinctive suspicion and distrust of all authority in general, and of concentrated political and economic power especially." Few would want to be without the tradition, and it is a young journalist of poor spirit who does not set out to uncover the machinations of some malefactor of great wealth and his political collaborators. Yet there is a cost, as Roger Starr suggests in his wistful wish that Lincoln Steffens's *The Shame of the Cities* might be placed on the restricted shelves of the schools of journalism. Steffens has indeed, as Starr declares, continued "to haunt the city rooms of the country's major newspapers." The question to be asked is whether, in the aftermath of Steffens, the cities were better, or merely more ashamed of themselves. Looking back, one is impressed by the energy and capacity for governance of some of the old city machines. Whatever else, it was popular government, of and by men of the people. One wonders: did the middle- and upper-class reformers destroy the capacity of working-class urban government without replacing it with anything better so that half-a-century later each and all bewail the cities as ungovernable? One next wonders whether something not dissimilar will occur now that the focus of press attention has shifted from City Hall to the White House. (And yet a miracle of American national government is the almost complete absence of monetary corruption at all levels, and most especially at the top.)

The muckraking tradition is well established. Newer, and likely to have far more serious consequences, is the advent of what Lionel Trilling has called the "adversary culture" as a conspicuous element in journalistic practice. The appearance in large numbers of journalists shaped by the attitudes of this culture is the result of a process whereby the profession thought to improve itself by recruiting more and more persons from middle- and upper-class backgrounds and trained at the universities associated with such groups. This is a change but little noted as yet. The stereotype of American newspapers is that of publishers ranging from conservative to reactionary in their political views balanced by reporters ranging from liberal to radical in theirs. One is not certain how accurate the stereotype ever was. One's impression is that twenty years and more ago the preponderance of the "working press" (as it liked to call itself) was surprisingly close in origins and attitudes to working people generally. They were not Ivy Leaguers. They now are or soon will be. Journalism has become, if not an elite profession, a profession attractive to elites. This is noticeably so in Washington where the upper reaches of journalism constitute one of the most important and enduring *social* elites of the city, with all the accoutrements one associates with a leisured class. (The Washington press corps is not leisured at all, but the style is that of men and women who *choose* to work.)

The political consequence of the rising social status of journalism is that the press grows more and more influenced by attitudes genuinely hostile to American society and American government. This trend seems bound to continue into the future. On the record of what they have been writing while in college, the young people now leaving the Harvard *Crimson* and the Columbia *Spectator* for journalistic jobs in Washington will resort to the Steffens style at ever-escalating levels of moral implication. They bring with them the moral absolutism of George Wald's vastly popular address, "A Generation in Search of a Future," that describes the Vietnam war as "the most shameful episode in the whole of American history." Not tragic, not heartbreaking, not vastly misconceived, but *shameful*. From the shame of the cities to the shame of the nation. But nobody ever called Boss Croker any name equivalent in condemnatory weight to the epithet "war criminal."

II

An ironical accompaniment of the onset of the muckraking style directed toward the Presidency has been the rise of a notion of the near-omnipotency of the office itself. This notion Thomas E. Cronin describes as the "textbook President." Cronin persuasively argues that in the aftermath of Franklin Roosevelt a view of the Presidency, specifically incorporated in the textbooks of recent decades, was developed which presented seriously "inflated and unrealistic interpretations of Presidential competence and beneficence," and which grievously "overemphasized the policy change and policy accomplishment capabilities" of the office. . . .

If the muckraking tradition implies a distrust of government, it is nonetheless curiously validated by the overly trusting tradition of the "textbook Presidency" which recurrently sets up situations in which the Presidency will be judged as having somehow broken faith. . . .

Here, too, there is a curious link between the Presidency and the press. The two most important *Presidential* newspapers are the New York *Times* and the Washington *Post* (though the *Star* would be judged by many to have the best reporting). Both papers reflect a tradition of liberalism that has latterly been shaped and reinforced by the very special type of person who *buys* the paper. (It is well to keep in mind that newspapers are capitalist enterprises which survive by persuading people to buy them.) Theirs is a "disproportionately" well-educated and economically prosperous audience. The geographical areas in which the two papers circulate almost certainly have higher per-capita incomes and higher levels of education than any of comparable size in the nation or the world. More of the buyers of these two papers are likely to come from "liberal" Protestant or Jewish backgrounds than would be turned up by a random sample of the population; they comprise, in fact, what James Q. Wilson calls "the Liberal Audience."[1] Both the working-class Democrats and the conservative Republicans, with exceptions, obviously, have been pretty much driven from office among the constituencies where the *Times* and the *Post* flourish. It would be wrong to ascribe this to the influence of the papers. Causality almost certainly moves both ways. Max Frankel of the *Times*, who may have peers, but certainly no betters as a working journalist, argues that a newspaper is surely as much influenced by those who read it as vice versa.

The readers of the New York *Times* and the Washington *Post*, then, are a special type of citizen: not only more affluent and more liberal than the rest of the nation, but inclined also to impose heavy expectations on the Presidency, and not to be amused when those expectations fail to be met. Attached by their own internal traditions to the "textbook Presidency," papers like the *Times* and the *Post* are reinforced in this attachment by the temperamental predilections of the readership whose character they inevitably reflect. Thus they help to set a tone of pervasive dissatisfaction with the performance of the national government, whoever the Presidential incumbent may be and whatever the substance of his policies.

III

A third circumstance working to upset the old balance of power between the Presidency and the press is the fact that Washington reporters depend heavily on more or less clandestine information from federal bureaucracies, which are frequently, and in some cases routinely, antagonistic to Presidential interests.

There is a view of the career civil service as a more or less passive executor of policies made on high. This is quite mistaken. A very great portion of policy ideas "bubble up" from the bureaucracy, and just as importantly, a very considerable portion of the "policy decisions" that go down never come to anything, either because the bureaucrats cannot or will not follow through. (The instances of simple inability are probably much greater than those of outright hostility.) Few modern Presidents have made any impact on the federal bureaucracies save by creating new ones. The bureaucracies are unfamiliar and inaccessible. They are quasi-independent, maintaining, among other things, fairly open relationships with the Congressional committees that enact their statutes and provide their funds. They are usually willing to work with the President, but rarely to the point where their perceived interests are threatened. Typically, these are rather simple territorial interests: not to lose any jurisdiction, and if possible to gain some. But recurrently, issues of genuine political substance are also involved.

At the point where they perceive a threat to those interests, the bureaucracies just as recurrently go to the press. They know the press; the press knows them. Both stay in town as Presidential governments come and go. Both cooperate in bringing to bear the most powerful weapons the bureaucracies wield in their own defense, that of revealing Presidential plans in advance of their execution. Presidents and their plans are helpless against this technique. I have seen a senior aide to a President, sitting over an early morning cup of coffee, rise and literally punch the front page of the New York *Times*. A major initiative was being carefully mounted. Success depended, to a considerable degree, on surprise. Someone in one of the agencies whose policies were to be reversed got hold of the relevant document and passed it on to the *Times*. Now everyone would know. The mission was aborted. There was *nothing* for the Presidential government to do. No possibility of finding, much less of disciplining, the bureaucrat responsible. For a time, or rather from time to time, President Johnson tried the technique of *not* going ahead with any policy or appointment that was leaked in advance to the press. Soon, however, his aides began to suspect that this was giving the bureaucracy the most powerful weapon of all, namely the power to veto a Presidential decision by learning of it early enough and rushing to the *Times* or the *Post*. (Or, if the issue could be described in thirty seconds, any of the major television networks.). . .

It is difficult to say whether the absolute level of such disloyalty to the Presidency is rising. One has the impression that it is. No one knows much about the process of "leaking" except in those instances where he himself has been involved. (*Everyone* is sooner or later involved. That should be understood.) The process has not been studied and little is known of it. But few would argue that the amount of clandestine disclosure is decreasing. Such disclosure is now part of the way we run our affairs. It means, among other things, that the press is fairly continuously involved in an activity that is something less than honorable. Repeatedly it benefits from the self-serving acts of government officials who are essentially hostile to the Presidency. This does the Presidency no good, and if an outsider may comment, it does the press no good either. Too much do they traffic in stolen goods, and they know it.

This point must be emphasized. The leaks which appear in the *Post* and the *Times*—other papers get them, but if one wants to influence decisions in Washington these are clearly thought to be the most effective channels—are ostensibly published in the interest of adding to public knowledge of what is going on. This budget is to be cut; that man is to be fired; this bill is to be proposed. However, in the nature of the transaction the press can only publish half the story—that is to say the information that the "leaker" wants to become "public knowledge." What the press *never* does is say who the leaker is and why he wants the story leaked. Yet, more often than not, this is the more important story: that is to say, what policy wins if the one being disclosed loses, what individual, what bureau, and so on. . . .

IV

The fourth of the five conditions making for an altered relation between the Presidency and the press is the concept of objectivity with respect to the reporting of events and especially the statements of public figures. Almost the first canon of the great newspapers, and by extension of the television news networks which by and large have taken as their standards those of the best newspapers, is that "the news" will be reported whether or not the reporter or the editor or the publisher likes the news. There is nothing finer in the American newspaper tradition. There is, however, a rub and it comes when a deicision has to be made as to whether an event really is news, or simply a happening, a non-event staged for the purpose of getting into the papers or onto the screen.

The record of our best papers is not reassuring here, as a glance at the experience of the Korean and the Vietnam wars will suggest. Beginning a bit before the Korean hostilities broke out, but in the general political period we associate with that war, there was a rise of right-wing extremism, a conspiracy-oriented politics symbolized by the name of Senator Joseph McCarthy, and directed primarily at the institution of the Presidency. There was, to be sure, a populist streak to this movement: Yale and Harvard and the "striped-pants boys" in the State Department were targets too. But to the question, "Who promoted Peress?" there was only one constitutional or—for all practical purposes—political answer, namely that the President did. McCarthy went on asking such questions, or rather making such charges, and the national press, which detested and disbelieved him throughout, went on printing them. The American style of objective journalism made McCarthy. He would not, I think, have gotten anywhere in Great Britain where, because it would have been judged he was lying, the stories would simply not have been printed.

Something not dissimilar has occurred in the course of the Vietnam war, only this time the extremist, conspiracy-oriented politics of protest has been putatively left-wing. . . . The Students for a Democratic Society, if that organization may be used as an exemplar, was (at least in its later stages) nominally revolutionist, dedicated to the overthrow of the capitalist-imperialist-fascist regime of the United States. . . . Peter Berger, a sociologist active in the peace movement, has demonstrated quite persuasively—what others, particularly persons of European origin like himself have frequently seemed to sense—that despite the leftist ring of the slogans of SDS and kindred groups, their ethos and tactics are classically fascist: the cult of youth, the mystique of the street, the contempt for liberal democracy, and the "totalization of friend and foe [with] the concomitant dehumanization of the latter," as in the Nazi use of *"Saujuden"* ("Jewish pigs").

In any case, the accusations which have filled the American air during the period of Vietnam have been no more credible or responsible than those of McCarthy during the Korean period, and the tactics of provocation and physical intimidation have if anything been more disconcerting. Yet the national press, and especially television, have assumed a neutral posture, even at times a sympathetic one, enabling the neo-fascists of the Left to occupy center stage throughout the latter half of the 60's with consequences to American politics that have by no means yet worked themselves out. (It took Sam Brown to point out that one consequence was to make the work of the anti-war movement, of which he has been a principal leader, vastly more difficult.)

Would anyone have it otherwise? Well, yes. Irving Kristol raised this question in an article that appeared before the New Left had made its presence strongly felt on the national scene, but his views are doubtless even more emphatic by now. He wrote of the "peculiar mindlessness which pervades the practice of journalism in the United States," asserting that the ideal of objectivity too readily becomes an excuse for avoiding judgment. If McCarthy was lying, why print what he said? Or why print it on the front page? If the SDS stages a confrontation over a trumped-up issue, why oblige it by taking the whole episode at face value? Here, let it be said, the editorials of the *Times* and the *Post* have consistently served as a thoughtful corrective to the impressions inescapably conveyed by the news columns. But the blunt fact is that just as the news columns were open to astonishingly false assertions about the nature of the American national government during the McCarthy period, they have been open to equally false assertions—mirror images of McCarthyism indeed—during the period of Vietnam. And although it is impossible to prove, one gets the feeling that the slanderous irresponsibilities now being reported so dutifully are treated with far more respect than the old.

The matter of a policy of "genocide" pursued by the national government against the Black Panthers is a good example. By late 1969, preparing a preface to a second edition of *Beyond the Melting Pot*, Nathan Glazer and I could insist that the charge that twenty-eight Panthers had been murdered by the police was on the face of it simply untrue. Yet in that mindless way of which Kristol writes, the *Times* kept reprinting it. Edward Jay Epstein has brilliantly explained the matter in a recent article in the *New Yorker*. What he finds is an immense fraud. No such policy existed. There was no conspiracy between the Department of Justice, the FBI, and various local police forces to wipe out the Panthers. Yet that fraudulent charge has so profoundly affected the thinking of the academic and liberal communities that they will probably not even now be able to see the extent to which they were deceived. The hurt that has been done to blacks is probably in its way even greater. None of it could have happened without the particular mind-set of the national press.

If the press is to deserve our good opinion, it must do better in such matters. And it should keep in mind that the motivation of editors and reporters is not always simply and purely shaped by a devotion to objectivity. In the course of the McCarthy era James Reston recalled the ancient adage which translated from the Erse proposes that "If you want an audience, start a fight." This is true of anyone who would find an audience for his views, or simply for himself. It is true also of anyone who would find customers for the late city edition. T. S. Matthews, sometime editor of *Time*, retired to England to ponder the meaning of it all. In the end, all he could conclude was that the function of journalism was entertainment. If it is to be more—and that surely is what the Rosenthals and Bradlees and Grunwalds and Elliotts want—it will have to be willing on occasion to forgo the entertainment value of a fascinating but untruthful charge. It will, in short, have to help limit the rewards which attend this posture in American politics.

V

The final, and by far the most important, circumstance of American journalism relevant to this discussion is the absence of a professional tradition of self-correction. The mark of any developed profession is the practice of correcting mistakes, by whomsoever they are made. This practice is of course the great invention of Western science. Ideally, it requires an epistemology which is shared by all respected members of the profession, so that when a mistake is discovered it can be established as a mistake to the satisfaction of the entire professional community. Ideally, also, no discredit is involved: to the contrary, honest mistakes are integral to the process of advancing the field. Journalism will never attain to any such condition. Nevertheless, there is a range of subject matter about which reasonable men can and will agree, and within this range American journalism, even of the higher order, is often seriously wide of the mark. Again Irving Kristol:

> It is a staple of conversation among those who have ever been involved in a public activity that when they read the Times the next morning, they will discover that it has almost never got the story quite right and has only too frequently got it quite wrong. . . .

This is so, and in part it is unavoidable. Too much happens too quickly: that the Times or the Post or the Star should appear once a day is a miracle. (Actually they appear three or four times a day in different editions.) But surely when mistakes are made they ought to be corrected. Sometimes they are, but not nearly enough. It is in this respect that Kristol is right in calling journalism "the underdeveloped profession."

VI

In the wake of so lengthy an analysis, what is there to prescribe? Little. Indeed, to prescribe much would be to miss the intent of the analysis. I have been hoping to make two points—the first explicitly, the second largely by implication. The first is that a convergence of journalistic tradition with evolving cultural patterns has placed the national government at a kind of operating disadvantage. It is hard for government to succeed: this theme echoes from every capital of the democratic world. In the United States it is hard for government to succeed and just as hard for government to appear to have succeeded when indeed it has done so. This situation can be said to have begun in the muckraking era with respect to urban government; it is now very much the case with respect to national government, as reflected in the "national press" which primarily includes the New York Times, the Washington Post, Time, Newsweek, and a number of other journals.

There is nothing the matter with investigative reporting; there ought to be more. The press can be maddeningly complacent about real social problems for which actual counter-measures, even solutions, exist. . . . The issue is not one of serious inquiry, but of an almost feckless hostility to power.

The second point is that this may not be good for us. American government will only rarely and intermittently be run by persons drawn from the circles of those who own and edit and write for the national press; no government will ever have this circle as its political base. Hence the conditions are present for a protracted conflict in which the national government keeps losing. This might once have been a matter of little consequence or interest. It is, I believe, no longer such, for it now takes place within the context of what Nathan Glazer has so recently described in these pages[2] as an "assault on the reputation of America . . . which has already succeeded in reducing this country, in the eyes of many American intellectuals, to outlaw status. . . ." In other words, it is no longer a matter of this or that administration; it is becoming a matter of national morale, of a "loss of confidence and nerve," some of whose possible consequences, as Glazer indicates, are not pleasant to contemplate. . . .

Obviously the press of a free country is never going to be and never should be celebratory. Obviously government at all levels needs and will continue to get criticism and some of it will inevitably be harsh or destructive, often enough justifiably so. Obviously we will get more bad news than good. Indeed the content of the newspapers is far and away the best quick test of the political structure of a society. . . .

Nonetheless there remains the question of balance. Does not an imbalance arise when the press becomes a too-willing outlet for mindless paranoia of the Joseph McCarthy or New Left variety? Does it not arise when the press becomes too self-satisfied to report its own mistakes with as much enterprise as it reports the mistakes of others? . . .

. . . Freedom of the press is a constitutional guarantee in the United States: how that freedom is excercised should remain a matter for the professional standards of those who exercise it. Here, however, there is really room for improvement. First is the simple matter of competence. The very responsibility of the national press in seeking to deal wilth complex issues produces a kind of irresponsibility. The reporters aren't up to it. They get it all wrong. It would be astonishing were it otherwise.

Further, there needs to be much more awareness of the quite narrow social and intellectual perspective within which the national press so often moves. There are no absolutes here; hardly any facts. But there *is* a condition that grows more, not less, pronounced. The national press is hardly a "value-free" institution. It very much reflects the judgment of owners and editors and reporters as to what is good and bad about the country and what can be done to make things better. It might be hoped that such persons would give more thought to just how much elitist criticism is good for a democracy. Is this a shocking idea? I think not. I would imagine that anyone who has read Peter Gay or Walter Laqueur on the history of the Weimar Republic would agree that there are dangers to democracy in an excess of elitist attack. A variant of the Jacksonian principle of democratic government is involved here. Whether or not ordinary men are capable of carrying out any governmental task what-soever, ordinary men are going to be given such tasks. That is what it means to be a democracy. We had best not get our expectations too far out of line with what is likely to happen, and we had best not fall into the habit of measuring all performance by the often quite special tastes, preferences, and interests of a particular intellectual and social elite. . . .

As to the press itself, one thing seems clear. It should become much more open about acknowledging mistakes. The *Times* should have printed Dr. Henderson's letter. Doubtless the bane of any editor is the howling of politicians and other public figures claiming to have been misquoted. But often they *are* misquoted. . . .

As for government itself, there is not much to be done, but there is something. It is perfectly clear that the press will not be intimidated. Specific efforts like President Kennedy's to get David Halberstam removed as a *Times* correspondent in Vietnam almost always fail, as they deserve to do.[3] Non-specific charges such as those leveled by Vice President Agnew get nowhere either. They come down to an avowal of dislike, which is returned in more than ample measure, with the added charge that in criticizing the press the government may be trying to intimidate it, which is unconstitutional.

What government can do and should do is respond in specific terms to what it believes to be misstatements or mistaken emphases; it should address those responses to specific stories in specific papers and it should expect that these will be printed (with whatever retort the journal concerned wishes to make). Misrepresentations of government performance must never be allowed to go unchallenged. The notion of a "one-day story," and the consoling idea that yesterday's papers are used to wrap fish, are pernicious and wrong. Misinformation gets into the bloodstream and has consequences. The *Times* ought by now to have had a letter from the Chairman of the Civil Service Commission pointing out the mistakes in the November 15 story on minority employment, and the even more important omissions. If the first letter was ignored, he should have sent another. Similarly the *Times* ought long since have had a letter from an HEW official exposing the errors of its coverage of federal aid to black colleges. Failing that, someone should have called in the education writers of the *Times* and asked why they let other men misreport their beat. Etc. Hamilton's formulation has not been bettered: the measure of effective government is energy in the executive.

In the end, however, the issue is not one of politics but of culture. The culture of disparagement that has been so much in evidence of late, that has attained such an astonishing grip on the children of the rich and the mighty, and that has exerted an increasing influence on the tone of the national press in its dealings with the national government, is bad news for democracy. Some while ago the late Richard Hofstadter foresaw what has been happening:

> *Perhaps we are really confronted with two cultures (not Snow's), whose spheres are increasingly independent and more likely to be conflicting than to be benignly convergent: a massive adversary culture on the one side, and the realm of socially responsible criticism on the other.*

But given what has been happening to the press in recent years and what is likely to go on being the case if current trends should continue on their present path, where is such "socially responsible criticism" to come from?

Or rather, where is it to appear in a manner that will inform and influence the course of public decision-making?

NOTES

1. See his article, "Crime and the Liberal Audience" in *Commentary*, January 1971.
2. "The Role of the Intellectuals," *Commentary*, February 1971.
3. See Halberstam's account of the incident in "Getting the Story in Vietnam," *Commentary*, January 1965.

Response to Daniel Moynihan

Max Frankel

[T]he central point [of Daniel Moynihan's article] . . . I take to be Mr. Moynihan's anguish about a reversal in the "old balance of power" between President and press. He thinks the press is well on the way to upsetting that "balance" to the detriment of effective government.

I found it odd, and negligent, that he never even attempted to define either the *old* balance of power or *any* balance that he deems desirable. This makes it a rather difficult thesis to rebut, especially after he gets through conceding the President's "near limitless capacity" to make news, to dominate events of public concern, to reward friends and punish enemies (and not only in the press corps), and to carry off "formidable deceptions." He can, of course, do much more. He can exhort, rally, and inspire. He can ruin and degrade. He can breathe life into American attitudes and, often, institutions. Or he can distort and discard them. And surely at the apex of anyone's list of Presidential powers is the power to make war, nuclear war, ten-year war, undeclared war, unchecked war, unpopular war, holy war, or pointless war. (If some of our histories are correct in suggesting that the Hearst and Pulitzer press were once able to goad or frighten the country and its President into war, then it would seem that there has been, indeed, a most remarkable shift in the balance of power, though hardly in the direction Mr. Moynihan suggests.)

But if I read the story correctly, he is not even talking about the collective, though incoherent, power of the press and the television. He is talking largely about the dangerous power of the New York *Times* and the Washington *Post*. This is flattering, but hardly persuasive. The great majority of black citizens, whose thoughts he wishes to protect from their own leaders and agitators, do not read either of those newspapers. The papers that they read, across the country, would probably score quite well

Reprinted from *Commentary*, by permission; copyright © 1971 by the American Jewish Committee. Reprinted with permission of the author, then Chief Washington Correspondent, now Editor of the Editorial Page, of *The New York Times*.

on his special loyalty test. As for television, I will let him decide, after some months in civilian life, whether it favors the champions of the space program or its critics, whether it is dominated by the ethics of our President or those of his critics, whether on balance it proclaims the old American and governmental virtues, or the virtues of what he calls, in Lionel Trilling's phrase, the "adversary culture."

But all right. It is the *Eastern* press that is threatening us. How?

Point One is that our muckraking tradition has fallen into the hands of a new breed of reporter of middle- and upper-class background, Ivy League, elitist. In Washington, this group constitutes a *social* elite, "with all the accoutrements one associates with a leisured class." We are not leisured, he quickly notes, but our "style is that of men and women who *choose* to work." And the political consequence of this social status is that "the press grows more and more influenced by attitudes genuinely hostile to American society and American government." And the evidence for this is that we have been brainwashed by the "moral absolutism" of George Wald!

Others have taken this absurd standard of pedigree and tallied the preponderance of non-Ivy degrees in the upper reaches of the Washington press corps. Still others, indeed, have noted with a little more relevance that the upper reaches are, in fact, dominated by the "silent generation" that has allegedly cowed into docility in the era of Eisenhower and Joe McCarthy. As for the "charges" of social elitism and our "style of leisure"—these really would have been better expressed if he had simply repeated, "effete snobs."

But how very odd that, in a paragraph devoted to the debunking of moral absolutism—in which Mr. Moynihan complains that people call the Vietnam war shameful instead of tragic, heartbreaking, or misconceived—he would dare to characterize the attitudes of reporters in the press not as wrong, or tragic, or misconceived, but as "hostile to American society and American government." Wow! Let's make it effete and *un-American* snobs.

We are, of course, guilty of having switched, over the last generation, to a more educated corps of reporters, if only to keep up with the credentials and footwork of the holders of public office (and our new critics). The fact is that we are not nearly smart enough yet to cope with the scientific, technological, pseudo-sociological expertise that is peddled to the public by both the government and its critics. And it is a further fact, and perhaps one of the most enduring attractions of our business, that any bright lad of proletarian or other origin can rid himself of the social and hierarchical pressures of our society to participate, as a journalist, in the political process of our country. . . .

It is also true, and more relevant to the essay's point, that there are among some of the newest recruits to our business young men and women who are impatient with the "objective" or, more accurately, "neutral" standards of journalism to which their elders aspired. Some of them share Mr. Moynihan's sense of that standard's inadequacy and wish to adjust it. A few of them are impatient with *any* standard that would prevent them from placing their own views before the public. It is an important subject and an interesting debate that news writers have conducted periodically over the decades. More of this in sequence.

Point Two suggests that along with hostility toward the Presidency we purvey an absurdly inflated picture of the President's importance and ability to influence events, thus setting a tone of pervasive dissatisfaction with the performance of government, under any President. The *Times* and the *Post* are particularly guilty here, it is argued, because Mr. Moynihan agrees with my contention that a newspaper is as much influenced by those who read it as vice versa.

This is apples and oranges.

We Americans do have an exaggerated expectation of our Presidents and only a handful of them ever fulfill their own promise and boast, even in hindsight. Such is the power and aura of this office that a politician, no matter how poorly regarded over the years, how often suspected and vilified and run down, can assume the office and earn at once not just what you call a "honeymoon" period of grace but a new reputation for nobility and intelligence. And when he begins in lofty manner, promising to heal some of the nation's wounds and to lower his voice, he is made to feel welcome and given the chance to appear as he wishes to appear before his countrymen. The press reflects these expectations of the public and records the efforts of our Presidents and Presidential candidates to nurture them. This faith is either an element of Presidential power, to be cherished and applied with skill by those who can, or it is a terrible burden, as Mr. Moynihan would have it.

If it is a burden, then only a President who insists from the start that he does *not* know everything, cannot change too much, and will aspire only to a modest program of action can correct the nation's view. How about a President who will work for a *year* of peace at a time, instead of a *generation?* Or one who begins by saying that a new Attorney General will *not* solve much of our crime problem? Or one who tells us how many loafers there really are on welfare and how much more sophisticated he has become, once in office, about the "welfare mess"?

We do try to match promise against performance and cumulatively we manage, I think, to draw a pretty good portrait of the strengths and weaknesses of the Presidency and any particular occupant thereof. But those who find the underlying truths obscured, must begin by noting not the power for occasional deception in the White House but the *habit* of *regular* deception in our politics and administration.

By and large, it is the President and the federal government who establish the agenda of public discussion and they must choose whether their purpose shall be uplifting and educational or merely manipulative. It is the damnable tendency toward manipulation that forces us so often into the posture of apparent adversaries.

We have indeed progressively lost our naiveté about the truthfulness of Presidents and government, starting with the U-2 affair a decade ago. A. J. Liebling found the awakening after U-2 to be the "beginning of wisdom" in the country and in the press. We lost the habit of reporting as fact what was only a contention or claim of our highest officials. And there is nothing in the record of the current administration, ten years later, to break us of the new habit of treating virtually every official utterance as a carefully contrived rendering that needs to be examined for the missing word or phrase, the sly use of statistics, the slippery syntax or semantics. Planes fly to "interdict supplies" but not in support of combat infantry, until such support becomes an "ancillary" benefit and until, finally, it becomes exposed as the *real* purpose of the flights. Troops do not engage in "ground combat" as long as they hover *two feet above the ground* in helicopters. Estimates of the gross national product turn out, within weeks, to be only targets.

If this shift from simple credulity to informed skepticism is the change of balance Mr. Moynihan deplores, then I plead guilty.

He will have to take it on faith that we practice this skepticism not in the spirit of persecution or prosecution, but from a sense of wishing to serve our readers with reports of what is really going on. I will not deny that, once discovered, governmental trickery in and of itself often becomes more "newsworthy" than the report itself. But a President or government dedicated to truth-telling and eager to inform the public could very rapidly turn the wolves of the press into lambs.

My contention that readers shape a newspaper as much as it shapes them bears on this, but only indirectly.

Our skepticism *does* reflect that of our readers and it is mutually reinforcing. As George Reedy so wisely reflected in thinking back on his tour as President Johnson's press secretary, "The reality is that a President has no press problems (except for a few minor administrative technicalities), but he does have political problems, all of which are reflected in their most acute form by the press.". . .

We reflect, or refract, but we do not simply create skepticism or dissatisfaction.

But I was speaking in a still larger sense. What is it, I asked, that makes newspapers accept some value judgments and not others? Why do we write in a different spirit about one kind of crime, say simple murder, than we do about another, say civil disobedience? Why do Northern and Western newspapers write, unquestionably, from the point of view of those who regard official segregation as not only illegal but also wrong, while some Southern newspapers give the racist equal standing in the court of opinion?

This is how I came to my answer that we are mutually influenced by the attitudes and values of our communities. The newspaper that is candidly written from the viewpoint of the home folks finds nothing wrong in sports coverage that is candidly partisan for the home team. But when the teams in contention are from the same community, the coverage suddenly turns "neutral." Why? Because the community is divided. We covered World War II from the partisan viewpoint of the Allies. Not so, by and large, the war in Vietnam. We did not, on a large scale, question or ignite debate on the crossing of the 38th Parallel in Korea in 1950, but we did examine and feed controversy on the bombing across the 17th Parallel in Vietnam. Not because we alone decided that one war was more clearly just than another, or one frontier more inviolate than another, but because the communities to which we reported were divided on the issue of Vietnam in sufficient degree to alter our perspective.

If I am right, then the interconnection is quite different from the one Mr. Moynihan suggests. A President does not enhance his power to govern by converting a few reporters or selling them on his point of view. He will more likely gain the trust—if not always the active support—of the press by gaining the trust and confidence of the community.

Point Three is that we are "fairly continuously" involved in the receipt of information passed to us by disloyal bureaucrats. Mr. Moynihan terms this as something "less than honorable" on our part, though he implies that receiving special information from bureaucrats who are "loyal" is okay. He says no one knows much about the process of "leaking" and that it has not been "studied."

Well, I know a great deal about it. The first thing that needs to be said is that the *deliberate* disclosure of information for the purpose of injuring the President is relatively rare. But what is rarer still is that such information finds its way into print without "the other side," whatever that may be in our judgment, being questioned about the matter and given a chance to discuss the deeper issues and even the motives of those who may have done the leaking. The great majority of deliberate "leaks" are not secret documents and papers, but guarded suggestions that a reporter look into a matter that he might otherwise neglect. More often than not, he is not even told what he will find.

And the absolute majority of unwanted "leaks" are not deliberate at all. They result from a diligent study of public papers and diligent inquiry among dozens of officials, with reporters carefully playing one set of clues against another, until they find a part of what they seek. Most of these officials make themselves available not because they wish to abet the effort but because over time they have found their accessibility to be desirable for loyal purposes. It is true that in this process, when reporters have some interesting facts but by no means all the facts, and find themselves shut out by government, they will then publish what they know for the purpose of lighting a fire that will smoke out a good deal more. For even when a first, unwanted story is incomplete or superficial, if it touches on an important subject it will almost always arouse the attention and curiosity of other reporters who will, together, move it much closer to the essence of the tale.

Yet even if deliberate "leaking" were as harmful as Mr. Moynihan suggests, is it his contention that the press should ignore such information and pretend it was never received? That would be an interesting discussion indeed.

Point Four deals with the "rub" that he finds adhering to our concept of objectivity. It comes, he observes, "when a decision has to be made as to whether an event really is news, or simply a happening, a non-event staged for the purpose of getting into the paper or onto the screen." (I note that television has been allowed back into the defendant's box.)

It is not the experience with Joe McCarthy that should be used to instruct us on this point. We were deficient in treating him—in part because we reflected and responded to the deficiency and gullibility of our communities—but as long as men who remember this experience are alive, we will probably apply the lessons learned.

The difficulty comes in the way in which Mr. Moynihan states the problem: *"simply* a happening, a non-event staged for the purpose of getting into the papers." A quarter of a million persons marching on the White House? A series of "teach-ins"? An agitator yelling "burn"? A Vice President attacking the papers (and the screen)? Lee Harvey Oswald? The quest for recognition, to be heard, to be noticed, to be heeded—often takes the form of a happening staged for the purpose of getting into the papers, but it is rarely *"simply"* that in either motivation or consequence.

The problem for thoughtful journalism is that we can never be sure about motivation and we certainly cannot know consequence. And in some small measure, at least, we know that we contribute to consequence. These are horrendous problems and we lose sleep over them, but they are not solved by the automatic assumption in our editorial suites of the absolute power to decide that Moynihan deserves to be heard, and another man does not. And has he thought about the agitator who *may* be encouraged in his extremism because he finds it to be "newsworthy"? What would he do to project his cause and gain attention for himself if he were shut out of the news? Burn, perhaps, instead of only shouting "burn"?

Point Five raises the "absence of a professional tradition of self-correction." In one sense, of course, we correct ourselves every morning, a requirement and an opportunity that most other institutions, including the Presidency, lack.

Mr. Moynihan's evidence does not make this point very well, but there is need, in another sense, for more correction or expansion and amendment of what we report. Persons who figure in our news coverage do occasionally need more space to explain their points of view or involvement in affairs than is provided in existing columns for guest-writers and Letters to the Editor. And clearly the need is greater in some papers than others. But as I suggested earlier, such opportunity for correction is rarely denied to the White House. Men of power—or presumed power—are able to make their views known, almost by definition. It is ordinary citizens, sometimes, of late, including the editors of the Eastern press, who require an outlet.

If our Presidents are seriously concerned about "protracted conflict" with a large enough segment of our population and genuinely believe, with Mr. Moynihan, that they are steadily losing that conflict, they had better look well beyond the bearers of the bad news and certainly well beyond the morning paper. They might even look in a mirror.

CHAPTER TWELVE

BUREAUCRACY

The federal bureaucracy has no shortage of critics. In recent years, especially, it has come under heavy fire from public officials and private citizens alike. In the first of the two selections which follow, Charles Peters adds his voice to the chorus. He maintains that cumbersome removal procedures serve to shield the numerous incompetents who populate the bureaucracy, that the hallmark of the civil service system—the merit principle—is breached more often than it is honored, and finally, that the complete elimination of partisan considerations in the hiring of civil servants renders the bureaucracy less responsive to the president than it should be.

While Peters argues that the hiring and firing procedures lead to poor performance in the bureaucracy, O. B. Conaway., Jr. contends that such procedures are indispensable requirements if we hope to attract qualified individuals into the public service. Acknowledging that abuses have occurred under the current civil service system, he insists that they may be more appropriately viewed as exceptions rather than the rule.

A Kind Word for the Spoils System

Charles Peters

. . . [A]nyone who has had a reasonable amount of contact with the federal government has encountered people who should be fired. There are, of course, some superb civil servants—maybe ten per cent of the total—who have every right to become indignant at blanket criticism of government workers. There are another 50 to 60 per cent who range from adequate to good. Unfortunately, that leaves 30 to 40 per cent in the range downward from marginal to outright incompetent.

Yet fewer than one per cent are fired each year. This is because 93 per cent are under some form of civil service and are therefore virtually impossible to fire. We recently reported, for example, the story of an employee of the Internal Revenue Service whose discharge was overturned even though he had repeatedly reported for work dead drunk. His union successfully contended that the IRS should have established programs to detect and treat alcoholism among its employees. With that kind of thing the likely product of a series of hearings and appeals that could last for years, it is the rare administrator who will attempt to fire anyone.

Imagine yourself a supervisor with an employee who does nothing all day but read the paper and take coffee breaks. Thinking of firing him, you might turn to Title 5 of the U.S. Code and peruse parts 752.101 through 752.402 and 772.101 through 772.404, which describe one hearing and appeal right after another. By the time you reached the end of 772.404, you'd say the hell with it and toss him the sports section.

Something has to be done—even though Jimmy Carter may not want to face it now. You can't reform the government without having the power to choose the people who work within it.

UP FROM CIVIL SERVICE

I came to this position after a long journey through government that I began on the other side of the civil service question.

In the late 1950s, while working on the staff of the West Virginia legislature, I drafted a bill designed to transform a patronage-ridden personnel system into a civil service based on merit and offering genuine career protection for state employees. Wanting to get that bill enacted into law was one of the reasons I ran for the legislature in the next election, and it was a proud day in my life when the bill, bearing my name, was passed in the following session.

Then I came to Washington. Having seen the evils of too much political patronage, I was now exposed to the evils of too much civil service. The terrible disruption of continuity that came from massive personnel changes following each election in West Virginia was offset in Washington by the excessive defensiveness and caution of civil servants primarily devoted to the protection of the institution for which they worked. If you can be fired only if your job is abolished—as is practically the case with a civil servant—then your only fear is that your agency will be diminished in size in a way that might threaten your job. Furthermore, the civil servant is not accountable to the public he is supposed to be serving. If an Elizabeth Ray is found on Capitol Hill, the Congress, which has no civil service, can fire her and the electorate can unseat Wayne Hays. But what can we do if they both work at HUD or HEW?[1] Finally, the civil service takes two million people out of what it is fashionable to call the political process. (It used to be called just plain "politics," and the fact that, when we want it to sound good, we have to dress it up as "political process" is a sign of the depths of regard to which politics has sunk, about which more later.) Whatever you call it, it's quite a loss. Remember, 200,000 of them are superb people, and the Hatch Act forbids their making their political views known to us.[2]

It is widely assumed, on the other hand, that a political patronage system will result in unqualified people, not selected on merit, making decisions for partisan political reasons. Let's take a look at this assumption.

Why do political employees have to be unqualified? You can require by law that a politically appointed secretary be able to type 50 words a minute, just like the civil service appointee. As for selection on pure merit from all the applicants, that is not done now in the civil service. As Ann Pincus pointed out in "How to Get A Government Job" in our June issue, the present civil service is a patronage machine that instead of being run on a political basis is run on the basis of friendship. You get a civil service job by knowing someone who is in the agency where you want to work. He gives you an advance tip on the opening, writes a job description tailored to fit your experience, and then requests your name from the Civil Service Commission. Isn't it possible that a job might be filled better by politicians who are interested in putting together an administration that will do a good enough job to get them reelected? The same principle applies to most other decisions. Why shouldn't they be made on a partisan basis if the motive behind them is doing a good enough job to be reelected?

The only real advantage I have seen to the career civil servant is continuity. When I worked at the Peace Corps in the 1960s, we had a five-year limit on employment. The result was the stimulation offered by a steady infusion of new blood and a much more adventurous group of employees than are attracted by the security of the civil service tenure. There was, however, the same lack of continuity I had seen in West Virginia. By the time I left, staff meetings had taken on the character of a series of broken records, as I heard problems discussed again and again as if they were brand new and the agency had no experience to suggest their solutions.

There is one other reason for not doing away with civil service tenure completely. It's that, occasionally, unwise or corrupt political decisions may threaten institutions like federal agencies, thus making it in the self-preservative interest of the civil servants who work in them to blow the whistle on whatever wrongdoing is going on. The role of the FBI and the CIA during the Watergate scandals shows how crucially important the loyalty of the civil servant to his institution can be. When people in the White House wanted to contain the investigation, it was the civil servants who rebelled, who blew the whistle, who leaked to the press. Indeed, the Watergate stories of the FBI and the CIA illustrate both the good and bad sides of the civil servant's institutional loyalty: an essential if only occasional and self-preservative willingness to stand up to political authority gone wrong, coupled with a mindless and equally self-preservative dedication to covering up his institution's own sins.

So instead of abolishing the civil service, I would urge cutting it by 50 per cent, and filling the remaining half with political appointees who can be fired at any time.

(I don't mean to imply by this, of course, that we should keep all the present *jobs* and just change *people*; it's clear that besides the problem of untouchable incompetents, there's a problem of jobs that are useless no matter who's doing them. It's a particularly thorny situation, though, because *part* of almost every job is useful—in some cases it's only 10 per cent, but it's almost never nothing at all.)

Being able to fire people is important for two reasons: 1) to permit you to hire the people you want and to get rid of those you don't want, and 2) to make it possible for you to attract the kind of risk-takers who are repelled by the safe civil service and the political emasculation it entails.

The problem with achieving all this is that for years Americans have been brainwashed by textbooks that make politics sound bad and civil service sound shiny clean. I suspect it all began when the Italian and Irish immigrants took over the elective offices in Boston and the Wasps had to figure out how to salvage something for themselves. "Politicians are inept, partisan, crooked; we are able, objective and virtuous," was their refrain, and it sounded good to their friends across the Charles at Harvard, who then put it into their textbooks from whence the doctrine spread across the land. Whatever its origin, the idea that politics and politicians are bad is now ingrained in many Americans. Not long ago a governor of my state, trying to appeal to this feeling, said of himself, "I am not a politician, I am a statesman."

We have an idiotic regard for people who are "above" politics. James Forrestal, then Secretary of Defense and one of countless possible examples, was praised by *The New York Times* for being above politics when he didn't support Truman in 1948. He and the *Times* were astounded when Truman fired him. Forrestal was a Coriolanus. For him being above politics really meant being above the mob.

We have too many Forrestals now, and what they don't understand is that being above the mob means being above the practice of democratic politics. They, and a good many of the rest of us, have forgotten that democratic politics is supposed to be the way we determine who governs this country. My colleague James Fallows recently wrote in the *Texas Monthly* that we need "the politicians, whose job is openly to ask other people for support. They can't be shy or coy or proud about it: they have to try to persuade. . . . You can't last long in such a calling if you close your ears to those who disagree; in order to persuade, you must first understand.

On the other extreme, we have those who never have to persuade anyone of anything—or at least not very often. The exalted physician is the classic example. However kind he may be, people come to him only as supplicants, and he speaks to them with the voice of resonant authority. Professors, writers, and others of the ilk are in the same boat. They don't have to listen to the other side because they can pronounce rather than persuade. There are 'politics' in these professions, no doubt—but the politics is usually such a seamy, backstairs business that no one can treat it respectably. In-house politics is a dirty little game in most professional worlds; consequently anyone who actually makes his living this way can hardly merit respect. If you are really good, the thinking goes, you won't have to scramble; people will come to you with offers. This is why the intellectual community was so delighted by Walter Mondale's withdrawal from the presidential race. By pulling out he said, in effect, that anyone who is willing to run for President doesn't deserve the job. Oh joyous confirmation of all existing prejudice! We happy, enlightened few deserve to run the country—but of course we won't demean ourselves to try.

There is no better illustration of this attitude and its currency among conservatives and liberals alike than the recent Supreme Court case of *Elrod v. Burns,* in which Justices Brennan, Marshall, White, Stewart, and Blackmun joined in ruling that a newly elected Democratic sheriff could not fire Republican political appointees from the previous administration. Firing the appointees would violate their First Amendment rights, the Court rules, because dismissal would punish them for having exercised those rights when they supported the losing Republican candidate for sheriff.

This is outrageous reasoning. Are the learned judges going to contend that my First Amendment rights are threatened when I run for office and am defeated? Of course not.

But is my freedom of political belief any less threatened if I run for election and lose my elected job when I'm defeated than if I support a candidate and lose my appointed job when he's defeated?

Political freedom is the freedom to run for office, to support others who run for office, and to win or lose as the electorate may decide. But the *Elrod* case says that everyone who had a political job on the day it was decided will now keep it for life. There is now no freedom for those who want to gain office by supporting other candidates who might convince the electorate they could do a better job—and who would do a better job if they could take their own team into office with them.

The Court excluded policy-making jobs from its ruling, arguing that that omission alone would be sufficient to keep the system responsive to the electorate.

What the Court forgets is that, if the government is to work, policy implementation is just as important as policy making. No matter how wise the chief, he has to have the right Indians to transform his ideas into action, to get the job done.

NOTES

1. We could eliminate the Hatch Act, of course, but that would give the civil servants the political power to make their jobs even more invulnerable to politics.
2. U.S. Departments of Housing and Urban Development and Health, Education and Welfare.

A Kind Word for the Merit System

O. B. Conaway, Jr.

The objective of any system of personnel management, public or private, is to create and maintain a work force that can and will accomplish the objectives of the organization it serves, whether it is the building of automobiles or the control of their use on the highways. The creation of an effective work force is a complicated task that requires professional expertise in many fields. Modern personnel management includes at minimum manpower planning, job classification, recruitment, examinations, placement, compensation, training, employee relations which usually include collective bargaining, the insurance of equal opportunity for all in appointments and promotions, efforts to maintain productivity at the highest possible level, and the administration of health and retirement systems.

These various personnel functions are usually found in both private and public organizations, but most of them are carried out in a very different manner in the public sector primarily because the Congress of the United States decided almost one hundred years ago that personnel administration in the national government should be based on merit principles. Prior to the passage of the Pendleton Act (1883), which is the foundation of the present merit system, positions in the national government were filled by political action, and there had been a large number of cases of corruption and incompetency as well as constant pressure by job seekers on government officials.

The basic merit principle, as defined in the Pendleton Act of 1883, is that appointments to and promotions in the national civil service should be made on the basis of relative ability as determined by "open, fair, honest, impartial competitive examination." The Pendleton Act also provided limited security of tenure for the employees it affected by prohibiting their

Prepared especially for this volumn by O. B. Conaway, Jr.

removal for refusing to be active in political campaigns and attempted to insure their political neutrality by forbidding them to "coerce the political action of any person" and prohibiting political assessments of or by them or by any other officials of the government."[1]

The concept of governments staffed with the best qualified men and women determined openly by competitive examinations and governmental work forces that were politically neutral appealed strongly to the large number of persons who in this period were attempting to eliminate widespread corruption from the governments of the country. Merit personnel administration thus became one of the great objectives of the strong reform movements of the late 19th and early 20th centuries.

Although the Pendleton Act has not been amended significantly since its passage, the principles of merit personnel administration have been reaffirmed recently by Congress in the Intergovernmental Personnel Act of 1970 and the Civil Service Reform Act of 1978. The principles of merit personnel administration with which federal personnel management must be consistent as defined in the Civil Service Reform Act of 1978 were:

(1) Recruitment should be from qualified individuals from appropriate sources in an endeavor to achieve a work force from all segments of society, and selection and advancement should be determined solely on the basis of relative ability, knowledge, and skills, after fair and open competition which assures that all receive equal opportunity.

(2) All employees and applicants should receive fair and equitable treatment in all aspects of personnel management without regard to political affiliation, race, color, religion, national origin, sex, marital status, age, or handicapping condition, and with proper regard for their privacy and constitutional rights.

(3) Equal pay should be provided for work of equal value, with appropriate consideration of both national and local rates paid by employers in the private sector, and appropriate incentives and recognition should be provided for excellence in performance.

(4) All employees should maintain high standards of integrity, conduct, and concern for the public interest.

(5) The Federal work force should be used efficiently and effectively.

(6) Employees should be retained on the basis of the adequacy of their performance; inadequate performance should be corrected, and employees should be separated who cannot or will not improve their performance to meet required standards.

(7) Employees should be provided effective education and training in cases in which education and training would result in better organizational and individual performance.

(8) Employees should be—

(A) protected against arbitrary action, personal favoritism, or coercion for partisan political purposes, and

(B) prohibited from using their official authority for the purpose of interfering with or affecting the result of an election or a nomination for election.

(9) Employees should be protected against reprisal for the lawful disclosure of information which the employees reasonably believe evidences—

(A) a violation of law, rule, or regulation,

(B) mismanagement, a waste of funds, or an abuse of authority, or

(C) a substantial and specific danger to public health or safety.

The Pendleton Act placed about 10 percent of the Federal employees at the time in the merit system and provided that other positions could be transferred into it by an executive order of the president. The number of positions in the merit system of the national government grew slowly until the 1930s, but at present, more than 90 percent of all civil service workers are hired and retained in accordance with merit principles. All of the states have a merit system in which some or all of their positions have been placed. A few of the state systems were established late in the 19th century, but most of them date from the 1930s. The cities of the country, too, generally have merit systems that include part or all of their employees, particularly policemen and firemen. Only a few of the largest counties have merit systems unless they are incorporated in a comprehensive state merit system.

Although merit personnel administration has been widely accepted by the governments of the country and has received more support by Congress in recent years than ever before, some people question whether a personnel system founded on the principles listed above serves a government as well as possible. The major criticism of the opponents of merit personnel administration, in whole or in part, deserve consideration. Since they usually have been directed at the merit system of the national government, the following discussion is in that context.

One of the major criticisms of the Federal merit system often made by journalists, party leaders, congressmen, candidates for office, and some incumbent presidents has been that the party in power cannot actually control policy formulation and implementation in the government because too many of its highest officials hold positions in the merit system and have such secure tenure that they do not have to be responsive to the policies of the incumbent administration and, in fact, can sabotage them. Thus, these critics argue that more positions should be filled by the party that won the last election. This problem has long been recognized in public personnel administration, and many efforts have been made to solve it. There is no conflict between requiring that the great majority of the positions in a government be filled by competitive examination and allowing the chief executive to appoint a sufficient number of officials to enable him to control the executive branch during his administration. If he could not do so, the winning of an election would be meaningless.

The positions that the president, or his political appointees, may fill now include not only the secretaries of departments and the heads of agencies and their deputies and personnel aides, but also approximately 1600 positions in the competitive service that have been excepted from competitive examination on the grounds that the incumbents participate significantly in the determination of the major political policies of the administration, or are deeply involved in the advocacy of administration programs and support of their controversial aspects, or serve principally as personal assistants to or advisors of a presidential appointee or other major political figures.

There have been many controversies over whether a particular position should be excepted and the number of positions that should be excepted. The only means of settling them has been a close evaluation of the duties of the position in the administration of the time.

The Civil Service Reform Act of 1978 gave the chief executive strong and specific powers over almost all high ranking officials in the competitive service. The Act established a Senior Executive Service composed of the officials in the three highest grades of the Civil Service (16 through 18) in the great majority of the government's agencies. The Act also required each agency to establish a Senior Executive Service appraisal system with performance requirements for each senior executive as well as criteria for performance including improvements in quality of work or service, cost efficiency and timeliness of performance. Any senior executive who receives an unsatisfactory rating may be reassigned within the Senior Executive Service or demoted from it. Senior executives who receive two unsatisfactory ratings in any period of five years must be removed from the service as must any senior executive who twice in three years receives less than fully successful ratings. Conversely, senior executives whose work is evaluated as exceptionally meritorious may be given large cash bonuses. It would seem that any member of the Senior Executive Service would be fully aware that he hardly could meet the criteria for retention in the service, much less promotion or bonuses, if he opposed or impeded the policies of the administration in power.

Another frequent criticism of the merit system is that employees who have permanent appointments are almost impossible to fire for incompetency or other reasons because the process of doing so is complicated and extremely time consuming. In considering this criticism, the first facts are that employees who have been given permanent status may be fired only for cause—such as incompetency—and the process of firing an employee cannot be either arbitrary or summary but must meet the requirements of due process. During the early and mid-seventies, more than 20,000 persons were involuntarily separated from the Federal service each year, and it seems reasonable to assume that at least an equal number resigned rather than contend with a removal proceeding.

The Civil Service Reform Act of 1978 revised the removal procedure of the government by limiting the appeals of an employee from an adverse agency decision to one, whereas prior to this act two or more appeals were possible. At present if a Federal agency acts to remove an employee "for such cause as will promote the efficiency of the service" the employee is entitled to:

1. At least thirty days advance written notice stating the specific reasons for the proposed action.

2. A reasonable time, but not less than seven days, to answer orally and in writing and to furnish affidavits and other documentary evidence in support of the answer.

3. Be represented by an attorney or other representative.

4. A written decision and the specific reasons therein at the earliest practicable date.

5. Appeal to the Merit System Protection Board from the agency's decision.

The protections of a permanent employee from being fired capriciously or for political reasons are a very important part of the merit concept. It is hardly likely that the national government could attract and retain competent employees unless they were given reasonable job security so long as their performance was satisfactory.

The agencies of the national government often are criticized as being overstaffed, presumably on the grounds of employee tenure and bad management. It probably is true that some agencies are or have been overstaffed at times, despite continuing efforts to relate their work forces to their program responsibilities. The control agencies of the government, particularly the Office of Management and Budget and the Civil Service Commission, now the Office of Personnel Management, have given a great deal of attention to this problem and have tried to control it by such measures as accurate job classification, manpower analysis, production standards, and limits on the personnel an agency may employ. The management controls of the national government have been refined during the past twenty-five years to such an extent that it is doubtful that there is a great deal of overstaffing in the federal agencies unless they have special political status.

The most effective approach to reducing the number of federal employees is to continually evaluate the need for the various programs of the government. This approach is seldom attractive to political leaders inasmuch as government agencies or programs exist because they are desired by citizens who enjoy the services they provide. It is far easier for a political leader to attribute overstaffing vaguely to the near impossibility of reducing the "permanent" civil service than to significantly reduce or eliminate services provided by the government.

The overstaffing criticism is closely related to the charge made frequently in some newspapers, journals, and political campaigns that government employees are less productive than the employees of private organizations because of their security of tenure—that is, the public employees do not work as hard as they can or should because they cannot be fired. Since governmental programs cannot be measured by profit or loss, and few governmental operations are generally similar to those of private organizations, the criticism is both difficult to substantiate or to answer. However, it should be noted that the managers of federal agencies have been concerned with productivity since the development of modern personnel administration in the 1930s. Work standards have been established when feasible in the various agencies. Personnel rating systems have long been used, and productivity has been a principal subject of government training programs. Moreover, the Civil Service Reform Act of 1978 requires each department and agency to establish a performance appraisal system that will be based on performance standards that will permit the accurate evaluation of job performance on the basis of objective criteria. All decisions to reward, promote, retain or remove employees will be linked to this evaluation.

A typical effort to increase productivity is the current project of a group of federal agencies—the Bureau of Labor Statistics, the General Accounting Office, the Office of Personnel Management, the Office of Management and Budget—to collect data and develop productivity measures for those federal activities whose quantitative outputs can be counted from year to year and related to the manpower used in their production.

The salaries of public employees has been a much discussed subject, usually with the conclusion that they are too high. Actually, the national government and those of most states and cities have long striven for pay scales generally equivalent to those in the private sector for comparable work. Only in recent years has that goal been reached approximately for the majority of federal employees. The government pays comparable salaries, however, only for low and middle level positions. While federal government departments and agencies require a very high level of administrative leadership, being at least as large and complicated as most private organizations, there never has been any attempt to pay public executives salaries comparable to those paid in the private sector for comparable responsibilities. Salaries in the federal merit system range from

$6,561 to $47,500. The salary of the secretary of a federal department is $66,000. On the other hand, it is not uncommon for top corporate executives in this country to earn a salary in excess of $300,000 a year.

Some observers of the federal government have maintained that if direct political patronage is very limited, there is a great deal of "personal patronage" in the sense of government officials hiring their friends. While there doubtless have been such cases in the federal service, it is highly likely that they have been relatively few among the 200,000 persons the government hires each year. The qualifications of all individuals proposed for appointment are reviewed by agency personnel offices and in some cases by the central personnel agency. Occasionally, the charge is made that an official has had a position classified in such a manner that only a friend can meet its qualifications. This perversion of the merit system has no doubt occurred but probably only very rarely. Job classifications are usually written by classification specialists and are standardized for most positions. In the federal system, job classifications are subject to review by the central personnel agency.

The problems and criticisms of merit personnel administration discussed above indicate that it has not been easy to establish and maintain and has required continuous adjustment to administrative needs and political changes. Obviously, merit personnel administration has not appealed to some individuals and groups, but their criticisms should be rigorously analyzed.

No personnel officers, administrators, observers, or members of the Congress have acclaimed the merit system as we know it as either perfect or perfectly administered. Yet the consensus is that merit personnel administration is the best system yet devised for staffing a public agency with the best personnel possible selected with equal opportunity for all citizens. It does not seem too much to say that the governments of this country must offer men and women positions they cannot be removed from unless there is cause; otherwise, they cannot attract the qualified personnel their increasingly complicated programs require. Staff members should be protected from political coercion, prevented from using their offices for partisan purposes, and paid adequately both in salary and in fringe benefits. After almost a century of experience in this country with merit personnel administration, in which its use by its respective governments has expanded steadily, those who maintain that the concept as defined above should be changed radically or abandoned must assume the burden of specific proof.

NOTE

1. For a full discussion of the Pendleton Act and the circumstances of its enactment see Paul Van Riper, *History of the United States Civil Service* (Evanston, Ill.: Row, Peterson and Co., 1958), chapter 5, on which this discussion of the act is largely based.

CHAPTER THIRTEEN

THE JUDICIARY

THE SUPREME COURT

While few would contend that the Supreme Court should not have the power to interpret the Constitution, there is considerable disagreement over how the nine justices should approach this awesome responsibility. On one side of this debate are those who advocate "judicial restraint," while on the other are those who favor "judicial activism."

Sam Irvin, a former U.S. Senator from North Carolina and for a time a member of that state's Supreme Court, comes down hard on the side of judicial restraint. He argues that the justices of the Supreme Court are obligated to interpret the Constitution solely on the basis of the language contained therein. Where the language is ambiguous, the justices must place themselves in the place of the framers of that document and interpret such language as they believe the framers would have. If provisions of the Constitution are inadequate and require change, then it must come solely through a constitutional amendment, and not through judicial fiat. In this connection, Irvin is highly critical of the Warren Court which he feels substituted its own ideological preferences for the true meaning of the Constitution.

Ramsey Clark, the U.S. Attorney General during the Johnson administration, sides with those who would take a more activist approach to interpreting the Constitution. Noting that the Founding Fathers could not have anticipated the fundamental political, social and economic alterations which have occurred in our society, Clark argues that interpretation of the Constitution must be made in light of these changes. To this extent, the Constitution may be viewed as an evolving document. To interpret the Constitution literally, is to wed us to the past, thereby denying us the ability to cope with the present.

In Support of
Judicial Restraint

Sam J. Ervin, Jr.

In discussing the question whether the role of the Supreme Court is that of policymaker or that of adjudicator, I will use the term "Founding Fathers" to designate the men who drafted and ratified the Constitution.

The Constitution answers this question with unmistakable clarity. There is not a syllable in it which gives the Supreme Court any discretionary power to fashion policies based on such considerations as expediency or prudence to guide the course of action of the government of our country. On the contrary, the Constitution provides in plain and positive terms that the role of the Supreme Court is that of an adjudicator, which determines judicially legal controversies between adverse litigants.

In assigning this role to the Supreme Court, the Founding Fathers were faithful to the dream which inspired them to draft and ratify the Constitution, and to their action in rejecting in the Constitutional Convention repeated proposals that the Supreme Court should act as a council of revision as well as a court and, in its capacity as a council of revision, possess discretionary power to veto all acts of Congress the justices deemed unwise, no matter how much those acts harmonized with the Constitution.[1]

These things do not gainsay that some Supreme Court justices have been unhappy with the role assigned them by the Constitution and have undertaken to usurp and exercise policymaking power. But their usurpations have not altered the rightful role of the Supreme Court. Murder and larceny have been committed in every generation, but that fact has not made murder meritorious or larceny legal. . . .

From Sam J. Ervin, Jr., "First Lecture," in *Role of the Supreme Court: Policymaker or Adjudicator?* (Washington, D.C.: American Enterprise Institute for Public Policy Research, 1970). © American Enterprise Institute, 1970. Reprinted with permission.

THE CONSTITUTION

Let me indicate what the Founding Fathers did in the Constitution to give our nation a government of laws and to preserve for themselves and their posterity the blessings of liberty.

To make our nation "an indestructible union composed of indestructible states,"[2] they delegated enumerated governmental powers to the federal government, and reserved all other governmental powers to the states. To further fragmentize political power, they allocated federal legislative power to the Congress, federal executive power to the President, and federal judicial power to the Supreme Court and "such inferior courts as the Congress may from time to time ordain and establish."[3]

To further forestall tyranny, they forbade federal and state governments to do specified things inimical to freedom, and conferred upon individuals enumerated liberties enforceable against government itself. And, finally, to make government by law secure, they made the Constitution and laws enacted by Congress pursuant to it the supreme law of the land, and imposed upon all public officials, both federal and state, as well as upon the people the duty to obey them.[4]

While they intended the Constitution to endure throughout the ages as the nation's basic instrument of government, the Founding Fathers realized that useful alterations of the Constitution would be suggested by experience. Consequently they made provision for its amendment in one way, and one way only, i.e., by concurrent action of Congress and the states as set forth in Article V.[5] By so doing, they ordained that "nothing new can be put into the Constitution except through the amendatory process" and "nothing old can be taken out without the same process."[6]

THE ROLE OF THE SUPREME COURT

A policy is a definite or settled course of action adopted and followed by government. The power to make policy is discretionary in nature. It involves the making of choices on the basis of expediency or prudence among alternative ways of action.

The power to make policy in a government of laws resides with those who are authorized to participate in the lawmaking process.

The Founding Fathers made policy when they ordained and established the Constitution, which determines the fundamental policies of our country.

Since Article I of the Constitution grants Congress the power to make laws and requires every bill passed by it to be presented to the President for his approval or disapproval before it takes effect, the Congress and the President have policymaking power. Moreover, Article V confers upon the Congress and the states, acting in conjunction, limited policymaking power, i.e., the power to amend the Constitution.

Article III denies the Supreme Court policymaking power in plain and positive terms. It does this by making the Supreme Court a court of law and equity and by granting to it "judicial power" only. Under this Article, the Supreme Court has no power whatever except the power to hear and determine cases between adverse litigants, which are within the scope of its original or appellate jurisdiction.

Article III denies the Supreme Court policymaking power in another way. When it is read in conjunction with the supremacy clause of Article VI, Article III obligates Supreme Court justices to base their decisions in the cases they hear upon the Constitution, the laws, and the treaties of the United States, and thus forbids them to take their personal notions as to what is desirable into account in making their rulings.

For this reason, Supreme Court justices are endowed with power to interpret any provision of the Constitution or any law or treaty which is determinative of the issue arising in a case coming before them.

THE POWER TO INTERPRET THE CONSTITUTION

The power to interpret the Constitution is an awesome power. This is so because, in truth, constitutional government cannot exist in our land unless this power is exercised aright.

Chief Justice Stone had this thought in mind when he stated this truth concerning Supreme Court justices:

> While unconstitutional exercise of power by the executive and legislative branches of the government is subject to judicial restraint, the only check upon our exercise of power is our own sense of self-restraint. [7]

The power to interpret the Constitution, which is allotted to the Supreme Court, and the power to amend the Constitution, which is assigned to Congress and the states acting in conjunction, are quite different. The power to interpret the Constitution is the power to ascertain its meaning, and the power to amend the Constitution is the power to change its meaning.

Justice Cardozo put the distinction between the two powers tersely when he said:

> We are not at liberty to revise while professing to construe. [8]

Justice Sutherland elaborated upon the distinction in this way:

> The judicial function is that of interpretation: it does not include the power of amendment under the guise of interpretation. To miss the point of difference between the two is to miss all that the phrase "supreme law of the land" stands for and to convert what was intended as inescapable and enduring mandates into mere moral reflections. [9]

America's greatest jurist of all times, Chief Justice John Marshall, established these landmarks of constitutional interpretation:

1. That the principles of the Constitution "are designed to be permanent."[10]

2. That "the enlightened patriots who framed our Constitution, and the people who adopted it, must be understood . . . to have intended what they have said."[11]

3. That the Constitution constitutes a rule for the government of Supreme Court justices in their official action.[12]

Since it is a court of law and equity, the Supreme Court acts as the interpreter of the Constitution only in a litigated case whose decision of necessity turns on some provision of that instrument. As a consequence, the function of the Court is simply to ascertain and give effect to the intent of those who framed and ratified the provision in issue. If the provision is plain, the Court must gather the intent solely from its language, but if the provision is ambiguous, the Court must place itself as nearly as possible in that condition of those who framed and ratified it, and in that way determine the intent the language was used to express. For these reasons, the Supreme Court is duty bound to interpret the Constitution according to its language and history.[13] . . .

THE WARREN COURT

During most of our history, Supreme Court justices were faithful to the dream of the Founding Fathers. They accepted the Constitution as the rule for their official action, and decided constitutional issues in accordance with its precepts.

Unfortunately, however, this has not been true during recent years. Shortly before 1953, Supreme Court justices began to substitute their personal notions for constitutional provisions under the guise of interpreting them, and provoked one of their colleagues, Justice Robert H. Jackson, into making this righteous outcry:

> Rightly or wrongly, the belief is widely held by the practicing profession that this Court no longer respects impersonal rules of law but is guided in these matters by personal impressions which from time to time may be shared by a majority of the Justices. Whatever has been intended, this Court also has generated an impression in much of the judiciary that regard for precedents and authorities is obsolete, that words no longer mean what they have always meant to the profession, that the law knows no fixed principles.[14]

With the advent of the Warren Court, this practice increased in frequency and intensity; and the Supreme Court decisions irreconcilable with the Constitution became in Milton's colorful phrase as "thick as autumnal leaves that strow the brooks in Vallombrosa."

I use the terms "Warren Court" and "justices of the Warren Court" to designate Chief Justice Warren and Justices Douglas, Brennan, Goldberg, Fortas, and Marshall who repeatedly undertook to revise the Constitution while professing to interpret it. Candor compels the confession that despite his eloquent protests against their misuse of the due process clauses of the Fifth and Fourteenth Amendments, Justice Black often aligned himself with the justices of the Warren Court; and that although the other justices who served at various times during the incumbency of Chief Justice Warren, namely, Justices Reed, Frankfurter, Jackson, Burton, Clark, Minton, Harlan, Stewart, and White, were rather steadfast in their adherence to the Constitution, some of them joined the Warren Court on some occasions in handing down revolutionary decisions inconsistent with the words and history of that instrument.[15]

The tragic truth is that under the guise of interpreting them, the Warren Court repeatedly assigned to constitutional provisions meanings incompatible with their language and history.

By so doing, it has impeded the President and his subordinates in the performance of their constitutional duty to execute the laws.

At times it has undertaken to abridge the constitutional powers of Congress as the nation's lawmaker, and at other times it has undertaken to stretch the legislative power of Congress far beyond their constitutional limits. And sometimes it has thwarted the will of Congress by imputing to congressional acts constructions which cannot be harmonized with their words.

What the Warren Court has done to the power allotted or reserved to the states by the Constitution beggars description. It has invoked the due process and equal protection clauses of the Fourteenth Amendment as *carte blanche* to invalidate all state action which Supreme Court justices think undesirable.

This is tragic, indeed, because nothing is truer than this observation attributed to Justice Brandeis by Judge Learned Hand:

> *The States are the only breakwater against the ever pounding surf which threatens to submerge the individual and destroy the only kind of society in which personality can survive.*

Besides, the Warren Court twisted some constitutional provisions awry to deny individuals basic personal and property rights.

All of the decisions of which I complain have tended to concentrate power in the federal government in general and the Supreme Court in particular.

The time presently allotted to me does not permit me to analyze or even enumerate these decisions.

These things mean little or nothing to those who would as soon have our country ruled by the arbitrary, uncertain, and inconstant wills of judges as by the certain and constant precepts of the Constitution. But they mean everything to those of us who love the Constitution and believe it evil to twist its precepts out of shape even to accomplish ends which may be desirable.

If desirable ends are not attainable under the Constitution as written, they should be attained in a forthright manner by an amendment under Article V, and not by judicial alchemy which transmutes words into things they do not say. Otherwise, the Constitution is a meaningless scrap of paper.

Nobody questions the good intentions of the justices of the Warren Court. They undoubtedly were motivated by a determination to improve and update the Constitution by substituting their personal notions for its principles. But candor compels the confession that their usurpations call to mind these trenchant observations of Daniel Webster:

> Good intentions will always be pleaded for every assumption of power. It is hardly too strong to say that the Constitution was made to guard the people against the dangers of good intentions. There are men in all ages who mean to govern well, but they mean to govern. They promise to be good masters, but they mean to be masters.

Those who champion or seek to justify the activism of the Warren Court assert with glibness that the Constitution is a living document which the Court must interpret with flexibility.

When they say the Constitution is a living document, they really mean that the Constitution is dead, and that activist justices as its executors may dispose of its remains as they please. I submit that if the Constitution is, indeed, a living document, its words are binding on those who pledge themselves by oath or affirmation to support it.

What of the cliché that the Supreme Court should interpret the Constitution with flexibility? If those who employ this cliché mean by it that a provision of the Constitution should be interpreted with liberality to accomplish its intended purpose, they would find me in hearty agreement with them. But they do not employ the cliché to mean this. On the contrary, they use the cliché to mean that the Supreme Court should bend the words of a constitutional provision to one side or the other to accomplish an objective the provision does not sanction. Hence, they use the cliché to thwart what the Founding Fathers had in mind when they fashioned the Constitution.

The genius of the Constitution is this: the grants of power it makes and the limitations it imposes are inflexible, but the powers it grants extend into the future and are exercisable with liberality on all occasions by the departments in which they are vested.

SAVING THE CONSTITUTION

As the result of the assumptions of power of the Warren Court, the people of our nation are now ruled in substantial areas of their lives by the partial wills of Supreme Court justices rather than by the impartial precepts of the Constitution. . . .

It is obvious to those who love the Constitution and are willing to face naked reality that the Warren Court took giant strides down the road of usurpation, and that if the course set by it is not reversed, the dream of the Founding Fathers will vanish and the most precious liberty of the people—the right to constitutional government—will perish.

Despite their perilous state, the dream of the Founding Fathers can be rekindled and the precious right of the people to constitutional government can be preserved if those who possess the power will stretch forth saving hands while there is yet time.

Who are they that possess this saving power?

They are Supreme Court justices, who are able and willing to exercise self-restraint and make the Constitution the rule for the government of their official action; Presidents, who will nominate for membership on the Supreme Court persons who are able and willing to exercise self-restraint and make the Constitution the role for the government of their official action; and senators, who will reject for Supreme Court membership nominees who are either unable or unwilling to exercise self-restraint and make the Constitution the rule for the government of their official action.

And, finally, if Supreme Court justices, Presidents, and senators fail them, the people may employ their own saving power. Through Congress and the states, they may adopt a constitutional amendment similar to my proposal which would compel Presidents and senators to make appointments to the Supreme Court from among persons recommended to them by the chief justices of the states. The people can rely upon the chief justices of the states to restrict their recommendations to persons who revere the federal system ordained by the Constitution and who will not sanction the concentration of power which always precedes the destruction of human liberties.

Let me add that lawyers who love the Constitution can aid the cause by practicing this preachment of Chief Justice Stone:

> Where the courts deal, as ours do, with great public questions, the only protection against unwise decisions, and even judicial usurpations, is careful scrutiny of their action, and fearless comment upon it.

In closing I make a conditional prophesy. If those who possess the power to rekindle the dream of the Founding Fathers and to preserve the right of the people to constitutional government do not act, Americans will learn with agonizing sorrow the tragic truth taught by Justice Sutherland:

The saddest epitaph which can be carved in memory of a vanished liberty is that it was lost because its possessors failed to stretch forth a saving hand while yet there was time.

NOTES

1. United States: Formation of the Union, pp. 147, 152, 165, 167, 422, 429, 548, 752, 753, 756, 848, 849, 852.
2. Texas v. White, 7 Wall. 700.
3. Article III, Section 1.
4. Article VI.
5. James Madison: The Federalist, No. 43.
6. Ullman v. U.S., 350 U.S. 422.
7. U.S. v. Butler, 297 U.S. 1, 78-79.
8. Sun Printing and Publishing Association v. Remington Paper and Power Co., 235 N.Y. 338, 139 N.E. 470.
9. West Coast Hotel Co. v. Parrish, 300 U.S. 379, 404, 81 L.ed. 703, 715.
10. Marbury v. Madison, 1 Cranch. 137, 175.
11. Gibbons v. Ogden, 9 Wheat. 1, 188.
12. Marbury v. Madison, 1 Cranch. 137.
13. Gibbons v. Ogden, 9 Wheat. 213, Ex Parte Bain, 121 U.S. 1; Lake County v. Rollins, 130 U.S. 662.
14. Brown v. Allen, 344 U.S. 443, 535.
15. See e.g., Justice White in Reitman v. Mulkey, 387 U.S. 369 (1967); and Justice Stewart in Jones v. Mayer Co., 392 U.S. 409 (1968).

In Support of
Judicial Activism

Ramsey Clark

We demean the Constitution of the United States by this endless metaphysical debate over "strict construction." There are real constitutional issues to be faced, perhaps even constitutional crises. They will require all the vision and courage we can muster. The false notion that men who wrote those words 183 years ago—distant age—could foresee the unforeseeable, or that we can look back and in words alone, or from their intent in the context of 1787, divine the authors' precise meaning as applied to current facts is contrary to all human experience. Our problems, actual and immense, cannot be solved by such conjury. We are fortunate that nature spares us from the foresight that would be required to give truth to the doctrine of strict construction, because the only thing worse than such an impossibility would be its possibility.

Change is the dominant fact of our times. Population and technology, the major dynamics, create more change in a decade than centuries witnessed heretofore. Life changes, the meanings of words change, the needs of man change. The Constitution, born in a fundamentally different epoch, must have the durability and wisdom to grow, to encompass essentially new situations, to meet new needs. It can.

To invoke the Founding Fathers against change is to charge them with seeking to deny subsequent generations that to which they were wholly committed for their own. To vest the Supreme Law of the Land with some religious attachment to the status quo is to deny its very meaning and disable the Ship of State in the turbulent seas of change. The purpose behind the doctrine of strict construction as utilized today is not to find specific guidance where none can exist. It is to resist change: to stay where we are, do as we have done and offer no hope. We can no longer afford this.

From Ramsey Clark, "Second Lecture," in *Role of the Supreme Court: Policymaker or Adjudicator?* (Washington, D.C.: American Enterprise Institute for Public Policy Research, 1970). © American Enterprise Institute, 1970. Reprinted with permission.

The results of efforts to invoke the doctrine of strict construction dot our legal history. Their consequences have often been disastrous.

A high water mark came in *Scott* v. *Sandford,* the "Dred Scott" decision, in 1857. There, the Supreme Court held that it lacked jurisdiction to determine whether Congress had power to ban slavery in the territories north of Missouri, or whether a slave voluntarily taken into a free state by his master thereby became free, because on a narrow and technical reading of some of the words of the Constitution, it concluded that no slave could be a "citizen" for purposes of federal jurisdiction. The language of the Constitution as readily read otherwise. Having disclaimed jurisdiction, the Court then proceeded, because strict constructionists are human and have their purposes, to answer these nation-shattering questions in the negative, ruling out not only a judicial, but a legislative solution to the slavery issue and thereby failing to do what it could to prevent the most calamitous war in our history. The majority sought to justify these tragic rulings, by pleading obedience to strict construction, saying:

> No one, we presume supposes that any change in public opinion or feeling, in relation to this unfortunate race . . . shall induce the court to give to the words of the Constitution a more liberal construction in their favor than they were intended to bear when the instrument was framed and adopted.

In 1918, a bare majority of the Supreme Court again showed what strict construction can mean. Reading the Commerce Clause alone, it said the federal government is powerless to prevent interstate shipment of the products of child labor. *Hammer* v. *Dagenhart,* 247 U.S. 251 (1918). The Constitution by that construction—unsupported incidentally in the language of the charter—did not empower the Congress to prevent virtual slave labor of ten- and 12-year-old children working in sweatshops 70 hours or more a week for subsistence wages. These men were not deciding issues on the basis of some clear understanding of intentions from 1787. The men in the Hall at Philadelphia could not foresee such questions, much less their answers. They were cruelly used by justices who would decide by fiat what words meant to them, then grace themselves in the mantle of the Founding Fathers. The experience and sympathies of the Court's majority were closer to the cotton mill owners who destroyed children than to justice and humane concerns, and they resisted change. If the majority opinion in *Hammer* v. *Dagenhart* prevailed today, the union would be a shambles. Can the commerce of 1787 be equated with the commerce of 1970? . . .

. . .The words of the Constitution matter greatly, but they do not suffice to solve the problems of another day. They are the place of beginning, not of ending. To begin and end, poring over words to find meanings they do not contain denies us the benefits of experience, the strength of growth and the wisdom of the spirit of the Constitution.

Strict construction is at best a convenient argument with which to support or attack particular judicial decisions. How many of us are really prepared to have our Constitution construed solely by its words and their intention when written? There is, after all, not a word in the Constitution about many of our most important protections. The hallowed presumption of innocence, and the requirement that guilt in criminal cases be proven beyond a reasonable doubt are not found in the words of the Constitution. Nor does the Constitution say that state governments may not trample upon freedom of speech or press or religion, that state legislatures must be fairly apportioned, or that any of us have any "right to privacy."

Even the most distinguished advocates of strict construction do not interpret the Constitution from its words when they address principles where words fail. Thus the Supreme Court's most prominent advocate of strict construction has fought tirelessly to preserve our First Amendment freedoms against interference by state governments and to require fair apportionment of state legislatures. The Constitution does not say this. And our foremost senatorial spokesman for strict construction champions the cause of the "right of privacy," believing that the Constitution itself prevents intrusion into the private lives of government employees by government snoopers armed with wiretaps, bugs, or computers. On these crucial issues, even the strict constructionists must look to the spirit of the Constitution and to the requirements of a free society.

It is hardly surprising that the words of the Constitution, even supplemented by their historical context, do not resolve the great questions of our time. In 1791, when the ink on the Constitution was hardly dry, President Washington, who had chaired the Convention, Thomas Jefferson, and Alexander Hamilton were unable to agree among themselves on whether the "necessary and proper clause" authorized the federal government to charter a national bank. Eventually the matter was resolved not on the basis of some nonexistent "plain meaning" of the constitutional language, but on the best judgment the statement of the day could make as to what was an appropriate rule for a constitutional federal government considering the general powers delegated to it. The crises which we face today, the great constitutional questions which are put to the Supreme Court for resolution, are far more difficult. Mass society, urban poverty, racism, vast industry, huge labor unions, tall skyscrapers, automobiles, jet aircraft, television, nuclear energy, environmental pollution, mass assemblies and protests, the interdependence of nations and individuals create issues undreamed of in the philosophies of the Founding Fathers.

The Constitution guides by general principle—a light that recognizes the existence of change. By its very nature it must embody a whole theory in a quick phrase—to regulate commerce—the general welfare—due process of law—the equal protection of the laws. Hundreds, thousands of cases are required to give the phrase a growing content, but the Constitution sets the tone. If it were to be specific, it could not be a Constitution nor hope to maintain a theory and framework of government with general powers and limitations.

The nature of the Constitution and the decisional process by which its principles are extended to new conditions have been recognized from the beginning.

Perhaps the most famous and profound expression was by Chief Justice John Marshall in *McCulloch* v. *Maryland*, 4 Wheat. 316 (1819): ". . . we must never forget that it is a Constitution we are expounding. . . . [a] Constitution intended to endure for ages to come, and consequently, to be adapted to the various crises of human affairs." Words of immutable meaning cannot be adapted to crises, and nations bound to them fail. But in truth there are no immutable words. To say there are is only to place the power to divine their meaning in some high priest. This has never led to truth. As Benjamin Cardozo observed in *The Truth of Law*, "Magic words and incantation are fatal to our science (law) as they are to any other." Learned Hand, a blunt man, said "There is no surer way to misread any document than to read it literally." *Guiseppe* v. *Walling*, 144 F.2d 608, 624 (2d Cir. 1944).

Cardozo demonstrated in *The Nature of the Judicial Process* that "The great generalities of the Constitution have a content and significance that vary from age to age. . . . A *Constitution* states . . . principles for an expanding future," pp. 17, 83. . . .

The essential qualities to give integrity, force, and vitality to the Constitution are deep commitment to its spirit, stern self-discipline in relating that spirit to present facts, understanding of the history and function of law in society, and sensitivity to the expanding future. A dictionary, smallness of spirit, and fear of change will not empower an old piece of parchment to curtail conduct of people that new conditions compel.

Perhaps the major question of our times is whether institutions can change to cope with the vast dynamics of mass urban population and burgeoning technology. The answer is far from clear. Can government be responsive to the needs of its people? Will technology master man? Can violence as an international and interpersonal problem solver be conditioned from human capability? Can we assure human dignity? Will racism divide people who must live together with dignity, respect, and love? . . .

The United States Supreme Court, inherently the most conservative institution within our system of government, has addressed itself to the present and future more effectively than any other agent of our society. Somehow, these last 20 years, it has detected the greatest needs of our times in the cases that have found their way to its forum and has acted to meet those needs.

The reapportionment cases, beginning with *Baker* v. *Carr,* 369 U.S. 186 (1962), in essence liberate government from the nineteenth century. Without that liberation, legislative bodies could not possibly address themselves meaningfully to the crushing problems of the people. The decisions were constitutional necessities. To have held otherwise would have crippled the spirit of a constitution that serves the people.

In *Brown* v. *Board of Education,* 347 U.S. 483 (1954), and a multitude of other civil rights cases, the Court addressed itself to the one huge wrong of the American nation—racism—and caused us to begin to do what decency and justice require. The spirit of the Constitution was clear on this subject. What other meaning can the Thirteenth, Fourteenth, and Fifteenth Amendments have? The failure was in the people. To now blame the Court for upholding the Constitution is hardly to respect that document or to seek fulfillment of its word.

Finally, in a whole series of cases we sometimes describe under the heading of civil liberties, the Supreme Court, enforcing the Constitution, recognized the great crisis in the meaning of the individual in our times—in human dignity. It said things we should have known all along. If we are to have equal justice, the poor, the ignorant, the sick, and despised as well as the rich and powerful must have "the assistance of counsel for his defense." *Gideon* v. *Wainwright,* 372 U.S. 335 (1963). No longer can police question persons in their custody without advising them of their rights. *Miranda* v. *Arizona,* 384 U.S. 436 (1966). Fulfillment of constitutional rights is no mere game. We insist on them. Government has an obligation to give them vitality, not seek their waiver. The educated know their rights, the rich have their lawyers; the powerful, however capable of crime, will be protected. So must the poor, the ignorant, and the powerless. So Danny Escobedo and Ernest Miranda could not be convicted by their own confessions when they were denied constitutional rights.

If we care for the future, our concern must not be that the Supreme Court had the wisdom and courage to face the central issues of our times, but that other institutions have done so little not only to seek solutions but to fulfill the critically important constitutional rights decreed by the Court.

. . .

COURTS AND CRIMINAL JUSTICE

Although crime is a social affliction with which all societies must cope, the problem has become especially acute in the United States, where an increasing number of Americans view it as one of the major social problems confronting the nation. While students of American society have offered a variety of sociological explanations for our crime problem, Ernest Van den Haag argues that much of the blame must be laid at the doorstep of the courts. Specifically, he contends that because of their insistence upon a variety of procedural safeguards for the accused, our criminal courts have rendered the trial process seemingly endless and the chances of conviction highly remote. In doing so, he contends that the courts have destroyed the two primary deterrents to crime, namely, swiftness *and* certainty *of punishment.*

Charles Silberman, on the other hand, argues that the indictments made against our criminal justice system by Van den Haag and others are simply untrue. In part, he says, this is because some of their data are incorrect; and in part, also because they misinterpret some of their evidence. Far from being ineffectual, Silberman concludes that our courts function in both a rational and just manner.

The Ineffectiveness of the Criminal Justice System

Ernest van den Haag

The penalties served by offenders in the U.S. and, above all, the probability of serving them are extremely low. For more than two-thirds of all felonies there are no arrests. And according to Maurice A. Nadjari, New York state special prosecutor, "there are 97,000 felony arrests in New York City in a year . . . and only 900 defendants are tried to the point of reaching a verdict."[1] This means that less than 1 percent of the arrested are tried. The rest either plead guilty to a lesser offense or are released because it is felt that no conviction could be obtained. The percentage of those punished (as distinguished from the percentage of those tried) for a crime is suggested by a study made in Atlanta, which showed that out of 278 adults arrested for assault, 63 were convicted and 23 served a jail sentence.[2] Surely part of the explanation for the difference between the U.S. and foreign crime rates lies in these figures: American crime rates are high because punishment rates are low. From 1960 to 1970 the crime rate increased 144 percent (reported crime increased 176 percent; the difference is accounted for by the increase in population). Reported arrests increased only 31 percent. The number of convicted offenders decreased from 117 to 95 per 100,000 population. Thus, arrest rates declined. And so did rates of conviction. In 1960 118 persons per 100,000 were in prison in the U.S.; in 1970 96 persons, a drop of more than 20 percent. This decline occurred while crime rates rose 144 percent. *Res ipsa loquitur:* The matter speaks for itself. The difficulty is in the courts.

Calls for higher rates of punishment used to come exclusively from the right side of the political spectrum. But, as crime has spread to middle class areas and suburbs, second thoughts appear to have seized persons who could normally be counted on to be more solicitous of offenders than of their victims. The trend is not universal, but it is unmistakable. The

Excerpted from *Punishing Criminals: Concerning a Very Old and Painful Question,* by Ernest van den Haag, pp. 158-173, © 1975 Basic Books, Inc., Publishers, New York.

following will illustrate both the growing outcry for more punishment and the determined opposition.

Margot Hentoff, a far from conservative New York writer, wrote the passages quoted here after she went to court with her husband, who had been mugged. She published her essay in the antiestablishmentarian *Village Voice*, a weekly New York City paper characterized by free-floating, non-party leftism.

> . . . As I remembered [the night court], the prisoners used to be mostly hookers, gamblers, and old derelicts who had been found drunk and helpless on the street. But this time it was different. A horde of menacing suspects (with a history of arrest upon arrest for crimes against people) were marched before the judge and, in one way or another, most of them were able to walk out of the building that night with either conditional discharges or extremely meetable bail—especially meetable since many of them had just ripped off enough money to meet it.

> After a while, considering what lay ahead in those cases which were not disposed of, it became clear that a complainant would have to appear in court as many times as the suspect, that he was not going to get any of his money back, and that the final disposition of the case would probably send the suspect back out into the city to continue his profitable and only minimally perilous career. In fact, it was a toss-up as to who would be most inconvenienced by the crime—the victim, the perpetrator, or the police.

> . . . It struck me that it was indeed true that New York was not so much a city full of criminals as it was a city plagued by a hard core of felons who go about their daily business almost outside the reach of the law . . . in a judicial system which neither corrects the behavior of the antisocial nor removes them from the rest of us. . . .

ACTUAL PUNISHMENT

Given the offense, actual punishment depends on the probability of (1) apprehension, (2) conviction, (3) the plea entered (or the charge sustained) and the sentence imposed, and (4) the sentence actually served. Most convictions are obtained upon guilty pleas to charges involving far lower penalties than the charges originally made: most offenders are punished not for the offense charged or committed but for a lesser one. And a great deal of time elapses between the offense and the punishment.

Offenders are granted parole for one-third of their federal sentences, unless they seriously misbehave while in prison, and they may be paroled earlier, as they are in most states. In fact, a life sentence usually means imprisonment for from seven to fifteen years. In some states parole is available after shorter periods (six months in Florida). Parole boards, however well intentioned, have few rational rules for deciding whether or not to parole. Finally, if the judge puts the convicted defendant on probation, he does not have to serve time in jail at all if he behaves lawfully over a given supervised period. And in most cases supervision is a formality.

Let me illustrate. . . .

[A]ccording to the New York Times (Jan. 27, 1975), "Almost eight of every ten defendants accused of homicide in New York plead guilty to a reduced charge and are freed on probation or receive a prison term of less than 10 years. Of those receiving a maximum 10-year term, most will be eligible for parole in three years." (Eighty percent of the defendants charged with homicide in 1973 pleaded guilty; 4.5 percent received life sentences, whereas 28.5 percent received a maximum of five years and 20 percent received a conditional discharge, or probation.)

The New York Times also reported (Feb. 8, 1975) that Hosie S. Turner was convicted of murder after a month-long trial in October 1973. His prior record included "sixteen convictions for robbery, burglary, larceny, parole violation, drug possession and sale. . . . He invariably was allowed to plead guilty to a lesser charge." The practice of reducing charges and imposing minor penalties on persons with a long record of violent crimes continues, according to the New York Times (Feb. 11, 1975). In 1974 nearly 80 percent of all felony arrests in New York City were disposed of by the city criminal court by reducing the charges to misdemeanors. . . .

Whatever the faults of the sitting judges, they cannot be saddled with the whole blame. They must labor under laws, procedures, precedents, and appeals court decisions that so favor the defendants as to compel courts to reduce charges of which defendants are, in many cases, clearly guilty. . . .

DELAYS

About 18,000 murders were committed in 1972 in the U.S. The homicide rate per 100,000 persons increased from 4.5 in 1963 to 9.3 in 1973. This figure, remarkably high by any standard, includes only reported murders and excludes negligent manslaughter and about 55,000 vehicular homicides. In 1972 London (about the size of New York) had 113 murders; New York, 1,700. London had 3,000 robberies; New York, 78,000. London had 150 rapes; New York, 3,300.

All parts of the criminal justice system must share the blame for the fact that so small a proportion of all crimes committed—about 1 percent—ever lead to actual imprisonment of the offender in the U.S. The police can never catch all criminals. Could they catch more? Many people claim that police departments in most cities are riddled with inefficiency, politics, and corruption, and that our criminals are more, and our police less, effective than in most of the Western countries.[3] Others claim that our police are hamstrung by our solicitude for suspects. At any rate, the behavior of our courts is more important, and most scandalous by far. The sheer incompetence and occasional corruption of many politically selected judges cannot be ignored. But the rules under which even the best-run courts have to operate play much the greater role. Some of these rules are enacted by legislatures. Many more have accumulated as a result of past decisions of appellate courts, including the U.S. Supreme Court. In effect, the courts have become nearly hamstrung by the accumulation of their own past attempts at perfection.[4]

The probability of convicting the guilty is greatly reduced in the U.S. by (a) delay, (b) the exclusionary rule, and (c) literally endless appeals allowed defendants from state to federal courts. Furthermore, many offenders are classified as juvenile delinquents to be "reformed" rather than punished, and others—far too many—are excused as mentally incompetent. "Reform"—custody for juveniles and incompetents—often means inappropriate terms: too indefinite, too long, or too short. Reformative institutions for juveniles have not been shown to be more effective than simple imprisonment. Incompetents referred to psychiatric institutions may be kept for life or for a few months, depending on utterly capricious psychiatric judgments.

As for the conviction of competent adults guilty of crime, there are innumerable time-wasting procedural hindrances. Some illustrations will have to do. . . . Joseph W. Bishop, Jr., professor of law at Yale University, in a review of Macklin Fleming's book, *The Price of Perfect Justice*, affords the layman a glance at what happens.

> . . . the incarceration of even the most obviously guilty criminal is a task comparable to landing a barracuda with a trout-rod and a dryfly. . . . [There are] numerous techniques by which an accused with an astute, well-paid, and/or zealous lawyer can delay or frustrate his prosecution, litigate the same issue (which may have little or nothing to do with his guilt or innocence) in several different courts, state and federal, and should he actually be convicted, attack the constitutionality of that conviction by endless appeals and petitions for habeas corpus. He can start before trial by seeking to enjoin the prosecution on the ground that its threat chills an asserted constitutional right. He can attack the indictment by claiming some ethnic or other group to which he claims to belong—people with Spanish surnames, young people, old people, people with low incomes, people with little education, etc., etc., ad infinitum—were inadequately represented on the panel from which the grand jury was drawn. This issue can be litigated, appealed, and reviewed by collateral process in both state and federal courts for months and years. Similar attacks can be made on the composition of the trial jury. Likewise, he can seek to disqualify the trial judge for alleged bias and appeal the judges' refusal to disqualify himself. He can assert that appointed defense counsel is incompe-

tent, before, during, and after the trial. He can demand that he be allowed to represent himself. If the request is denied and he loses his case, he can appeal on that ground; if it is granted, he can appeal on that ground also, arguing that the trial judge should have recognized his unfitness to be his own lawyer. He can move to suppress evidence, even when its truth and relevance are unquestioned, on the ground that it was obtained illegally; Justice Fleming itemizes twenty-six separate state and federal proceedings in which a defendant can challenge the lawfulness of a single search or seizure. Moreover, he can petition for habeas corpus ad libitum, *hoping finally to find a federal judge who agrees with him and disagrees with all the other judges, for the doctrine of* res judicata—*that an issue finally determined by a court cannot be reopened—does not apply to* habeas corpus, *and a single federal district judge can spring a convict whose arguments have been unanimously rejected by a state's supreme court and other federal judges. If all else fails, the petitioner can argue that the inadequacy of the prison's law library denies him due process or the equal protection of the laws. These . . . are only a small sampling of Justice Fleming's catalogue (all documented by actual cases) of the devices which make it a labor of Sisyphus to put a criminal in jail and keep him there. One who loses at every step can almost claim that that very fact shows he has been denied equal protection of the laws.* [5]

Some illustrative comparisons may cast light on our timewasting procedures. Lord Haw-Haw (William Joyce) was tried in England after the Second World War for broadcasting for the Nazis. He was found guilty by a jury after a three-day trial in September 1945. By December he had exhausted his appeals and was hanged January 3, 1946. Tokyo Rose (Iva D'aquino) was tried in the U.S. for broadcasting for the Japanese. When her trial started, after many delays, it lasted two months. She was found guilty and sentenced to ten years. The last of her numerous appeals was rejected four and a half years later. These are not isolated cases; they are typical. The longest criminal trial in England lasted forty-eight days and the longest murder trial twenty-one. The trial of the Manson "family" in California lasted nine months. Selection of the jury for Bobby Seale (acquitted) took five months. In England it usually takes a few minutes. There is no evidence that the quality of English justice, or juries, is inferior to our own. Other practices that contribute to unjustifiable delays and to uncertainty are too numerous to list. The requirement of jury unanimity often means that the government has to retry a defendant several times to reach a verdict, or give up and let him go. A two-thirds majority might do as well—after all, it suffices to amend the Constitution. As it is, our judicial system seems more designed to blunt the deterrent force of punishment in the rare cases in which it is imposed and to protect defendants' rights than to protect society from crime. It certainly works that way.

Many minor cases in the U.S. are never tried even when they reach the courts. Between ten and twenty postponements are not uncommon. When defense lawyers suspect their client can be shown to be guilty, they delay—with the consent of the judge—until witnesses disappear or become unwilling to waste another day in court. Without witnesses or complainants, the defendant is safely acquitted. Trial judges, although given rules about expeditious trials, often have no choice. If they do not grant adjournments, the appellate courts may reverse the decision despite the rules.[6]. . .

Moralists and the media often lament the unwillingness of the public to come to the aid of victims of a crime being committed, to help pursue the criminal, or to testify to what they have seen. In a notorious New York City case, Kitty Genovese was murdered under the eyes of many people who literally shut their windows as the dying woman was being pursued and repeatedly attacked by her murderer. Of course, the moralists are right. Yet none bothers to explain what happens all too often to those who try to help, if only by calling the police.[7] They get into a lot of trouble and look in vain for protection by the authorities. A man who in self-defense shoots a burglar or assailant is more likely to be arrested for illegal possession of weapons than to be congratulated. It can be quite dangerous, and in any case is hardly rewarding, to denounce the corner heroin dealer to the police, or the numbers runner, or to testify to a gang murder, or to become unpopular with a neighborhood gang of juveniles.

Whereas the protection offered victims and witnesses is minimal, the protection given suspects often is nearly impenetrable. Known criminals can live undisturbed in the community, having to fear only other criminals. With so small a percentage of all crimes punished, it is a marvel that the overwhelming majority of people remain law-abiding. They do. But we seem to live off the capital of the past. Crime is rising rapidly; the cautionary adage "crime does not pay" is becoming an old wives' tale.

THE EXCLUSIONARY RULE

English justice, renowned for fairness, does without the "exclusionary rule," which in the U.S. excludes from admission as evidence anything—documents, photographs, tapes, weapons, information—seized without legal authority. A confession made before the suspect has been offered a lawyer is inadmissible. (No lawyer has ever been known to encourage his client to confess to the police.) Evidence found as a result of an inadmissible confession is ruled inadmissible, too. So is evidence seized in a search of persons or places not authorized by warrant or wholly justified by circumstances. The "exclusionary rule" was established in federal courts[8] and has been steadily enlarged and applied to state proceedings.[9] Only in 1974[10] did the courts begin to limit the rule.

The exclusion of hearsay evidence is perhaps defensible. (Perhaps. Juries can, after all, distinguish with the help of the lawyers for the two sides.) The exclusion of previous conviction records is unwarranted. To be sure, the previous record tells nothing about the offense at issue. But in practice, verdicts are probability decisions. Previous convictions do help form a judgment about probabilities. If a bishop is accused of robbery, one wants to scrutinize the evidence carefully and give him the benefit of the doubt. If a man with previous convictions for robbery is accused once more of the same crime, one must scrutinize the evidence carefully, to be sure, but one is justifiably more inclined to believe the victim or the witnesses.

Unlawful conduct by the police should be punished. But not by letting a murderer benefit from the error, the impropriety, or the offense of an overzealous law-enforcement officer who obtained the evidence—e.g., the weapon used—without a search warrant. If we want to discourage unlawful police actions, must we do it in so roundabout a way at the price of freeing guilty persons? Must society punish itself rather than the guilty law-enforcement officer? No other country in the world does. Nor does our exclusionary rule keep the police more law-abiding than they are elsewhere.

The rule has caused our trials to take place in a legal wonderland. Courts, instead of trying to find out if the defendant is guilty or innocent, spend their time determining whether or not the evidence that might prove his guilt is admissible.[11] Any newspaper is entitled to publish illegally obtained information. No court is entitled to weigh illegally obtained evidence.

The exclusionary rule has not worked as intended. It has not led to more lawful, but only to less effective, law enforcement. It should be abolished. . . . Lawful and effective law enforcement depend on wholly different matters, such as the recruitment, training, and discipline of the police force. As a matter of fact, the exclusionary rule, by permitting policemen to pretend to enforce the law while deliberately making enough errors to have the evidence excluded and the defendants acquitted, has helped in protecting lawless policemen as well as civilian criminals. It has victimized innumerable law-abiding citizens by letting known criminals go scot free.

The following letter is unusual in as much as the writer bothered to complain and to come to court as cften as she did, vastly amusing the defendant.

> In early October, 1972, I was mugged at the front door of my house in Hollis Hills, Queens. The mugger was caught within three hours of my report to the police. I pressed charges and six hearings over a span of six months ensued. When my father and I walked into the sixth hearing, the defendant, his wife, and his brother-in-law were overly friendly, waving, smiling, and bidding us good luck. All the evidence which helped catch the mugger was offered: (1) description of car—year, type, color; (2) license plate number—one number off, M instead of W; (3) $40 in the mugger's pocket in the exact bills I reported

missing; (4) an autoharp pick—he did not even know what an autoharp is; (5) an almost exact approximation of his height and weight; (6) accurate description of his clothing, etc. . . . The mugger was freed after the sixth hearing because of an illegal search of vehicle by the policeman.

Last night on Channel 5 news, there was an item about the $1 rapist, who was finally caught after raping about 25 women in Queens. His name, Leroy Hamlin, was the same man who had mugged me . . . Mr. Hamlin had several previous arrests prior to mugging me.[12]

PLEA BARGAINING

We have created other difficulties. Appeals are riskless for the defendant: penalties cannot be increased nor partial acquittals overturned. The prosecution cannot appeal. This makes it safe for judges to help produce acquittals if they so want. At any rate, they become defense-minded: if a judge errs against the defendant, an appeal is likely and he may be overruled. If he errs against the prosecution, the judge is safe. No appeal is possible. Hence, when in doubt, it is in the judge's interest to rule for the defense.

Since it is difficult, chancy, expensive, and far too time-consuming to obtain conviction through trial in our courts, prosecutors must resort to plea bargaining, however guilty the defendant. More than 90 percent of all cases are settled by striking a bargain: the defendant is allowed to plead guilty to a lesser charge than the one originally brought so that in exchange for his lower punishment the trial can be avoided.[13] The defendant and his lawyer know that the prosecution cannot afford trial despite sufficient evidence. Prosecutors must bargain. The risk, the cost, the time-wasting procedures, and the uncertainties of our legal processes cause the interests of justice to be protected best by avoiding trial if the accused is willing to plead guilty to a lesser charge. But these risks and uncertainties have been created largely by the courts themselves.

There is nothing intrinsically wrong with plea bargaining. Defense and prosecution, under the supervision of the judge, may anticipate the outcome of a trial and decide through a bargaining process to accept the anticipated outcome without going through the trial. This well may be in the best interests of all concerned. There is a great deal wrong, however, with the conditions largely created by the past decisions of the courts, that compel prosecutors to allow the defendant routinely to get away with a lesser penalty than that prescribed by law for the offenses he actually committed. In effect, the penalties prescribed by law for the actual offenses are not the penalties applied in most cases, and the penalties applied are not the penalties served. The bargaining power of defense and prosecution depends on the anticipated outcome of the trial and the likely sentence. If it has to be anticipated that the defendant cannot be convicted because of inadmissible evidence, or that if convicted the sentence will be light, the prosecution cannot obtain more by bargaining than it could by trial.

The degeneration of the plea bargaining process is illustrated in the following news story (*New York Times*, May 10, 1975).

> *Julio Vasquez, a 31-year-old former convict, was sentenced to a minimum of 15 years and a maximum of life imprisonment yesterday for killing an off-duty police officer . . .*
>
> *Mr. Vasquez had a criminal record that included 11 arrests in the last 12 years on robbery, assault and other charges, and five convictions that led to prison terms of less than one year each. His earlier sentences had been arrived at through plea bargaining, which means that he was permitted to plead to a lesser charge in exchange for a guilty plea.*

The courts are overwhelmed because of the rise of crime, but even more because of their own time-wasting procedures and inefficiencies, which, in part, account for the rise in crime. They must reform themselves or be reformed. Courts also might be helped by dejudicializing and decriminalizing acts that can be dealt with otherwise. "No fault" traffic accident or divorce regulations are a step in the right direction. It also would help if courts were divested of jurisdiction over such offenses as housing violations and other matters that could be dealt with administratively. The judicial apparatus is too cumbersome to be used where it can be replaced without major disadvantages. But, in the main, courts must help themselves by changing their procedures. . . .

NOTES

1. The *New York Times*, Sept. 24, 1974.
2. Quoted by U.S. Attorney General William B. Saxbe, *loc. cit.* James Q. Wilson found that of about 10,000 persons arrested in one year in California for robbery, only 1,300 were incarcerated. The police released 40 percent. Of the remainder, only 33 percent were charged with a felony; 20 percent had the charge dismissed at preliminary hearings. See "Crime and Law Enforcement," in Kermit Gordon, ed., *Agenda for a Nation* (Washington, D.C.: Brookings Institution, 1968.)
3. We must forgo suggestions about better police manpower allocation and utilization. There is a voluminous and growing literature on the topic to which the reader can refer.
4. An excellent summary of what has happened is found in Macklin Fleming, *The Price of Perfect Justice* (Basic Books, 1974).
5. *Commentary*, July 1974, pp. 101-104.
6. Many of the above data are drawn from Macklin Fleming's "The Law's Delay" (*The Public Interest*, Summer 1973). A somewhat different light is cast on the matter in Martin A. Levin, "Delay in the Criminal Courts" (*The Journal of Legal Studies*, Jan. 1975).

7. Foundations support many projects but do not help and reward (a) people injured in *bona fide* attempts to help the police arrest offenders; (b) people injured in *bona fide* attempts to come to the assistance of victims of violent crime, or (c) *bona fide* victims of violent crime.
8. *Weeks* v. *U.S.* 232 U.S. 383, 1914.
9. *Mapp* v. *Ohio* 367 U.S. 643 (1961).
10. So far in grand jury proceedings only: *U.S.* v. *Calandra* (1974), 414 U.S. 338 (1974).
11. The rule is extended to exclude evidence tainted by unlawful acts, arrests, surveillances, searches or confessions; the case against Daniel Ellsberg was thrown out of court after many weeks of trial because of governmental misconduct. There was such misconduct, and it should be punished—but not by dismissing the case against the defendant. The misconduct of the government was wholly irrelevant to the guilt or innocence of the defendant. No evidence whatever was produced by it. The rule shortchanged both defense and prosecution. But if the governmental misconduct had produced evidence, why should it be disregarded? Why should those who misconducted themselves not be punished instead?
12. *The New York Times*, April 12, 1975.
13. To be sure, the suspect may have been "overcharged"—he may be guilty of only some of the offenses he is charged with, and only of the lesser ones. But quite often he is allowed to plead to far less than what he is actually guilty of.

Perry Mason in Wonderland: What Happens in Criminal Court

Charles E. Silberman

. . . To read most critics of criminal sentencing policy, one would think that incarceration was a rare, almost idiosyncratic, event—that most criminals escape punishment altogether, or, at most, receive a slap on the wrist. Ernest van den Haag rails against "the fact that so small a proportion of all crimes committed—about 1 percent—ever lead to actual imprisonment of the offender in the U.S." Other scholars liken the judicial process to a funnel, with large numbers of arrested offenders being poured into the courts at the top, and a mere handful exiting into prisons from the bottom.

The metaphor is misleading, and van den Haag's statistics are plain wrong. Nationwide, at least one-third of the adults who are arrested on a felony charge, half or more of those who are formally charged with a crime, and about two-thirds of those who are convicted, serve time in jail or prison. Whether or not more people should be locked up is a question on which reasonable people may disagree. But it is one thing to attack judicial leniency if the "punishment rate," to use van den Haag's term, is only 1 percent; it is quite another matter if the rate turns out to be 65 percent.

How did the impression arise that criminals typically escape punishment? Figure 1, developed by the Crime Commission's Science and Technology Task Force to illustrate the so-called "funneling effect," provides a useful starting point.[1] . . .

At first glance, the diagram seems to confirm the thesis that the courts permit the overwhelming majority of criminals to escape scot-free: some 2,780,000 Index crimes reported to the police in 1965 resulted in 63,000 offenders going to prison, a punishment rate of only 2.3 percent. If one begins with the number of arrests, rather than of reported crimes—a more appropriate starting point if we are to assess the role of the courts, rather than of the police—punishment still seems to be a rare event. (The courts

2,780,000 Index Crimes Reported

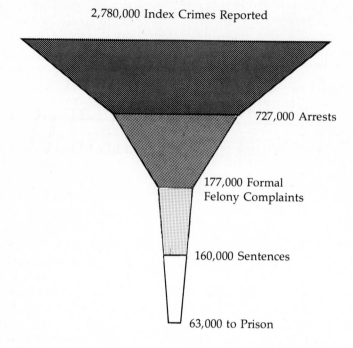

727,000 Arrests

177,000 Formal
Felony Complaints

160,000 Sentences

63,000 to Prison

Figure 1 Funneling effect from reported crimes through prison sentence.

cannot be blamed for the fact that the police cleared only 26 percent of reported Index crimes through arrest.) Although 727,000 arrests were made for an Index crime, only 177,000 people were formally charged with a felony; the statistics imply that only one felon in four was prosecuted, and one in twelve actually punished.

The statistics are grossly misleading. The fact that only one arrested suspect in four was prosecuted for a felony does not mean that the other three were turned loose. Some 260,000 arrestees were transferred to juvenile court—a mandatory procedure when the police arrest someone below the age at which the criminal courts have jurisdiction. Of the 467,000 adults who were arrested for an Index crime—the proper base from which to analyze the performance of the adult courts—charges were dropped against 128,000, or 27 percent.

That left 339,000 people—73 percent of the total—who were prosecuted for a crime. Charges were reduced to a misdemeanor in 162,000 cases, in exchange for a guilty plea; of the 177,000 who were charged with a felony, 130,000 pleaded guilty and another 30,000 were convicted after a bench or jury trial.[2] All told, therefore, 322,000 defendants were convicted on either a felony or misdemeanor charge—69 percent of all those who were arrested, and 95 percent of those who were prosecuted. (Whether more defendants should have been prosecuted is a question I will consider below, when I examine why prosecutors release individuals whom the police have arrested.)

How many were punished? The answer depends on how one defines punishment. Critics of sentencing policy often write—and the Crime Commission's diagram of the funnel effect was drawn—as if a prison term were the only form of punishment convicted offenders receive. It is not; a considerably larger number of offenders are sentenced to jail than to prison. By and large, offenders are sent to prison only if their sentence exceeds one year; those receiving shorter sentences usually serve them in jail. Whether jail terms of less than one year constitute *sufficient* punishment is another question. But it is a strange and arbitrary view of sentencing to write as if jail did not constitute punishment at all.

In fact, a jail sentence constitutes far more severe punishment than comparable time in prison. Because they are thought of as temporary detention centers for people awaiting trial, jail cells generally are smaller and more crowded than prison cells, and they afford even less privacy.[3] According to a report prepared for the American Correctional Association, the majority of American jails "are not properly heated, ventilated nor lighted; they do not have the necessary facilities for the preparation and service of food; proper and adequate provision for bathing and laundering are missing; sanitary arrangements are, for the most part, primitive and in a bad state of repair. . . . in general, complete idleness is the order of the day. Filth, vermin, homosexuality and degeneracy are rampant, and are the rule rather than the exception." Richard Velde, the conservative administrator of the Law Enforcement Assistance Administration during the Ford presidency, described American jails as "without question, brutal, filthy cesspools of crime—institutions which serve to brutalize and embitter men to prevent them from returning to a useful role in society."[4]

With this perspective in mind, let me return to the question of how many of the adults who were arrested for an Index crime in 1965 were punished. As shown in Figure 1, 63,000 received prison terms; 103,000 offenders served time in jail, and another 21,000 initially sentenced to probation wound up in prison or jail as a result of having violated the terms of their probation. All told, 187,000 offenders were incarcerated—40 percent of all those who were arrested, 55 percent of those who were charged with a crime, and 58 percent of those who were convicted. (The fact that so many probationers ended up behind bars suggests that being sentenced to probation constitutes punishment, too.)

Those figures go back more than a decade; there is no evidence that the courts have become any more lenient. Carl Pope of the Criminal Justice Research Center in Albany, New York, has analyzed what happened to everyone arrested for a felony in two urban counties in California in the period 1969-71—some 17,649 adults in all. Charges were dropped against

27 percent, leaving 12,925 who were prosecuted. (Convictions were secured in 90 percent of the cases.) Some 1,141 convicted felons were sentenced to prison, and 5,042 offenders drew time in jail. All told, 35 percent of those who were arrested, 48 percent of those actually charged with a crime, and 53 percent of those convicted were sentenced to jail or prison. (Incarceration rates were higher for more serious crimes; for example, 46 percent of those arrested for burglary were sentenced to jail or prison.) And these figures understate the number who were incarcerated: some of those who were sentenced to probation spent time in jail awaiting trial, and others were locked up for violating the terms of their probation. If both groups were included, the incarceration rate would be around 40 percent.[5] . . .

For all the talk about the decline in punishment and the hobbling effect of the Warren Court, moreover, what data are available indicate that contemporary criminal courts prosecute, convict, and incarcerate a larger proportion of those arrested for a felony today than did the courts of the 1920s. Take two examples:

- Of the 12,543 people arrested for a felony in Chicago in 1926, only 2,449—19.5 percent—were convicted, three-quarters of them on a lesser charge than the one for which they were arrested; charges were dropped in about 70 percent of the cases. Jail or prison sentences, mostly the latter, were given to 1,892 offenders—15.1 percent of the number initially arrested.

- Some 4,514 people were arrested on felony charges in 1924 in Kansas City and St. Louis. Charges were dropped in 70 percent of the cases, and convictions obtained in 27 percent. The incarceration rate was 19 percent, divided almost equally between prison and jail sentences.[6]

By itself, the fact that proportionately more offenders are punished now than in the 1920s, or that fewer cases drop out of court, does not demonstrate that the courts are fulfilling their crime-control function in an adequate way. To assess the courts' performance, we need to know a lot more about the reasons for judges and prosecutors taking the actions they do. Why do prosecutors and judges dismiss all charges against one arrested felon in three? Why do prosecutors and judges permit another third to plead guilty to a misdemeanor, instead of being tried on the felony charges on which they were arrested? And why do judges sentence only about half of those who are convicted to time in jail or prison?

The most popular (and most enduring) explanation puts the blame on archaic procedures and excessive concern for the rights of defendants. "Our dangers do not lie in too little tenderness to the accused," Judge Learned Hand wrote in 1923. "Our procedure has been always haunted by the ghost of the innocent man convicted. It is an unreal dream. What we need to fear is the archaic formalism and watery sentiment that obstructs, delays, and defeats the prosecution of crime." More than a half-century later, President Gerald Ford echoed this sentiment. "For too long, law has centered its attention more on the rights of the criminal defendant than on the victim of crime," Ford told the Congress in 1975. "It is time for law to concern itself more with the rights of the people it exists to protect."

Arguments of this sort are rooted in ideological preferences rather than in empirical research. When the data are assembled and analyzed, it becomes clear that the pendulum has not swung too far. Only a handful of criminals go free or escape punishment because of exclusionary rules, search-and-seizure laws, collateral attacks or appeals, and other "technicalities" designed to protect defendants' rights. As part of their study of robbery in California, Floyd Feeney and Adrianne Weir analyzed what happened to a sample of 260 Oakland and Los Angeles robbery arrests. Not a single case was lost on "search-and-seizure" grounds; not a single case involved any serious legal issue involving interrogation; no evidence was excluded as a result of the Miranda rule, which requires policemen to inform suspects of their rights before questioning them; and not a single identification of a suspect was lost to the prosecution because of violation of the Supreme Court's rules governing identification of suspects in line-ups.[7]

Nor are the Oakland data atypical in any way. "Many believe that offenders escape punishment because of 'technicalities' induced by Supreme Court rulings or because of unwarranted leniency of judges," Brian Forst and his colleagues at the Institute for Law and Social Research have written. After analyzing what happened to everyone arrested for a street crime, and why, over a six-year period, the INSLAW researchers found both beliefs to be untrue, concluding that "the public needs to discard its myths and begin to ask 'Why?' "[8]

In New York City, the Vera Institute analyzed a sample of felony cases to determine why arrests did not stand up in court. The researchers found that exclusionary rules played no discernible role at all in the dismissal or reduction of charges in six of the seven offense categories—assault, rape, murder and attempted murder, robbery, burglary, and grand larceny—that were analyzed in depth. And a Rand Corporation study of the prosecution of adult felony defendants in Los Angeles County, the largest prosecutor's office in the United States, found that only 3 percent of the burglary arrests were dismissed because of an illegal search and seizure, unlawful arrest, or other violation of defendants' rights; none of the burglary arrests were reduced to misdemeanors for those reasons. . . .

It is only in cases of so-called "victimless crimes" that any significant number of seemingly guilty offenders go free because tainted evidence— evidence acquired as a result of an illegal search, seizure, or arrest—is excluded from court; and even here, the number is considerably smaller than critics assume. In the Vera Institute sample, a number of gun possession cases *were* dismissed—but not because of search-and-seizure problems; the dismissals occurred because there was no evidence to connect the defendants with the guns (or, in one case, because there was no gun at all). Search-and-seizure problems did affect the outcome of some of the cases that remained, almost all of them involving defendants with minor records or none at all. Because the prosecutors themselves had doubts about the legality of the searches or arrests that uncovered the guns, they accepted guilty pleas to a misdemeanor count, preferring the certainty of a misdemeanor conviction to the possibility that the case would be dismissed altogether if it went to trial.[9] . . .

When charges against an arrested felon are dropped or reduced to a misdemeanor, it usually is not because prosecutors and judges are unduly lenient, nor because their heavy caseloads force them to give away the courthouse. Nor, as we have seen, is it because the exclusionary rule "punishes the constable by letting the criminal go free." For the most part, prosecutors drop felony charges or reduce them to a misdemeanor because they doubt the defendant's guilt, because they lack the evidence needed to prove his guilt, or because they feel the crime was not serious enough, or the defendant not sufficiently culpable, to warrant the stigma and punishment that a felony conviction would bring.

To understand what happens in criminal court, then, we need to look to the nature of the cases themselves—particularly to the fact that so high a proportion of them are felonies only in the technical sense of the term. According to the authors of the Vera Institute study of felony arrests, "at the root of much of the crime brought to court is anger—simple or complicated anger between two or more people who know each other."[10] In New York City, they found, the victim and offender had a prior relationship in nearly half the "victim crimes" that were brought to court.[11] The proportions ranged from a low of 21 percent in auto theft cases to a high of 69 percent in assault and 83 percent in rape arrests. But even with robbery and burglary, which we think of as crimes committed exclusively by strangers, victims and offenders were acquainted in 36 percent and 39 percent of the cases, respectively. . . .

By and large, prosecutors distinguish between "real crimes"—crimes committed by strangers—and "junk (or garbage) cases," i.e., those which grow out of a dispute between people who know one another. As the Vera Institute study makes clear, this dichotomy is central to any understanding of what happens in criminal court. Take robbery: the Vera researchers found that the defendant was convicted in 88 percent of the "stranger robbery" cases, but in only 37 percent of the robberies in which there was a prior relationship between victim and offender. In the stronger robberies, moreover, prosecutors and judges rarely accepted a plea to a misdemeanor; more than three-quarters of the convictions were on a felony charge, compared to only 14 percent of the prior relationship cases. . . .

It would be hard to exaggerate the significance of this discovery. Until the Vera and INSLAW researchers analyzed the reasons why some arrests stand up in court and others do not, no one had realized how much of a criminal court's workload involves cases in which victims and offenders know one another; nor had anyone understood the degree to which this affects what happens to those cases. Prosecutors and judges view stranger crimes as more serious offenses than crimes involving a prior relationship between victim and offender; but they concentrate their resources on stranger crimes, too, because it is so much harder to get a conviction in prior relationship cases.

The reason, quite simply, is that when they know the offender, victims often refuse to press charges, to testify against the offender, or to cooperate with the prosecutor in other ways. No single factor has so large an impact on what happens to felons after they have been arrested: "complainant noncooperation" accounted for more than two-thirds of the dismissals of "victim felonies" in New York, and well over half in Washington, D.C.[12]

There are many reasons victims refuse to cooperate with the authorities. Sometimes they are afraid of retaliation on the part of the offender or his friends; occasionally, too, victims and witnesses lose interest after they have made several appearances in court only to have the case postponed. In larceny cases, victims often press charges as a way of forcing the offender to make restitution; once they have recovered the stolen money or property, they drop charges. (In one such case in the Vera sample, an employer-complainant actually rehired his employee-offender after restitution had been made.)

Frequently, victims decline to press charges or testify out of a reluctance to let authorities (or their families) learn about their own activities. . . .

Most of the time, however, victims refuse to cooperate because they have become reconciled with the offender after one or the other has calmed down or sobered up. Prior-relationship assault cases usually involve domestic disputes that the police could not settle without an arrest, and prior-relationship robberies and burglaries often grow out of a dispute over money between husbands and wives, lovers or friends. . . .

Whether a crime involves strangers, relations, or friends, the weight that prosecutors and judges give to it reflects their evaluation of what the case is "worth." In effect, decisions about the worth of a case are decisions about the nature and amount of punishment the offender deserves—in particular, whether he needs to be incarcerated or not. "Good guys should get breaks, and bad guys shouldn't," a California prosecutor explains, meaning that charging and sentencing decisions are based in good measure on an evaluation of the offender's culpability and of his commitment to a criminal (or law-abiding) way of life.[13]

A gun possession case in the Vera sample provides a clear example of the way the "good guy-bad guy" dichotomy affects dispositions. The defendant was arrested when a policeman saw him walking along the street with what appeared to be a gun bulging out of his back pocket; the defendant claimed that he was a maintenance worker at Shea Stadium, that he had found the gun there, and that he was taking it to the station house up the block—the direction in which he was walking. The policeman made a felony arrest nonetheless, explaining that the man "had no license. He hadn't gone through the right procedures to turn in a gun, and he had a record from way back." (The real reason may have been that the defendant had "flunked the attitude test.") Technically, the policeman was correct; there were no evidentiary problems and the prosecution had a strong case. But after hearing his story at arraignment, the ADA and the judge felt that the defendant was telling the truth. Equally important, the defendant's prior arrests had been twenty years earlier; he had had no trouble with the law since then, and he had been working steadily at Shea Stadium for more than ten years. As a result, the prosecutor and the judge agreed to dismiss the charge. "I'm very stringent on weapons charges," the judge explained, but "I couldn't see any criminal intent here." To the prosecutor, "it was a nothing case."

Decisions about the worth of a case also reflect judgments about the seriousness of the offense itself. In general, prior-relationship crimes are considered less serious than those involving strangers; but stranger crimes also may be ranked in ways that do not correspond to the letter of the law. In New York City, nighttime commercial burglaries are almost routinely reduced to misdemeanors; since stores, offices, and warehouses normally are not occupied at night, prosecutors, judges, and even policemen view such offenses as nuisance crimes. Residential burglaries, on the other hand, are considered "real" crimes; they evoke considerable fear and anguish, and since a burglar can never be certain that no one is home, the possibility of violence is always present. . . .

What appear to be departures from the norms—instances, say, in which "real criminals" get a "walk" or are permitted to plead guilty to a misdemeanor—usually turn out, on examination, to be cases the prosecutor was reluctant to take to trial. Sometimes the problem is the nature of the evidence itself. Robbery victims are not always able to identify the offender, even when he is caught with the victim's wallet in his possession; a prosecutor will prefer to accept a guilty plea to possession of stolen property or some other lesser offense, rather than risk acquittal on the robbery charge if the defendant should insist on going to trial. Frequently, too, a victim may identify the offender from mug shots but fail to recognize him in a line-up; sometimes a victim identifies the offender if he is caught shortly after the crime, but becomes uncertain about the identification a few weeks later. Identification problems are more frequent in muggings and strong-arm robberies than in armed robberies; the latter offense usually involves a face-to-face confrontation, whereas muggers and strong-arm robbers frequently approach their victims from the rear.[14]

Even when there are no evidentiary problems as such, prosecutors may accept a guilty plea to a misdemeanor or lesser felony because the victim or key witness lacks credibility. If the victim was drunk or "stoned" at the time the crime occurred, the defense attorney may be able to discredit his testimony; victims with long criminal records or records of drug addiction may also have their credibility undermined at the preliminary hearing or at a trial. In such cases, prosecutors are likely to prefer the certainty of conviction on a misdemeanor or lesser felony to the possibility of acquittal on the original felony charge. . . .

In deciding where to concentrate their scarce resources, prosecutors generally consider the defendant's "convictability," in addition to the seriousness of his offense. If the choice is between two cases, one a robbery, the other a larceny, in which the evidence of guilt is about the same, prosecutors naturally concentrate on the robbery. But the choice usually is more troublesome—say, between prosecuting a larceny case in which the evidence of guilt is overwhelming and a robbery case in which conviction is uncertain.

Most prosecutors will emphasize the former—in part because they like to win and, more importantly, because they do not like to lose. In general, prosecutors care less about winning than about not losing; to lose any significant number of cases weakens their sense of self and undermines their credibility in the courtroom and in the larger community. Most prosecutors believe that they should not press charges unless they are convinced of the defendant's guilt. . . .

Even when evidence of guilt is overwhelming and the case involves a "bad guy" who has committed a serious crime, prosecutors prefer to settle the case through a guilty plea to a lesser felony, so long as the lesser charge carries an appropriate sentence. The reason is that taking a case to trial always involves some risk of acquittal; what seems to be an airtight case may come apart, and one can never be sure of the impression witnesses or the defendant may make, or of the way a jury will react to them.

It is a rare prosecutor, therefore, who does not prefer the certainty of a negotiated plea to the uncertainty of a trial. Even the Watergate Special Prosecution Force, which had unusually able prosecutors and a call on virtually unlimited resources, settled the overwhelming majority of its cases through negotiated pleas. "In assessing the likelihood that the evidence will convince a jury of the defendant's guilt when presented under the conditions of a trial," the Force wrote in its report, "prosecutors recognize that their familiarity with all the facts of a case and their assessment of the credibility of witnesses cannot necessarily be transferred to a trial jury, where evidence is strictly limited by trial rules and cross-examination can leave unpredictable impressions."

One of the cases in the Vera sample helps explain why prosecutors avoid trials if they can: a seemingly guilty defendant was acquitted against all the odds. Charged with first-degree sexual abuse and assault, the defendant had a record of five convictions, including a prison term for rape. The case went to trial only because the defendant rejected his lawyer's advice and refused the bargain offered by the prosecutor; he also insisted on taking the stand, despite his prior record. "My client had a long record, his story was unconvincing, he was crazy," his attorney recalled. "He would jump up and down in the court yelling that everyone was lying," as a result of which he had to be handcuffed to the rail in the courtroom. "But he was my client and insisted on his innocence, so we went to trial—handcuffs and all." Despite the fact that the complainant—a fifteen-year-old-girl—made an unusually credible witness, the man was acquitted. When asked about his prior record, he responded, "I pleaded guilty in the past—five times—because I committed those crimes. This time I didn't do anything and I didn't plead because I'm not guilty." The jury believed him, even though his own lawyer did not. . . .

More felons would be convicted . . . if detectives did a better job of collecting evidence and presenting it to the prosecutor; in good measure, the courts are taking the blame for what the police fail to do. Although detectives contribute relatively little to the identification of offenders or to their arrest, as we have seen, careful investigation is needed to collect the additional evidence required to demonstrate guilt. But once an arrest has been made, policemen have little incentive to collect additional evidence or to "waste" time preparing the evidence for submission to the prosecutor; their job satisfaction comes from making arrests, and the traditional reward system reinforces this outlook.

The result, all too often, is that prosecutors do not receive the information they need to convert an arrest into a conviction. Sometimes necessary information is not collected; frequently, the information is collected, but it remains in the patrolman's or detective's head and is not transmitted to prosecutors in the detail and form they need. . . .

Even so, prosecutors bear much of the responsibility for the gaps in the information they receive; it is rare for them to give policemen guidance about the kind of information they need and why they need it, and even rarer to explain why charges have been reduced or dismissed. To be sure, prosecutors often *think* that they have explained their actions to the police; in one study of police-prosecutor relations, half the prosecutors who were queried said they routinely told the police the reasons why cases were disposed of through plea bargaining. Policemen saw things differently; only 19 percent said they were informed as a matter of routine, and more than a third reported that they were "seldom" or "never" given the reasons for prosecutorial dispositions.[15] . . .

The picture I have been drawing of criminal courts bears little resemblance to the popular image. Just as the Sherlock Holmes legend has shaped our image of the police, what might be called the Perry Mason myth dominates thinking about criminal courts. In the popular view, adults who have been arrested for a crime retain Perry Mason, or some equally able and telegenic, but mythic, defense lawyer, to defend them. In short order, but after the defense lawyer's staff of investigators have combed the country in search of evidence to support the defendant's alibi, his fate is determined by a jury trial in a dignified, attractive wood-paneled and marble-floored courtroom. Indeed, the focal point of the whole legal process—its very essence and reason for being—is the jury trial, designed to determine the defendant's innocence or guilt. The jury discovers the truth through trial by combat between two equally armed (or, if the lawyer is Perry Mason, unequally armed) lawyers who adhere to the sportsman-like rules of the game because of the careful attention of a wise and scrupulously objective judge.

This is not the system most defendants encounter. Jury trials are rare events, occurring in only 5 to 10 percent of criminal cases in the United States. Perry Masons are equally rare: if a defendant is represented by counsel at all—many are not—the lawyer is likely to be a member of the staff of the local public defender service or an attorney assigned by the court. In either situation, defendants do not choose their lawyers, and they are likely to view the attorneys assigned to their defense as agents of the prosecution. In the 90 to 95 percent of the cases that are not tried, guilt and innocence are determined by the prosecutor or judge in negotiation with the defendant or his attorney.

Such is the hold of the Perry Mason myth that most discussions of the way criminal courts operate sound as though plea bargaining represented some recent fall from grace. Even those who favor the practice usually apologize for their position. They write as if universal jury trials had been the norm until quite recently, and they defend plea bargaining as an unfortunate departure from the norm that is necessary if courts are to handle the explosive increase in their caseloads.

If trials are the norm and plea bargaining simply a device by which big-city courts dispose of their heavy caseloads, one would expect to find relatively little plea bargaining in smaller cities and rural areas, where caseloads are light. But the overwhelming majority of criminal cases are disposed of by negotiated pleas in every part of the United States, rural as well as urban, small cities as well as large. . . .

Clearly, plea bargaining stems from causes more deeply rooted in the judicial process than court congestion. To be sure, heavy backlogs and inadequate trial facilities may distort the plea bargaining process. To keep the assembly line moving, prosecutors sometimes recommend, and judges impose, more lenient sentences than they think desirable; this happens far less often than critics allege. More important, jailed defendants who assert their innocence and who might be acquitted at trial sometimes are forced to choose between pleading guilty and gaining their freedom, and pleading not guilty and remaining in jail. There can be no excuse for plea bargaining under circumstances of that sort. But what is indefensible is not plea bargaining as such, but a bail system that makes defendants' liberty contingent on the financial resources at their disposal, and court congestion that keeps defendants rotting in jail for months on end, awaiting trial. . . .

. . Proponents of abolition assume that the question to be resolved in a criminal case is always simple and clear-cut: Is the defendant guilty or not guilty of committing the crime with which he is charged? If the answer is Not guilty, the defendant should be freed; if it is Guilty, he should receive the "proper" punishment for the offense. To convict a defendant of any lesser charge, in this view, or to sentence him to any lesser punishment, is a perversion of justice.

It is a curious notion of justice to tie it so completely to the prosecutor's uncontrolled discretionary decision about the crime with which an offender will be charged. Opponents of plea bargaining attribute an objectivity to the charging decision that most prosecutors would be loath to claim; as Professor Arnold Enker has written, the opponents of plea bargaining seem to assume that there is "an objective truth existing in a realm of objective historical fact" that can best be ascertained through a jury trial. But the "truth" of an offense usually is neither objective nor absolute; it is embodied in the way "the facts" are interpreted and in the significance attached to them, as much as in the facts themselves.

In the great majority of criminal cases, "the facts" are not in dispute. What is at issue—what needs to be adjudicated—is the significance that should be attached to the facts. Decisions about the seriousness of the offense and the degree of the offender's culpability involve complex and often highly subjective judgments about such factors as premeditation, intent, force, credibility, negligence, threat, recklessness, and harm. What is being adjudicated is not guilt or innocence, but the punishment the offender deserves.

Take one of the cases in the Vera Institute's sample. The facts seemed clear enough: the gate to a factory was broken one night and $2,000 in cash and inventory was stolen; the nineteen-year-old defendant was arrested inside the factory at 1 A.M. and charged with burglary. Initially, the ADA treated it as a serious crime, offering to reduce charges only to a lesser felony, which might have carried a term in jail or prison; the defendant refused to plead guilty. His attorney argued that "it was not a real burglary," pointing out that there had been forty other young men wandering around inside the factory a few minutes before the defendant's arrest; that the defendant had been the only one who had been caught; and that no money or stolen goods had been found on him. As a result, the ADA agreed to accept a plea to trespass—a misdemeanor—for which the defendant was sentenced to three years' probation. "He was found just wandering around, looking far from sinister," the judge explained, "and it wouldn't have been fair to punish the one who wasn't quick enough to get out when forty other men were equally guilty. . . . This was trespass, no more, and he had already been ten weeks in custody; any more time would have been damaging—and unjust."

When the facts *are* in dispute—when there is reasonable doubt that the defendant committed the crime with which he is charged—a jury trial is the most appropriate means of adjudication. Whether a defendant chooses to go to trial depends on his (and his attorney's) assessment of the risks that may be involved. Although the potential gain of complete acquittal is large, the price of defeat may be just as large. If the defendant is convicted of the highest charge against him, or if the judge is in the habit of imposing stiffer sentences on defendants who insist on a trial than on defendants who plead guilty to the same offense, conviction at trial may bring a long prison sentence. In deciding whether or not to go to trial, therefore, the defendant and defense lawyer weigh the strength of the evidence and the credibility of the witnesses who may be called, including the defendant himself. They also consider the sentence the defendant is likely to draw if he pleads guilty to a lesser charge; the stiffer the sentence, the smaller the risk attached to conviction at trial.

For that same reason, defendants may opt for trial in the opposite situation—one in which evidence of guilt is so overwhelming and the crime (or the offender's prior record) so serious that the defendant will draw "heavy time" whether he pleads guilty or not. In situations of this sort, defendants have little to lose and much to gain from a trial, since there always is *some* possibility of acquittal. In general, therefore, the more serious the offense, the larger the proportion of cases that are settled by trial. . . .

I have been arguing a heretical and paradoxical thesis: that a seemingly irrational and unjust adult judicial process produces results that are surprisingly rational and just. Exceptions—too many of them—do occur; but for the most part, prosecutors and judges use their discretion to carry out the intent, if not the precise letter, of the law, i.e., to prosecute, convict, and punish "real criminals," while showing appropriate leniency to those whose crimes are not serious, or who seem to pose no real danger to the community. . . .

NOTES

1. The President's Commission on Law Enforcement and the Administration of Justice, *Task Force Report: Science and Technology* (Washington, D.C.: U.S. Government Printing Office, 1967), p. 61.
2. In general, defendants convicted of a misdemeanor cannot be sentenced to more than one year in jail. Besides its longer sentence, a felony conviction

carries more of a stigma and may involve the loss of certain rights—to vote, for example, or to receive a license for specified occupations. (A bench trial is a trial before a judge, without a jury; although the Constitution guarantees the right to a jury trial in criminal cases, defendants may waive that right and choose a bench trial instead.)

3. At the time of the 1970 National Jail Census, 52 percent of the inmates were awaiting trial and 5 percent were awaiting sentencing; the remaining 43 percent were serving post-conviction sentences.

4. Quoted in Ronald L. Goldfarb, *Jails: The Ultimate Ghetto* (Garden City, N.Y.: Anchor Press/Doubleday, 1975), pp. 6, 21. See also Hans Mattick, "The Contemporary Jails of the United States: An Unknown and Neglected Area of Justice," in Daniel Glaser, ed., *Handbook of Criminology* (New York: Rand McNally, 1974); Edith Elizabeth Flynn, "Jails and Criminal Justice," in Lloyd E. Ohlin, ed., *Prisoners in America* (Englewood Cliffs, N.J.: Prentice-Hall, Inc., 1973), Ch. 2.

5. Carl E. Pope, *Offender-Based Transaction Statistics: New Directions in Data Collection and Reporting* (Washington, D.C.: Law Enforcement Assistance Administration National Criminal Justice Information and Statistics Service, 1975), pp. 20–21. See also Pope, *The Judicial Processing of Assault and Burglary Offenders in Selected California Counties* (Washington, D.C.: National Criminal Justice Information and Statistics Service, 1975), p. 17.

6. C. E. Gehlke, "Recorded Felonies: An Analysis and General Survey," Illinois Association for Criminal Justice, *Illinois Crime Survey* (Montclair, N.J.: Patterson Smith Reprint Series, 1968), Ch. 1; Gehlke, "A Statistical Interpretation of the Criminal Process," *Missouri Crime Survey* (Montclair, N.J.: Patterson Smith Reprint Series, 1968), Part VII.

7. Alan Carlson and Floyd Feeney, "Handling Robbery Arrestees: Some Issues of Fact and Policy," in Floyd Feeney and Adrianne Weir, eds., *The Prevention and Control of Robbery*, Vol. II (Davis, Calif.: The Center on Administration of Criminal Justice, University of California—Davis, 1973), Ch. 8, esp. p. 133.

8. *PROMIS Research Project: Highlights of Interim Findings and Implications* (Washington, D.C.: Institute for Law and Social Research 1977, mimeo), pp. 59–60.

9. *Felony Arrests: Their Prosecution and Disposition in New York City's Courts,* A Vera Institute of Justice Monograph (New York: The Vera Institute of Justice, 1977).

10. *Felony Arrests,* p. xv.

11. In "victimless crimes," such as gambling and prostitution, offenders have customers rather than victims. When arrests are made, the complainant usually is the arresting officer.

12. *Felony Arrests,* p. 20, Table E. See also *PROMIS Research Project.* I am indebted to Brian E. Forst, senior research analyst at INSLAW, for sharing the PROMIS findings with me before publication.

13. Lief H. Carter, *The Limits of Order* (Lexington, Mass.: D. C. Heath & Co., 1974), p. 174.

14. See Feeney and Weir, *Prevention and Control of Robbery*, Vol. II, pp. 92–93, and Vol. IV, p. 144.

15. McIntyre, "Impediments to Effective Police-Prosecutor Relationships," *American Criminal Law Review*, Vol. 13 (1975), p. 209.

CHAPTER FOURTEEN

CIVIL LIBERTIES

FREE SPEECH

At what point does it become necessary for society to restrict the freedoms granted to us in the First Amendment to the Constitution? Of the many questions that the Supreme Court has had to confront over the course of our history, this one has surely proved to be one of the most vexing. This question last became the subject of national debate as recently as 1978 when the city of Skokie, Illinois, sixty percent of whose residents are Jewish, passed an ordinance prohibiting members of the American Nazi Party from marching through its community. The American Nazi Party contended that this ordinance represented an unconstitutional infringement upon its right to freedom of speech. This view was shared by the American Civil Liberties Union (ACLU), an organization long reluctant to see any restrictions imposed upon freedom of expression. In this particular instance, however, the ACLU's position came under such heavy fire from within its own ranks that the organization decided to issue a pamphlet explaining why it felt compelled to defend the right of the American Nazi Party to parade through Skokie. The contents of this pamphlet appear as the first selection in this section.

In the second selection, George Will makes clear that he is not persuaded by those who contend that all manner of free expression is guaranteed by the First Amendment. On the contrary, he insists that the Constitution does not and should not provide any protection for the expression of views which are antithetical to the values upon which our republic is based. To argue otherwise is not only imprudent but also inconsistent with the intent of those who formulated the First Amendment.

Why Free Speech for Racists and Totalitarians

American Civil Liberties Union

Why does the ACLU defend free speech for Nazis, KKK members, and others who advocate racist or totalitarian doctrines?

Because we believe that the constitutional guarantees of freedom of speech and press would be meaningless if the government could pick and choose the persons to whom they apply. The ACLU's responsibility—since its founding in 1920—has been to make sure that all are free to speak, no matter what their ideas.

In what circumstances does the ACLU defend such people?

The ACLU defends the right of such persons to make speeches in which they express their beliefs; to print and distribute written material; to hold peaceful marches and rallies; to display their symbols, and to be members of groups which promote their doctrines.

Has the ACLU always defended such people?

Yes. Always. The ACLU's very first annual report describes a case in which the ACLU defended free speech for the KKK. We have been defending free speech for these groups—and all others—ever since.

ACLU defense is needed when the views of some people are unpopular and the government interferes with their ability to express their views peacefully. In times and places where the views of civil rights activists, pacifists, religious and political dissenters, labor organizers and others have been unpopular, the ACLU has insisted on their right to speak.

Throughout the history of the ACLU, we have adhered to Voltaire's principle that "I may disapprove of what you say, but I will defend to the death your right to say it."

From *Why the American Civil Liberties Union Defends Free Speech for Racists and Totalitarians* (New York: American Civil Liberties Union). Used with permission.

But does the First Amendment protect even those who urge the destruction of freedom? Does it extend to those who advocate the overthrow of our democratic form of government or who espouse violence?

In 1969, in an ACLU case involving a KKK leader who had urged at a rally in Hamilton County, Ohio, that Black Americans be sent back to Africa, the United States Supreme Court unanimously established the principle that speech may not be restrained or punished unless it "is directed to inciting or producing imminent lawless action and is likely to incite or produce such action." *(Brandenburg v. Ohio)*

In this, and in earlier cases involving advocates of draft resistance in World War I and leaders of the Communist Party during and following World War II, the Supreme Court made it clear that before a speaker can be suppressed there must be a clear and present danger that the audience will *act illegally and do what the speaker urges*—not just *believe* in what is advocated.

When Nazis or others like them choose to demonstrate in places like Skokie, Illinois, where hundreds of survivors of the concentration camps live, are they not creating a clear and present danger of violent reactions?

Speaking or marching before a *hostile* audience is not the same as inciting a *sympathetic* crowd to engage in illegal acts. The audience is not being urged to become violent and do bodily harm to the demonstrators. Hostile crowds must not be allowed to exercise a veto power over the speech of others by themselves creating a clear and present danger of disorder. Otherwise any of us could be silenced if people who did not like our ideas decided to start a riot.

It is common practice for speakers and demonstrators to carry their messages to hostile audiences—perhaps in the hope of making conversions, perhaps to attract attention, or perhaps to test the potential for restraint or for ugliness in their adversaries.

In hundreds of cases, the ACLU has defended the right to speak even when the speakers were so unpopular that opponents reacted violently. The Wobblies carried their unionization message to Western mining towns. That message was so unpopular that some of them were lynched. Jehovah's Witnesses distributed their tracts in Roman Catholic neighborhoods. They were stoned. Norman Thomas spoke in Mayor Frank Hague's Jersey City. He was pelted with eggs and narrowly escaped serious violence. Paul Robeson sang at a concert in Peekskill, New York. There was a riot. Civil rights activists in the 1960s chose to demonstrate in Mississippi and Alabama. Some of them were murdered. Opponents of the Vietnam war picketed military bases. Many of them were beaten. Martin Luther King, Jr. marched in the most racist neighborhoods of Chicago. And there was racial violence.

The duty of government is to permit speech and to restrain those who would disrupt it violently. Opponents of a point of view must be free to have their say, but not to make any public place off-limits for speech they don't like.

But isn't a demonstration in an intensely hostile area the same as falsely shouting "fire" in a crowded theater?

Speaking or marching with offensive messages in public places is not at all the same as falsely shouting "fire" in a crowded theater. The members of the crowd are not in a tightly enclosed arena where a panic would almost certainly follow by a sudden and unexpected cry of danger before any contrary view could be heard. They have come to the scene freely, probably knowing what to expect, and they may freely turn away if they are upset by what they see or hear. Just as speakers have a right to express themselves, listeners have a right to ignore them or, if they choose, to hold peaceful counter-demonstrations.

Hasn't the Supreme Court said that certain kinds of communication—like hurling epithets at another person—are so likely to lead to fighting that the speaker, and not the audience, is responsible? Isn't the display of a swastika or the burning of a cross the same as such "fighting words?"

The Supreme Court has made it clear that speech can be punished as "fighting words" only if it is directed at another person in an *individual, face-to-face encounter.* The Court has never applied this "fighting words" concept to nonverbal symbols displayed before a *general* audience (like the display of a swastika or a peace symbol or the burning of a cross or of an effigy of a political leader).

Why do the ACLU and the courts believe that prior restraints on free speech are so much worse than punishments after a speech has been made?

Prior restraints not only prevent *entirely* the expression of the would-be speaker, but they also deprive the public of its *right to know* what the speaker would have said.

When the Nixon Administration tried to impose a prior restraint on the Pentagon Papers, they told us that publication would injure the national security. When the Pentagon Papers were published, we discovered that they exposed misdeeds by the government, but did no damage to national security.

If the purpose of the First Amendment is to insure a free flow of ideas, of what value to that process are utterances which defame people because of their race or religion? Can't we prohibit group libel that merely stirs up hatred between peoples?

Legal philosopher Edmond Cahn dealt with this subject in a notable address delivered at the Hebrew University in Jerusalem in 1962. If there were a prohibition against group defamation, said Cahn:

"The officials could begin by prosecuting anyone who distributed the Christian Gospels, because they contain many defamatory statements not only about Jews but also about Christians; they show Christians failing Jesus in his hour of deepest tragedy. Then the officials could ban Greek literature for calling the rest of the world 'barbarians.' Roman authors would be suppressed because when they were not defaming the Gallic and Teutonic tribes they were disparaging the Italians. For obvious reasons, all Christian writers of the Middle Ages and quite a few modern ones could meet a similar fate. Even if an exceptional Catholic should fail to mention the Jews, the officials would have to proceed against his works for what he said about the Protestants and, of course, the same would apply to Protestant views on the subject of Catholics. Then there is Shakespeare who openly affronted the French, the Welsh, the Danes . . . Dozens of British writers from Sheridan and Dickens to Shaw and Joyce insulted the Irish. Finally, almost every worthwhile item of prose and poetry published by an American Negro would fall under the ban because it either whispered, spoke, or shouted unkind statements about the group called 'white.' Literally applied, a group-libel law would leave our bookshelves empty and us without desire to fill them."

History teaches us that group libel laws are used to *oppress* racial and religious minorities, not to protect them. For example, none of the anti-Semites who were responsible for arousing France against Captain Alfred Dreyfus was ever prosecuted for group libel. But Emile Zola was prosecuted for libelling the military establishment and the clergy of France in his magnificent *J'Accuse* and had to flee to England to escape punishment.

Didn't Weimar Germany's tolerance for free speech allow Hitler to achieve power?

No. The Weimar government did not uphold free speech. When Hitler and the Nazis violently interfered with the speech of their opponents, the Weimar government took no effective action to protect speech and restrain violence. Even murder of political opponents by the Nazis—where the murderers were known—went unpunished or virtually unpunished.

Why should someone who detests the Nazis and the KKK support defense of their right to speak?

In a society of laws, the principles established in dealing with racist views necessarily apply to all. The ACLU defended the right of Father Terminiello, a suspended Catholic priest, to give a racist speech in Chicago. In 1949, the U.S. Supreme Court agreed with our position in a decision that is a landmark in the history of free speech. Time and again, the ACLU was able to rely on the decision in *Terminiello v. Chicago* in defending free speech for civil rights demonstrators in the deep South. The Supreme Court cited its own decision in *Terminiello* in its leading decisions on behalf of civil rights demonstrators, *Cox v. Louisiana* and *Edwards v. South Carolina*. Similarly, the Supreme Court's decision in 1969 in *Brandenburg v. Ohio* upholding free speech for the KKK was the principal decision relied upon by a lower court the following year in overturning the conviction of Benjamin Spock for opposing the draft.

The principles of the First Amendment are indivisible. Extend them on behalf of one group and they protect all groups. Deny them to one group, and all groups suffer.

Doesn't providing racists and totalitarians with a legal defense give publicity to their cause and their ideas that they would otherwise not receive?

It is the attempts by communities to *prevent* such people from expressing themselves that gives them the press coverage they would ordinarily not receive. If providing a legal defense for their constitutional rights results in a continuation of the publicity, that is an unavoidable consequence of the events that were set in motion by the original denial of First Amendment guarantees. A fact that seems little understood by those who take a restrictive view toward speech they do not like is that attempts at suppression ordinarily increase public interest in the ideas they are trying to stamp out.

But doesn't the ACLU have more important things to do with its limited resources than to defend racists and totalitarians?

The ACLU has many important jobs to do and it devotes its resources to a wide range of civil liberties concerns—sexual equality; racial justice; religious freedom; the freedom to control one's own body; the constitutional rights of students, prisoners, mental patients, service personnel, juveniles, the elderly; and the rights of privacy for all of us. More than 6,000 court cases are undertaken each year by the ACLU to protect these rights.

But first among the freedoms we are dedicated to defending are those of speech, press and assembly, for they are the bedrock on which all other rights rest. We are involved in only five or six cases each year to defend free speech for racists or totalitarians. Even though this is only a tiny fraction of the ACLU's work, we think it is important.

We cannot remain faithful to the First Amendment by turning our backs when it is put to its severest test—the right to freedom of speech for those whose views we despise the most.

Nazis: Outside the Constitution

George F. Will

During World War II, Sol Goldstein lived in Lithuania, where Nazis threw his mother down a well with 50 other women and buried them alive in gravel. Today he lives in Skokie, Ill., where on April 20 Nazis wearing brown shirts and swastikas may demonstrate to celebrate Hitler's birthday.

Sixty percent of Skokie residents are Jewish, including thousands of survivors of the Holocaust. Aided by the American Civil Liberties Union, the Nazis have successfully challenged an injunction against demonstrations with swastikas, and almost certainly will succeed in challenging ordinances banning demonstrations involving military-style uniforms and incitements of hatred. After 60 years of liberal construction of the First Amendment, amost anything counts as "speech"; almost nothing justifies restriction.

The Nazis say they want to demonstrate in Skokie because "where one finds the most Jews, one finds the most Jew-haters." Beyond inciting hatred, the Nazis' aim is to lacerate the feelings of Jews. Liberals say the Skokie ordinances place unconstitutional restrictions on the Nazis' "speech." But Skokie's ordinances do not prohibit "persuasion," in any meaningful sense. The ordinances prohibit defamatory verbal and symbolic assault. What constitutional values do such ordinances violate?

The *Washington Post* says the rationale for striking down restrictions on advocacy of genocide is that "public policy will develop best through the open clash of ideas, evil ideas as well as benign ones." A typical Nazi idea is expressed on the poster depicting three rabbis—the Nazis call them "loose-lipped Hebes"—conducting the ritual sacrifice of a child. The *Post* does not suggest exactly how it expects the development of policy to be improved by "clashes" over ideas like that, or like the idea that Jews favor the "nigger-ization" of America.

Liberals quote Oliver Wendell Holmes's maxim that "the best test of

From George F. Will, "Nazis: Outside the Constitution," *The Washington Post*, February 2, 1978. © The Washington Post. Used with permission.

truth is the power of the thought to get itself accepted in the competition of the market." Liberalism is a philosophy that yields the essential task of philosophy—distinguishing truth from error—to the "market," which measures preferences (popularity), not truth. Liberals say all ideas have an equal "right" to compete in the market. But the right to compete implies the right to win. So the logic of liberalism is that it is better to be ruled by Nazis than to restrict them.

Liberals seem to believe that all speech—any clash between any ideas—*necessarily* contributes to the political ends the First Amendment is supposed to serve. But they must believe that the amendment was not intended to promote particular political ends—that there is no connection between the rationale for free speech and the particular purposes of republican government.

A wiser theory is in "The First Amendment and the Future of American Democracy," in which Prof. Walter Berns argues that the First Amendment is part of a political document. There are political purposes for protecting free speech, and some speech is incompatible with those purposes.

The purpose of the Constitution, he argues, is to establish a government faithful to the "self-evident" truths of the Declaration of Independence. Holmes said the Constitution was written for people of "fundamentally differing views." That would be an absurd idea about any constitutional community and is especially absurd about this one. The Founders thought rational persons could hardly avoid agreeing about "self-evident" fundamentals. The Founders believed in freedom for all speech that does not injure the health of the self-evidently proper kind of polity, a republic.

So the distinction between liberty and license, between permissible and proscribable speech, is implicit in the Constitution's purposes. Hence restraint can be based on the substance as well as the time, place and manner of speech.

Berns argues it is bizarre to say that the Constitution—a document designed to promote particular political ends—asserts the equality of ideas. There is no such thing as an amoral Constitution, neutral regarding all possible political outcomes.

American Nazis are weak, so liberals favor protecting Nazi swastikas and other "speech." Liberals say the pain to Jews is outweighed by the usefulness of the "clash of ideas" about "loose-lipped Hebes." Were the Nazis becoming stronger, liberals would favor protecting Nazi speech because the "market"—the best test of truth—would be affirming Nazi truth. Besides, restricting speech can be dangerous.

But it is not more dangerous than national confusion about fundamental values. Evidence of such confusion is the idea that restrictions on Nazi taunts and defamations are impermissible because the Constitution's fundamental value is political competition open equally to those who, if they win, will destroy the Constitution and then throw people down wells.

PORNOGRAPHY

The previous two selections suggest the divergence of opinion which exists on the matter of what we should be free to speak about in our society. No less is the disagreement on the question of what we should be free to read and see. This issue has been hotly debated in connection with a certain category of material which has been variously labelled as "pornographic" or "obscene."

Murray Hausknect feels that pornographic—as distinct from erotic—books, magazines, and films are personally offensive to most Americans, and for this reason he has no objection to zoning ordinances which limit where such materials may be shown and sold. Nor does he object to restricting children from access to such materials. He does not wish to go beyond this, however, arguing that the limited evidence available does not demonstrate that pornography undermines the moral fiber of our adult society and its institutions. Moreover, even if it did, Hausknect believes that censorship should still be rejected on the grounds that it would limit the public's right to make its own political choices.

Cynthia Epstein, on the other hand, identifies a certain class of pornography which she feels does indeed merit censorship. Also, in her judgment, we should not shy away from such a task. We do, after all, make individual as well as collective judgments about the nature of our lives all the time. Therefore, why should reading and viewing matter be exempt from similar scrutiny?

The Problem of Pornography: No Censorship

Murray Hausknecht

For a walker through Times Square or the downtown areas of many American cities a stop for a newspaper means a confrontation with the tastelessness of *Screw* and *Hustler*; a glance at a record shop window discloses an album-cover photograph, reproduced on a rooftop billboard, of a bound woman, while a nearby movie marquee promotes the dubious delights of an X-rated movie featuring children. One is overcome by a sense that the texture of public life has become coarsened and that some natural boundary between public and private worlds is being wantonly violated by a barrage of pornography. It is hard to resist crying out, Enough!

The cry, though, is or can be a prelude to a call for censorship, and the uneasiness that thought produces is reinforced by the reality of prosecutions against porno-film actors and the publisher of *Hustler*. One's discomfort is increased by the recognition that such prosecutions gain legitimacy from our disgust with the daily encounter with pornography. All of which prompts the questions, What can be done? What ought to be done?

By pornography I mean any written or visual representation of sexual behavior—explicitly and vividly presented—whose sole intent is sexual arousal. By "erotic writing" or "erotica" I mean an explicit representation of sex within a context in which it is treated as part of the human experience and in which the sexual material is not used solely to stimulate arousal. (Throughout, it is to be understood that what is said about "writing" applies also to movies.) In short, erotic writing is work that tries to achieve the traditional end of art. However, erotica can be converted by the reader into pornography; that is, it can be used simply for the purposes of arousal.

From Murray Hausknecht, "The Problem of Pornography," *Dissent* 25 (Spring 1978). Used with permission.

Pornography is usually condemned because it is equated with obscenity, that which is dirty, shameful, and degrading. If, however, we do not accept such traditional beliefs about sex, then the mere fact that pornography stimulates sexual excitement cannot, by itself, be grounds for condemnation. Pornography is also accused of other evils, as in Irving Kristol's pronouncement that "pornography . . . is inherently and purposefully subversive of civilization and its institutions."[1] On a less Spenglerian level this translates into accusations that pornography causes a breakdown in sexual morals and the family, and encourages juvenile delinquency, sex crimes, and other perversions. Whether pornography does have these far-reaching consequences is an empirical question, a difficult enough problem even without the assumption that an end to civilization is "inherently and purposefully" intended. This evokes a picture analogous to the old stereotype of the bearded anarchist gleefully working on the bombs that will destroy the regime. But all one really need assume about the poor hack scribbling away is that he hopes someone will become excited.

The National Commission on Obscenity and Pornography, which completed its work in 1970, sponsored a number of research studies ranging from the quasi-experimental to opinion surveys, and consequently we are in a better position than previously to deal with the empirical question. The results must be accepted with more than the usual reservations, since the methodological difficulties of social-psychological research are compounded by the nature of the problem. Even when the effect may be observed by direct measurement of physiological changes, the Heisenberg Uncertainty Principle complicates matters: the instrumentation measuring sexual arousal tends to inhibit response. In addition, none of the "experimental" studies assessed the long-range effects of pornography, and, for obvious reasons, no studies involved children. Still, with all their limitations, the findings seem to justify the following propositions:

1. Exposure to pornographic materials produces sexual arousal "in substantial proportions of males and females." Heterosexual materials rather than homosexual or sadomasochistic materials are more significant in producing arousal.

2. Continued exposure to pornography results in satiation of arousal and interest.

3. Established patterns of sexual behavior are not significantly altered by exposure to pornography. After exposure there is an increase in coital activity by those with an available sexual partner, but the effect disappears within 48 hours. Those without available partners or those who masturbate regularly show increases in masturbatory activity, but this too disappears within two days.

4. Exposures to pornographic stimuli have little or no effect on "established attitudinal commitments regarding either sexuality or sexual morality."

5. There is no relation between criminal sex offenses, other forms of crime, and juvenile delinquency and the use of pornography.[2]

Obviously, these findings can have only an indirect impact on popular beliefs about pornography. Research results by themselves no more inhibit attempts at censorships or legal prosecutions than scientific findings on race can by themselves eradicate prejudice and discrimination. It is possible to argue, though, that in the current cultural situation it is difficult to conceive of the antipornography forces mustering strength to bring back "the bad old days" when D. H. Lawrence and Henry Miller were under-the-counter items.

On the other hand, not withstanding the recent and rapid changes in attitudes toward sex, these very changes contribute to the strength of the antiabortion movement and the opposition to the Equal Rights Amendment. These antifeminist forces are reinforced by the zealous foes of pornography. The recent defeats of ERA, while not wholly a result of the fears and anxieties generated by "the sexual revolution," show how strong this opposition can be. The *Hustler* prosecution and that of the actors by district attorneys on the political make also indicate that traditional civil liberties problems have by no means been completely settled. Such legal actions have a "chilling effect" on free speech; they encourage self-censorship and caution among publishers and producers who are not a notably courageous lot. . . .

In the absence, then, of empirical evidence and plausible arguments one must remain skeptical of the presumed long-run consequences of pornography and erotica. But even if one were to grant that they undermine civilization and social institutions, the justification for censorship rests on grounds unacceptable to liberals and radicals.

To say that pornography and erotic writing endanger institutions is to say that they affect beliefs and opinion about the proper way to organize social relationships, about the appropriate means for accomplishing the tasks necessary to maintain society. These are *political* questions, and censorship would prohibit exposure to a full range of politically relevant perspectives. To defend censorship is to assume that existing social arrangements represent the best of all possible worlds, or, since we already know what the proper relationships among people ought to be, citizens need not be distracted by wrong and incorrect views. Even if one only believes that the present arrangements are more bearable than what would result from the unrestricted availability of pornography, our historical experience suggests that censorship more often than not kills what it is ostensibly designed to protect. Those prejudiced in favor of freedom must reject anything that interferes with people's right to free political choice.

Can nothing be done, then, to secure ourselves against the daily offense of pornography?

The arguments about pornography and its effects apply only to adults and not to children. Our lack of knowledge about its effects on children combined with the plausibility of arguments that they are at greater risk from pornography than adults favor retaining the present restrictions on children's access to it. Similarly, the use of children in pornographic movies can and ought to be prosecuted under child abuse laws. Beyond this we shall have to be satisfied with more limited goals.

All cities have zoning laws that separate, for example, industrial from residential land us. For most people pornography is like the noxious stink of a glue factory, and just as we locate the factory away from homes so we can zone to restrict our public encounters with pornography. We can limit the location and number of establishments dealing solely with pornography.

A zoning ordinance designed to protect residential areas from "adult bookstores" and porno movie houses would restrict them to business and entertainment districts where anonymity has always cloaked the pursuit of anomalous pleasures. In cities that have escaped the blight of urban renewal there are residential neighborhoods overlapping these districts; some are traditional "slums" while others are "respectable" middle-class areas. Residents of these neighborhoods, as well as those whose occupations bring them to the center of the city, will be more exposed to the offensiveness of pornography than others. But this location has always had similar disadvantages. Neighborhoods are "slums," in part, because their inhabitants already have to contend with such social pollutants as prostitution and drugs, and some of the most exclusive and expensive neighborhoods of Manhattan overlook the smoke and brutal ugliness of Consolidated Edison's generating plants. Similarly, in some cities pornography will defile public places to a greater extent than in others. When a city like New York tries to attract tourists as a great place to visit it encourages the trade in pornography. After all, the attraction of the metropolis always has been the promise of pleasures unavailable at home.

This modest proposal implies that here as elsewhere in the life of the society, we must bear the consequences of the beliefs that define us as political beings. Just as the commitment to freedom of speech or due process of law means that we put up with a flow of ethnic and racial scurrilities and the occasional freeing of an obvious criminal, so too we must continue to contend with the burden of pornography. Our consolation is the austere one that the alternative to freedom would prove rather more burdensome.

NOTES

1. *On the Democratic Idea in America* (New York: Harper & Row, 1972), p. 40.
2. U.S. Commission on Obscenity and Pornography, *The Report of the U.S. Commission on Obscenity and Pornography* (Washington, D.C.: U.S. Government Printing Office, 1970), pp. 163-243. Further analyses of the research done for the Commission are reported in a special issue of the *Journal of Social Issues*, vol. 29, no. 3, 1973.

For Selective Censorship

Cynthia Fuchs Epstein

In the small Ohio city where I used to work, it was common knowledge that every month or so the American Legion would show "dirty" movies. Members of the post would gather, and after the flag had been saluted and the padre had blessed the meeting and (ostentatiously) left the hall, all would settle down for an evening of beer and stag films. No one in the community, not even their wives or parents, openly objected. The Legion practice in southern Ohio was probably not very different from that in other areas. It was as American as motherhood and apple pie.

No doubt, many functions were served by men gathering in this fashion; almost tribal, a prototypical ritual of collective conscience according to the gospel of Emile Durkheim. Men and their brothers engaging in forbidden games, analogous to the secret societies in preliterate groups whose rituals serve to band men of maturity together, to initiate adolescent men to their ranks, and to set themselves apart from women. Practices that underscore men's particularity, often to their hierarchical advantage.

One might even argue that when pornography is legalized and publicly offered, it is no longer offered in a form that serves the *"weness"* of community but rather contributes to alienation and anomie. Pornography for the individual and not the group causes sex to become an anonymous experience. (A colleague has even instructed me that the best way to watch a pornographic movie is alone; to bring a friend is to introduce an element of "relationship," which dilutes or confuses the total porn experience.)

But perhaps we shouldn't simplistically sentimentalize pornography as a positive expression of group solidarity. We know, after all, that what is functional for the in-group may precipitate antagonisms to the out-group. What are the further consequences of pornography? Whom does it serve? Whom does it help? Whom does it harm?

Reprinted from Cynthia Fuchs Epstein, "The Problem of Pornography," *Dissent* 25 (Spring, 1978): 202-204. Used with permission.

We do not know much about the answers. Only the crudest measures have been used and I question the way the questions have been conceptualized and put. Sociologist Ned Polsky informs me that the incidence of child molestation went down in Denmark with the ending of all restrictions on pornography. He has argued that pornography provides the opportunity for persons to act out sexual needs vicariously or through fantasy that defuses possible antisocial expression. If this is so, the case for unlimited pornographic expression has some merit. Yet, one may ask, how truly related are the factors in this presumed causal relationship? As far as I know, no social scientist has ever done community studies to see what are the consequences of porn experiences for the "normal population," outside a laboratory setting. No one studied what happened to those American Legionnaires in Ohio after their monthly meetings, but I can speculate on what investigators would have found. Some probably managed to supress their aroused urges and some probably were put straight to bed, victims of the evening's beer. However, we can infer from findings of the 1970 Commission on Pornography that some, sexually aroused, mated with their wives with renewed vigor. And some (we are discovering this with alarming frequency) may have drunkenly beaten the wives who wouldn't. (The courts deny it is rape if the husband forces sex on his wife.) Others may have mused through the week about that pert waitress in the diner who is always really "asking for it anyway" and may have tried a tickle or some remarks. I don't think that even regression analysis will tell us whether the porn movies might have contributed to the events surmised above, or the drink, or the "we" spirit of the boys getting together without the women.

As I interview people whose opinions I value on the perplexing problem of censorship and freedom and pornography, which led me to these series of reflections, I find that some of my best male friends and colleagues (who are hardly Mr. Middle America in their intellect or taste) turn out to be porn-movie regulars. These are men of sensitivity, of civil libertarian mind, who write and act in their private lives as committed feminists. For them, in varying degrees, porn is a voyage into erotica; a way of touching base with their elemental being; a lift from a world of words and abstractions; a diversion or dream. They are not turned mean by exposure to pornography but are turned on or off to sexuality, depending on whether they've experienced the porn as "good" or "bad." They argue for license as freedom and contend that expression of sexuality in any form (save that which depicts and uses children) opens and expands the individual and collective opportunity structure.

If they were in fact models of most men, or if 95 percent (or 80 percent or 50 percent) of the legionnaires were like them, I could easily subscribe to unqualified freedom. I find fault in their reasoning although I concede they are accurate in part.

As Murray Hausknecht points out, there is porn, and there is porn that is erotica. There is the not so bad old stuff such as *Fannie Hill* and the work of Frank Harris, there is "literature" such as *Lady Chatterly's Lover*. There are also the X-rated movies in sections such as New York's 42nd Street, the monthly perusal of *Playboy*, a skim of *Penthouse* at the barber's, and glances at the covers of *Hustler* and similar magazines at the news stand.

The movies seen by my academic friends turn out to be not bad politically. Indeed, one colleague assures me that the movies he sees depict an equal enthusiasm by women and men for the satisfaction of erotic pleasures. Yet what of the pornographic literature and media that bears a message of inequality and exploitation? Take *The Story of O* and even the high art of Henry Miller, which the feminist community decries as debasing to women and evocative of ugly images regarding them. What of pornography that exploits the weak? Most of the colleagues whose wisdom I've sought claim not to be attracted to whips and chains and don't come much into contact with porn based on pleasure through brutality.

But there is a large business in pornography that depicts exploitation and brutalization of women, and men (though to a lesser degree). Pornography doesn't originate these views but it does aid and abet them. It legitimates a set of attitudes for a public unfortunately prepared to subscribe to the notion that pain can be pleasure, particularly on the part of women. This view, grounded in folk culture and corrupted Freudian psychology, has serious and dangerous political overtones.

In the absence of knowing just how much pornography is to blame, but suspecting its impact, I would like to curtail expression of certain kinds of messages that demean and hurt groups of people. Because I am for nonsexist terminology in text books and against the media presentation of black men and women as shuffling, illiterate, lazy and inept, or of Jews as crafty and avaricious, I am also against porn movies, television programs, and magazines that portray women—and men—as victims who love their victimization.

It is argued that censorship is dangerous because the censors are not qualified to make judgments. But those who question the qualifications of the censors—and who deny that *anyone* is qualified to censor—exercise standards of judgment in their everyday lives and indeed often make their living by making judgments.

These same persons, who deny any right to judge the presentation of sexual matter, impose standards of excellence in English composition, piano playing, or research techniques in their own fields. Outside their fields, they often express fury about bad films, theater, art, and home decoration. Who shall judge, they ask, and in the next moment they are judging, the worthiness of a political candidate, the system of Justice in the U.S., or when it became decent to travel in Spain or buy a Volkswagen. In fact, they judge and censor the use of poor grammar in texts, the behavior they consider inappropriate, and the spread of ideas they consider to be abhorrent.

Every society imposes standards of taste, of morality, and of behavior. One may not strike another person; to do so is to commit the crime of assault. One may not falsely accuse another person to his or her detriment; to do so is to commit the crime of assault. One may not falsely accuse another person to his or her detriment; to do so is to commit the crime of libel. It is not considered a limitation of one's personal freedom to be denied the right to freely express anger and hatred of a type that is detrimental to the health of society. Many otherwise responsible citizens have opposed such community measures as mandatory schooling, innoculation, fluoridation of the water, and prohibitions on dumping of raw sewage into public water. Which side were we on? Somehow any restriction on pornography is symbolic to some of an end to freedom of speech and an end to poetry and beauty.

Yet it is within the nature of social life to permit freedom in some areas and not others, to judge the cost of freedom and of its restrictions, and to make decisions about what social good may be served. We are capable of deciding to teach Bellow and not Irving Wallace in a course on the modern novel and surely we can decide to retain James Joyce and not *Hustler*. Many aspects of the good society entail decisions for less freedom and more restrictions. I can think of some right off: restrictions on cars that use large quantities of gasoline, tomatoes that are gassed to ripeness, possession of guns, littering, cigarette advertising, and the playing of transistor radios on public beaches. I also think it would not be too great a denial of freedom of personal expression or art in America to prohibit films indicating that the highest form of sensuality is to hack up your lover as the grande finale of the sex act. I believe we should censor pornography that insults, defames, and encourages assault on people, men or women. I believe that words and pictures have power. I fear the point of view that is insensitive to the implications of the pornography that is grounded in society's tolerance of brutality toward women or men. Clever as we are, I think we can work out a way to differentiate between the pornography that is bad for our culture, ourselves and our families, and that which is a frolic into the world of sensuality or even a tolerable vulgarity.

We've all marched to ban the bomb and to prevent radioactive fall-out even though some scientists said it wasn't clear how much fall-out was injurious to the health. Perhaps there's something to be said for an ounce of prevention in matters of the psyche.

CHAPTER FIFTEEN

CIVIL RIGHTS

In the recent case of Bakke v. Regents of the University of California *(1978), the United States Supreme Court ruled that the special admissions program for minorities at the Davis Medical School violated the Civil Rights Act of 1964. The Court ordered Davis officials to admit 38-year-old Allan Bakke, a white engineer who had scored higher on the entrance examination than any black applicant and yet was denied entrance because of the University's racial quota system. The ruling of the Court was widely acclaimed by some whites as a victory against "reverse discrimination."*

While the Supreme Court did not completely disallow the use of racial criteria in university admissions, it strongly discouraged use of racial quotas or other such preferential systems for minorities.

The Court was not unanimous in its opinion, however, and one of those who dissented was Justice Thurgood Marshall, a long-time civil rights advocate. In Justice Marshall's opinion, a portion of which is presented here, medical schools and other types of professional schools must give preferential treatment to blacks because of our past history of discrimination against blacks in this country. Without such a policy, blacks will continue to suffer the consequences of inequality.

Taking issue with racial quotas is Thomas Sowell, a professor of economics at UCLA. Sowell argues that a policy of racial quotas is unwarranted for a number of reasons. One is the assumption that the absence of blacks in professional positions is due solely to past discrimination. According to Sowell, this is not necessarily the case. Sowell also argues that a policy of racial quotas may actually be unfair to blacks because it places black students at a disadvantage in many colleges and universities. Finally, Sowell suggests that racial quotas are not even desired by a majority of blacks and may well lead to an increase, rather than a decrease, in racial tensions.

The Case for Racial Quotas

Thurgood Marshall

Mr. Justice MARSHALL.

. . . I do not agree that petitioner's admissions program violates the Constitution. For it must be remembered that, during most of the past 200 years, the Constitution as interpreted by this Court did not prohibit the most ingenious and pervasive forms of discrimination against the Negro. Now, when a State acts to remedy the effects of that legacy of discrimination, I cannot believe that this same Constitution stands as a barrier. . . .

I

B

The status of the Negro as property was officially erased by his emancipation at the end of the Civil War. But the long awaited emancipation, while freeing the Negro from slavery, did not bring him citizenship or equality in any meaningful way. Slavery was replaced by a system of "laws which imposed upon the colored race onerous disabilities and burdens, and curtailed their rights in the pursuit of life, liberty, and property to such an extent that their freedom was of little value." *Slaughter-House Cases*, 16 Wall. 36, 70, 21 L.Ed. 394 (1873). Despite the passage of the Thirteenth, Fourteenth, and Fifteenth Amendments, the Negro was systematically denied the rights those amendments were supposed to secure. The combined actions and inactions of the State and Federal Government maintained Negroes in a position of legal inferiority for another century after the Civil War.

The Southern States took the first steps to re-enslave the Negroes. Immediately following the end of the Civil War, many of the provisional

From *Regents of University of California v. Bakke,* 98 S. Ct. 2733 (1978).

legislatures passed Black Codes, similar to the Slave Codes, which, among other things, limited the rights of Negroes to own or rent property and permitted imprisonment for breach of employment contracts. Over the next several decades, the South managed to disenfranchise the Negroes in spite of the Fifteenth Amendment by various techniques, including poll taxes, deliberately complicated balloting processes, property and literacy qualifications, and finally the white primary.

Congress responded to the legal disabilities being imposed in the Southern States by passing the Reconstruction Acts and the Civil Rights Acts. Congress also responded to the needs of the Negroes at the end of the Civil War by establishing the Bureau of Refugees, Freedmen, and Abandoned Lands, better known as the Freedmen's Bureau, to supply food, hospitals, land and education to the newly freed slaves. Thus for a time it seemed as if the Negro might be protected from the continued denial of his civil rights and might be relieved of the disabilities that prevented him from taking his place as a free and equal citizen.

That time, however, was short-lived. Reconstruction came to a close, and, with the assistance of this Court, the Negro was rapidly stripped of his new civil rights. . . .

The Court began by interpreting the Civil War Amendments in a manner that sharply curtailed their substantive protections. See, *e.g.*, *Slaughter-House Cases, supra; United States v. Reese*, 92 U.S. 214, 23 L.Ed. 563 (1876); *United States v. Cruikshank*, 92 U.S. 542, 23 L.Ed. 588 (1876). Then in the notorious *Civil Rights Cases*, 109 U.S. 3, 3 S.Ct. 18, 27 L.Ed. 835 (1883), the Court strangled Congress' efforts to use its power to promote racial equality. In those cases the Court invalidated sections of the Civil Rights Act of 1875 that made it a crime to deny equal access to "inns, public conveyances . . ., theatres, and other places of public amusement." According to the Court, the Fourteenth Amendment gave Congress the power to proscribe only discriminatory action by the State. The Court ruled that the Negroes who were excluded from public places suffered only an invasion of their social rights at the hands of private individuals, and Congress had no power to remedy that. *Id.*, at 24-25, 3 S.Ct., at 31. "When a man has emerged from slavery, and by the aid of beneficent legislation has shaken off the inseparable concomitants of that state," the Court concluded, "there must be some stage in the progress of his elevation when he takes the rank of a mere citizen, and ceases to be the special favorite of the laws. . . ." *Id.*, at 25, 3 S.Ct., at 31. As Justice Harlan noted in dissent, however, the Civil War Amendments and Civil Rights Acts did not make the Negroes the "special favorite" of the laws but instead "sought to accomplish in reference to that race . . .—what had already been done in every State of the Union for the White race—to secure and protect rights belonging to them as freemen and citizens; nothing more." *Id.*, at 61, 3 S.Ct., at 57.

The Court's ultimate blow to the Civil War Amendments and to the equality of Negroes came in *Plessy v. Ferguson,* 163 U.S. 537, 16 S.Ct. 1138, 41 L.Ed. 256 (1896). In upholding a Louisiana law that required railway companies to provide "equal but separate" accommodations for whites and Negroes, the Court held that the Fourteenth Amendment was not intended "to abolish distinctions based upon color, or to enforce social, as distinguished from political equality, or a commingling of the two races upon terms unsatisfactory to either." *Id.,* at 544, 16 S.Ct., at 1140. Ignoring totally the realities of the positions of the two races, the Court remarked:

> *"We consider the underlying fallacy of the plaintiff's argument to consist in the assumption that the enforced separation of the two races stamps the colored race with a badge of inferiority. If this be so, it is not by reason of anything found in the act, but solely because the colored race chooses to put that construction upon it." Id., at 551, 16 S.Ct., at 1143.*

Mr. Justice Harlan's dissenting opinion recognized the bankruptcy of the Court's reasoning. He noted that the "real meaning" of the legislation was "that colored citizens are so inferior and degraded that they cannot be allowed to sit in public coaches occupied by white citizens." *Id.,* at 560, 16 S.Ct., at 1147. He expressed his fear that if like laws were enacted in other States, "the effect would be in the highest degree mischievous." *Id.,* at 563, 16 S.Ct., at 1148. Although slavery would have disappeared, the States would retain the power "to interfere with the full enjoyment of the blessings of freedom; to regulate civil rights, common to all citizens, upon the basis of race; and to place in a condition of legal inferiority a large body of American citizens. . . ." *Id.,* at 563, 16 S.Ct., at 1148.

The fears of Mr. Justice Harlan were soon to be realized. In the wake of *Plessy,* many States expanded their Jim Crow laws, which had up until that time been limited primarily to passenger trains and schools. The segregation of the races was extended to residential areas, parks, hospitals, theaters, waiting rooms and bathrooms. There were even statutes and ordinances which authorized separate phone booths for Negroes and whites, which required that textbooks used by children of one race be kept separate from those used by the other, and which required that Negro and white prostitutes be kept in separate districts. . . .

Nor were the laws restricting the rights of Negroes limited solely to the Southern States. In many of the Northern States, the Negro was denied the right to vote, prevented from serving on juries and excluded from theaters, restaurants, hotels, and inns. Under President Wilson, the Federal Government began to require segregation in Government buildings; desks of Negro employees were curtained off; separate bathrooms and separate tables in the cafeterias were provided; and even the galleries of the Congress were segregated. . . .

The enforced segregation of the races continued into the middle of the 20th century. In both World Wars, Negroes were for the most part confined to separate military units; it was not until 1948 that an end to segregation in the military was ordered by President Truman. And the history of the exclusion of Negro children from white public schools is too well known and recent to require repeating here. That Negroes were deliberately excluded from public graduate and professional schools—and thereby denied the opportunity to become doctors, lawyers, engineers, and the like—is also well established. It is of course true that some of the Jim Crow laws (which the decisions of this Court had helped to foster) were struck down by this Court in a series of decisions leading up to *Brown v. Board of Education of Topeka,* 347 U.S. 483, 74 S.Ct. 686, 98 L.Ed. 873 (1954). See, *e.g., Morgan v. Virginia,* 328 U.S. 373, 66 S.Ct. 1050, 90 L.Ed. 1317 (1946); *Sweatt v. Painter,* 339 U.S. 629, 70 S.Ct. 848, 94 L.Ed. 1114 (1950); *McLaurin v. Oklahoma State Regents,* 339 U.S. 637, 70 S.Ct. 851, 94 L.Ed. 1149 (1950). Those decisions, however, did not automatically end segregation, nor did they move Negroes from a position of legal inferiority to one of equality. The legacy of years of slavery and of years of second-class citizenship in the wake of emancipation could not be so easily eliminated.

II

The position of the Negro today in America is the tragic but inevitable consequence of centuries of unequal treatment. Measured by any benchmark of comfort or achievement, meaningful equality remains a distant dream for the Negro. . . .

When the Negro child reaches working age, he finds that America offers him significantly less than it offers his white counterpart. For Negro adults, the unemployment rate is twice that of whites,[1] and the unemployment rate for Negro teenagers is nearly three times that of white teenagers.[2] A Negro male who completes four years of college can expect a median annual income of merely $110 more than a white male who has only a high school diploma.[3] Although Negroes represent 11.5% of the population,[4] they are only 1.2% of the lawyers, and judges, 2% of the physicians, 2.3% of the dentists, 1.1% of the engineers and 2.6% of the college and university professors.[5]

The relationship between those figures and the history of unequal treatment afforded to the Negro cannot be denied. At every point from birth to death the impact of the past is reflected in the still disfavored position of the Negro.

In light of the sorry history of discrimination and its devastating impact on the lives of Negroes, bringing the Negro into the mainstream of American life should be a state interest of the highest order. To fail to do so is to ensure that America will forever remain a divided society.

III

. . . It is plain that the Fourteenth Amendment was not intended to prohibit measures designed to remedy the effects of the Nation's past treatment of Negroes. The Congress that passed the Fourteenth Amendment is the same Congress that passed the 1866 Freedmen's Bureau Act, an act that provided many of its benefits only to Negroes: Act of July 16, 1866, ch. 200, 14 Stat. 173. . . .

Since the Congress that considered and rejected the objections to the 1866 Freedman's Bureau Act concerning special relief to Negroes also proposed the Fourteenth Amendment, it is inconceivable that the Fourteenth Amendment was intended to prohibit all race-conscious relief measures. It "would be a distortion of the policy manifested in that amendment, which was adopted to prevent state legislation designed to perpetuate discrimination on the basis of race or color." *Railway Mail Association v. Corsi*, 326 U.S. 88, 94, 65 S.Ct. 1483, 1487, 89 L.Ed. 2072 (1945), to hold that it barred state action to remedy the effects of that discrimination. Such a result would pervert the intent of the framers by substituting abstract equality for the genuine equality the amendment was intended to achieve.

B

As has been demonstrated in our joint opinion, this Court's past cases establish the constitutionality of race-conscious remedial measures. Beginning with the school desegregation cases, we recognized that even absent a judicial or legislative finding of constitutional violation, a school board constitutionally could consider the race of students in making school assignment decisions. See *Swann v. Charlotte-Mecklenberg Board of Education*, 402 U.S. 1, 16, . . . (1971); *McDaniel v. Barresi*, 402 U.S. 39, 41, . . . (1971). . . .

> *. . . As we have held in* Swann, *the Constitution does not compel any particular degree of racial balance or mixing, but when past and continuing constitutional violations are found, some ratios are likely to be useful as starting points in shaping a remedy. . . ."*

As we have observed, "[a]ny other approach would freeze the status quo that is the very target of all desegregation processes." *McDaniel v. Barresi, supra,* 402 U.S. at 41, 91 S.Ct. at 1289.

Only last Term, in *United Jewish Organizations v. Carey,* 430 U.S. 144, 97 S.Ct. 996, 51 L.Ed. 229 (1977), we upheld a New York reapportionment plan that was deliberately drawn on the basis of race to enhance the electoral power of Negroes and Puerto Ricans; the plan had the effect of diluting the electoral strength of the Hasidic Jewish Community. We were willing in *UJO* to sanction the remedial use of a racial classification even though it disadvantaged otherwise "innocent" individuals. In another case last Term, *Califano v. Webster,* 430 U.S. 313, 97 S.Ct. 1192, 51 L.Ed.2d 360 (1977), the Court upheld a provision in the Social Security laws that discriminated against men because its purpose was " 'the permissible one

of redressing our society's long standing disparate treatment of women.' "
Id., at 317, 97 S.Ct. at 1195, quoting *Califano v. Goldfarb,* 430 U.S. 199, 209 n.
8, 97 S.Ct. 1021, 1028, 51 L.Ed.2d 270 (1977) (plurality opinion). We thus
recognized the permissibility of remedying past societal discrimination
through the use of otherwise disfavored classifications.

Nothing in those cases suggests that a university cannot similarly act
to remedy past discrimination.[6] It is true that in both *UJO* and *Webster* the
use of the disfavored classification was predicated on legislative or administrative action, but in neither case had those bodies made findings that
there had been constitutional violations or that the specific individuals to
be benefited had actually been the victims of discrimination. Rather, the
classification in each of those cases was based on a determination that the
group was in need of the remedy because of some type of past discrimination. There is thus ample support for the conclusion that a university can
employ race-conscious measures to remedy past societal discrimination,
without the need for a finding that those benefited were actually victims of
that discrimination.

IV

While I applaud the judgment of the Court that a university may consider
race in its admissions process, it is more than a little ironic that, after
several hundred years of class-based discrimination against Negroes, the
Court is unwilling to hold that a class-based remedy for that discrimination
is permissible. In declining to so hold, today's judgment ignores the fact
that for several hundred years Negroes have been discriminated against,
not as individuals, but rather solely because of the color of their skins. It is
unnecessary in 20th century America to have individual Negroes demonstrate that they have been victims of racial discrimination; the racism of
our society has been so pervasive that none, regardless of wealth or
position, has managed to escape its impact. The experience of Negroes in
America has been different in kind, not just in degree, from that of other
ethnic groups. It is not merely the history of slavery alone but also that a
whole people were marked as inferior by the law. And that mark has
endured. The dream of America as the great melting pot has not been
realized for the Negro; because of his skin color he never even made it into
the pot.

These differences in the experience of the Negro make it difficult for
me to accept that Negroes cannot be afforded greater protection under the
Fourteenth Amendment where it is necessary to remedy the effects of past
discrimination. . . .

It is because of a legacy of unequal treatment that we now must permit
the institutions of this society to give consideration to race in making
decisions about who will hold the positions of influence, affluence and
prestige in America. For far too long, the doors to those positions have

been shut to Negroes. If we are ever to become a fully integrated society, one in which the color of a person's skin will not determine the opportunities available to him or her, we must be willing to take steps to open those doors. I do not believe that anyone can truly look into America's past and still find that a remedy for the effects of that past is impermissible.

It has been said that this case involves only the individual, Bakke, and this University. I doubt, however, that there is a computer capable of determining the number of persons and institutions that may be affected by the decision in this case. For example, we are told by the Attorney General of the United States that at least 27 federal agencies have adopted regulations requiring recipients of federal funds to take *"affirmative action* to overcome the effects of conditions which resulted in limiting participation . . . by persons of a particular race, color, or national origin. Supplemental Brief for the United States as *Amicus Curiae* 16 (emphasis added). I cannot even guess the number of state and local governments that have set up affirmative action programs, which may be affected by today's decision.

I fear that we have come full circle. After the Civil War our government started several "affirmative action" programs. This Court in the *Civil Rights Cases* and *Plessy v. Ferguson* destroyed the movement toward complete equality. For almost a century no action was taken, and this nonaction was with the tacit approval of the courts. Then we had *Brown v. Board of Education* and the Civil Rights Acts of Congress, followed by numerous affirmative action programs. *Now,* we have this Court again stepping in, this time to stop affirmative action programs of the type used by the University of California. . . .

NOTES

1. U.S. Dept. of Labor, Bureau of Labor Statistics, Employment and Earnings, January 1978, at 170 (table 44).
2. *Ibid.*
3. U.S. Dept. of Commerce, Bureau of the Census, Current Population Reports, Series P-60, No. 105, at 198 (1977) (table 47).
4. U.S. Dept. of Commerce, Bureau of the Census, Statistical Abstract of the United States 25 (table 24).
5. *Id.,* at 407-408 (table 662)(based on 1970 census).
6. Indeed, the action of the University finds support in the regulations promulgated under Title VI by the Department of Health, Education, and Welfare and approved by the President, which authorize a federally funded institution to take affirmative steps to overcome past discrimination against groups even where the institution was not guilty of prior discrimination. 45 CFR sec. 80.3(b)(6)(ii).

Are Quotas Good for Blacks?

Thomas Sowell

Race has never been an area noted for rationality of thought or action. Almost every conceivable form of nonsense has been believed about racial or ethnic groups at one time or another. Theologians used to debate whether black people had souls (today's terminology might suggest that *only* black people have souls). As late as the 1920's, a leading authority on mental tests claimed that test results disproved the popular belief that Jews are intelligent. Since then, Jewish IQ's have risen above the national average and more than one-fourth of all American Nobel Prize-winners have been Jewish.

Today's grand fallacy about race and ethnicity is that the statistical "representation" of a group—in jobs, schools, etc.—shows and measures *discrimination*. This notion is at the center of such controversial policies as affirmative-action hiring, preferential admissions to college, and public-school busing. But despite the fact that far-reaching judicial rulings, political crusades, and bureaucratic empires owe their existence to that belief, it remains an unexamined assumption. Tons of statistics have been collected, but only to be interpreted in the light of that assumption, never to test the assumption itself. Glaring facts to the contrary are routinely ignored. Questioning the "representation" theory is stigmatized as not only inexpedient but immoral. It is the noble lie of our time.

AFFIRMATIVE-ACTION HIRING

"Representation" or "underrepresentation" is based on comparisons of a given group's percentage in the population with its percentage in some occupation, institution, or activity. This might make sense if the various

Reprinted from *Commentary*, by permission; copyright © 1978 by the American Jewish Committee.

ethnic groups were even approximately similar in age distribution, education, and other crucial variables. But they are not.

Some ethnic groups are a whole decade younger than others. Some are two decades younger. The average age of Mexican Americans and Puerto Ricans is under twenty, while the average age of Irish Americans or Italian Americans is over thirty—and the average age of Jewish Americans is over forty. This is because of large differences in the number of children per family from one group to another. Some ethnic groups have more than twice as many children per family as others. Over half of the Mexican American and Puerto Rican population consists of teenagers, children, and infants. These two groups are likely to be underrepresented in any adult activity, whether work or recreation, whether controlled by others or entirely by themselves, and whether there is discrimination or not.

Educational contrasts are also great. More than half of all Americans over thirty-five of German, Irish, Jewish, or Oriental ancestry have completed at least four years of high school. Less than 20 per cent of all Mexican Americans in the same age bracket have done so. The disparities become even greater when you consider quality of school, field of specialization, postgraduate study, and other factors that are important in the kind of high-level jobs on which special attention is focused by those emphasizing representation. Those groups with the most education—Jews and Orientals—also have the highest quality education, as measured by the rankings of the institutions from which they receive their college degrees and specialize in the more difficult and remunerative fields, such as science and medicine. Orientals in the United States are so heavily concentrated in the scientific area that there are more Oriental scientists than there are black scientists in absolute numbers, even though the black population of the United States is more than twenty times the size of the Oriental population.

Attention has been focused most on high-level positions—the kind of jobs people reach after years of experience or education, or both. There is no way to get the experience or education without also growing older in the process, so when we are talking about top-level jobs, we are talking about the kind of positions people reach in their forties and fifties rather than in their teens and twenties. Representation in such jobs cannot be compared to representation in a population that includes many five-year-olds—yet it is.

The general ethnic differences in age become extreme in some of the older age brackets. Half of the Jewish population of the United States is forty-five years old or older, but only 12 per cent of the Puerto Rican population is that old. Even if Jews and Puerto Ricans were identical in every other respect, and even if no employer ever had a speck of prejudice, there would still be huge disparities between the two groups in top-level positions, just from age differences alone.

Virtually every underrepresented racial or ethnic group in the United States has a lower than average age and consists disproportionately of children and inexperienced young adults. Almost invariably these groups also have less education, both quantitatively and qualitatively. The point here is not that we should "blame the victim" or "blame society." The point is that we should, first of all, *talk sense!* "Representation" talk is cheap, easy, and misleading; discrimination and opportunity are too serious to be discussed in gobbledygook.

The idea that preferential treatment is going to "compensate" people for past wrongs flies in the face of two hard facts:

1. Public-opinion polls have repeatedly shown most blacks opposed to preferential treatment either in jobs or college admissions. A Gallup Poll in March 1977, for example found only 27 per cent of non-whites favoring "preferential treatment" over "ability as determined by test scores," while 64 per cent preferred the latter and 9 per cent were undecided. (The Gallup breakdown of the U.S. population by race, sex, income, education, etc. found that "not a single population group supports affirmative action."[1])

How can you compensate people by giving them something they have explicitly rejected?

2. The income of blacks relative to whites reached its peak *before* affirmative-action hiring and has *declined* since. The median income of blacks reached a peak of 60.9 per cent of the median income of whites in 1970—the year before "goals" and "timetables" became part of the affirmative-action concept. "In only one year of the last six years," writes Andrew Brimmer, "has the proportion been as high as 60 per cent."[2]

Before something can be a "compensation," it must first be a benefit.

The repudiation of the numerical or preferential approach by the very people it is supposed to benefit points out the large gap between illusion and reality that is characteristic of affirmative action. So does the cold fact that there are few, if any, benefits to offset all the bitterness generated by this heavy-handed program. The bitterness is largely a result of a deeply resented principle, galling bureaucratic processes, and individual horror stories. Overall, the program has changed little for minorities or women. Supporters of the program try to cover up its ineffectiveness by comparing the position of minorities today with their position many years ago. This ignores all the progress that took place under straight equal-treatment laws in the 1960's—progress that has not continued at anywhere near the same pace under affirmative action.

Among the reasons for such disappointing results is that hiring someone to fill a quota gets the government off the employer's back for the moment, but buys more trouble down the road whenever a disgruntled employee chooses to go to an administrative agency or a court with a complaint based on nothing but numbers. Regardless of the merits, or the end result, a very costly process for the employer must be endured, and the threat of this is an incentive *not* to hire from the groups designated as special by the government. The affirmative-action program has meant mutually canceling incentives to hire and not to hire—and great bitterness and cost from the process, either way.

If blacks are opposed to preferential treatment and whites are opposed to it, who then is in favor of it, and how does it go on? The implications of these questions are even more far-reaching and more disturbing than the policy itself. They show how vulnerable our democratic and constitutional safeguards are to a relative handful of determined people. Some of those people promoting preferential treatment and numerical goals are so convinced of the rightness of what they are doing that they are prepared to sacrifice whatever needs to be sacrificed—whether it be other people, the law, or simply honesty in discussing what they are doing (note "goals," "desegregation," and similar euphemisms). Other supporters of numerical policies have the powerful drive of self-interest as well as self-righteousness. Bureaucratic empires have grown up to administer these programs, reaching into virtually every business, school, hospital, or other organization. The rulers and agents of this empire can order employers around, make college presidents bow and scrape, assign schoolteachers by race, or otherwise gain power, publicity, and career advancement— regardless of whether minorities are benefited or not.

While self-righteousness and self-interest are powerful drives for those who have them, they can succeed only insofar as other people can be persuaded, swept along by feelings, or neutralized. Rhetoric has accomplished this with images of historic wrongs, visions of social atonement, and a horror of being classed with bigots. These tactics have worked best with those most affected by words and least required to pay a price personally: non-elected judges, the media, and the intellectual establishment.

The "color-blind" words of the Civil Rights Act of 1964, or even the protections of the Constitution, mean little when judges can creatively reinterpret them out of existence. It is hard to achieve the goal of an informed public when the mass media show only selective indignation about power grabs and a sense of pious virtue in covering up the failures of school integration. Even civil libertarians—who insist that the Fifth Amendment protection against self-incrimination is a sacred right that cannot be denied Nazis, Communists, or criminals—show no concern when the government routinely forces employers to confess "deficiencies" in their hiring processes, without a speck of evidence other than a numerical pattern different from the government's preconception.

PREFERENTIAL ADMISSIONS

Preferential admissions to colleges and universities are "justified" by similar rhetoric and the similar assumption that statistical underrepresentation means institutional exclusion. Sometimes this assumption is buttressed by notions of "compensation" and a theory that (1) black communities need more black practitioners in various fields; and that (2) black students will ultimately supply that need. The idea that the black community's doctors, lawyers, etc. should be black is an idea held by white liberals, but no such demand has come from the black community, which has rejected preferential admissions in poll after poll. Moreover, the idea that an admissions committee can predict what a youth is going to do with his life years later is even more incredible—even if the youth is one's own son or daughter, much less someone from a wholly different background.

These moral or ideological reasons for special minority programs are by no means the whole story. The public image of a college or university is often its chief financial asset. Bending a few rules here and there to get the right body count of minority students seems a small price to pay for maintaining an image that will keep money coming in from the government and the foundations. When a few thousand dollars in financial aid to students can keep millions of tax dollars rolling in, it is clearly a profitable investment for the institution. For the young people brought in under false pretense, it can turn out to be a disastrous and permanently scarring experience.

The most urgent concern over image and over government subsidies, foundation grants, and other donations is at those institutions which have the most of all these things to maintain—that is at prestigious colleges and universities at the top of the academic pecking order. The Ivy League schools and the leading state and private institutions have the scholarship money and the brand name visibility to draw in enough minority youngsters to look good statistically. The extremely high admissions standards of these institutions usually cannot be met by the minority students—just as most students in general cannot meet them. But in order to have a certain minority body count, the schools bend (or disregard) their usual standards. The net result is that thousands of minority students who would normally qualify for good, non-prestigious colleges where they could succeed, are instead enrolled in famous institutions where they fail. For example, at Cornell during the guns-on-campus crisis, fully half of the black students were on academic probation, despite easier grading standards for them in many courses. Yet these students were by no means unqualified. Their average test scores put them in the top quarter of all American college students—but the other Cornell students ranked in the top 1 per cent. In other words, minority students with every prospect of success in a normal college environment were artificially turned into failures by being mismatched with an institution with standards too severe for them.

When the top institutions reach further down to get minority students, then academic institutions at the next level are forced to reach still further down, so that they too will end up with a minority body count high enough to escape criticism and avoid trouble with the government and other donors. Each academic level, therefore, ends up with minority students underqualified for that level, though usually perfectly qualified for some other level. The end result is a systematic mismatching of minority students and the institutions they attend, even though the wide range of American colleges and universities is easily capable of accommodating those same students under their normal standards.

Proponents of "special" (lower) admissions standards argue that without such standards no increase in minority enrollment would have been possible. But this blithely disregards the fact that when more *money* is available to finance college, more low-income people go to college. The GI Bill after World War II caused an even more dramatic increase in the number of people going to college who could never have gone otherwise—and without lowering admissions standards. The growth of special minority programs in recent times has meant both a greater availability of money and lower admissions standards for black and other designated students. It is as ridiculous to ignore the role of money in increasing the numbers of minority students in the system as a whole as it is to ignore the effect of double standards on their maldistribution among institutions. It is the double standards that are the problem, and they can be ended without driving minority students out of the system. Of course, many academic hustlers who administer special programs might lose their jobs, but that would hardly be a loss to anyone else.

As long as admission to colleges and universities is not unlimited, someone's opportunity to attend has to be sacrificed as the price of preferential admission for others. No amount of verbal sleight-of-hand can get around this fact. None of those sacrificed is old enough to have had anything to do with historic injustices that are supposedly being compensated. Moreover, it is not the offspring of the privileged who are likely to pay the price. It is not a Rockefeller or a Kennedy who will be dropped to make room for quotas; it is a De Funis or a Bakke. Even aside from personal influence on admissions decisions, the rich can give their children the kind of private schooling that will virtually assure them test scores far above the cut-off level at which sacrifices are made.

Just as the students who are sacrificed are likely to come from the bottom of the white distribution, so the minority students chosen are likely to be from the top of the minority distribution. In short, it is a forced transfer of benefits from those least able to afford it to those least in need of it. In some cases, the loose term "minority" is used to include individuals who are personally from more fortunate backgrounds than the average American. Sometimes it includes whole groups, such as Chinese or Japanese Americans, who have higher incomes than whites. One-fourth of all employed Chinese in this country are in professional occupations— nearly double the national average. No amount of favoritism to the son or daughter of a Chinese doctor or mathematician today is going to compensate some Chinese of the past who was excluded from virtually every kind of work except washing clothes or washing dishes.

The past is a great unchangeable fact. *Nothing* is going to undo its sufferings and injustices, whatever their magnitude. Statistical categories and historic labels may seem real to those inspired by words, but only living flesh-and-blood people can feel joy or pain. Neither the sins nor the sufferings of those now dead are within our power to change. Being honest and honorable with the people living in our own time is more than enough moral challenge, without indulging in illusions about rewriting moral history with numbers and categories. . . .

However futile the various numerical approaches have been in their avowed goal of advancing minorities, their impact has been strongly felt in other ways. The message that comes through loud and clear is that minorities are losers who will never have anything unless someone gives it to them. The destructiveness of this message—on society in general and minority youth in particular—outweighs any trivial gains that may occur here and there. The falseness of the message is shown by the great economic achievements of minorities during the period of equal-rights legislation before numerical goals and timetables muddied the waters. By and large, the numerical approach has achieved nothing, and has achieved it at great cost.

Underlying the attempt to move people around and treat them like chess pieces on a board is a profound contempt for other human beings. To ignore or resent people's resistance—on behalf of their children or their livelihoods—is to deny our common humanity. To persist dogmatically in pursuit of some abstract goal, without regard to how it is reached, is to despise freedom and reduce three-dimensional life to cardboard pictures of numerical results. The false practicality of results-oriented people ignores the fact that the ultimate results are in the minds and hearts of human beings. Once personal choice becomes a mere inconvenience to be brushed aside by bureaucrats or judges, something precious will have been lost by all people from all backgrounds.

A multi-ethnic society like the United States can ill-afford continually to build up stores of intergroup resentments about such powerful concerns as one's livelihood and one's children. It is a special madness when tensions are escalated between groups who are basically in accord in their opposition to numbers games, but whose legal establishments and "spokesmen" keep the fires fueled. We must never think that the disintegration and disaster that has hit other multi-ethnic societies "can't happen here." The mass internment of Japanese Americans just a generation ago is a sobering reminder of the tragic idiocy that stress can bring on. We are not made of different clay from the Germans, who were historically more enlightened and humane toward Jews than many other Europeans—until the generation of Hitler and the Holocaust.

The situation in America today is, of course, not like that of the Pearl

Harbor period, nor of the Weimar republic. History does not literally repeat, but it can warn us of what people are capable of, when the stage has been set for tragedy. We certainly do not need to let emotionally combustible materials accumulate from ill-conceived social experiments.

NOTES

1. Gallup Opinion Index, June 1977, Report 143, p. 23.
2. *Black Enterprise,* April 1978, p. 62. A newly released RAND study similarly concludes that very little credit should be given to government affirmative-action programs for any narrowing of the income gap between white and black workers. The RAND researchers write, "our results suggest that the effect of government on the aggregate black-white wage ratio is quite small and that the popular notion that . . . recent changes are being driven by government pressure has little empirical support" (New York *Times,* May 8, 1978).

CHAPTER SIXTEEN

CHARACTERIZATIONS OF THE AMERICAN POLITICAL SYSTEM

Up to this point, the selections in this reader have focused narrowly upon various political institutions and processes. These final two selections, however, examine our political system at a more general level. Specifically, they attempt to characterize the structure of power in our political system. C. Wright Mills' book, The Power Elite, *represents one of the most ambitious treatments of this subject. In it, he argues that all decisions of at least national consequence are determined by a power elite—a group of individuals who occupy the top positions in three different sectors of our national life. The members of this power elite can move with relative ease from the top of one sector to another. While Mills is not prepared to say that these individuals conspire with one another, he contends that they quite naturally hold similar views of the world because of common interests and backgrounds. Mills expresses concern about this power elite because many of them are not held accountable to the electorate for the exercise of their power. Also, in his judgment, the interests of this elite do not necessarily coincide with the public interest.*

Arnold Rose, author of the second selection, contends that the structure of power in the American political system is not as monolithic as Mills would have us believe. He notes that the group which Mills designates as power elite is not unified in its views and goals and that the evidence does not suggest this group is all that successful in bringing about the adoption of policies favoring its own interests. This is so because our society is in fact composed of a multiplicity of competing interests, no one of which is able to call the tune all of the time.

The Power Elite

C. Wright Mills

2

We study history, it has been said, to rid ourselves of it, and the history of the power elite is a clear case for which this maxim is correct. Like the tempo of American life in general, the long-term trends of the power structure have been greatly speeded up since World War II, and certain newer trends within and between the dominant institutions have also set the shape of the power elite and given historically specific meaning to its fifth epoch:

I. Insofar as the structural clue to the power elite today lies in the political order, that clue is the decline of politics as genuine and public debate of alternative decisions—with nationally responsible and policy-coherent parties and with autonomous organizations connecting the lower and middle levels of power with the top levels of decision. America is now in considerable part more a formal political democracy than a democratic social structure, and even the formal political mechanics áre weak.

The long-time tendency of business and government to become more intricately and deeply involved with each other has, in the fifth epoch, reached a new point of explicitness. The two cannot now be seen clearly as two distinct worlds. It is in terms of the executive agencies of the state that the rapprochement has proceeded most decisively. The growth of the executive branch of the government, with its agencies that patrol the complex economy, does not mean merely the "enlargement of government" as some sort of autonomous bureaucracy: it has meant the ascendancy of the corporation's man as a political eminence.

During the New Deal the corporate chieftains joined the political directorate; as of World War II they have come to dominate it. Long interlocked with government, now they have moved into quite full direction of the economy of the war effort and of the postwar era. This shift of the corporation executives into the political directorate has accelerated the long-term relegation of the professional politicians in the Congress to the middle levels of power.

II. Insofar as the structural clue to the power elite today lies in the enlarged and military state, that clue becomes evident in the military ascendancy. The warlords have gained decisive political relevance, and the military structure of America is now in considerable part a political structure. The seemingly permanent military threat places a premium on the military and upon their control of men, material, money, and power; virtually all political and economic actions are now judged in terms of military definitions of reality: the higher warlords have ascended to a firm position within the power elite of the fifth epoch.

In part at least this has resulted from one simple historical fact, pivotal for the years since 1939: the focus of elite attention has been shifted from domestic problems, centered in the 'thirties around slump, to international problems, centered in the 'forties and 'fifties around war. Since the governing apparatus of the United States has by long historic usage been adapted to and shaped by domestic clash and balance, it has not, from any angle, had suitable agencies and traditions for the handling of international problems. Such formal democratic mechanics as had arisen in the century and a half of national development prior to 1941, had not been extended to the American handling of international affairs. It is, in considerable part, in this vacuum that the power elite has grown.

III. Insofar as the structural clue to the power elite today lies in the economic order, that clue is the fact that the economy is at once a permanent-war economy and a private-corporation economy. American capitalism is now in considerable part a military capitalism, and the most important relation of the big corporation to the state rests on the coincidence of interests between military and corporate needs, as defined by warlords and corporate rich. Within the elite as a whole, this coincidence of interest between the high military and the corporate chieftains strengthens both of them and further subordinates the role of the merely political men. Not politicians, but corporate executives, sit with the military and plan the organization of war effort.

The shape and meaning of the power elite today can be understood only when these three sets of structural trends are seen at their point of coincidence: the military capitalism of private corporations exists in a weakened and formal democratic system containing a military order already quite political in outlook and demeanor. Accordingly, at the top of this structure, the power elite has been shaped by the coincidence of interest between those who control the major means of production and those who control the newly enlarged means of violence; from the decline of the professional politician and the rise to explicit political command of the corporate chieftains and the professional warlords; from the absence of any genuine civil service of skill and integrity, independent of vested interests.

The power elite is composed of political, economic, and military men, but this instituted elite is frequently in some tension: it comes together only on certain coinciding points and only on certain occasions of "crisis." In the long peace of the nineteenth century, the military men were not in the high councils of state, not of the political directorate, and neither were the economic men—they made raids upon the state but they did not join its directorate. During the 'thirties, the political man was ascendant. Now the military and the corporate men are in top positions.

Of the three types of circle that compose the power elite today, it is the military that has benefited the most in its enhanced power, although the corporate circles have also become more explicitly intrenched in the more public decision-making circles. It is the professional politician that has lost the most, so much that in examining the events and decisions, one is tempted to speak of a political vacuum in which the corporate rich and the high warlord, in their coinciding interests, rule.

It should not be said that the three "take turns" in carrying the initiative, for the mechanics of the power elite are not often as deliberate as that would imply. At times, of course, it is—as when political men, thinking they can borrow the prestige of generals, find that they must pay for it, or, as when during big slumps, economic men feel the need of a politician at once safe and possessing vote appeal. Today all three are involved in virtually all widely ramifying decisions. Which of the three types seems to lead depends upon "the tasks of the period" as they, the elite, define them. Just now, these tasks center upon "defense" and international affairs. Accordingly, as we have seen, the military are ascendant in two senses: as personnel and as justifying ideology. That is why, just now, we can most easily specify the unity and the shape of the power elite in terms of the military ascendancy.

But we must always be historically specific and open to complexities. The simple Marxian view makes the big economic man the *real* holder of power; the simple liberal view makes the big political man the chief of the power system; and there are some who would view the warlords as virtual dictators. Each of these is an oversimplified view. It is to avoid them that we use the term "power elite" rather than, for example, "ruling class."*

---

*"Ruling class" is a badly loaded phrase. "Class" is an economic term; "rule" a political one. The phrase, "ruling class," thus contains the theory that an economic class rules politically. That short-cut theory may or may not at times be true, but we do not want to carry that one rather simple theory about in the terms that we use to define our problems; we wish

Insofar as the power elite has come to wide public attention, it has done so in terms of the "military clique." The power elite does, in fact, take its current shape from the decisive entrance into it of the military. Their presence and their ideology are its major legitimations, whenever the power elite feels the need to provide any. But what is called the "Washington military clique" is not composed merely of military men, and it does not prevail merely in Washington. Its members exist all over the country, and it is a coalition of generals in the roles of corporation executives, of politicians masquerading as admirals, or corporation executives acting like politicians, of civil servants who become majors, of vice-admirals who are also the assistants to a cabinet officer, who is himself, by the way, really a member of the managerial elite.

Neither the idea of a "ruling class" nor of a simple monolithic rise of "bureaucratic politicians" nor of a "military clique" is adequate. The power elite today involves the often uneasy coincidence of economic, military, and political power.

3

Even if our understanding were limited to these structural trends, we should have grounds for believing the power elite a useful, indeed indispensable, concept for the interpretation of what is going on at the topside of modern American society. But we are not, of course, so limited: our conception of the power elite does not need to rest only upon the correspondence of the institutional hierarchies involved, or upon the many points at which their shifting interests coincide. The power elite, as we conceive it, also rests upon the similarity of its personnel, and their personal and official relations with one another, upon their social and psychological affinities. In order to grasp the personal and social basis of the power elite's unity, we have first to remind ourselves of the facts of origin, career, and style of life of each of the types of circle whose members compose the power elite.

The power elite is *not* an aristocracy, which is to say that it is not a political ruling group based upon a nobility of hereditary origin. It has no compact basis in a small circle of great families whose members can and do

to state the theories explicitly, using terms of more precise and unilateral meaning. Specifically, the phrase "ruling class," in its common political connotations, does not allow enough autonomy to the political order and its agents, and it says nothing about the military as such. It should be clear to the reader by now that we do not accept as adequate the simple view that high economic men unilaterally make all decisions of national consequence. We hold that such a simple view of "economic determinism" must be elaborated by "political determinism" and "military determinism"; that the higher agents of each of these three domains now often have a noticeable degree of autonomy; and that only in the often intricate ways of coalition do they make up and carry through the most important decisions. Those are the major reasons we prefer "power elite" to "ruling class" as a characterizing phrase for the higher circles when we consider them in terms of power.

consistently occupy the top positions in the several higher circles which overlap as the power elite. But such nobility is only one possible basis of common origin. That it does not exist for the American elite does not mean that members of this elite derive socially from the full range of strata composing American society. They derive in substantial proportions from the upper classes, both new and old, of local society and the metropolitan 400. The bulk of the very rich, the corporate executives, the political outsiders, the high military, derive from, at most, the upper third of the income and occupational pyramids. Their fathers were at least of the professional and business strata, and very frequently higher than that. They are native-born Americans of native parents, primarily from urban areas, and, with the exceptions of the politicians among them, overwhelmingly from the East. They are mainly Protestants, especially Episcopalian or Presbyterian. In general, the higher the position, the greater the proportion of men within it who have derived from and who maintain connections with the upper classes. The generally similar origins of the members of the power elite are underlined and carried further by the fact of their increasingly common educational routine. Overwhelmingly college graduates, substantial proportions have attended Ivy League colleges, although the education of the higher military, of course, differs from that of other members of the power elite.

But what do these apparently simple facts about the social composition of the higher circles really mean? In particular, what do they mean for any attempt to understand the degree of unity, and the direction of policy and interest that may prevail among these several circles? Perhaps it is best to put this question in a deceptively simple way: in terms of origin and career, who or what do these men at the top represent?

Of course, if they are elected politicians, they are supposed to represent those who elected them; and, if they are appointed, they are supposed to represent, indirectly, those who elected their appointers. But this is recognized as something of an abstraction, as a rhetorical formula by which all men of power in almost all systems of government nowadays justify their power of decision. At times it may be true, both in the sense of their motives and in the sense of who benefits from their decisions. Yet it would not be wise in any power system merely to assume it.

The fact that members of the power elite come from near the top of the nation's class and status levels does not mean that they are necessarily "representative" of the top levels only. And if they were, as social types, representative of a cross-section of the population, that would not mean that a balanced democracy of interest and power would automatically be the going political fact.

We cannot infer the direction of policy merely from the social origins and careers of the policy-makers. The social and economic backgrounds of the men of power do not tell us all that we need to know in order to understand the distribution of social power. For: (1) Men from high places may be ideological representatives of the poor and humble. (2) Men of humble origin, brightly self-made, may energetically serve the most vested and inherited interests. Moreover (3), not all men who effectively represent the interests of a stratum need in any way belong to it or personally benefit by policies that further its interests. Among the politicians, in short, there are sympathetic *agents* of given groups, conscious and unconscious, paid and unpaid. Finally (4), among the top decision-makers we find men who have been chosen for their positions because of their "expert knowledge." These are some of the obvious reasons why the social origins and careers of the power elite do not enable us to infer the class interests and policy directions of a modern system of power.

Do the high social origin and careers of the top men mean nothing, then, about the distribution of power? By no means. They simply remind us that we must be careful of any simple and direct inference from origin and career to political character and policy, not that we must ignore them in our attempt at political understanding. They simply mean that we must analyze the political psychology and the actual decisions of the political directorate as well as its social composition. And they mean, above all, that we should control, as we have done here, any inference we make from the origin and careers of the political actors by close understanding of the institutional landscape in which they act out their drama. Otherwise we should be guilty of a rather simple-minded biographical theory of society and history.

Just as we cannot rest the notion of the power elite solely upon the institutional mechanics that lead to its formation, so we cannot rest the notion solely upon the facts of the origin and career of its personnel. We need both, and we have both—as well as other bases, among them that of the status intermingling.

But it is not only the similarities of social origin, religious affiliation, nativity, and education that are important to the psychological and social affinities of the members of the power elite. Even if their recruitment and formal training were more heterogeneous than they are, these men would still be of quite homogeneous social type. For the most important set of facts about a circle of men is the criteria of admission, of praise, of honor, of promotion that prevails among them; if these are similar within a circle, then they will tend as personalities to become similar. The circles that compose the power elite do tend to have such codes and criteria in common. The co-optation of the social types to which these common values lead is often more important than any statistics of common origin and career that we might have at hand.

There is a kind of reciprocal attraction among the fraternity of the successful—not between each and every member of the circles of the high and mighty, but between enough of them to insure a certain unity. On the slight side, it is a sort of tacit, mutual admiration; in the strongest tie-ins, it proceeds by intermarriage. And there are all grades and types of connection between these extremes. Some overlaps certainly occur by means of cliques and clubs, churches and schools.

If social origin and formal education in common tend to make the members of the power elite more readily understood and trusted by one another, their continued association further cements what they feel they have in common. Members of the several higher circles know one another as personal friends and even as neighbors; they mingle with one another on the golf course, in the gentleman's clubs, at resorts, on transcontinental airplanes, and on ocean liners. They meet at the estates of mutual friends, face each other in front of the TV camera, or serve on the same philanthropic committee; and many are sure to cross one another's path in the columns of newspapers, if not in the exact cafes from which many of these columns originate. As we have seen, of "The New 400" of cafe society, one chronicler has named forty-one members of the very rich, ninety-three political leaders, and seventy-nine chief executives of corporations.

"I did not know, I could not have dreamed," Whittaker Chambers has written,

> of the immense scope and power of Hiss' political alliances and his social connections, which cut across all party lines and ran from the Supreme Court to the Religious Society of Friends, from governors of states and instructors in college faculties to the staff members of liberal magazines. In the decade since I had last seen him, he had used his career, and, in particular, his identification with the cause of peace through his part in organizing the United Nations, to put down roots that made him one with the matted forest floor of American upper class, enlightened middle class, liberal and official life. His roots could not be disturbed without disturbing all the roots on all sides of him.[1]

The sphere of status has reflected the epochs of the power elite. In the third epoch, for example, who could compete with big money? And in the fourth, with big politicians, or even the bright young men of the New Deal? And in the fifth, who can compete with the generals and the admirals and the corporate officials now so sympathetically portrayed on the stage, in the novel, and on the screen? Can one imagine *Executive Suite* as a successful motion picture in 1935? Or *The Caine Mutiny*?

The multiplicity of high-prestige organizations to which the elite usually belong is revealed by even casual examination of the obituaries of the big businessman, the high-prestige lawyer, the top general and admiral, the key senator: usually, high-prestige church, business associations, plus high-prestige clubs, and often plus military rank. In the course of their lifetimes, the university president, the New York Stock Exchange chairman, the head of the bank, the old West Pointer—mingle in the status sphere, within which they easily renew old friendships and draw upon them in an effort to understand through the experience of trusted others those contexts of power and decision in which they have not personally moved.

In these diverse contexts, prestige accumulates in each of the higher circles, and the members of each borrow status from one another. Their self-images are fed by these accumulations and these borrowings, and accordingly, however segmental a given man's role may seem, he comes to feel himself a "diffuse" or "generalized" man of the higher circles, a "broad-gauge" man. Perhaps such inside experience is one feature of what is meant by "judgment."

The key organizations, perhaps, are the major corporations themselves, for on the boards of directors we find a heavy overlapping among the members of these several elites. On the lighter side, again in the summer and winter resorts, we find that, in an intricate series of overlapping circles; in the course of time, each meets each or knows somebody who knows somebody who knows that one.

The higher members of the military, economic, and political orders are able readily to take over one another's point of view, always in a sympathetic way, and often in a knowledgeable way as well. They define one another as among those who count, and who, accordingly, must be taken into account. Each of them as a member of the power elite comes to incorporate into his own integrity, his own honor, his own conscience, the viewpoint, the expectations, the values of the others. If there are no common ideals and standards among them that are based upon an explicitly aristocratic culture, that does not mean that they do not feel responsibility to one another.

All the structural coincidence of their interests as well as the intricate, psychological facts of their origins and their education, their careers and their associations make possible the psychological affinities that prevail among them, affinities that make it possible for them to say of one another: He is, of course, one of us. And all this points to the basic, psychological meaning of class consciousness: Nowhere in America is there as great a "class consciousness" as among the elite; nowhere is it organized as effectively as among the power elite. For by class consciousness, as a psychological fact, one means that the individual member of a "class" accepts only those accepted by his circle as among those who are significant to his own image of self.

Within the higher circles of the power elite, factions do exist; there are conflicts of policy; individual ambitions do clash. There are still enough divisions of importance within the Republican party, and even between Republicans and Democrats, to make for different methods of operations. But more powerful than these divisions are the internal discipline and the community of interests that bind the power elite together, even across the boundaries of nations at war.[2]

4

Yet we must give due weight to the other side of the case which may not question the facts but only our interpretation of them. There is a set of objections that will inevitably be made to our whole conception of the power elite, but which has essentially to do with only the psychology of its members. It might well be put by liberals or by conservatives in some such way as this:

"To talk of power elite—isn't this to characterize men by their origins and associations? Isn't such characterization both unfair and untrue? Don't men modify themselves, especially Americans such as these, as they rise in stature to meet the demands of their jobs? Don't they arrive at a view and a line of policy that represents, so far as they in their human weaknesses can know, the interests of the nation as a whole? Aren't they merely honorable men who are doing their duty?"

What are we to reply to these objections?

I. We are sure that they are honorable men. But what is honor? Honor can only mean living up to a code that one believes to be honorable. There is no one code upon which we are all agreed. That is why, if we are civilized men, we do not kill off all of those with whom we disagree. The question is not: are these honorable men? The question is: what are their codes of honor? The answer to that question is that they are the codes of their circles, of those to whose opinions they defer. How could it be otherwise? That is one meaning of the important truism that all men are human and that all men are social creatures. As for sincerity, it can only be disproved, never proved.

II. To the question of their adaptability—which means their capacity to transcend the codes of conduct which, in their life's work and experience, they have acquired—we must answer: simply no, they cannot, at least not in the handful of years most of them have left. To expect that is to assume that they are indeed strange and expedient: such flexibility would in fact involve a violation of what we may rightly call their character and their integrity. By the way, may it not be precisely because of the lack of such character and integrity that earlier types of American politicians have not represented as great a threat as do these men of character?

It would be an insult to the effective training of the military, and to their indoctrination as well, to suppose that military officials shed their military character and outlook upon changing from uniform to mufti. This background is more important perhaps in the military case than in that of the corporate executives, for the training of the career is deeper and more total.

"Lack of imagination," Gerald W. Johnson has noted,

> is not to be confused with lack of principle. On the contrary, an unimaginative man is often a man of the highest principles. The trouble is that his principles conform to Cornford's famous definition: "A principle is a rule of inaction giving valid general reasons for not doing in a specific instance what to unprincipled instinct would seem to be right."[3]

Would it not be ridiculous, for example, to believe seriously that, in psychological fact, Charles Erwin Wilson represented anyone or any interest other than those of the corporate world? This is not because he is dishonest; on the contrary, it is because he is probably a man of solid integrity—as sound as a dollar. He is what he is and he cannot very well be anything else. He is a member of the professional corporation elite, just as are his colleagues, in the government and out of it; he represents the wealth of the higher corporate world; he represents its power; and he believes sincerely in his oft-quoted remark that "what is good for the United States is good for the General Motors Corporation and vice versa."

The revealing point about the pitiful hearings on the confirmation of such men for political posts is not the cynicism toward the law and toward the lawmakers on the middle levels of power which they display, nor their reluctance to dispose of their personal stock.[4] The interesting point is how impossible it is for such men to divest themselves of their engagement with the corporate world in general and with their own corporations in particular. Not only their money, but their friends, their interests, their training—their lives in short—are deeply involved in this world. The disposal of stock is, of course, merely a purifying ritual. The point is not so much financial or personal interests in a given corporation, but identification with the corporate world. To ask a man suddenly to divest himself of these interests and sensibilities is almost like asking a man to become a woman.

III. To the question of their patriotism, of their desire to serve the nation as a whole, we must answer first that, like codes of honor, feelings of patriotism and views of what is to the whole nation's good, are not ultimate facts but matters upon which there exists a great variety of opinion. Furthermore, patriotic opinions too are rooted in and are sustained by what a man has become by virtue of how and with whom he has lived. This is no simple mechanical determination of individual character by social conditions; it is an intricate process, well established in the major tradition of modern social study. One can only wonder why more social scientists do not use it systematically in speculating about politics.

IV. The elite cannot be truly thought of as men who are merely doing their duty. They are the ones who determine their duty, as well as the duties of those beneath them. They are not merely following orders: they give the orders. They are not merely "bureaucrats": they command bureaucracies. They may try to disguise these facts from others and from themselves by appeals to traditions of which they imagine themselves the instruments, but there are many traditions, and they must choose which ones they will serve. They face decisions for which there simply are no traditions.

Now, to what do these several answers add up? To the fact that we cannot reason about public events and historical trends merely from knowledge about the motives and character of the men or the small groups who sit in the seats of the high and mighty. This fact, in turn, does not mean that we should be intimidated by accusations that in taking up our problem in the way we have, we are impugning the honor, the integrity, or the ability of those who are in high office. For it is not, in the first instance, a question of individual character; and if, in further instances, we find that it is, we should not hesitate to say so plainly. In the meantime, we must judge men of power by the standards of power, by what they do as decision-makers, and not by who they are or what they may do in private life. Our interest is not in that: we are interested in their policies and in the *consequences* of their conduct of office. We must remember that these men of the power elite now occupy the strategic places in the structure of American society; that they command the dominant institutions of a dominant nation; that, as a set of men, they are in a position to make decisions with terrible consequences for the underlying populations of the world.

5

Despite their social similarity and psychological affinities, the members of the power elite do not constitute a club having a permanent membership with fixed and formal boundaries. It is of the nature of the power elite that within it there is a good deal of shifting about, and that it thus does not consist of one small set of the same men in the same positions in the same hierarchies. Because men know each other personally does not mean that among them there is a unity of policy; and because they do not know each other personally does not mean that among them there is a disunity. The conception of the power elite does not rest, as I have repeatedly said, primarily upon personal friendship.

As the requirements of the top places in each of the major hierarchies become similar, the types of men occupying these roles at the top—by selection and by training in the jobs—become similar. This is not mere deduction from structure to personnel. That it is a fact is revealed by the heavy traffic that has been going on between the three structures, often in very intricate patterns. The chief executives, the warlords, and selected politicians came into contact with one another in an intimate, working way during World War II; after that war ended, they continued their associations, out of common beliefs, social congeniality, and coinciding interests. Noticeable proportions of top men from the military, the economic, and the political worlds have during the last fifteen years occupied positions in one or both of the other worlds: between these higher circles there is an interchangeability of position, based formally upon the supposed transferability of "executive ability," based in substance upon the co-optation by cliques of insiders. As members of a power elite, many of those busy in this traffic have come to look upon "the government" as an umbrella under whose authority they do their work.

As the business between the big three increases in volume and importance, so does the traffic in personnel. The very criteria for selecting men who will rise come to embody this fact. The corporate commissar, dealing with the state and its military, is wiser to choose a young man who has experienced the state and its military than one who has not. The political director, often dependent for his own political success upon corporate decisions and corporations, is also wiser to choose a man with corporate experience. Thus, by virtue of the very criterion of success, the interchange of personnel and the unity of the power elite is increased.

Given the formal similarity of the three hierarchies in which the several members of the elite spend their working lives, given the ramifications of the decisions made in each upon the others, given the coincidence of interest that prevails among them at many points, and given the administrative vacuum of the American civilian state along with its enlargement of tasks—given these trends of structure, and adding to them the psychological affinities we have noted—we should indeed be surprised were we to find that men said to be skilled in administrative contacts and full of organizing ability would fail to do more than get in touch with one another. They have, of course, done much more than that: increasingly, they assume positions in one another's domains.

The unity revealed by the interchangeability of top roles rests upon the parallel development of the top jobs in each of the big three domains. The interchange occurs most frequently at the points of their coinciding interest, as between regulatory agency and the regulated industry; contracting agency and contractor. And, as we shall see, it leads to co-ordinations that are more explicit, and even formal.

The inner core of the power elite consists, first, of those who interchange commanding roles at the top of one dominant institutional order with those in another: the admiral who is also a banker and a lawyer and who heads up an important federal commission; the corporation executive whose company was one of the two or three leading war materiel producers who is now the Secretary of Defense; the wartime general who dons civilian clothes to sit on the political directorate and then becomes a member of the board of directors of a leading economic corporation.

Although the executive who becomes a general, the general who becomes a statesman, the statesman who becomes a banker, see much more than ordinary men in their ordinary environments, still the perspectives of even such men often remain tied to their dominant locales. In their very career, however, they interchange roles within the big three and thus readily transcend the particularity of interest in any one of these institutional milieux. By their very careers and activities, they lace the three types of milieux together. They are, accordingly, the core members of the power elite.

These men are not necessarily familiar with every major arena of power. We refer to one man who moves in and between perhaps two circles—say the industrial and the military—and to another man who moves in the military and the political, and to a third who moves in the political as well as among opinion-makers. These in-between types most closely display our image of the power elite's structure and operation, even of behind-the-scenes operations. To the extent that there is any "invisible elite," these advisory and liaison types are its core. Even if—as I believe to be very likely—many of them are, at least in the first part of their careers, "agents" of the various elites rather than themselves elite, it is they who are most active in organizing the several top milieux into a structure of power and maintaining it.

The inner core of the power elite also includes men of the higher legal and financial type from the great law factories and investment firms, who are almost professional go-betweens of economic, political and military affairs, and who thus act to unify the power elite. The corporation lawyer and the investment banker perform the functions of the "go-between" effectively and powerfully. By the nature of their work, they transcend the narrower milieu of any one industry, and accordingly are in a position to speak and act for the corporate world or at least sizeable sectors of it. The corporation lawyer is a key link between the economic and military and political areas; the investment banker is a key organizer and unifier of the corporate world and a person well versed in spending the huge amounts of money the American military establishment now ponders. When you get a lawyer who handles the legal work of investment bankers you get a key member of the power elite.

During the Democratic era, one link between private corporate organizations and governmental institutions was the investment house of Dillon, Read. From it came such men as James Forrestal and Charles F. Detmar, Jr.; Ferdinand Eberstadt had once been a partner in it before he branched out into his own investment house from which came other men to political and military circles. Republican administrations seem to favor the investment firm of Kuhn, Loeb and the advertising firm of Batten, Barton, Durstine and Osborn.

Regardless of administrations, there is always the law firm of Sullivan and Cromwell. Mid-West investment banker Cyrus Eaton has said that

> Arthur H. Dean, a senior partner of Sullivan & Cromwell of No. 48 Wall Street, was one of those who assisted in the drafting of the Securities Act of 1933, the first of the series of bills passed to regulate the capital markets. He and his firm, which is reputed to be the largest in the United States, have maintained close relations with the SEC since its creation, and theirs is the dominating influence on the commission.[5]

There is also the third largest bank in the United States: the Chase National Bank of New York (now Chase-Manhattan). Regardless of political administration, executives of this bank and those of the International Bank of Reconstruction and Development have changed positions: John J. McCloy, who became Chairman of the Chase National in 1953, is a former president of the World Bank; and his successor to the presidency of the World Bank was a former senior vice-president of the Chase National Bank.[6] And in 1953, the president of the Chase National Bank, Winthrop W. Aldrich, had left to become Ambassador to Great Britain.

The outermost fringes of the power elite—which change more than its core—consist of "those who count" even though they may not be "in" on given decisions of consequence nor in their career move between the hierarchies. Each member of the power elite need not be a man who personally decides every decision that is to be ascribed to the power elite. Each member, in the decisions that he does make, takes the others seriously into account. They not only make decisions in the several major areas of war and peace; they are the men who, in decisions in which they take no direct part, are taken into decisive account by those who are directly in charge.

On the fringes and below them, somewhat to the side of the lower echelons, the power elite fades off into the middle levels of power, into the rank and file of the Congress, the pressure groups that are not vested in the power elite itself, as well as a multiplicity of regional and state and local interests. If all the men on the middle levels are not among those who count, they sometimes must be taken into account, handled, cajoled, broken or raised to higher circles.

When the power elite find that in order to get things done they must reach below their own realms—as is the case when it is necessary to get bills passed through Congress—they themselves must exert some pressure. But among the power elite, the name for such high-level lobbying is "liaison work." There are "liaison" military men with Congress, with certain wayward sections of industry, with practically every important element not directly concerned with the power elite. The two men on the White House staff who are *named* "liaison" men are both experienced in military matters; one of them is a former investment banker and lawyer as well as a general.

Not the trade associations but the higher cliques of lawyers and investment bankers are the active political heads of the corporate rich and the members of the power elite.

> *While it is generally assumed that the national associations carry tremendous weight in formulating public opinion and directing the course of national policy, there is some evidence to indicate that interaction between associations on a formal level is not a very tight-knit affair. The general tendency within associations seems to be to stimulate activities around the specific interests of the organization, and more effort is made to educate its members rather than to spend much time in trying to influence other associations on the issue at hand.*

. . . As media for stating and re-stating the over-all value structure of the nation they (the trade associations) are important. . . . But when issues are firmly drawn, individuals related to the larger corporate interests are called upon to exert pressure in the proper places at the strategic time. The national associations may act as media for co-ordinating such pressures, but a great volume of intercommunication between members at the apex of power of the larger corporate interests seems to be the decisive factor in final policy determination.[7]

Conventional "lobbying," carried on by trade associations, still exists, although it usually concerns the middle levels of power—usually being targeted at Congress, and, of course, its own rank and file members. The important function of the National Association of Manufacturers, for example, is less directly to influence policy than to reveal to small businessmen that their interests are the same as those of larger businesses. But there is also "high-level lobbying." All over the country the corporate leaders are drawn into the circle of the high military and political through personal friendship, trade and professional associations and their various subcommittees, prestige clubs, open political affiliation, and customer relationships. "There is . . . an awareness among these power leaders," one firsthand investigator of such executive cliques has asserted, "of many of the current major policy issues before the nation such as keeping taxes down, turning all productive operations over to private enterprises, increasing foreign trade, keeping governmental welfare and other domestic activities to a minimum, and strengthening and maintaining the hold of the current party in power nationally."[8]

There are, in fact, cliques of corporate executives who are more important as informal opinion leaders in the top echelons of corporate, military, and political power than as actual participants in military and political organizations. Inside military circles and inside political circles and "on the sidelines" in the economic area, these circles and cliques of corporation executives are in on most all major decisions regardless of topic. And what is important about all this high-level lobbying is that it is done within the confines of that elite.

6

The conception of the power elite and of its unity rests upon the corresponding developments and the coincidence of interests among economic, political, and military organizations. It also rests upon the similarity of origin and outlook, and the social and personal intermingling of the top circles from each of these dominant hierarchies. This conjunction of institutional and psychological forces, in turn, is revealed by the heavy personnel traffic within and between the big three institutional orders, as well as by the rise of go-betweens as in the high-level lobbying. The conception of the power elite, accordingly, does *not* rest upon the assumption that American history since the origins of World War II must be understood as a secret plot, or as a great and co-ordinated conspiracy of the members of this elite. The conception rests upon quite impersonal grounds.

There is, however, little doubt that the American power elite—which contains, we are told, some of "the greatest organizers in the world"—has also planned and has plotted. The rise of the elite, as we have already made clear, was not and could not have been caused by a plot; and the tenability of the conception does not rest upon the existence of any secret or any publicly known organization. But, once the conjunction of structural trend and of the personal will to utilize it gave rise to the power elite, then plans and programs did occur to its members and indeed it is not possible to interpret many events and official policies of the fifth epoch without reference to the power elite. "There is a great difference," Richard Hofstadter has remarked, "between locating conspiracies *in* history and saying that history *is*, in effect, a conspiracy. . . ."[9]

The structural trends of institutions become defined as opportunities by those who occupy their command posts. Once such opportunities are recognized, men may avail themselves of them. Certain types of men from each of the dominant institutional areas, more far-sighted than others, have actively promoted the liaison before it took its truly modern shape. They have often done so for reasons not shared by their partners, although not objected to by them either; and often the outcome of their liaison has had consequences which none of them foresaw, much less shaped, and which only later in the course of development came under explicit control. Only after it was well under way did most of its members find themselves part of it and become gladdened, although sometimes also worried, by this fact. But once the co-ordination is a going concern, new men come readily into it and assume its existence without question.

So far as explicit organization—conspiratorial or not—is concerned, the power elite, by its very nature, is more likely to use existing organizations, working within and between them, than to set up explicit organizations whose membership is strictly limited to its own members. But if there is no machinery in existence to ensure, for example, that military and political factors will be balanced in decisions made, they will invent such machinery and use it, as with the National Security Council. Moreover, in a formally democratic polity, the aims and the powers of the various elements of this elite are further supported by an aspect of the permanent war economy: the assumption that the security of the nation supposedly rests upon great secrecy of plan and intent. Many higher events that would reveal the working of the power elite can be withheld from public knowledge under the guise of secrecy. With the wide secrecy covering their operations and decisions, the power elite can mask their intentions, operations, and further consolidation. Any secrecy that is imposed upon those in positions to observe high decision-makers clearly works for and not against the operations of the power elite.

There is accordingly reason to suspect—but by the nature of the case, no proof—that the power elite is not altogether "surfaced." There is nothing hidden about it, although its activities are not publicized. As an elite, it is not organized, although its members often know one another, seem quite naturally to work together, and share many organizations in common. There is nothing conspiratorial about it, although its decisions are often publicly unknown and its mode of operation manipulative rather than explicit.

It is not that the elite "believe in" a compact elite behind the scenes and a mass down below. It is not put in that language. It is just that the people are of necessity confused and must, like trusting children, place all the new world of foreign policy and strategy and executive action in the hands of experts. It is just that everyone knows somebody has got to run the show, and that somebody usually does. Others do not really care anyway, and besides, they do not know how. So the gap between the two types gets wider.

When crises are defined as total, and as seemingly permanent, the consequences of decision become total, and the decisions in each major area of life come to be integrated and total. Up to a point, these consequences for other institutional orders can be assessed; beyond such points, chances have to be taken. It is then that the felt scarcity of trained and imaginative judgment leads to plaintive feelings among executives about the shortage of qualified successors in political, military, and economic life. This feeling, in turn, leads to an increasing concern with the training of successors who could take over as older men of power retire.[10] In each area, there slowly arises a new generation which has grown up in an age of co-ordinated decisions.

In each of the elite circles, we have noticed this concern to recruit and to train successors as "broad-gauge" men, that is, as men capable of making decisions that involve institutional areas other than their own. The chief executives have set up formal recruitment and training programs to man the corporate world as virtually a state within a state. Recruitment and training for the military elite has long been rigidly professionalized, but has now come to include educational routines of a sort which the remnants of older generals and admirals consider quite nonsensical.

Only the political order, with its absence of a genuine civil service, has lagged behind, creating an administrative vacuum into which military bureaucrats and corporate outsiders have been drawn. But even in this domain, since World War II, there have been repeated attempts, by elite men of such vision as the late James Forrestal's, to inaugurate a career service that would include periods in the corporate world as well as in the governmental.[11]

What is lacking is a truly common elite program of recruitment and training; for the prep school, Ivy League College, and law school sequence of the metropolitan 400 is not up to the demands now made upon members of the power elite.[12] Britishers, such as Field Marshall Viscount Montgomery, well aware of this lack, recently urged the adoption of a system "under which a minority of high-caliber young students could be separated from the mediocre and given the best education possible to supply the country with leadership." His proposal is echoed, in various forms, by many who accept his criticism of "the American theory of public education on the ground that it is ill-suited to produce the 'elite' group of leaders . . . this country needs to fulfill its obligations of world leadership."[13]

In part these demands reflect the unstated need to transcend recruitment on the sole basis of economic success, especially since it is suspect as often involving the higher immorality; in part it reflects the stated need to have men who, as Viscount Montgomery says, know "the meaning of discipline." But above all these demands reflect the at least vague consciousness on the part of the power elite themselves that the age of co-ordinated decisions, entailing a newly enormous range of consequences, requires a power elite that is of a new caliber. Insofar as the sweep of matters which go into the making of decisions is vast and interrelated, the information needed for judgments complex and requiring particularized knowledge,[14] the men in charge will not only call upon one another; they will try to train their successors for the work at hand. These new men will grow up as men of power within the co-ordination of economic and political and military decision.

7

The idea of the power elite rests upon and enables us to make sense of (1) the decisive institutional trends that characterize the structure of our epoch, in particular, the military ascendancy in a privately incorporated economy, and more broadly, the several coincidences of objective interests between economic, military, and political institutions; (2) the social similarities and the psychological affinities of the men who occupy the command posts of these structures, in particular the increased interchangeability of the top positions in each of them and the increased traffic between these orders in the careers of men of power; (3) the ramifications, to the point of virtual totality, of the kind of decisions that are made at the top, and the rise to power of a set of men who, by training and bent, are professional organizers of considerable force and who are unrestrained by democratic party training.

Negatively, the formation of the power elite rests upon (1) the relegation of the professional party politician to the middle levels of power, (2) the semi-organized stalemate of the interests of sovereign localities into which the legislative function has fallen, (3) the virtually complete absence of a civil service that constitutes a politically neutral, but politically relevant, depository of brainpower and executive skill, and (4) the increased official secrecy behind which great decisions are made without benefit of public or even Congressional debate.

As a result, the political directorate, the corporate rich, and the ascendant military have come together as the power elite, and the expanded and centralized hierarchies which they head have encroached upon the old balances and have now relegated them to the middle levels of power. Now the balancing society is a conception that pertains accurately to the middle levels, and on that level the balance has become more often an affair of intrenched provincial and nationally irresponsible forces and demands than a center of power and national decision.

But how about the bottom? As all these trends have become visible at the top and on the middle, what has been happening to the great American public? If the top is unprecedentedly powerful and increasingly unified and willful; if the middle zones are increasingly a semi-organized stalemate—in what shape is the bottom, in what condition is the public at large? The rise of the power elite, we shall now see, rests upon, and in some ways is part of, the transformation of the publics of America into a mass society.

NOTES

1. Whittaker Chambers, *Witness* (New York: Random House, 1952), p. 550.
2. For an excellent introduction to the international unity of corporate interests, see James Stewart Martin, *All Honorable Men* (Boston: Little Brown, 1950).
3. Gerald W. Johnson, "The Superficial Aspect," *New Republic*, 25 October 1954, p. 7.
4. See the Hearings before the Committee on Armed Services, United States Senate, Eighty-third Congress, First Session, On Nominees Designate Charles E. Wilson, Roger M. Keyes, Robert T. Stevens, Robert B. Anderson, and Harold E. Talbott, 15, 16, and 23 January 1953 (Washington, D.C.: U.S. Government Printing Office, 1953).
5. Hearings before the Subcommittee on Study of Monopoly Power of the Committee on the Judiciary, House of Representatives, Eighty-first Congress, First Session, Serial No. 14, Part 2-A (Washington, D.C.: U.S. Government Printing Office, 1950), p. 468.
6. Cf. *The New York Times*, 6 December 1952, p. 1.
7. Floyd Hunter, "Pilot Study of National Power and Policy Structures," Institute for Research in Social Science, University of North Carolina, Research Previews, vol. 2, No. 2, March 1954 (mimeo), p. 8.
8. Ibid., p. 9.
9. Richard Hofstadter, *The Age of Reform* (New York: Knopf, 1955), pp. 71-2.
10. Cf. Hans Gerth and C. Wright Mills, *Character and Social Structure* (New York: Harcourt, Brace, 1953).

11. Cf. Mills, "The Conscription of America," *Common Sense,* April 1945, pp. 15 ff.
12. Cf. "Twelve of the Best American Schools," *Fortune,* January 1936, p. 48.
13. Speech of Field Marshal Viscount Montgomery at Columbia University as reported in *The New York Times,* 24 November 1954, p. 25.
14. Cf. Dean Acheson, "What a Secretary of State Really Does," *Harper's,* December 1954, p. 48.

Power Is Pluralistic

Arnold M. Rose

The belief that an "economic elite" controls governmental and community affairs, by means kept hidden from the public, is one that can be traced at least as far back in American history as the political attacks of some Jeffersonians on some Hamiltonians at the end of the eighteenth century. Scarcely any lower-class political movement in the United States has failed to express the theme that the upper classes successfully used nondemocratic means to thwart democratic processes. Perhaps the widest popular use of the theme was achieved by the Populist movement in the decades following 1890. Anarchism and Marxism were imports from Europe that accepted the theme as one of the essential elements of their ideologies. The history of the United States also provides ample factual examples to strengthen credence in the theme. The literature of exposure, especially that of the "muckrakers" in the first decade of the twentieth century, provides details as to how economically privileged individuals and groups illegally bought and bribed legislators, judges, and executive heads of government to serve their own desires for increased wealth and power.

The belief is not entirely wrong. But it presents only a portion of relevant reality and creates a significant misimpression that in itself has political repercussions. A more balanced analysis of the historical facts would probably arrive at something like the following conclusion: Segments of the economic elite have violated democratic political and legal processes, with differing degrees of effort and success in the various periods of American history, but in no recent period could they correctly be said to have controlled the elected and appointed political authorities in large measure. The relationship between the economic elite and the political authorities has been a constantly varying one of strong influence, co-operation, division of labor, and conflict, with each influencing the other in changing proportion to some extent and each operating independently of the other to a large extent. Today there is significant political control and limitation of certain activities over the economic elite, and there are also some significant processes by which the economic elite uses its wealth to help elect some political candidates and to influence other political authorities in ways which are not available to the average citizen. Further, neither the economic elite nor the political authorities are monolithic units which act with internal consensus and coordinated action with regard to each other (or probably in any other way). In fact there are several economic elites which only very rarely act as units within themselves and among themselves, and there are at least two political parties which have significantly differing programs with regard to their actions toward any economic elite, and each of them has only a partial degree of internal cohesion.[1] On domestic issues, at least, it is appropriate to observe that there are actually four political parties, two liberal ones and two conservative ones, the largest currently being the national Democratic party, which generally has a domestic policy that frustrates the special interests of the economic elite. This paragraph states our general hypothesis, and we shall seek to substantiate it with facts that leave no significant areas of omission. Merely to provide it with a shorthand label, we shall call it the "multi-influence hypothesis," as distinguished from the "economic-elite-dominance" hypothesis.

*   *

. . . Specifically, this study presents evidence against the following statements of Mills:

> There is no effective countervailing power against the coalition of the big businessmen—who, as political outsiders, now occupy the command posts— and the ascendant military men—who with such grave voices now speak so frequently in the higher councils.

> While the professional party politicians may still, at times, be brokers of power, compromisers of interests, negotiators of issues, they are no longer at the top of the state.

> The executive bureaucracy becomes not only the center of power but also the arena within which all conflicts of power are resolved or denied resolution. Administration replaces electoral politics. . . .

Implicit in these and other remarks are Mills's political assumptions that (1) voting means little or nothing; (2) there is no significant difference between the two major political parties; (3) the economic-military elite has an interest in all major political issues against the interest of the masses, and that the former interest is always victorious over the latter; (4) the Legislative branch of government is subordinate to the Executive branch. . . .

Mills adopts an economic determinism which we cannot accept. He points to the fact that most congressmen are of upper-class or middle-class origin . . ., and assumes that they must therefore reflect the economic interests of businessmen and other members of the economic elite. Even when a congressman does not have an upper-class or middle-class background, he is assumed to take orders from the economic elite. These assumptions neglect the vast amount of social welfare legislation, particularly since the 1930's, and of other legislation designed to protect the interests of the working classes. They neglect the fact that some of the wealthiest of elected government officials have been among those leading in the fight for such legislation. The aristocratic Franklin Roosevelt doubtless represented the interests of the working masses better than his "average man" political opponent of 1936, Alfred Landon; and a similar comparison could be made between the wealthy John Kennedy and his opponent of more nearly average wealth, Richard Nixon. Of course, Mills can consider Landon and Nixon as "lieutenants" of the economic elite, but he cannot get around the fact that Roosevelt, Kennedy, and such other liberal politicians as W. Averill Harriman, Joseph Clark, Herbert Lehman, Stuart Symington, and G. Mennen Williams are members of the upper economic class. It may be true that military leaders have growing power in government circles, but they have not succeeded in getting much of the legislation they have asked for, nor has any President allowed them to speak freely in public. It is not illuminating to be told by Mills that "a small group of men are now in charge of the executive decisions" . . ., for there has always been, and must continue to be, leadership in a democracy; this is even part of the definition of "executive." The significant question is in whose interests the political elite acts and whether it is checked by the mass of voters and of interest groups. There is every evidence that the masses of the American people today are better off economically, both absolutely and relatively, than they were in the past, and that this has been largely due to government intervention, supported by the majority of the voters.

It is explicit in Mills's . . . analyses that the elected legislators have no power in and of themselves. At most, they are "lieutenants" who carry out the orders of the economic elite, who—Mills claims—have taken over the direction of the government through appointment to the top policy-making offices in the federal Executive. In fact, a considerable number of statutes originate in the Congress rather than in the Executive branch— more than in European parliamentary regimes—and many of these are responses to the wishes of private pressure groups, including those of the economic elite. Yet, there are also some bills that are originated by the congressmen themselves, sometimes in opposition to the wishes of both the Executive branch and the pressure groups. Congress also controls the purse strings, and the areas of taxation and appropriations involve far more creative opportunities than is generally understood.

Administrations since 1933 have been diligent in efforts to solve social problems, and have sought enabling statutes and appropriations from the Congress, a large number with success, some after a delay, and others with failure. In most cases Congress has "improved" and the bills submitted to it by the Executive before passing them, and that has been its chief role. But in some outstanding instances, it has initiated or expanded legislation on its own when it felt the Executive branch was evasive or dilatory. The Civil Rights Act of 1964 and the Medicare Act of 1965 provide examples of liberal legislation enacted by Congress with provisions that went much beyond what the Administration requested. Congress's annual allocation of funds for medical research and often for medical facilities is usually greater than that requested by the President, and in 1965 Congress doubled the educational program for veterans that the President requested, and made a special allocation, that the President did not request, for schools in areas of high federal employment.[2]

There are a number of other general points to be made against the Mills thesis . . . :

1. The important facts of political power and political influence are not "secret" or "hidden" or "behind the scenes" most of the time. Pressure groups—of which many represent economic interests—and public opinion operate on legislative and executive branches of government. But only a small proportion of federal legislators and executives are "in the control of" an economic elite. At state and local levels, a larger proportion of legislators seek their positions to serve special economic interests, but even whey they do, many of their votes are in accord with their ideological conception of what the public interest is.

There is a circularity in Mills's reasoning because of his beliefs that the top economic elite effects its control of American society secretly and that the political elite consists of lieutenants of the commanding economic elite. From these premises he deduces that the *actions* of the political elite are generally the only means by which the wishes and interests of the commanding economic elite can be ascertained by the outside observers, and that the *words* of the political elite are mere window dressing to mislead the masses into voting for them. There are several factual questions at issue here—the extent to which there is a discrepancy between the words and deeds of the political elite, and the extent to which the deeds of the political elite do not reflect the interests and wishes of the public. But aside from these factual questions, there is dubious logic in reasoning that the political elite constantly proves its subordination to the economic elite by its actions, where there is no independent way of ascertaining what the commanding economic elite really wants because of its secret modes of operating. The economic elite in fact does often expound its wishes—in the programs and campaigns of the National Association of Manufacturers, the United States Chamber of Commerce, and more specialized groups such as the American Medical Association. . . . [T]he President and the majority of the Congress more often go against these programs than support them, although the businessmen are more likely to get their way when they seek narrow economic advantages from the independent regulatory commissions and the military procurement agencies. Are the National Association of Manufacturers, the Chamber of Commerce, and the American Medical Association merely engaging in window dressing to fool the public as to their true wishes when they come out with a program or campaign?

Secrecy in politics has many functions other than the desire to hide the control that may be exercised by the economic elite on the politicians. The New York Reform Democratic party leader, Edward U. Costikyan,[3] says:

> The nature of politics and politicians is to reach decisions privately. This often leads the public to believe that secrecy is a screen to shield wrongdoing. It usually isn't. Generally it shields a desire for privacy, as well as some confusion, and some selfishness. . . .

Thus, the existence of secrecy in some political actions cannot by itself be taken as evidence that it hides business control of politics. Just how much secrecy there is in politics is an open question on which there is little evidence. Public ignorance of certain actions taken by politicians does not mean that there is secrecy; it often simply reflects the failure of the news media to report actions that were taken openly. Politicians interviewed by this author invariably stated, when asked about the frequency of the decisions they take in secret, that they occasionally found it expedient to act in secret, but that the secret usually "leaked out" in a matter of days or weeks. They all averred that the value of secrecy to them was temporary, and that they assumed, when they took secret actions, that the secret would likely ultimately become public. They also stated that many of the supposedly secret actions they took were not secret at all: newspaper and other mass media reporters were just not present, and when the news releases were finally issued, the reporters excused their own failure to be present by asserting that the decision-making had occurred secretly. . . .

2. Mills and his followers have been critical of those political scientists like Dahl who hold that political power is pluralistic in the United States. Our position is not simply that power is pluralistic in American society, but that the society itself is pluralistic. The different spheres of life do not interpenetrate each other in the way that in India, for example, religious values and institutions permeate the average man's political, economic, family, artistic, educational, and other spheres of life. Or in the way that, in Hitler's Germany, or Stalin's Russia, political values similarly permeated all the other spheres of life. In the United States (and many other countries), practically every person has differentiated roles and values for

the various spheres of life, and so power too usually does not significantly cross the boundaries of each sphere in which it is created. As Merton has put it: "Men with power to affect the economic life-chances of a large group may exert little interpersonal influence in other spheres: the power to withhold jobs from people may not result in directly influencing their political or associational or religious behavior."[4]

3. Since 1933, Democrats have won the great majority of the elections, naming all the Presidents but one (Eisenhower),* dominating all the Congresses but two (1946-48, 1952-54), and electing a considerable major-ity of the governors and state legislatures. Yet the majority of businessmen have strongly supported the Republican party. Businessmen have not only not dominated the political scene, but have shown an increasing sense of frustration and bitterness at being "left out" in political decisions.

In 1960, the Committee on Economic Development conducted an attitude survey of bankers. One of the findings was that they felt that Congress ignored them and their interests. They pointed to the much lighter controls on their competitors, the savings and loan associations and the credit unions. In their belief this could be attributed to the "fact" that Congressmen were more likely to place their savings in these latter associations than in banks, and that, because of the high rate of bank failures in the early 1930's, banks were still regarded with suspicion—in spite of the many reforms in procedure that banks had made since then.

The brief two years (1952-54) when the Republicans controlled both the presidency and the Congress must have seemed like a "Restoration" for the majority of businessmen, and it was during this atypical period that C. Wright Mills must have written the bulk of The Power Elite. But alienation from government increased during the late years of the Eisenhower presidency as the Administration proved unable to achieve any of the major goals of the businessmen. They became even more antagonistic and truculent toward government when President Kennedy forced back the steel price rise . . . and they went so far as to pull the Business Advisory Council out of its semiofficial relationship to the government. It was not until a politically extremist minority seized control of the majority of the Republican state organizations that a significant group of big businessmen exhibited a desire to take an accommodating position toward the Democrats. Big businessmen worked out a pragmatic relationship with President Lyndon Johnson[5] which they had refused to do with Presidents Roosevelt, Truman, and Kennedy—but their subordinate role in the Johnson Administration was shown by the fact that more welfare and "reform" legislation was passed by the 1964-65 Congress under Johnson's stimulation, than by any Congress since 1933.

4. Mills contends that the American top elite has a common prove-

*Since this was written, one other Republican President, Richard Nixon, has been elected and another, Gerald Ford, succeeded to the office—Editors.

nance: He says that they are upper-class people, who attend the same preparatory schools and private colleges, associate with each other throughout their lives, and pass on their power to their offspring. This picture is certainly not true for the top elected government officials. Very few sons of presidents, governors, and congressmen ever achieve top political positions. The men in these positions have the most diverse social origins. Of presidents in the twentieth century, only the two Roosevelts (sixth cousins to each other) were from the upper upper class, and only one came from a very wealthy family (Kennedy, whose family background is *nouveau riche*); Truman, Eisenhower, and Johnson could be said to have come from the lower middle class, and the others had somewhat higher middle-class family backgrounds. The Middle West provided as many presidents as did the East, and the small towns provided more than the opulent cities or suburbs. The majority did not attend the upper-class private schools or colleges. The great majority of the top elected officials of the United States have experienced a considerable amount of upward social mobility in comparison with their parents, not only in prestige and power, but also in education and wealth.

Studies by Newcomer, and by Warner and Abegglen, suggest that there is more social mobility in the economic elite than Mills claims.[6] In Newcomer's sample of big business executives in the early 1950's, 7.5 per cent were sons of workers, as compared to 4.2 per cent for the executives of 1900; in Warner and Abegglen's study of 8,562 businessmen from 1900 to 1950 there was an increase of 8 per cent in the proportion of executives whose fathers were laborers and a decrease of 10 per cent in those whose fathers were owners of businesses. But Mills is almost completely wrong about the absence of social mobility among the political elite.

Dwight D. Eisenhower, General of the Armies and President of the United States, appointer of many top-level business executives to the leading decision-making posts in government, must have been considered by Mills a leading member of the power elite. Yet he was one of the few in top decision-making posts who publicly warned against a "military-industrial complex" as a threat to the United States. On the significant occasion of his Farewell Address, this leader of the Establishment seemed to give support to one of C. Wright Mills's central theses:

> In the councils of Government, we must guard against the acquisition of unwarranted influence, whether sought or unsought, by the military-industrial complex. The potential for the disastrous rise of misplaced power exists and will persist. We must never let the weight of this combination endanger our liberties or democratic processes.

Many individuals not persuaded by the scholar Mills were persuaded by the President Eisenhower.[7] Yet a closer reading of Eisenhower's speech shows that he was on a different track than Mills. In the first place, Eisenhower placed the danger in the future; Mills had the economic-military power elite already in control of the nation. Secondly, Eisenhower was arguing for the autonomy of government; Mills identified the government as a tool of the elite. Thirdly, Eisenhower—a leading figure in Mills's elite—was publicly denouncing the threat posed by that presumed elite, whereas Mills held that the members of the elite were like-minded and operated more or less in secret.

It is clear that Eisenhower was worried about the huge size of the armaments industry, and its consequent potential for using its great economic power to influence many areas of government, education, and science. . . . Eisenhower may also have worried about conflict of interest on the part of the nation's military leaders: As direct purchasers from the armaments industry, and as relatively low-paid government servants who could "retire" at an early age, were they not in danger of making decisions influenced by the fact that they could go into high-salaried jobs in one or another munitions firm after they retired? When Eisenhower made his statement, Congress was considering a bill to require retiring military procurement officers to wait two years before accepting a position in one of the supplying firms. But this may not be a long enough waiting period to prevent conflict of interest, and the law could not apply to civilians working for the Defense Department or to military officers not directly engaged in procurement. There were all sorts of ways of unduly influencing a military procurement officer: The military supply firms even set up a trade association, called the National Security Industrial Association, which has been in existence since World War II, to enhance their relationships with military leaders. Provision of information and gossip, wining and dining, and other standard techniques of lobbying were used on the military procurement officers. General Eisenhower was concerned about the conflict of interest on the part of his brother officers, and anxious to maintain the tradition of military independence and service.

Yet Eisenhower's conception of his role as President, as a mere enforcer of laws and mediator of the various conflicting forces in the Executive branch, did much to enhance the very dangers he called attention to. It was his successors, Kennedy and Johnson, because they had a conception of the dominant and decisive role of the presidency, who set industry back several times when it sought an inflationary rise in prices, and whose appointed Secretary of Defense, Robert McNamara, maintained his dominance over the military in all matters. These Presidents were political leaders, who saw a superordinate government as the check on any potential military-industrial complex. . . .

NOTES

1. The two political parties sometimes agree on almost identical specific pieces of legislation, but mainly in the areas of foreign policy and national defense, practically never in regard to their programs or actions with respect to an economic elite.

2. *The New York Times,* April 5, 1966, p. 21.
3. *Behind Closed Doors: Politics in the Public Interest* (New York: Harcourt, Brace and World, 1966), Preface.
4. Robert K. Merton, "Patterns of Influence: A Study of Interpersonal Influence and of Communication Behavior in a Local Community," in Paul F. Lazarsfeld and Frank N. Stanton (eds.), *Communication Research: 1948-1949* (New York: Harper, 1949), p. 217.
5. David T. Bazelton, "Big Business and the Democrats," *Commentary,* 39 (May 1965), 39-46.
6. Mabel Newcomer, *The Big Business Executive* (New York: Columbia University Press, 1955); W. Lloyd Warner and James C. Abegglen, *Big Business Leaders in America* (New York: Harper, 1955).
7. I do not know if Mills welcomed Eisenhower's statement. Among those who accepted it as verification of Mills's thesis were Fred J. Cook, *The Warfare State* (New York: Macmillan, 1962); and Marc Pilisuk and Thomas Hayden, "Is There a Military Industrial Complex which Prevents Peace?" *Journal of Social Issues,* 21 (July 1965), 67-117. The latter mentions many others.